INTERPRETING CONSTITUTIONS

Interpreting Constitutions

A Comparative Study

Edited by
JEFFREY GOLDSWORTHY

OXFORD
UNIVERSITY PRESS

OXFORD
UNIVERSITY PRESS

Great Clarendon Street, Oxford OX2 6DP

Oxford University Press is a department of the University of Oxford.
It furthers the University's objective of excellence in research, scholarship,
and education by publishing worldwide in

Oxford New York

Auckland Cape Town Dar es Salaam Hong Kong Karachi
Kuala Lumpur Madrid Melbourne Mexico City Nairobi
New Delhi Shanghai Taipei Toronto

With offices in

Argentina Austria Brazil Chile Czech Republic France Greece
Guatemala Hungary Italy Japan Poland Portugal Singapore
South Korea Switzerland Thailand Turkey Ukraine Vietnam

Oxford is a registered trade mark of Oxford University Press
in the UK and in certain other countries

Published in the United States
by Oxford University Press Inc., New York

First published 2006

British Library Cataloguing in Publication Data

Data available

Library of Congress Cataloging in Publication Data

Interpreting constitutions : a comparative study / edited by
Jeffrey Goldsworthy.
p. cm.
Includes index.
ISBN-13: 978–0–19–927413–0 (alk. paper) 1. Constitutional law—
Methodology. 2. Constitutional law—Philosophy. I. Goldsworthy,
Jeffrey Denys.
K3165.I58 2006
342.02—dc22   2005030777

Typeset by Newgen Imaging Systems (P) Ltd., Chennai, India
Printed in Great Britain
on acid-free paper by
Biddles Ltd., King's Lynn

ISBN 0–19–927413–4 978–0–19–927413–0

3 5 7 9 10 8 6 4 2

Contents

Detailed Table of Contents

Preface

This book describes how the highest courts in six major federations (or in one case, quasi-federation) have interpreted their constitutions, compares their interpretive methodologies and philosophies, and explores the reasons for differences between them. The six countries are Australia, Canada, Germany, India, the United States, and South Africa. Each is the subject of a separate chapter, written by a leading authority in the field, which describes not only the interpretive methodology currently employed by their highest court, but how it has changed since the constitution was first adopted. The book ends with a concluding chapter that compares these methodologies, and attempts to explain differences between them in terms of different social, historical, institutional, and political circumstances.

I would like to thank all my collaborators for agreeing to participate in this project, and for their enthusiasm, advice and assistance throughout. We met twice to co-ordinate the project, in Seattle in February 2003, and in Berkeley in March 2004. I thank the Law Schools of Seattle University, and the University of California, Berkeley (through the agency of Dan Farber), for kindly providing us with meeting rooms.

The project was funded by a Discovery Grant awarded by the Australian Research Council in 2003, which provided financial assistance to enable the contributors to meet, and for editorial and research assistance and indexing. I thank the Council for its generous assistance. I also thank Fiona Galbraith and Caterina Popa for providing invaluable editorial and research assistance.

Finally, I thank the staff at Oxford University Press—John Louth, Gwen Booth, Rebecca Smith, Rowena Lennon, and Jude Chillman—for their advice, their patience in awaiting the manuscript, and their meticulous care in preparing it for publication.

List of Contributors

Professor Jeffrey Goldsworthy holds a Personal Chair in the Faculty of Law at Monash University, Melbourne, Australia. He is the author of *The Sovereignty of Parliament, History and Philosophy* (Clarendon Press, Oxford, 1999), a co-editor of *Protecting Human Rights; Instruments and Institutions* (Oxford University Press, Oxford, 2003) and two other books of essays, and the author of many book chapters and journal articles dealing with constitutional history, theory, and interpretation, including 'Originalism in Constitutional Interpretation' (1997) 1 *Federal Law Review* 1–50; 'Dworkin as an Originalist' (2000) 17 *Constitutional Commentary* 49–78; 'Interpreting the *Constitution* in Its Second Century' (2000) 24 *Melbourne University Law Review* 677–710; and 'Raz on Constitutional Interpretation' (2003) 22 *Law and Philosophy* 167.

Professor Peter W. Hogg is a former Dean, and now Professor Emeritus, of Osgoode Hall Law School of York University, Toronto, and Scholar in Residence, Blake, Cassels & Graydon, LLP, Toronto. He is Canada's most eminent and influential constitutional scholar. He is the author of the leading two-volume treatise *Constitutional Law of Canada* (4th edn, supplemented, Carswell, Ontario, 1997), *Liability of the Crown* (with PJ Monahan) (3rd edn, Law Book, N.S.W., 2000), and numerous articles and book chapters, which have frequently been cited by the Canadian judiciary.

Professor Heinz Klug is a Professor of Law at the University of Wisconsin. He is the author of *Constituting Democracy: Law, Globalism and South Africa's Political Reconstruction* (Cambridge University Press, 2000), and many articles in the fields of comparative constitutionalism, land reform, water law, and human rights, particularly dealing with South Africa. He previously taught law at the University of the Witwatersrand in Johannesburg, worked with two South African Ministries on water law and land tenure issues, served on the African National Congress Land Commission, and was a team member on the World Bank mission to South Africa on Land Reform and Rural Restructuring.

Professor Donald P. Kommers is Joseph and Elizabeth Robbie Professor of Political Science and Professor of Law, University of Notre Dame, United States. He is the leading Anglo-American authority on German constitutional law. He is the author of the acclaimed work *The Constitutional Jurisprudence of the Federal Republic of Germany* (2nd edn, Duke University Press, Durham, NC, 1997), the 3rd edition of which is in preparation. He is also the co-author, with John Finn and Gary Jacobsohn, of *American Constitutional Law: Essays, Cases, and Comparative Notes* (New York: Rowman and Littlefield, 2004). In addition, he has published dozens of articles on various aspects of American and comparative constitutional law. He is currently writing a book entitled *Red, Black, and Gold: Germany's Constitutional Odyssey*.

Professor S. P. Sathe is Honorary Director of the Institute of Advanced Legal Studies, and former Principal of the ILS Law College, Pune. He is one of India's leading public law scholars, and the author of numerous books, book chapters, and journal articles, including

The Tribunal System in India (NM Tripathi, 1996), *Administrative Law* (7th edn, Butterworths, India, 2004), and *Judicial Activism in India, Transcending Borders and Enforcing Limits* (Oxford University Press, New Delhi, 2001).

Professor Mark V. Tushnet is Carmack Waterhouse Professor of Constitutional Law at Georgetown University Law Center in Washington D.C., United States. He is a leading American constitutional scholar, and author of numerous books including *Red, White, and Blue: a Critical Analysis of Constitutional Law* (Harvard University Press, Cambridge, Mass., 1988), *Remnants of Belief: Contemporary Constitutional Issues* (Oxford University Press, New York, 1996) (with Louis M. Seidman), *Making Constitutional Law: Thurgood Marshall and the Supreme Court, 1961–1991* (Oxford University Press, New York, 1997), and *Taking the Constitution Away From the Courts* (Princeton University Press, Princeton, 1999). He is also a leading comparative constitutionalist, being the joint author of *Comparative Constitutional Law* (Foundation Press, New York, 1999) (with Vicki Jackson).

Abbreviations

AC	Appeal Cases
AIR	All India Reporter
BVerfGE	Entscheidungen des Bundesverfassungsgericht [Decisions of the Federal Constitutional Court]
CAD	Constituent Assembly Debates
CDU	Christian Democratic Union
CSU	Christian Social Union
CLR	Commonwealth Law Reports
DLR	Dominion Law Reports
FC	Federal Court
FCC	Federal Constitutional Court
FCCA	Federal Constitutional Court Act
FCR	Federal Court Reporter
FDP	Free Democratic Party
FRG	Federal Republic of Germany
GDR	German Democratic Republic
GG	Grundgesetz [Basic Law]
HCA	High Court of Australia
ILR	Indian Law Reports
JILI	Journal of the Indian Law Institute
SC	Supreme Court
SCC	Supreme Court Cases
SCJ	Supreme Court Journal
SCR	Supreme Court Reporter or Supreme Court Reports
SPD	Social Democratic Party
VLR	Victorian Law Reports
VSC	Victorian Supreme Court

Introduction

Jeffrey Goldsworthy

The Challenges of Constitutional Interpretation

The provisions of national constitutions, like other laws, are often ambiguous, vague, contradictory, insufficiently explicit, or even silent as to constitutional disputes that judges must decide. In addition they sometimes seem inadequate to deal appropriately with developments that threaten principles the constitution was intended to safeguard, developments that its founders either failed, or were unable to anticipate.

How judges resolve these problems through 'interpretation' is problematic and controversial, mainly because legitimate interpretation can be difficult to distinguish from illegitimate change. Judges believed to have improperly changed a constitution while purporting to interpret it are vulnerable to criticism for usurping the prescribed power of amendment, violating their duty of fidelity to law, flouting the principles of democracy and federalism (if the amending procedure requires special majorities to protect regional interests), and straying beyond their legal expertise into the realm of politics.

How judges interpret other laws can also be controversial, but the stakes are much higher where constitutions are concerned. As fundamental laws, they allocate and regulate the powers of government and the rights of citizens. Their interpretation can have profound effects on the institutional structure of society, and the exercise of political power within it. It can affect the distribution of powers or rights between organs of government (legislature, executive, and judiciary), levels of government (national and state), and government and citizen. Moreover, legislatures can readily change other laws if they disapprove of the way judges have interpreted them, but constitutions are usually much more difficult to amend, and erroneous or undesirable judicial interpretations therefore more difficult to correct (except by the judges themselves).

On the other hand, the greater difficulty of amending constitutions might be regarded as a reason for judges to be more creative when interpreting them, compared with other laws. Consider the extent to which judges should remedy failures on the part of the constitution's founders to expressly provide for problems, whether or not they should have anticipated them. When interpreting statutes judges are often reluctant to rectify failures of that kind, preferring to leave it to the legislature to do so. But when dealing with a constitution, it is arguable that they should be more willing to provide a solution. If, because of the founders' oversight, a constitution might fail to achieve one of its main purposes, the potential consequences are grave. They include the danger of constitutional powers being abused, of the democratic process or the federal system being subverted, of human rights being violated, and so on. If the constitution is difficult to amend formally, or if amendment requires action by the very politicians who pose the threat that needs to be checked, there may be good moral reasons for the judges to act. Yet there is an obvious risk of such reasoning being used to justify extensive judicial rewriting of the constitution, especially if the founders' purposes are pitched at a very abstract level ('they wanted to achieve a just society, and this is necessary to achieve justice'). Judges are not supposed to be 'statesmen', appointed to fill the shoes of the founders and continue the task of constitution-making as an on-going enterprise, correcting mistakes and omissions wherever they see them.

When constitutional provisions need to be interpreted can be as controversial as how they should be interpreted. When, for example, is a provision ambiguous? When its words, read literally, are capable of bearing more than one meaning? Or only when the ambiguity persists, after taking into account admissible evidence of the intentions, purposes, or understandings of those who adopted it? And when should such evidence be admissible? These are only some of the difficult questions that arise.

Much of the controversy surrounding constitutional interpretation concerns two issues. The first is a version of a conundrum that has perplexed lawyers for millennia: should the interpretation of a law be governed mainly by its 'letter', or by its 'spirit'? Should a constitution be regarded as a set of discrete written provisions, authoritative because they were formally adopted or enacted, or as a normative structure whose written provisions are founded on, and derive their authority from, more abstract principles and values that may not be expressly stated? To what extent should 'implications' and 'unwritten principles' be recognised and given effect?

The second issue is the extent to which the meaning of a constitution can, and should, be determined by the original intentions, purposes, or understandings of its founders. This issue pits so-called 'non-originalists' against 'originalists'. The former argue that the interpretation of a constitution in the modern world should be guided by contemporary needs and values, rather than the 'dead hand of the past'. The latter reply that such an approach would allow judges too much power to change the constitution according to their own political ideologies, contrary to the procedure for formal amendment prescribed by the constitution itself.

Both issues pose the following question: if the courts are the 'guardians' of their nation's constitution, what exactly is it that they are guarding? Is it a set of reasonably fixed rules and principles, laid down at the founding, that must not be changed except by formal amendment? Or does the force of those rules and principles ultimately depend on abstract principles and values, whose effective protection may justify considerable judicial creativity in response to perceived threats?

Comparing Interpretive Methods and Philosophies

There is a vast, theoretically sophisticated, literature dealing with these difficult normative, conceptual, and ontological questions, especially in the United States where they have been debated for longer than anywhere else. But as well as asking how courts *should* interpret constitutions, it can be of considerable interest to ask how in fact they *have* interpreted them, not only in one's own country but also elsewhere.

The American literature includes detailed studies of how the Supreme Court has interpreted its Constitution since it was adopted, the main outlines of which are to some extent familiar to constitutional lawyers elsewhere. But the practices of courts in other countries are much less well known. There are many differences between the Constitution and constitutional tradition of the United States, and those of other countries, which have affected the interpretive practices of their courts. Yet no substantial comparative study of constitutional interpretation in different countries seems to have been undertaken before, at least in the English language. Interpretive methodologies and philosophies have been largely ignored even in texts devoted to comparative constitutional law. The current leading text, for example, mentions constitutional interpretation only in passing.[1]

We live in an era of 'cosmopolitan constitutionalism', in which lawyers and judges increasingly look beyond their own borders and borrow ideas from other jurisdictions.[2] The time is ripe for a comparative study of the methods by which constitutions have been interpreted. It should be of considerable interest to constitutional lawyers, judges, and legal theorists. Comparing legal practices in different countries can help broaden one's horizons, expand one's sense of what is possible, and dispel any sense of false necessity. Learning how foreign courts tackle similar constitutional problems may reveal that one's own courts 'simply fail to address adequately arguments that apparently sensible people in other nations have addressed.'[3] Of course, it does not follow that practices appropriate in one country are universally applicable: another benefit of comparative study is that it can help explain differences by reference to institutional, political, social, and cultural circumstances. On the other hand, if it turns out that some approaches to constitutional interpretation are almost universal, that might strengthen the case in their favour.

Such a study should also be of interest to political scientists, who rightly regard constitutional courts as political institutions that wield enormous power. Whenever judges develop the law they exercise political power, and when that law is the nation's constitution, they exercise the highest political power that exists in a state. Political scientists often maintain that courts regularly change constitutions

---

[1] V Jackson and M Tushnet, *Comparative Constitutional Law* (Foundation Press, New York, 1999).
[2] See S Choudhry, *The Migration of Constitutional Ideas* (Cambridge University Press, Cambridge, 2005) (forthcoming).   [3] Jackson and Tushnet (n 2) 145.

through interpretation, but they rarely examine legal arguments with sufficient care to distinguish between different kinds of change, or consider the extent to which courts have legal authority (as opposed to political power) to do so. Like other political actors, courts are supposed to be constrained by laws, including the very laws they are charged with interpreting. Any study of the behaviour of political actors in a society that claims to abide by the rule of law must include an account of how effectively their exercise of power is ruled by law.[4] How courts exercise their power to interpret constitutions—what considerations they take into account, explicitly or implicitly, and why—should be of vital interest to any student of constitutional politics.

This comparative study is primarily descriptive and explanatory, rather than prescriptive. It describes and compares the interpretive methods that have in fact been employed by courts in six countries, and the interpretive philosophies that have guided them, and it also seeks explanations for differences between their practices. The study includes some scope for critical comment, but only incidentally, and it certainly does not purport to propose a universal theory of how constitutions ought to be interpreted.

The study is limited to six countries to enable each to be examined in more depth than would otherwise have been possible. Australia, Canada, Germany, India, South Africa, and the United States were chosen for comparison because:

(a) they each possess a written, federal (or quasi-federal[5]) constitution that has been the subject of interpretation by an independent judiciary;

(b) their constitutions vary widely in age, from the oldest written constitution (that of the United States) to one of the youngest (that of South Africa);

(c) the interpretation of each constitution, except for South Africa's, has had some influence on the design and interpretation of later ones;

(d) they are institutionally, politically, socially, and culturally diverse.

They provide an opportunity to compare judicial responses to similar (and dissimilar) challenges in very different contexts.

An Outline of What Follows

Six scholars, all leading experts in their respective fields, have each contributed a chapter describing and explaining the interpretive methods and philosophies that have guided courts in the country they are familiar with, and how these have evolved since its constitution was first enacted. These chapters are arranged in

---

[4] The concept of the 'rule of law' is, of course, a notoriously contested one, and itself the subject of political debate.

[5] The South African Constitution is at most quasi-federal, and often described as a system of cooperative governance rather than federalism.

chronological order, from the oldest to the youngest constitution, to make it easier for readers to see how the interpretation of older constitutions has influenced the design and interpretation of later ones. The book concludes with a chapter in which I summarize and compare the information provided in the earlier chapters, attempt to explain significant differences between the interpretive practices of these courts, and draw some conclusions.

Before work on these chapters commenced, the authors met in person to agree on a common set of issues for examination. To facilitate comparisons it was agreed that, as far as practicable, these issues would be discussed in the same order in each chapter. The authors were permitted to depart from that order if there were a good reason for doing so. As it turned out, it was not possible for them to closely follow the same template: each had a distinctive story to tell, which had to be told in its own way.

These chapters begin with an introduction to the constitution in question: when, how, and by whom it was adopted or enacted, its main structural elements (the main institutions, powers, and rights that it creates and confers), and the method it prescribes for its own amendment. They then describe the court or courts that have had primary responsibility for interpreting the constitution, how their judges are appointed, how they select, hear, and decide cases, the extent to which their independence is protected, workload issues, and the legal culture in which they operate.

After describing the main types of interpretive problems these courts have faced, and their causes, the chapters turn to the interpretive methodologies that have been employed to resolve them. Only rarely do express constitutional provisions require specific considerations to be taken into account. For the most part, the courts have drawn on interpretive norms found in pre-existing general law, especially those governing the interpretation of statutes, or in the constitutional jurisprudence of other countries. A recurring issue has been the extent to which constitutions differ from statutes, and require different methods of interpretation. Most of the courts recognise that there are substantial differences, due to the intended longevity of constitutions, their inclusion of broad, abstract terms, and the difficulty of amending them.

Interpretation everywhere is guided by similar considerations, including the ordinary or technical-legal meanings of words, evidence of their originally intended meaning or purpose, 'structural' or 'underlying' principles, judicial precedents, scholarly writings, comparative and international law, and contemporary understandings of justice and social utility. The chapters discuss how these diverse considerations are combined to reach an overall conclusion, and whether they are prioritized or weighed up in some overall balance.

The chapters pay particular attention to the extent to which evidence of original intention or purpose is treated as significant, including whose intentions or purposes, the level of abstraction at which they are framed, and limits imposed on the kinds of historical evidence that is admitted. They also examine on what basis and to what extent courts have been willing to recognize and enforce unwritten, supposedly implied powers, immunities, obligations and rights.

The chapters examine whether the courts' interpretive practices have changed over time, the apparent reasons for any changes, and whether the courts apply the same interpretive principles to different areas of constitutional law, such as federalism, separation of powers, and individual rights.

The chapters then reflect on the institutional, political, social, and cultural contexts that might help to explain differences between the practices of these courts. Contextual factors include interpretive traditions preceding the enactment of each constitution; judicial personnel (including selection, training, and background); the way in which cases are brought and argued before each court; the style in which judgments are written; the extent to which courts have been influenced by the practices of foreign courts; the prevailing legal and political culture, including traditional conceptions of the nature of law and the proper role of courts; attitudes and reactions of the other branches of government towards perceived judicial 'activism'; the difficulty of formally amending the constitution; and the extent to which judges have felt compelled to 'stretch' their constitutional authority in order to deal with problems such as corruption, oppression, and injustice.

The authors were invited to conclude their chapters with some overall critical observations, on issues such as whether the courts have been either too legalistic or too creative, and the contribution they have made to their societies.

The book ends with my attempt to summarise the information provided in the earlier chapters, compare the approaches of the various national courts, explain significant differences between them, and draw some conclusions.

1

The United States: Eclecticism in the Service of Pragmatism

Mark Tushnet

Constitutional interpretation in the United States is decisively shaped by three features. The US Constitution is old, it is quite difficult to amend, and some of its provisions—notably, those involving fundamental rights—are stated in relatively abstract terms. Because it is old, changes in technology, knowledge, the economic order, and society more broadly not infrequently create a need to adapt constitutional arrangements, both those establishing and organizing the government and those protecting rights. Because the US Constitution is difficult to amend, interpretation, rather than amendment, must carry the burden of adjusting those constitutional arrangements as seems necessary. And, because the Constitution uses abstract terms, someone must specify the meaning of those terms in particular contexts, a task that has fallen almost naturally, though not inevitably, to judges.

The traditions of constitutional interpretation in the United States make it possible, and indeed relatively easy, to use interpretation as the vehicle for constitutional adaptation. The distinction between interpretation and alteration is accordingly quite thin. The interpretive traditions are decidedly eclectic. Interpretation relies on the words of the text as understood when they were made part of the Constitution, general propositions about how institutional arrangements promote constitutionalism, ideas about the values of democracy and individual autonomy, and much more.

The many interpretive tools at hand allow courts to fashion constitutional interpretations, and so the Constitution, so that it does the jobs the courts think need to be done at any specific time. Examples pervade US constitutional history. As judicial visions of the national economy changed, so did the courts' interpretation of national power to regulate commerce among the states. As technology posed what the justices came to see as new threats to personal privacy, the justices devised new constitutional doctrines. Under these circumstances, describing the US Supreme Court's constitutional interpretations as creative may be misleading. Creativity was probably inevitable given the age, brevity, and terms of the Constitution the Court was interpreting.

The Constitution's Origins and Structure

Formation of the Constitution

The US Constitution is a short document, adopted in 1789 and amended only 27 times since. During and after the Revolutionary War of 1776–1783 the states in what became the United States formed a rough alliance among governments. After independence, the states created a confederation, embodied in the Articles of Confederation for the United States. The Articles of Confederation established a legislative body for the confederation, with some powers over matters affecting all the states. The Articles did not establish a national executive, and for all practical purposes no national courts either. The Confederation Congress was a weak institution because it could act effectively only with the essentially unanimous agreement of the states, and lacked power to impose taxes to support national programs, relying instead on frequently ignored requests to states for revenue.

Dissatisfaction among nationally oriented political elites led to efforts to revise the Articles of Confederation. The first effort failed when too few states sent delegates to a convention held in Annapolis, Maryland, in 1786. The Confederation Congress itself authorized a convention to consider amendments to the Articles, which convened in Philadelphia, Pennsylvania, in the summer of 1787. Presided over by George Washington, the leader of the armed forces during the Revolutionary War and the nation's most revered figure, and with intellectual leadership by major political thinkers such as James Madison, the delegates rather quickly decided to go beyond their charge of proposing amendments to the Articles of Confederation and instead drafted a new Constitution for the United States, one that would replace the defective Confederation with a set of institutions that would allow the people in the United States to select enforceable policies on matters that concerned them all and—importantly—would allow the United States to act decisively in international affairs.

The Articles of Confederation stated that they could be amended only if all the states agreed. The drafters of the new Constitution substituted a different procedure for putting the Constitution into effect. The proposed Constitution said that it would go into effect when nine (of the then 13) states agreed to it. To avoid anticipated difficulties from existing state legislatures, whose powers the new Constitution would reduce, the drafters insisted on ratification by special conventions, called in each state to deal solely with the question of ratification. As the ratification campaign proceeded in individual states, suggestions for amending the proposal repeatedly arose. Allowing ratification of an amended document, or ratification conditional on quick adoption of amendments, raised serious problems of coordinating action among the states. The new Constitution's supporters insisted that the document be put to an up-or-down vote, although they promised that, were the Constitution to be adopted, the first Congress would place on its early agenda widely supported amendments such as a Bill of Rights.[1]

In some states ratification was easy, in others hard fought, with opponents emphasizing fears about what a powerful national government could do. The most important ratification fights took place in the largest states, especially Virginia and New York. During the public debate in New York over ratification, James Madison and Alexander Hamilton, with some small contributions from John Jay, wrote a series of newspaper articles, later collected as *The Federalist Papers*, that, though not especially influential in shaping the immediate debate, became immensely important sources for insight into the solutions the framers proposed for the problems they identified.

Basis of the Constitution: Popular versus State Sovereignty

The Constitution proposed in 1787 was ratified by the requisite nine states and went into effect in 1789. The fact that ratification occurred state by state produced constitutional controversies in the nation's first 60 years over whether the national government was best understood as an expression of the will of the people of the United States as a whole, or rather as an agreement among the pre-existing states. Advocates of the former view seemed to have the better case. The Constitution's Preamble begins, 'We the People of the United States,' a phrase that was chosen after rejecting a formulation that referred to the people of the states taken one by one. Ratification occurred in conventions organized on a state-by-state basis because that was the only practical way to achieve ratification; a national referendum, for example, was out of the question not only because of the impossibility of conducting such a referendum in 1787–88 but also because of the framers' discomfort with direct participation by the people in making fundamental law.

The controversy persisted, though, because Southern defenders of slavery—or at least of the right of states to adopt slavery—believed that their interests would be protected better by a conceptualization of the national government as the product of the agreement of the states than by one treating it as the result of a decision by the people of the United States as a whole. South Carolina Senator John C. Calhoun developed a 'states' rights' account of the Constitution that authorized individual states, which had agreed to the Constitution in the first place, to interpose their authority against assertions of national power that a state's legislature believed to be unconstitutional. Calhoun also argued that the state-based origins of the Constitution required that the national government act only with the agreement of what he called concurrent majorities, that is, majorities in each of the nation's regions.

---

[1] On the strategies in the ratification struggle, see J Rakove *Original Meanings: Politics and Ideas in the Making of the Constitution* (AA Knopf, New York, 1996).

Calhoun's approach to the Constitution, and states' rights theories of the Constitution more generally, suffered a severe blow with the North's victory in the Civil War and with the adoption of several clearly nationalizing amendments in the War's aftermath. Still, states' rights theories of the Constitution persisted in popular culture, particularly in the South's defense of its system of racial segregation. Strikingly, they were revived in a dissenting opinion written by Supreme Court Justice Clarence Thomas in a 1995 decision.[2] The case involved attempts by individual states to impose limits on the number of terms their representatives could serve in the national legislature. The Supreme Court held the attempts unconstitutional because states lacked the power to control the composition of the national legislature except in ways specified in the Constitution itself, which did not impose term limits. Justice Thomas, for himself and three other dissenters, argued that the Constitution was created by the people of the states, who therefore retained the power to structure their participation in the national government as they choose. Justice Thomas acknowledged that the Constitution itself might limit that power, but, finding nothing in the Constitution that specifically barred the people of any state from imposing term limits, he would have allowed them to impose such limits. Justice Thomas's approach does not amount to a complete revival of earlier theories, because it focuses on the people—or peoples—of the original states, rather than on states as corporate entities.

The Legislature and the Executive

The original Constitution was primarily concerned with organizing a national government with sufficient power to accomplish national ends. It began with a Preamble, which has not been taken as identifying any legally enforceable propositions, asserting that the Constitution's purposes were 'to form a more perfect union, establish justice, insure domestic tranquility, provide for the common defense, promote the general welfare, and secure the blessings of liberty to ourselves and our posterity.'

The Constitution then devoted three Articles to creating the national legislature, an executive, and the judicial branch. Article I creates a national legislature with two houses. Members of the House of Representatives serve two-year terms, and are chosen directly by the people from districts within the states. Each state is entitled to one representative. With that as a constraint, the Constitution strives to ensure that each state has representation in the House proportionate to its share of the nation's population. In the 1960s the Supreme Court interpreted the requirement that representatives be chosen 'by the People' to require equal representation *within* each state.[3] The Senate consists of two members from each state, each of whom serves for six years. Initially the Constitution provided for the

---

[2] *US Term Limits v Thornton* 514 US 779 (1995).

[3] *Wesberry v Sanders* 376 US 1 (1964) held unconstitutional an apportionment that meant that the single member representing Atlanta, Georgia, had two to three times as many constituents as

selection of Senators by state legislators, in the hope that Senators chosen in that way would be more sensitive to the interests of the states as such and that indirect election would fill the Senate with individuals who were able to take a longer view of the nation's needs than representatives directly responsible to the people. Popular dissatisfaction with indirect election, fuelled by a more general movement toward direct democracy, led to the replacement of indirect by direct election in an amendment adopted in 1913, a change that undermined the argument that senators were particularly responsive to the interests of the states as such. Until the late 20th century, though, the Senate remained a more deliberative body than the House of Representatives, and party discipline was weaker there as well.

Article I begins with the words, 'All legislative powers herein granted shall be vested' in the national legislature. The theory behind this formulation was that the national legislature would have only those powers that were enumerated later in Art I, with all other powers remaining in the state governments. The list of enumerated powers contains some quite specific ones, such as the power to establish post offices and post roads, and some seemingly general ones, such as the power to regulate commerce among the several states. In addition, a sweeping clause gives Congress the power to 'make all laws which shall be necessary and proper for carrying into execution the foregoing powers, and all other powers vested by this Constitution in the government of the United States.' The 1789 Constitution did not contain a residual clause of the sort other constitutions have, but the Tenth Amendment, adopted in 1791, has the form of such a clause, providing, 'The powers not delegated to the United States by the Constitution, nor prohibited by it to the states, are reserved to the states respectively, or to the people.' As the Supreme Court later said, this provision states the 'truism' that whatever has not been granted to Congress is reserved to the states, but does nothing to identify what has been granted.[4] In failing to identify or enumerate the residual powers of the states, even in general terms, the Tenth Amendment lacks content independent of the Constitution's enumeration of powers to the national government.

Large constitutional controversies have arisen around the definition of the scope of the powers enumerated in Art I. In the nation's early years those controversies were compounded by a legal-political theory that treated governmental powers as exclusive, in the sense that a power granted to one government could not be exercised by another. So, for example, if Congress had the power to regulate commerce among the several states, state legislatures could not do so. Expansive definitions of the national power to regulate interstate commerce would therefore disable states from acting even when Congress had not, a troubling result that the Supreme Court struggled to overcome, not entirely successfully.

members representing other districts in the state. Later decisions insisted on quite stringent applications of the rule that congressional districts within each state have equal numbers of constituents, eg *Karcher v Daggett* 426 US 725 (1983) (finding unconstitutional districts that deviated from strict numerical equality by as little as 0.7 per cent between the largest and smallest districts).

[4] *United States v Darby* 312 US 100, 124 (1941).

Eventually the theory that powers were exclusive was abandoned,[5] to be replaced by the more satisfactory one that all government powers were generally concurrent. With that theory in hand, questions of state power arose only when a state law conflicted with some existing national law, and the Constitution itself specified, in the Supremacy Clause of Art VI, that in such cases national law prevailed.

Article II deals with the national executive, a president with a four-year term.[6] The president is elected indirectly. Voters cast their ballots not for a presidential candidate, but for 'electors' who, in modern times, have pledged their votes to a specific candidate. The more important feature of the indirect election is that votes for presidential electors are not aggregated nation-wide. Instead, they are allocated state-by-state, with each state having one elector for each member of the House of Representatives from that state, and two for its Senators. The effect of this allocation is to give smaller states disproportionate influence over the choice of the president. That influence is offset, to some degree, by the tradition embodied in state laws in all but two states that the winner of a plurality of the votes cast for president receives *all* of the state's electoral votes. Another effect of the allocation is that, occasionally (most recently in the 2000 elections), a presidential candidate who receives fewer votes than his opponent will become president.

The Constitution's drafters devoted relatively little thought to defining the president's powers carefully, in part because they knew that George Washington would be the first president. Article II begins with the words, 'The executive power shall be vested,' omitting the words 'herein granted,' suggesting that the president has all powers that can be fairly described as executive in light of British legal history and theorizing about separation of powers by practical political theorists. Yet, other provisions in Art II suggest that the president's inherent executive power might be limited; for example, Art II specifically states that the president 'may require the opinion, in writing, of the principal officer in each of the executive departments, upon any subject relating to the duties of their respective offices,' a provision that seems unnecessary if the president's inherent executive powers are broad.

The Supreme Court

Article III creates the structure of the national judiciary. It provides that there shall be a Supreme Court. Congress is given the power, but not the duty, to create subordinate courts in the national system (referred to in the United States as federal courts), the assumption being that for many matters cases could be processed through the existing state courts and then reviewed by the US Supreme

---

[5] The first case so holding, *Willson v Blackbird Creek Marsh Co* 27 US (2 Pet) 245 (1829), was relatively obscure, but major cases later in the ante bellum period confirmed the abandonment of the exclusive-powers theory, though the cases were decided by highly fractured Courts. See *The License Cases* 46 US (5 How) 504 (1847); *The Passenger Cases* 48 US (7 How) 283 (1849).

[6] The Twenty-Second Amendment, adopted in 1951, limits the president to serving two terms.

Court if necessary. From the beginning, Congress has established lower federal courts, whose jurisdiction has gradually expanded to the point where today nearly every question of national law can be considered in the first instance by a lower federal court.

The Supreme Court is a general high court, not a specialized constitutional court. It has the power to interpret national statutes and even, formally, to develop purely state law, though that power historically was rarely exercised and today never is.[7] The Supreme Court today has almost complete control over its docket,[8] granting review of only a small fraction of the several thousand petitions for review submitted to it. The number of decisions the Court hands down each year has dropped over the past two decades from approximately 150 to approximately 80. These include important statutory interpretation cases as well as constitutional ones. In recent years constitutional cases have made up about half of the Court's docket, with statutory cases occupying the other half.

The Supreme Court is authorized by the Constitution to decide 'cases and controversies.' The Court has interpreted this provision to preclude it from issuing advisory opinions and to require it to decide constitutional questions only when they are presented in a concrete case in which the legal rights of contending parties are at stake. Sporadically the Supreme Court has taken the 'case or controversy' requirement quite seriously, imposing what seem to be significant limitations on the class of litigants who have standing to raise constitutional questions. More often, though, the 'case or controversy' requirement poses only a small obstacle to a well-counselled litigant who wishes to obtain a constitutional determination from the Supreme Court. For example, the Supreme Court has rejected the proposition that legislators have standing to challenge statutes that they believe unconstitutionally grant legislative power to the president (thereby diminishing the objecting legislators' own power),[9] but only a year later entertained and upheld essentially the same challenge when presented to it by a different litigant.[10] In another case the Court denied standing to a person who claimed that federal executive officials had failed to comply with environmental laws that, the litigant said, protected endangered species in other nations, but indicated that had she purchased a ticket to travel to observe the endangered species in their native habitats, she would have had standing.[11] These and other justiciability requirements create some barriers to those who would raise constitutional claims, but in general the

---

[7] The Supreme Court also has the power to develop a national common law for matters of peculiarly national importance, such as the rules determining the boundaries of the states when, for example, the rivers dividing states change course.

[8] The Court gained control over its docket gradually. For about 100 years it had no discretion to decline to hear cases. Starting at the end of the 19th century, and culminating in the so-called Judges Act of 1925, the Court was given discretion over an increasing fraction of its docket. Some areas of mandatory jurisdiction remained, the most important of which involved certain kinds of challenges to state and national laws. Most of that jurisdiction was shifted into the discretionary domain in the 1970s and 1980s.   [9] *Raines v Byrd* 521 US 811 (1997).

[10] *Clinton v New York* 524 US 417 (1998).

[11] *Lujan v Defenders of Wildlife* 504 US 555 (1992).

requirements preclude the courts from hearing only a small number of almost randomly chosen cases.[12] The fact that the Court's docket is discretionary allows it to articulate justiciability doctrines that authorize quite extensive consideration of constitutional questions by lower courts, and then to avoid deciding such questions when the justices conclude that prudence counsels against intervention.

Supreme Court justices serve life terms, subject only to removal by impeachment (with charges brought by the House of Representatives and tried in the Senate) for misconduct.[13] The number of justices is set by statute, not by the Constitution. Historically, the size of the Court has been manipulated to achieve political goals, at least when there were plausible public policy grounds for changing the Court's size. In 1937, though, President Franklin D. Roosevelt's so-called Court-packing plan, aimed at increasing the Court's size to ensure that his political programs would not be held unconstitutional, failed despite Roosevelt's personal popularity. Today the nation's political culture has come to accept nine as the optimal, and for all practical purposes fixed, size for the Supreme Court.

Supreme Court justices are chosen by the president and confirmed by the Senate, which acts by majority vote on nominations. The criteria for choosing Supreme Court justices have varied. Basic legal ability has always been important. Some nominations, particularly those in the 19th century, have been patronage awarded by the president to an important political supporter, or to someone affiliated with an important political faction. Other nominations have gone to personal friends of the president. In the late 20th century, Democratic presidents typically saw Supreme Court nominations as part of ordinary interest group politics, seeking to name people to the Court whose appointments would strengthen the president's position with important interest groups. Republican presidents did something similar, although for them the constituency they sought to satisfy tended to be one focused more directly on the composition of the courts.

Supreme Court decisions in the 1950s, including decisions dealing with segregated education, prayer in public schools, and the rights of political dissenters, particularly Communists, generated substantial political controversy, which influenced the appointment process. Drawing support from academic theorists who identified what they called the 'countermajoritarian difficulty' with judicial review, the Court's critics challenged its supposed activism. The charge of activism stuck, even as the Supreme Court's composition changed. One result was a rhetoric about Supreme Court nominations that emphasized technical expertise as a central qualification for a position on the Supreme Court, and the view that nominees should be 'above' politics, at least in the partisan sense. As a result, an informal norm may have developed requiring that a Supreme Court nominee

---

[12] There is a sense in the cases that issues regarding foreign affairs are particularly insusceptible to judicial resolution, but neither the formal doctrines nor the Court's own decisions actually articulate a clear presumption against adjudicating claims implicating foreign affairs.

[13] No justices have been removed from office by the impeachment process, although Justice Abe Fortas resigned in anticipation of a serious effort to impeach him.

have some judicial experience immediately prior to service on the Court. That would be a change from historic practices, which allowed the appointment of justices from the Senate, such as Hugo Black, or state governorships, such as Earl Warren.

Judicial independence is guaranteed by life tenure and a constitutional ban on reducing the salaries of judges. Formally, there are some mechanisms by which the legislature can try to discipline federal judges. Judges can be impeached for misconduct, Congress can limit the jurisdiction of the courts when it expects unfavourable decisions, and Congress can control the overall court budget, even to the point of freezing judicial salaries during periods of inflation. In practice, none of these methods of discipline has proven effective. No Supreme Court justice has been removed from office via impeachment, and no significant restrictions on jurisdiction have been enacted. The only serious means of political control over the courts is entirely prospective, as political actors determine who will be nominated and confirmed as federal judges. This does give political actors some input into the perspective the judges bring to the general task of constitutional interpretation, but that input still leaves the judges with quite a substantial amount of independence.

Constitutional Amendment

Article V of the Constitution requires that any amendment first be proposed by a two-thirds majority of either both Houses of Congress, or the state legislatures, and then passed by three-quarters of either the state legislatures or special state conventions (the choice between these alternatives being made by Congress). This procedure has been used only 27 times. The structures created in the 1789 Constitution therefore remain in place. Some constitutional amendments tinker with those structures. The Twelfth Amendment, for example, revised the provisions dealing with the indirect election of the president, which had become awkward with the unanticipated rise of nationally organized political parties. The Twentieth Amendment moved forward the date on which a newly elected president took office by two months, responding to the reduced need to accommodate travel difficulties in the modern world.

There are, of course, other more important amendments. The opponents of the original Constitution objected that it failed to include a Bill of Rights, thereby creating a national government with enough power to override treasured rights. The Constitution's supporters responded that the original Constitution did indeed contain some protections for individual rights and, more broadly, that the enumeration of national powers in Art I functioned to protect against rights-violations. Neither claim was particularly persuasive, and the Constitution's supporters retreated, saying that they would support constitutional amendments to cure such defects as soon as the Constitution was ratified and Congress took office. Honouring that promise, James Madison, representing Virginia in the first

House of Representatives, introduced a dozen amendments. Ten were adopted in Congress and ratified by the states, taking effect in 1791.[14]

The first ten amendments are the Bill of Rights. Since 1791 only 17 additional amendments have been added to the Constitution. They fall into two broad categories.[15] As mentioned earlier, some are adjustments, sometimes small, sometimes more significant, in the structure of the national government. Others are rights-protecting and expanding, typically enforcing newer notions of equality. The most significant of the rights-protecting amendments were adopted immediately after the Civil War. The Thirteenth Amendment abolished slavery. The Fourteenth Amendment contains a general guarantee of equality and requires that states provide everyone with due process of law when they deprive people of liberty or property, a provision the Supreme Court interpreted to require that states adhere to the detailed requirements of the Bill of Rights. The Fifteenth Amendment guaranteed the right to vote without regard to race; a guarantee extended to women in 1920 and to young adults in 1971.

The roster of successful constitutional amendments is so short because the amendment process is so difficult. Even constitutional proposals that enjoy substantial public support often fail to make it through the amendment process.[16] In the 1970s the Equal Rights Amendment, which would have guaranteed equal rights to women, failed to obtain sufficient ratifications by state legislatures. In the 1990s constitutional amendments to overturn Supreme Court decisions barring governments from enforcing laws against flag-burning as a means of political protest failed to gain the two-thirds vote in both houses of Congress and were never submitted to the states for ratification. Yet, in both instances, surveys indicated that far more than a majority of the American people—although not always two-thirds or three-quarters of the people—supported the proposals.

Another reason for the small number of amendments is that a culture has arisen strongly cautioning against amending the Constitution at all. Sometimes politicians who probably oppose specific amendments on the merits argue not against the specific proposal but instead mount general arguments against changing the Constitution in response to possibly transitory public urges. Such arguments appear to persuade enough members of the public that politicians who vote against popular amendments suffer relatively little political damage.

The US Constitution, then, is old, short, and stable—in a world where change produces political innovations and pressures to adapt constitutional structures and rights to new circumstances. Constitutional interpretation has been the only

[14] One of the amendments sent to the states languished for 200 years, eventually securing the requisite number of ratifications in 1992. The Twenty-seventh Amendment delays the effective date of salary increases for members of Congress until after an election occurs.

[15] The Sixteenth Amendment, authorizing the national government to impose an income tax, overturned a Supreme Court decision holding a national income tax unconstitutional.

[16] For an overview of the historical experience in the amendment process, see DE Kyvig *Explicit and Authentic Acts: Amending the US Constitution, 1776–1995* (University Press of Kansas, Lawrence, 1996).

method available as a practical matter in US constitutional law to deal with change and its consequences for the constitutional order.

Problems and Methods of Interpretation

The US Constitution does not expressly provide for judicial review, but lawyers in the framing generation were essentially unanimous in agreeing that courts had *some* power of judicial review.[17] Without a constitutional provision conferring the power of judicial review, the Constitution unsurprisingly lacks any provisions dealing with how it is to be interpreted.[18]

General Problems of Constitutional Interpretation

The major problems of constitutional interpretation in the United States arise from three features of the Constitution and the structures it creates. First, some of the terms used in the Constitution to deal with issues of enduring importance are rather general. What is 'commerce,' for example? What does 'due process' require? What are the 'privileges or immunities' of US citizens? Second, and related, the technical or widely understood meanings of such terms at the time they were inserted into the Constitution often seem archaic and unsuited to dealing with the social and economic issues that have emerged over the years. Third, the Constitution does a good job of describing how each of the three branches of government should operate internally, but does little to specify how the branches should relate to each other.

The authors of *The Federalist Papers* offered solutions to the first and third of these problems, but those solutions did not endure. As to the first, James Madison agreed that some of the Constitution's terms were 'more or less equivocal,' but said that 'their meaning [would] be liquidated and ascertained by a series of particular discussions and adjudications.'[19] As the nation grappled with the new Constitution, its decision-makers would specify what the uncertain terms meant, narrowing over time the range of interpretive options.

[17] Precisely what that power was, though, was indeed a matter of contention. Some advocated a narrow departmentalist view, according to which courts could invalidate legislation that, in the judges' view, violated the Constitution's provisions dealing with the judiciary itself. Others advocated a broader departmentalist view, according to which each branch had the power to act on its own constitutional interpretations—which, in some situations, would lead to a contest over power between or among the branches. Few advocated judicial supremacy, according to which the judges' own interpretations of the Constitution prevailed as a matter of law over the contrary interpretations offered by the other branches.

[18] Two constitutional amendments do contain interpretive directives. The Ninth Amendment provides, 'The enumeration in the Constitution, of certain rights, shall not be construed to deny or disparage others retained by the people,' and the Eleventh Amendment provides, 'The Judicial power of the United States shall not be construed to extend' to a list of described suits against states.

[19] *The Federalist* no 37.

Madison's solution to the problem of vagueness depends on a vision of precedent-based decision-making that proved impossible to sustain. The vision required various kinds of stability—in the problems presented to the courts, in the views of judges about the values the Constitution protected, and in the judges' willingness to subordinate their views about those values to the views expressed in the precedents—that simply did not exist.

Two persistent controversies in US constitutional law illustrate these difficulties: the question of the scope of Congress's power to regulate interstate commerce, and the question of whether the Constitution protects fundamental rights against infringements by state governments.

Writers in the years surrounding the Constitution's framing regularly referred to a trio of economic activities: agriculture, manufacturing, and commerce. The latter referred primarily to the sale and purchase of goods, secondarily to the activity of transporting goods for sale. The Supreme Court first confronted the question of what the word *commerce* meant in the Constitution in a case involving the constitutionality of a federal statute giving a steamboat operator a license to operate between New York and New Jersey.[20] The word's traditional meaning clearly encompassed the navigation statute, although one party to the case argued otherwise. Chief Justice John Marshall used the occasion to offer a more far-reaching definition: 'Commerce, undoubtedly, is traffic, but it is something more: it is intercourse. It describes the commercial intercourse between nations, and parts of nations, in all its branches, and is regulated by prescribing rules for carrying on that intercourse.'[21] By first drawing a distinction between commerce and commercial intercourse and then holding that Congress's power extended to the latter, Marshall CJ effectively erased the earlier line separating commerce on the one hand from manufacturing and agriculture on the other.

Marshall CJ's definition appears to have been motivated by his vision of an expanding national economy, which he believed required regulation by the national legislature, which could take a wide view of the economy's needs, rather than by more parochial state legislatures. And, indeed, as the economy expanded, Congress responded by adopting more regulations under the Commerce Clause. In 1895 the Supreme Court tried to resuscitate the distinction between commerce, which Congress could regulate, and manufacturing, which it could not.[22] Economic and social pressures produced powerful social movements favouring national regulation of the manufacturing and sale of goods. Congress responded by enacting laws attempting to restrict the sale and distribution of mislabelled food and drugs, and the employment of child labour in manufacturing enterprises. Sometimes the Court invalidated these laws, sometimes it upheld them. The Court's decisions seemed inconsistent to many contemporaneous

---

[20] *Gibbons v Ogden* 22 US 1 (1824).   [21] ibid 189–190.
[22] *United States v EC Knight Co* 156 US 1 (1895).

observers. The decisions illuminate the problems with Madison's precedent-based solution to the problem of vagueness. Bound by the newly revived distinction between manufacturing and commerce, the Court developed alternative tests for determining whether the Constitution limited Congress's power. The two most prominent were the so-called 'stream of commerce' test, which allowed Congress to regulate activities that were part of the flow of commerce, and the even more expansive 'affecting commerce' test, which allowed Congress to regulate activities that affected commerce as Marshall CJ had defined it.

Conceptually, it was possible to assemble these three tests into a coherent whole, but in doing so the Court discovered that the limits on congressional power were insubstantial and not defensible in terms of any sensible account of *why* Congress's powers should be limited. The upshot of the story is that the meaning of the vague term *commerce* was not 'liquidated and ascertained' by a series of decisions. Instead, the series of decisions articulated alternative definitions of the word, which could be deployed as judges with varying views about the scope of congressional power gained and lost support on the Court.

The Supreme Court's treatment of fundamental rights is similar. The first ten amendments, usually referred to as the Bill of Rights, were interpreted early on as protecting rights such as freedom of expression only against actions by the national government.[23] The national controversy over slavery led many to believe that constitutional guarantees against violations of fundamental rights by state governments were needed as well. The Fourteenth Amendment, adopted after the end of the Civil War, was the response to that concern.

The Fourteenth Amendment protects people against deprivations of liberty and property 'without due process of law' by state governments, and bars states from enacting laws that 'abridge the privileges or immunities of citizens of the United States.' The natural, non-technical reading of these provisions is that the first deals with the procedures states may use, and that the second identifies substantive limits on state power. That reading is supported by the precedential background. In 1823, Supreme Court Justice Bushrod Washington, writing in a case he heard as a trial judge, interpreted the provision in the 1789 Constitution that guaranteed the citizens of each state 'the privileges and immunities of the citizens in the several states.' This was designed to prevent one state from discriminating against citizens of other states, but interpreting it required Washington J to define the term *privileges and immunities*. He gave it an expansive reading:

[p]rotection by the government; the enjoyment of life and liberty, with the right to acquire and possess property of every kind, and to pursue and obtain happiness and safety; subject

---

[23] *Barron v Baltimore* 32 US (7 Pet) 243 (1833). The First Amendment specifically states that 'Congress shall make no law' limiting free speech; other provisions in the Bill of Rights, such as the Fifth Amendment, guaranteeing due process of law, do not refer in terms only to the national government, but *Barron* stated the general understanding in holding that the Fifth Amendment required only the national government to comply with the Due Process clause.

nevertheless to such restraints as the government may justly prescribe for the general good of the whole.[24]

The drafters of the Fourteenth Amendment knew of, and relied on, Washington J's expansive definition.[25] The Supreme Court found that definition *too* expansive, threatening to replace state legislative authority with federal judicial authority over too wide a range. It held that the Fourteenth Amendment's clause identified only a small set of rights, those that were inherent in being a *national* citizen such as the right to diplomatic protection, hardly an issue in connection with state governments, and the somewhat more important right to travel from one state through another on the way to the national capital.[26]

This did not end the effort to obtain protection of fundamental rights against state violations. The text litigants relied on simply shifted from the Privileges or Immunities Clause to the Due Process Clause. Relying on a long tradition from which the words *due process* derived, litigants—and rather soon the Supreme Court—argued that the Due Process Clause protected everyone against arbitrary government actions. The next step was simple: Actions that deprived people of fundamental rights were, by definition, arbitrary, and therefore violated the Due Process Clause. The migration of protection of fundamental rights from one constitutional provision to another one provides another example of the way in which constitutional meaning need not be 'liquidated and ascertained' in a series of decisions.

As to the third problem, that of the relation among the three branches of government, Madison offered a theory, not of interpretation, but of political interaction. The branches would relate to each other as one power-holder to another, each seeking to achieve the most it could in a sort of bargaining process. First, he wrote, the Constitution connected 'the interest of the man'—the occupant of a position in the national government—with 'the constitutional rights of the place.'[27] Seeking to protect their own interests, political actors would simultaneously protect the institution of which they were a part. And, when 'ambition [was] made to counteract ambition,' the political branches would—through politics, not through the application of reason in adjudications—work out the way the Constitution arranged power.[28]

Madison's solution to the third problem was more successful than the one he offered for the first problem. Persistent controversies over the roles of Congress and the president in connection with war illustrate how the Constitution has been 'interpreted' by political practice rather than by reasoned decision. The Constitution gives Congress the power to 'declare War,' gives the president the executive power, and makes the president the commander in chief of the armed forces. Originally the Constitution's drafters proposed that Congress be given the power to make

[24] *Corfield v Coryell* 6 Fed Cas 546 no 3230 (CC ED Pa 1823).
[25] They did not believe that the replacement of the word *and* by the word *or* had any substantive implications.   [26] *The Slaughterhouse Cases* 83 US 36 (1873).
[27] *The Federalist* no 51.   [28] ibid.

war, but that proposal was modified when critics pointed out that only the president was in a position to, as they put it, repel sudden attacks.

In 1977 Congress enacted the War Powers Resolution (a statute despite its name), which purports to place procedural and substantive limits on what the president can do in deploying US military forces abroad. According to the statute, for example, the president must report to Congress on substantial deployments when the armed forces might engage in war-like activities, and must get approval within 60 days of such deployments. Since its enactment, presidents have taken the position that the War Powers Resolution is an unconstitutional infringement on the powers the president has as commander in chief and chief executive. Even so, they have regularly submitted the reports required by the Resolution, usually saying that they are doing do out of courtesy rather than compulsion. And, because substantial military operations typically require special appropriations of funds from Congress, presidents have been careful to line up support for their most controversial actions before the armed forces are deployed—even though they have not always sought explicit prior authorization for the deployments. Congress's power to control appropriations gives it a significant 'bargaining chip' in the informal negotiations between the president and Congress over who has the power to do what with respect to the use of US military forces.

The political accommodations reached by the president and Congress simply *are* what the Constitution means with respect to war powers, as Madison's solution suggested. Similar examples of inter-branch negotiation and accommodation suggest that Madison's solution to the problems created by the Constitution's failure to specify how the branches are to relate to each other is a quite general one.

That solution is not completely satisfactory, though. The difficulty is that the two sides invoke, not merely their political resources, but the rhetorical resources offered by the Constitution's terms. In the war powers discussions, for example, 'declare War' and 'repel sudden attacks' are rhetorical weapons on Congress's side, met by 'commander in chief' on the president's side. With the rise of judicial review, Americans have come to expect that the courts will specify what the Constitution's terms mean. Yet, the Supreme Court has assiduously refrained from intervening in the war powers discussion. In consequence, constitutional rhetoric is thrown around by partisans on both sides, with no referee to help the public understand the Constitution's true bearing on the disputes. Madison's solution was to use politics to displace constitutional rhetoric as a means of resolving separation-of-powers problems, but the Constitution's terms inevitably interject themselves in discussions of those problems. Madison's approach fails to grapple with that fact.

The Supreme Court might in principle resolve separation-of-powers disputes. But its interventions in other separation-of-powers disputes have had a curiously formalistic tone, demonstrating little awareness of the political context in which those disputes are set—and, as a result, having little effect on the actual resolution of the disputes. The best example is a long-standing controversy over the so-called legislative veto, a practice that allowed Congress to override decisions made by executive officials to whom Congress had delegated some authority, without revoking the delegation or indeed enacting a statute submitted to the president for signature. The legislative veto operated in this way: The executive action was reported to Congress. One or both houses could then pass a resolution of disapproval. If such a resolution was passed, the action did not take effect. Notably, these resolutions of disapproval were not submitted to the president for signature or veto.

The Supreme Court held the legislative veto unconstitutional.[29] According to the Court, the legislative veto was inconsistent with the Constitution's requirement that all bills be submitted to the president for signature, defining 'bills' as legislative actions affecting the legal rights of persons outside the legislative branch. The Court's opinion was widely criticized for its formalism and incoherence; for example, one could plausibly contend that a person had no legal rights until the time for exercising the legislative veto over an executive action affecting him or her had passed.

More important, the Court's decision failed to appreciate *why* Congress enacted statutes authorizing legislative vetoes. They were designed to deal with a pervasive problem in the modern administrative state. Legislatures lack the time and resources to deal with problems through detailed legislative schemes. To accomplish their desired goals, they delegate their authority to executive officials. But, they need to ensure that their delegates carry out the policies the legislatures actually want implemented. The legislative veto is one among many mechanisms for legislative oversight of authority delegated to executive officials. Eliminating it accomplishes almost nothing, because Congress has found it easy to substitute alternatives that are nearly as good—some of which, indeed, intrude on executive prerogatives more substantially than the legislative veto did. Here too Madison seems to have had the right answer. His solution was undermined, again, by the widespread acceptance of the Supreme Court as the Constitution's ultimate interpreter.

Early Examples of Constitutional Interpretation

The use of abstract terms in the Constitution and the fact that new laws had to be judged against an old Constitution meant that neither text nor precedent would be sufficient to determine what the Constitution meant. In the nation's early years the question of constitutional interpretation was not examined in any sustained theoretical inquiry. Discussions of constitutional interpretation relied on the then-prevailing common sense about how one interpreted *any* documents, including ordinary contracts and statutes, with some modest modifications to take account of the fact that the document being interpreted was a constitution.

---

[29] *Immigration and Naturalization Service v Chadha* 462 US 919 (1983).

Three early discussions of constitutional interpretation illustrate the views of the Constitution's first generation of interpreters. James Madison believed that Congress lacked the power to create a national bank, which Alexander Hamilton, his compatriot in the battle over the Constitution, favoured as George Washington's Secretary of the Treasury. Madison delivered a major speech on the subject in the House of Representatives in 1791. He prefaced his analysis of the constitutional question by 'laying down' some rules for interpretation:

An interpretation that destroys the very characteristic of the government cannot be just. Where a meaning is clear, the consequences, whatever they may be, are to be admitted— where doubtful, it is fairly triable by its consequences. In controverted cases, the meaning of the parties to the instrument, if it be collected by reasonable evidence, is a proper guide. Contemporary and concurrent expositions are a reasonable evidence of the meaning of the parties. In admitting or rejecting a constructive authority, not only the degree of its incidentality to an express authority, is to be regarded, but the degree of its importance also; since on this will depend the probability or improbability of its being left to construction.[30]

These rules are not quite banalities, but they rather clearly are unlikely to provide strong guidance in any difficult case.

Two generations later Francis Lieber, an expatriate German who became a celebrated public intellectual in the United States, wrote the first sustained exposition of statutory and constitutional interpretation. Lieber's book, *Legal and Political Hermeneutics* (1837), contained a longer list of rules for interpretation. So, for example: 'Words are . . . to be taken as the utterer probably meant them to be taken.' Lieber elaborated a set of subsidiary rules as well. 'The construction ought to harmonize with the substance and general spirit of the text,' for example. Because they were adopted after serious deliberation, constitutions 'should be closely construed in most cases.' Again, these are useful but hardly conclusive.[31]

Probably the most influential statement about constitutional interpretation came, unsurprisingly, from Chief Justice John Marshall and the Supreme Court. The issue in *McCulloch v Maryland*[32] was, once again (but for the first time in the Supreme Court), the constitutionality of the statute creating the Bank of the United States. No enumerated power specifically gave Congress the power to create a bank, and indeed the constitutional convention expressly considered whether to enumerate that power and decided against doing so. The issue before the Court, then, was whether the power to create a bank could be inferred from any of the other enumerated powers. The Court said that Congress did have the power to create the Bank. That answer, Marshall CJ wrote, flowed from 'a fair construction of the whole instrument.'[33] Echoing Madison and foreshadowing Lieber, Marshall CJ said that it was 'essential to just construction, that many words which import something excessive, should be understood in a more

---

[30] *Speech on the Bank of the United States* House of Representatives 2 February 1791 (J Madison).
[31] Lieber's work was widely read and almost immediately ignored.
[32] *McCulloch v Maryland* 17 US 316 (1819).   [33] ibid 406.

mitigated sense—in that sense which common usage justifies.'[34] In construing constitutional terms, 'the subject, the context, the intention of the person using them, are all to be taken into view.'[35]

Constitutions could not deal in detail with everything the governments they created would do:

A constitution, to contain an accurate detail of all the subdivisions of which its great powers will admit, and of all the means by which they may be carried into execution, would partake of the prolixity of a legal code, and could scarcely be embraced by the human mind. It would probably never be understood by the public.[36]

Instead, 'only its great outlines should be marked, its important objects designated, and the minor ingredients which compose those objects be deduced from the nature of the objects themselves.'[37] So, he concluded, 'In considering this question, then, we must never forget, that *it is a constitution we are expounding*.'[38] Marshall CJ supplemented this point with his observation a few pages later that the Constitution was 'intended to endure for ages to come, and, consequently, to be adapted to the various crises of human affairs.'[39]

Marshall CJ's opinion in the *McCulloch* case became the touchstone for everyone who defended the idea of a living Constitution. Commentators occasionally suggested that Marshall CJ's observation about the need for the Constitution to be adapted to unanticipated crises did indeed provide support for the idea of a living Constitution with respect to the *powers* of government, but was less apt when questions arose about interpreting the Constitution's old provisions to deal with new intrusions on individual rights. Still, Marshall CJ's formulations became part of the common sense about interpreting the Constitution.

The *McCulloch* opinion does more than articulate general propositions about constitutional interpretation. The details of Marshall CJ's argument provide an almost complete catalogue of the techniques of constitutional interpretation used in US constitutional law. After using the opinion to illustrate the techniques, this Chapter examines the techniques in more detail.

Marshall CJ did not begin his discussion of whether Congress had the power to create the bank by citing any specific constitutional language. Instead, he observed that a national bank had been created by the first Congress after full discussion there and by Hamilton and Thomas Jefferson within the president's cabinet. The long-standing judgment of the political branches, reflected in practice, should make 'a considerable impression' on the courts: 'It would require no ordinary share of intrepidity to assert that a measure adopted under these circumstances was a bold and plain usurpation.'[40] Marshall CJ then qualified his reliance on practice: 'These observations belong to the case; but they are not made under the impression that, were the question entirely new, the law would be found irreconcilable with the constitution.'[41]

---

[34] *McCulloch v Maryland* 414.   [35] ibid 415.   [36] ibid 407.   [37] ibid.
[38] ibid 407.   [39] ibid 415.   [40] ibid 402.   [41] ibid.

Marshall CJ next turned to an exposition of the general theory of the Constitution's creation. Maryland's lawyers contended that the national government's powers had been delegated to it from the states, not from the people, and that the states therefore were 'truly sovereign.' Examining the Constitution's history, Marshall CJ rejected the argument. The national government got its authority from the people of the states acting in special conventions called solely for the purpose of ratification, not from the standing state legislatures.[42]

Only after these points did Marshall CJ even mention the constitutional text. He acknowledged that the text did not specifically say that Congress had the power to create a national bank. But, he noted, the Tenth Amendment, declaring that the powers not delegated to the national government were reserved to the states, 'omits the word "expressly".'[43] The list of enumerated powers defined the 'great outlines' of the national government's powers, leaving the 'minor ingredients' to be 'deduced from' the enumerated powers.[44] Marshall CJ pointed to the power to collect taxes, borrow money, and raise and support armies and navies. A national bank, according to Marshall CJ, was one of the 'usual means' of carrying out those enumerated powers.[45] 'The exigencies of the nation may require that the treasure raised in the north should be transported to the south.'[46] Without a national bank, 'these operations [would be] difficult, hazardous, and expensive.'[47]

Maryland agreed that Congress has some choice of methods to implement its enumerated powers, but contended that the choice was limited by the final clause in the section enumerating Congress's powers, the Necessary and Proper Clause. Marshall CJ's discussion of the clause began by observing that it was placed in the section of the Constitution granting Congress power, rather than in the section limiting that power, a point to which he returned later in the opinion, when he added that the clause's terms 'purport to enlarge, not to diminish the powers vested in the government. It purports to be an additional power, not a restriction on those already granted.'[48]

Marshall CJ continued by expounding on the ordinary meaning of the word *necessary*. According to Marshall CJ, 'in the common affairs of the world' and 'in approved authors,' the word 'frequently imports no more than that one thing is convenient, or useful, or essential to another.'[49] It 'admits of all degrees of comparison,' a point Marshall CJ bolstered by pointing to another constitutional provision that prohibited states from laying duties on imports 'except what may be absolutely necessary for executing its inspection laws.'[50]

Marshall CJ then examined the effects of a restrictive interpretation of the Necessary and Proper Clause. Congress had the power to establish post offices and post roads, and based on that power it had made it a crime to steal from the mails.

---

[42] This rejects the proposition that the Constitution emanated from the states in their corporate capacities, but not the different theory, discussed earlier, that it emanated from the peoples of the several states coordinating their separate decisions.   [43] *McCulloch v Maryland* (n 32) 406.
[44] ibid 407.   [45] ibid 409.   [46] ibid 409.   [47] ibid 408.   [48] ibid 420.
[49] ibid 413.   [50] ibid 414.

The criminal statute was 'essential to the beneficial exercise of the power, but not indispensably necessary to its existence.'[51]

Maryland objected that Marshall CJ's argument that enumerated powers themselves gave Congress the power to implement them made the Necessary and Proper Clause redundant. Marshall CJ replied that the clause might have been included out of a 'desire to remove all doubts respecting the right to legislate on that vast mass of incidental powers which must be involved in the constitution, if that instrument be not a splendid bauble.'[52]

The case raised a second question. Maryland had imposed a tax on the operations of the national bank and, even if Congress had the power to create the bank, still Maryland's tax might be constitutionally permissible. Among the arguments Marshall CJ developed against Maryland's position, one has continuing relevance. Maryland argued that its tax was permissible because people in other states, who benefited from the bank's existence, should be confident that Maryland would not impose a tax so large as to interfere with the bank's operations. Marshall CJ replied, 'Would the people of any one State trust those of another with a power to control the most insignificant operations of their State government? We know they would not.'[53] People have confidence in the governments in which they are represented, and '[i]n the legislature of the Union alone, are all represented. The legislature of the Union alone, therefore, can be trusted by the people with the power of controlling measures which concern all, in the confidence that it will not be abused.'[54]

Marshall CJ's idea here is that political representation is an important means by which the people guard against abusive exercises of power. Maryland's argument failed because people in other states, who might be affected by Maryland's actions, were not represented in that state's legislature. Political representation could not protect against an abusive tax. Marshall CJ's idea supports a more general proposition about constitutional interpretation: Constitutional provisions should be interpreted so as to enhance the ability of the people to use their power as voters to protect them against over-reaching by legislatures.

McCulloch did not implicate one other approach to constitutional interpretation that already had arisen in the Supreme Court. Can judges go beyond the constitutional text and invoke unwritten principles of justice in deciding cases? Two Supreme Court justices discussed that question in *Calder v Bull* (1798).[55] The case involved the constitutionality of a Connecticut statute authorizing the state courts to re-hear an already decided case invalidating a will. The claim was that this statute violated the federal Constitution's ban on state 'ex post facto' laws. The justices agreed that it did not, because the ban applied only to laws that made a crime out of something that was legal at the time it was done. In describing the point of constitutional limitations, Justice Samuel Chase said that the

[51] *McCulloch v Maryland* (n 32) 416.   [52] ibid 421.   [53] ibid 431.   [54] ibid.
[55] 3 US 386 (1798).

Constitution rested on 'certain vital principles' that limited government power—even if those principles were not set out in the Constitution itself:

It is against all reason and justice, for a people to entrust a Legislature with SUCH powers; and, therefore, it cannot be presumed that they have done it. . . . To maintain that our Federal, or State, Legislature possesses such powers, if they had not been expressly restrained; would, in my opinion, be a political heresy, altogether inadmissible in our free republican governments.[56]

Chase J gave as examples a statute that made a person the judge in his own case, and a statute that simply took property from one person and transferred it to another. Nothing found in the written Constitution as it stood in 1798 specifically made such statutes unconstitutional,[57] and yet to Chase J they were.

Justice James Iredell disagreed. For Iredell J, the Constitution did limit government, but only in the ways specified in its text:

If . . . the Legislature of the Union, or the Legislature of any member of the Union, shall pass a law, within the general scope of their constitutional power, the Court cannot pronounce it to be void, merely because it is, in their judgment, contrary to the principles of natural justice.[58]

Iredell J continued by identifying a theme that would eventually come to predominate in theorizing about constitutional interpretation—the inability of anyone to identify the constraints natural justice (or, in later treatments, any other constitutional theory) placed on government. In Iredell J's terms, 'The ideas of natural justice are regulated by no fixed standard,'[59] and so those ideas provided no sound basis for judicial invalidation of a statute. References to natural justice and similar concepts persisted in Supreme Court decisions nonetheless. In effect, the Court never chose between the positions offered by Chase and Iredell.

I turn now to a more detailed examination of the methods of interpretation sketched in *McCulloch* and *Calder v Bull*.

Text

Ordinary meaning

Interpretation of course begins with the constitutional text, and sometimes ends there. Many of the provisions setting out the structure of the national government are indisputably clear, the conventional examples being the provisions using numerical terms such as the one specifying that each state shall have two Senators,

---

[56] *McCulloch v Maryland* 388–389.

[57] The Fifth Amendment contains a due process clause and a provision that private property shall not be taken for public use without just compensation, which can be read to require that all takings be for public purposes. These provisions could readily be interpreted to make Chase J's hypothetical statutes unconstitutional. Chase J had state laws in mind, though, and, as discussed earlier, early interpreters took the Fifth Amendment to restrict only the national government.

[58] *Calder v Bull* (n 55) 399.   [59] ibid.

or the one setting forth the rule that a person must be 35 years old to be eligible for the presidency.

Occasionally even apparently transparent constitutional language can be over-ridden. A useful example is provided by the Emoluments Clause, which provides: 'No Senator or Representative shall, during the time for which he was elected, be appointed to any civil office under the authority of the United States, which shall have been created, or the emoluments whereof shall have been increased during such time.' Sometimes the following situation arises: Congress enacts a statute increasing the salaries of members of the president's Cabinet. During that same term of Congress, the president finds it politically useful to name a member of Congress to the Cabinet. To accommodate the president, Congress enacts a new statute returning the salary of the particular Cabinet position to its level at the start of the congressional term. This practice, which has become known as the 'Saxbe fix' after Ohio Senator and Attorney General William Saxbe, has become uncontroversial, although the Supreme Court has never addressed its constitutionality. It is rather clearly in severe tension with the Constitution's language. The salary *was* increased during the affected person's term in Congress, and the fact that it was later decreased seems irrelevant in light of the Constitution's wording.

Technical meaning

The foregoing example involves interpretation according to the ordinary meaning of constitutional language. Some constitutional terms had technical meanings when they were inserted into the Constitution. The *Ex Post Facto* Clause at issue in *Calder v Bull* is an example. The core idea behind the clause is that there is something particularly unjust about changing the law to a person's disadvantage at a time when the person can do nothing to conform his or her conduct to the new law—after the fact almost literally. The injustice is not obviously different when the law takes away a person's property by changing the rules under which the property was already acquired, or when the law makes a person's completed actions illegal when they were lawful at the time they were done. Yet, in the *Calder* case the justices agreed that the *Ex Post Facto* Clause applied only to criminal statutes, not to the civil statute changing the distribution of property pursuant to a will.

Another, more complex, example involves the Constitution's two Due Process Clauses. The ordinary meaning of those clauses would make them applicable to the procedures used to deprive people of property or liberty. Yet, by the time they were inserted into the Constitution, the term *due process* had acquired an additional technical meaning. It was the modern version of the phrase *law of the land* used in Magna Charta, and had come to mean that neither executive actions nor legislation could be unreasonable or arbitrary.[60] That is, the term *due process* had come to incorporate some substantive limitations on government power.

---

[60] For a discussion, see JV Orth *Due Process of Law* (University North Carolina Press, Chapel Hill, 2003).

Notably, interpretations that rely on technical meanings are inevitably originalist. The technical meaning at the time of adoption controls, not ordinary understanding (either then or at the time interpretation occurs).

Textual structure

The overall structure of the constitutional text also provides the basis for interpreting particular provisions. *McCulloch* provides two examples of what Akhil Amar has recently called *intratextualism*.[61] By contrasting the word *necessary* in the Necessary and Proper Clause with the phrase *absolutely necessary* in the clause dealing with state inspection laws, Marshall CJ was able to establish that the Constitution contemplated the possibility that necessity admitted of degrees. And, by observing that the Necessary and Proper Clause was included in the enumeration of Congress's powers, Marshall CJ was able to undermine the state's argument that the clause should operate as a limitation on the other enumerated powers.

'Holistic' interpretation

The relation between one constitutional provision and amendments added later has received some attention recently. The issue is whether an amendment not directed at a particular existing constitutional provision can be invoked to justify a new interpretation of that provision. In *United States v Morrison*, the Supreme Court held that a provision of the Violence Against Women Act 2000 was unconstitutional.[62] The provision gave a civil remedy in the national courts to victims of gender-motivated violence. Congress attempted to justify the provision by establishing that violence against women had a serious adverse impact on interstate commerce. The Court held that Congress lacked power under the Commerce Clause to enact the provision, because acts of violence against women were not themselves commercial in nature. Proponents of holistic interpretation argue that later adopted amendments, such as the Nineteenth Amendment guaranteeing women the right to vote, should be used to inform the interpretation of the Commerce Clause.[63] This approach, while attracting some academic support, has not yet worked its way into the Court's interpretive jurisprudence.

Text and practice

The 'Saxbe fix' is little more than 100 years old. It indicates that long-standing practice can sometimes validate statutes that might otherwise be held unconstitutional. The Supreme Court has never been entirely clear about the relation between text and practice. Marshall CJ opened his opinion in the *McCulloch* case by observing that the national bank had been in existence for many years, and took that practice to have some weight. He then immediately qualified his reliance on practice, specifically attempting to overcome the inference that he was relying

---

[61] AR Amar 'Intratextualism' (1999) 112 Harvard L Rev 748.   [62] 529 US 598 (2000).
[63] eg VC Jackson 'Holistic Interpretation: Fitzpatrick v Bitzer' (2001) 53 Stanford L Rev 1259.

on practice because otherwise Congress lacked the power to create the bank. The Court has been persistently ambivalent about the relation between text and practice. Justice William Rehnquist once wrote: 'Past practice does not, by itself, create power,'[64] but that observation was preceded by a quotation from Justice Felix Frankfurter, that 'a systematic [and] unbroken practice . . . may be treated as a gloss' on specific constitutional terms—at least those terms that require glossing because their meaning is subject to fair dispute.[65]

Constitutional Structure

Professor Charles Black emphasized the importance of structural considerations in interpreting the Constitution.[66] Black's primary example was a 1965 case challenging the constitutionality of a state law barring members of the armed forces from voting in state elections, even though the soldiers satisfied the state's general requirement that only state residents could vote.[67] The Supreme Court held the statute unconstitutional as a violation of the Constitution's Equal Protection Clause. The case was a simple one from the standpoint of constitutional doctrine in 1965, although the application of the Equal Protection Clause to voting rights had been controversial earlier. Black argued that there was a simpler and better way to deal with the case. The state statute, according to Black, manifested a hostility to the national government and its employees that was inconsistent with the structural premises of the union: States could not treat national soldiers as an occupying or foreign force.

Structural considerations have been important in cases dealing with the relation between the states and the nation. When California took advantage of a congressional statute that purported to authorize states to provide public assistance to recent migrants from another state at only the level the new residents had received in the states they had left, the Supreme Court invoked a constitutional right to travel protected by the Privileges and Immunities Clause to invalidate the statute.[68] Again, the holding was not doctrinally innovative. The Court took that clause as expressing an idea of national unity, to the effect that states were not allowed to treat migrants from other states as foreigners. The Privileges and Immunities Clause does indeed express that idea, but once again the Court could have relied on inferences from the structure of the national government to support its conclusion.

The foregoing cases illustrate how structural considerations can support nationalist conclusions. Such considerations have been used more recently, and more prominently, to support conclusions protecting the states against the

---

[64] *Dames & Moore v Regan* 453 US 654, 686 (1981).

[65] *Youngstown Sheet & Tube Co v Sawyer* 343 US 579, 610–611 (1952).

[66] CL Black Jr *Structure and Relationship in Constitutional Law* (Louisiana State University Press, Baton Rouge, 1969).   [67] *Carrington v Rash* 380 US 89 (1965).

[68] *Saenz v Roe* 526 US 48 (1999).

nation. The cases involve two kinds of immunities of state governments from national action. The first is an immunity from substantive regulations imposed by the national government, the second is an immunity from suit for violations of substantive regulations that the national government has the power to impose.

The substantive immunity protects states against what the Supreme Court calls the commandeering of their legislative or executive branches in the service of national goals. The Supreme Court has as yet invoked the anti-commandeering principle only twice. In one case, the Court held that Congress could not require state legislatures to enact legislation, complying with federal standards, that had the effect of determining where in a state a nuclear waste disposal site would be located.[69] In the other, the Court held that Congress could not require local law enforcement officers to devote 'reasonable' efforts to verify whether gun purchasers were eligible under federal law to buy the guns.[70] In neither case could the Court rely on specific constitutional language protecting states against these forms of commandeering. Indeed, in the gun-control case, Justice Antonin Scalia explicitly noted that there was 'no constitutional text speaking to this precise question.'[71] The Court relied on 'historical understanding and practice' and on 'the structure of the Constitution' to support its conclusion.[72] For the Court, that structure was one in which the states retained important elements of sovereignty. It cited various constitutional provisions, including the Constitution's ban on changing a state's boundaries without its consent and, more generally, the presupposition that states would have citizens of their own. Allowing the national government to commandeer state governments would, according to the Court, reduce the protection of liberty provided by the division of power between national and state governments.

The relation between structural reasoning and constitutional text is shown even more clearly in the cases involving state immunity from suit. Two contextual features are important. First, the cases involve nationally imposed substantive rules that do not violate the anti-commandeering principle. States must comply with the substantive requirements, which include minimum wage laws and anti-discrimination laws. Second, there is a specific constitutional provision dealing with state immunity from suit. The Eleventh Amendment provides that the federal judicial power shall not be construed to extend to suits against states by citizens of other states. By its terms, the Eleventh Amendment applies only to suits brought in the national courts, and does not apply to suits brought, in those courts or in state courts, by a state's own citizens against it.

The Supreme Court has held that the constitutional structure bars Congress from requiring that states submit to suits in the national courts or in state courts, brought against them by their own citizens for violating substantive obligations

---

[69] *New York v United States* 488 US 1041 (1992).
[70] *Printz v United States* 521 US 98 (1997).   [71] ibid 905.   [72] ibid.

Congress has the power to impose on the states.[73] The constitutional text is unavailing here, but the Court relied on the assumptions about state sovereignty held by the framing generation. Allowing Congress to require that states submit to suit would, according to the Court, be inconsistent with the combination of national and state sovereignty that characterized the government of the United States taken as a whole. In the Court's view, other remedies, such as suits by the national government to enforce its laws, or suits by individuals against officials rather than the state, are better means of enforcing national law while respecting the sovereignty the states retain in a national union.

Although structural analysis has been used most often to deal with questions implicating the federal structure of the United States, it can be used in cases implicating individual rights as well. Here the relevant structural feature, or pre-supposition, is the one Chase J alluded to in *Calder v Bull*, that all governments in the United States are limited governments. Justice Chase's argument is that not all the limitations on government power are enumerated in the Constitution. The difficulty, common to all structuralist arguments, those dealing with federalism as well as individual rights, is to identify the precise content of the limitations on government power that the government's structure imposes. Notably, structuralist arguments are brought into play most often when there is little specific constitutional language to work with, which means that there is relatively little other material to impose discipline on the results offered via structuralist arguments.

Perhaps the best role of structural arguments is as a supplement to other arguments. So, for example, in the gun-control case, Scalia J relied on historic practice—there, the absence of any significant acts of commandeering by the national government—and the Court's own precedents to justify the outcome.[74] The Supreme Court's first major right-to-privacy case offers another example. *Griswold v Connecticut* (1965) invalidated a state law making it a crime to use contraceptive devices.[75] Justice William O. Douglas's opinion for the Court listed a number of constitutional provisions—the First, Fourth, and Fifth Amendments, among others—that had 'penumbras, formed by emanations from those guarantees that help give them life and substance.'[76] Douglas J's formulation has been widely derided by scholars and Supreme Court justices. Others have suggested that Douglas J's opinion should be understood either as invoking the structural pre-supposition that government power is limited or as one that could be strengthened by using that structural pre-supposition to supplement the reliance on specific constitutional provisions.[77]

[73] *Florida Prepaid Postsecondary Ed Expense Bd v College Savings Bank* 527 US 629 (1999); *Alden v Maine* 527 US 766 (1999).

[74] *Printz* (n 70). The dissent in that case mounted a substantial challenge to Scalia J's account of historic practice, but said almost nothing about his interpretation of the Court's precedents, because the recently decided nuclear waste disposal case was really the only relevant precedent, and the dissenters disagreed with that decision.   [75] 381 US 479 (1965).

[76] ibid 484.

[77] The parallels between the *Griswold* case (n 75), which political conservatives criticize, and the anti-commandeering and immunity cases, which such conservatives defend, have not been overlooked.

'Representation-reinforcing Review'

Marshall CJ's opinion in the *McCulloch* case rejected Maryland's tax on the national bank because the people of the nation as a whole, who benefited from the bank, were not represented in the legislature that imposed the tax, in contrast to Congress where, Marshall CJ said, 'all are represented.' John Hart Ely gave this approach to constitutional interpretation its modern name, 'representation-reinforcing review.'[78] According to this approach, constitutional provisions should be interpreted so as to reinforce the nation's system of democratic representation. Doing so emphasizes the legitimacy of legislation that gets enacted in a fully democratic process and, conversely, emphasizes the questionable democratic legitimacy of laws enacted when we can identify some representational defect in the legislative process. For some advocates, the approach also has the advantage of focusing on what they believe to be relatively uncontroversial questions of process, relegating more controversial questions about the law's substance to the background.

Representation-reinforcing review draws on a general account of the democratic process, and may perhaps be better described as a theory of the constitution itself rather than as a method of constitutional interpretation. Still, ideas about the adequacy of representation have influenced some interpretations the Court has offered. Probably the best way to understand the theory of representation-reinforcing review is that it provides a general guideline applicable to all constitutional provisions, advising judges to apply particular constitutional provisions more aggressively when the judges can identify some representational defect in the processes that led to the challenged statute's enactment.

Ely derived his theory from the work of the Warren Court and from what has been called the most celebrated footnote in constitutional law,[79] footnote four of Justice Harlan Fiske Stone's opinion in *United States v Carolene Products* (1938).[80] The Court had little difficulty in upholding a congressional ban on the interstate shipment of filled milk, a low-cost substitute for whole milk, applying an extremely deferential standard for determining whether a statute violated the economic right of the filled milk producers to engage in ordinary commercial activity. Stone J's footnote four said that a less deferential standard would be applied when the constitutional challenge rested on specific constitutional guarantees like those in the Bill of Rights rather than on what the Court took to be the generalities of the Due Process Clause. The footnote then turned to concerns about representation:

It is unnecessary to consider now whether legislation which restricts those political processes which can ordinarily be expected to bring about repeal of undesirable legislation, is to be subjected to more exacting judicial scrutiny under the general prohibitions of the 14th Amendment than are most other types of legislation . . . Nor need we enquire

---

[78] JH Ely *Democracy and Distrust: A Theory of Judicial Review* (Harvard University Press. Cambridge Mass., 1980).
[79] LF Powell 'Carolene Products Revisited' (1982) 82 Columbia L Rev 1087, 1087.
[80] 304 US 144 (1938).

whether similar considerations enter into the review of statues directed at particular religious . . . or national . . . or racial minorities; [or] whether prejudice against discrete and insular minorities may be a special condition, which tends seriously to curtail the operation of those political processes ordinarily to be relied upon to protect minorities, and which may call for a correspondingly more searching judicial inquiry . . .[81]

Exclusions from voting are good examples of the first category Stone J's footnote identifies. The US Constitution protects the right to vote against denials based on a number of particular grounds, such as race and gender, but it contains no general right to vote. The Supreme Court invoked representation-reinforcing ideas in subjecting exclusions from the franchise not covered by those particular provisions to exacting review under the Equal Protection Clause.[82] Also in this first category are laws suppressing speech: Those who would like to change the content of the law cannot do so if they are penalized for saying what they think. Such laws might well be covered by the specific guarantee of the First Amendment, but Stone J's thought might be that representation-reinforcement concerns could be used to determine that Amendment's precise coverage in situations of interpretive ambiguity.

Representation-reinforcing ideas also provide strong support for a long-standing doctrine invalidating state laws that discriminate against commerce originating in another state as violations of the so-called 'dormant' Commerce Clause. The Commerce Clause on its face is simply a grant of power to Congress, but the Supreme Court has relied on it as the source of a doctrine that allows the courts to invalidate laws that interfere with the development of a nation-wide market. The best explanation for the doctrine is Marshall CJ's in *McCulloch*: State laws that discriminate against commerce originating elsewhere adversely affect the people of other states, who do not have an opportunity to have their views considered in the enacting legislature.[83]

Stone J's concern about laws based on prejudice against discrete and insular minorities seems to have been designed to address state laws discriminating against African Americans. When he wrote African Americans were widely excluded from the franchise by formal and informal means, including physical coercion. Ely devoted a great deal of effort attempting to work out the implications of Stone J's

[81] ibid 152 n 4.

[82] eg *Kramer v Union Free School District* 395 US 621 (1969) (invalidating the denial of the right to vote in local school board elections to persons who neither owned property in the district nor had children enrolled in the district's schools).

[83] Stone J relied on the representation-reinforcing idea in a dormant Commerce Clause case, writing in *South Carolina Highway Dept v Barnwell Bros* 303 US 177 (1938), that the doctrine rested on 'the thought, often expressed in judicial opinion, that, when the regulation is of such a character that its burden falls principally upon those without the state, legislative action is not likely to be subjected to those political restraints which are normally exerted on legislation where it affects adversely some interests within the state.' (At 185 n 2). Fully rationalizing the dormant Commerce Clause doctrine on representation-reinforcing grounds is, however, quite difficult and leads to elaborate and not always persuasive distinctions. For one analysis, see M Tushnet 'Rethinking the Dormant Commerce Clause' [1975] Wisconsin L Rev 125.

insight in situations where the 'discrete and insular minorities' had full access to the voting booth. Most commentators believe that Ely's efforts are not fully satisfactory. In some ways the deepest criticism is that, in situations of full enfranchisement, it is not discrete and insular minorities that are at a disadvantage, but dispersed majorities.[84] Consider the filled-milk case. Its primary beneficiaries are the well-organized special interest group of milk producers, who can raise funds to lobby Congress for the statute, while those who feel its burdens are low-income consumers who would be able to purchase more filled milk than whole milk, but are unable to organize themselves as an effective counter-lobby.[85]

Original Understanding

Reacting to what they perceived as the unjustified activism of the Supreme Court in the 1960s, political conservatives began to develop what they eventually called a jurisprudence of original intention. Reference to the framers' understandings had always been part of constitutional interpretation, but rarely were decisions justified solely by invoking original understanding. Modern political conservatives urged that only original understandings be used in constitutional interpretation.

After some mis-steps,[86] the jurisprudence of original understanding eventually settled on the proposition that the Constitution's terms should be interpreted by giving them the meaning they had among the general (or generally educated and politically attentive) public at the time they were inserted into the Constitution.[87] Supreme Court opinions rely on the dictionaries that were available in 1789, for example, to establish the meaning of words like *arrest*.[88] Occasionally the jurisprudence of original understanding degenerates into bizarre disputes like one between Justices Scalia and David Souter over the proper way to read several sentences in the *Federalist Papers*,[89] but the difficulties with this form of originalism are more serious.

One problem echoes difficulties with versions of originalism that focus on intent rather than understanding. The nation's history made it clear that some constitutional arrangements were aimed at extending existing British practices,

---

[84] The basic argument was made by B Ackerman 'Beyond Carolene Products' (1985) 98 Harvard L Rev 713.

[85] Again, the full analysis is more complex, as it would have to take into account the ability of filled-milk producers to represent (virtually, to use the term common in political theory) the consumers.

[86] The mis-steps typically involved formulating the jurisprudence as one of original *intent*, which created large difficulties about identifying whose intent counted, about whether understandings about likely outcomes should count among the intentions or indeed should exhaust what counted as an intention, and, probably most important, about how to go about aggregating the intentions of many individuals.

[87] Most originalist scholarship focuses on the 1789 Constitution and the 1791 Bill of Rights, but originalism's interpretive principles are equally applicable to the Reconstruction Amendments.

[88] *Atwater v City of Lago Vista* 532 US 318, 330 (2001).

[89] *Printz* (n 70) 911–12 (Scalia J for the Court), 972–73 (Souter J dissenting).

while others were aimed at repudiating those practices. Yet, without recourse to original intentions of some sort, it proved difficult indeed to explain why some words were to be interpreted as endorsing British practices, others as repudiating them. This reflected a deeper difficulty. The jurisprudence of original understanding attempted to reproduce the processes of legal reasoning of the late 18th century to determine what constitutional provisions mean. Yet, lawyers in the late 18th century agreed, more or less, on how to engage in legal reasoning, but they disagreed, often quite substantially, about what the outcomes of that reasoning would be in particular instances. Words were understood to mean things because they fit into larger conceptions of the political order, but in the cases that interest today's interpreters, disagreements about those larger conceptions cascade down—in the 18th century no less than today—into disagreements about what an ordinary person would understand the words to mean. So, for example, everyone agreed that the states were to retain some sort of sovereignty within the new national government, but disagreement was pervasive over what the components of that sovereignty were.

The second difficulty with the jurisprudence of original understanding arises from changes in society, economy, and the values held by the society. Slavery provides the most dramatic example. The 1789 Constitution and the 1791 Bill of Rights were written for a society in which slavery was well-established in part of the country, and legal almost everywhere else. Somehow people in the late 18th century were able to see in the Constitution's words, as they understood them, a charter for liberty from the British and from potential domestic tyrants, and yet were unable to see in those same words condemnation of slavery. Today it is trivially easy for an interpreter to give the original Constitution's words meanings that at least make slavery a constitutionally problematic institution, but that seemingly was not so in 1789 and 1791.

In discussions of the problem change poses for originalist approaches to constitutional interpretation, the term *commerce* has been the one receiving most attention. In the 1930s the Supreme Court adopted interpretations of that term that gave the national government essentially unrestricted power to enact statutes that regulated or banned activities that had even the slightest connection to interstate commerce. Those interpretations were in some tension with original understandings, and the results were inconsistent with the proposition, well-established at the time of the Constitution's adoption, that the national government was one of limited powers. In the 1990s the Supreme Court began to rethink Commerce Clause doctrine. Its decisions were rather limited, though, because a return to original understandings threatened to make a great deal of the regulation adopted in the 20th century unconstitutional.

Justice Thomas revived the idea that, as originally understood, commerce was distinguished from manufacturing and agriculture.[90] Were that idea to be adopted by the Court, national labour laws, national environmental laws, national

---

[90] *United States v Lopez* 514 US 549, 590–91 (1995) (Thomas J concurring).

anti-discrimination laws, and more might have come under a constitutional cloud. The Court was not prepared to take that step. Concurring in a decision that invalidated a national statute making it a crime to possess a gun near a school, Justice Anthony Kennedy, joined by Justice Sandra Day O'Connor, expressed concern about pushing the reconsideration of existing doctrine much beyond that point. The history of the Court's effort to limit the scope of the Commerce Clause, Kennedy J wrote, gave him 'pause,' but he emphasized that the Court's holding, while 'necessary,' was 'limited.'[91]

How can original understandings be accommodated to the fact of change? The most popular solution uses the metaphor of *translation* to capture what needs to be done.[92] Today's interpreters should do what a good translator does: We should understand the powers the Constitution confers and the rights it protects as if the Constitution's words were translated from the 18th century into our modern language. A good translation preserves the original meaning, but makes the composition understandable and relevant to the reader unfamiliar with the original language.

The metaphor of translation preserves the shell of a jurisprudence of original understanding, but leaches out everything inside the shell; it seems to be originalist, but is not. Ordinarily we translate the Constitution's words first by identifying the principles those words embodied at the time they were written into the Constitution, and then by determining how those principles apply to contemporary problems. If Congress was given the power to regulate commerce among the states in 1789 to ensure that market transactions would be conducted according to the same rules through the nation, in order to ensure economic growth, we translate the term *commerce* in a way that authorizes today's Congress to achieve the same goals.

The example illustrates the general problem with 'translation.' Conventionally called the 'level of generality' problem, it is that different interpreters will specify the principles underlying particular constitutional terms differently, some at an abstract level of generality, some at a more concrete level, and as a result will come up with different translations of the Constitution's original meaning. Contemporary disputes over affirmative action or positive discrimination illustrate the difficulty.

The Fourteenth Amendment bars states from denying the equal protection of the laws. The meaning of *equal protection* is clear enough in core applications: States may not impose disadvantages on African Americans simply because of their race. What, though, is the principle of equality embodied in the Equal Protection Clause? It might be a principle of anti-subordination, making constitutionally questionable statutes that impose disabilities on African Americans but not affirmative action programs that are not designed or intended to perpetuate subordination or a caste system. Or, it might be a principle of colour-blindness,

---

[91] *United States v Lopez* 568 (Kennedy J concurring).
[92] L Lessig 'Understanding Changed Readings: Fidelity and Theory' (1995) 47 Stanford L Rev 395 (1995); L Lessig 'Translating Federalism: United States v Lopez' [1995] Supreme Court Rev 125.

according to which governments are barred from taking race into account in any way in their decisions. The colour-blindness principle makes affirmative action programs constitutionally questionable.

The question of the provision's application to contemporary affirmative action programs arises precisely because we cannot tell from consulting the dictionaries used in 1868 what the provision's terms meant at the time. So, we have to have recourse to the principles that the provision was meant to write into the Constitution. Identifying those principles leads away from the meaning of the Constitution's words to the understandings held by people at the time. The latter inquiry is close to an intentionalist one: What principle did the people in 1868 intend to write into the Constitution? Unfortunately, with respect to almost every interesting controversy over the principles underlying particular constitutional provisions, we inevitably discover serious disagreement about what those principles were. Some people understood 'equal protection' to mean anti-subordination, others that it meant colour-blindness. The effort to translate the earlier term into contemporary terms leads to the interpreters reproducing the contemporary problems by discovering that, on the level of principle to which the translator must move, today's difficulties were present in the past.

Some version of a jurisprudence of original understanding remains an essential component of nearly all particular resolutions of interpretive controversies, but the effort in the 1980s to make such a jurisprudence the only component of constitutional interpretation failed.

Appeals to Justice

Several constitutional provisions employ terms that evoke moral judgments: 'Due process' resonates with ideas about fairness, 'equal protection of the laws' with ideas of equality. In giving these general terms content in particular cases, the Supreme Court sometimes has suggested that the underlying moral judgments can be read into the Constitution.[93] The Court's equal protection jurisprudence, for example, requires that legislation treating one group differently from another must be justified by some relevant difference between the groups. Relevance necessarily has some normative component. This is true even in the ordinary case, and more dramatically so in cases involving so-called suspect classifications, where the Court requires extremely good reasons for laws that impose disadvantages on groups that have historically been subjected to adverse treatment.

Specific textual referents are not the only reason for importing the conclusions of moral reasoning into the Constitution. On the most general level, the Court— and even more, political leaders reflecting deeply on the nature of the Constitution, such as Abraham Lincoln during the Civil War—sometimes treat

---

[93] Commentators, most notably R Dworkin, have gone further and argued that the conclusions drawn by those who engage in moral philosophy in a systematic way should be imported into the Constitution through the terms that invoke moral concepts.

the Constitution as an expression of the nation's commitment to 'establish justice' and 'secure the blessings of liberty,' in the Preamble's terms. The Preamble is not directly enforceable, but the concerns it expresses for justice and liberty easily inform the interpretation of specific, enforceable constitutional provisions.

The Court has relied on moral concepts to overcome the limitation that other interpretive approaches might impose on reaching conclusions that the justices believe correct. In *Harper v Virginia State Board of Elections*, the Supreme Court struck down a state requirement that people pay $1.50 annually before they could vote.[94] This poll tax was challenged as a violation of the Fourteenth Amendment's prohibition of laws that deny equal protection of the laws. Several obstacles stood in the way of invalidating the poll tax. When the Fourteenth Amendment was adopted, lawyers drew a sharp distinction between civil rights, which the Amendment was designed to protect, and political rights, which its framers thought it did not protect. The right to vote was the quintessential political right, and so, it would seem, inequalities in the distribution of the right to vote would be unaffected by the adoption of the Equal Protection Clause. That conclusion is confirmed by the fact that Congress believed it necessary it propose another amendment, the Fifteenth, to guarantee the right to vote against denials on the basis of race, and by the fact that a separate provision in the Fourteenth Amendment sought to encourage states to distribute the franchise broadly by depriving them of seats in the House of Representatives in proportion to their denial of votes to males over the age of 21. Even more, the Supreme Court had rejected constitutional challenges to the poll tax in 1937. In the face of these obstacles, the Court nonetheless found the poll tax unconstitutional. Justice William O Douglas wrote, 'the Equal Protection Clause is not shackled to the political theory of a particular era,' and that the Court has 'never been confined to historic notions of equality.' He concluded, 'Notions of what constitutes equal treatment for purposes of the Equal Protection Clause *do* change.'[95]

The Court's use of moral concepts in this way is explained best by combining the proposition that some constitutional provisions do appear to direct the courts to look to morality to give the provisions content, with the proposition that our understanding of morality is always imperfect. Notions of equality change because, it is said, we come to understand better what equality truly requires as we grapple with specific problems and reflect on the deep meaning of the Constitution's moral terms.

Yet, it is precisely the possibility that our *notions* of equality and other morally laden terms change that raises the most serious questions about the Court's reliance on such notions in interpreting the Constitution. Critics sometimes question the ability of Supreme Court justices, who are trained as ordinary lawyers, not moral or political philosophers, to engage in serious moral reflection— or, at least, more serious moral reflection than the legislators whose work they are

---

[94] 383 US 663 (1966).   [95] ibid 669.

reviewing engaged in. More important, though, is the persistent fact of moral disagreement even after serious reflection. What one person characterizes as a change responsive to deeper understanding of the underlying moral concept, another person characterizes as a wilful departure from the concept's meaning in the service of a result driven by preference rather than morality.

These criticisms have real force, but they overstate the extent to which constitutional interpretation by the courts actually relies on the importation of conclusions from systematic moral theorizing. Commentators have urged the Court to do so, but the actual references to moral concepts in Supreme Court opinions are more often gestures in the direction of such concepts than reliance on them. And, to the extent that the Constitution itself gestures in the same direction, it is hard to fault the justices for doing so as well.

Precedent

The modal Supreme Court opinion is almost certainly one that deals almost entirely with the Court's own precedents, mentioning the Constitution's text only as a starting point and ignoring almost entirely the original understanding of the text's words. In one sense this is hardly surprising. The Court's precedents serve as glosses on the text. Ordinarily one can work one's way backwards through the precedents to an opinion at the foundation of the line of precedents that does deal to a substantial extent with text and original understanding, albeit that sometimes the older precedents are like Marshall CJ's in the *McCulloch* case, dealing with the text by treating it as an exemplification of applied political theory. In addition, the Constitution's age makes precedents particularly important. The text has become so encrusted with precedent that looking past the precedents to the text might well disrupt practices deeply embedded in the constitutional system's on-going operation, as Thomas J's treatment of the word *commerce* suggests.

Precedent-based adjudication is a particular problem for those who believe that the only permissible basis for interpretation is the text as it was originally understood. Precedent matters, after all, only when it points in a direction different from the one indicated by the text or original understanding. The most devoted originalists do argue that erroneous precedents should simply be ignored,[96] but that is an eccentric position among US constitutionalists.

One reason for the rejection of such a purist position is that some of the Court's decisions seem rather clearly at odds with original understanding, and yet rejecting them is unthinkable in today's constitutional culture. The primary example is *Brown v Board of Education*, holding segregation of the public schools unconstitutional.[97] The correctness of that decision is a fixed point, perhaps the only fixed point, in contemporary constitutional law. Yet, it is difficult to defend on originalist

---

[96] eg G Lawson 'The Constitutional Case Against Precedent' (1994) 17 Harvard J L & Public Policy 23.   [97] 347 US 483 (1954).

grounds.[98] Even originalists need some account of the proper role of precedent in constitutional adjudication if they are to agree that *Brown* should not be overruled.

The more important questions about the role precedent should play in constitutional interpretation involve the conditions for overruling erroneous precedents. The justices agree that it should be easier to overrule constitutional precedents than statutory ones. Mistaken interpretations of statutes, they say, can be rectified by ordinary legislative processes. Mistaken constitutional interpretations, in contrast, are embedded in the law unless they are overturned through the difficult process of constitutional amendment.

Sometimes the Court takes the position that precedents can be overruled simply because today's Court disagrees with them. *Lawrence v Texas*, holding unconstitutional state laws against homosexual sodomy, overruled a decision rendered 17 years earlier because, the Court said, the precedent 'was not correct when it was decided.'[99] Such an approach gives precedent no independent weight. Precedent has that weight only when the judge, considering the question as an original matter, would reach a decision different from the one indicated by a fair reading of the precedents—that is, precedent matters only when the precedent is, from the judge's point of view, mistaken.

In *Lawrence* the Court gestured toward other criteria, although its judgment that the precedent was wrong clearly played the largest role. The Court's opinion mentioned that the precedent misconstrued the nature of the constitutional claim presented, and that two later cases cast some doubt on the precedent's rationale. These are among the concerns the Court has mentioned in discussing the propriety of overruling a constitutional precedent.

The controversial joint opinion of Justices O'Connor, Kennedy, and Souter in *Planned Parenthood of Southeastern Pennsylvania v Casey* contains a summary of the guidelines the justices said the Court uses:

> [The Court should consider] whether [the precedent] has been found unworkable; whether [the precedent] could be removed without serious inequity to those who have relied upon it or significant damage to the stability of the society governed by the rule in question; whether the law's growth in the intervening years has left [the precedent] a doctrinal anachronism discounted by society; and whether [the precedent's] premises of fact have so far changed . . . as to render its . . . holding somehow irrelevant or unjustifiable in dealing with the issue it addressed.[100]

The application of these guidelines is hardly mechanical. *Casey* involved the question of overruling the Supreme Court's basic abortion decision, *Roe v Wade*.[101] Discussing the reliance interest, the joint opinion's authors argued that reliance was established not by showing that specific individuals had relied on

---

[98] For one unsuccessful effort, see M McConnell 'Originalism and the Desegregation Decisions' (1995) 81 Virginia L Rev 947. [99] *Lawrence v Texas* 123 S Ct 2472, 2484 (2003).
[100] *Planned Parenthood of Southeastern Pennsylvania v Casey* 505 US 833, 855 (1992) (joint opinion of O'Connor, Kennedy, and Souter JJ). [101] 410 US 113 (1973).

Roe and that their on-going expectations would be defeated by overruling that decision, but that:

for two decades of economic and social developments, people have organized intimate relationships and made choices that define their views of themselves and their places in society, in reliance on the availability of abortion in the event that contraception should fail. The ability of women to participate equally in the economic and social life of the Nation has been facilitated by their ability to control their reproductive lives.[102]

And, in dealing with changed factual premises, the opinion justified the overruling of *Lochner v New York*,[103] which held that economic liberty enforced through the Due Process Clause made unconstitutional state laws requiring maximum hours, by referring to its 'fundamentally false factual assumptions about the capacity of a relatively unregulated market to satisfy minimal levels of human welfare,'[104] rather than by invoking the rather more obvious proposition that *Lochner* rested on normatively inappropriate assumptions about the relative freedom of workers and employers.

This discussion of the conditions for overruling or adhering to precedent should not obscure the more important point. Constitutional interpretation in the United States involves arguing about the implications of the Court's precedents far more than it involves any other interpretive approach.

Considerations of Administrability

Large swathes of American constitutional law do not involve interpreting the Constitution at all, at least directly. Instead, they are concerned with developing rules that allow the Constitution to be implemented in the nation's daily governance.[105] Many constitutional rules are linked to underlying constitutional text and values only by these considerations of administrability.

Many examples could be given, because rules justified by such considerations are pervasive. Two illustrations show why administrability matters. As noted earlier, the Supreme Court has implemented its doctrine that districts from which representatives are elected must satisfy a requirement of equal population by imposing a rule of strict mathematical equality, with an arbitrary exception that allows deviations of up to 10 per cent in districts for state legislatures. Plainly, neither general notions of equality in voting nor the more precise 'one person, one vote' rule dictates a rule as strict as the one the Court has applied. The justification for the Court's rule is that the only rule courts can reliably administer is one tied exclusively to strict mathematical equality. Any other rule would authorise arbitrary deviations from equality.

---

[102] *Casey* (n 100) 856.   [103] *Lochner v New York* 198 US 45 (1905).

[104] *Casey* (n 100) 861–862.

[105] The term *implemented* derives from RH Fallon Jr *Implementing the Constitution* (Harvard University Press, Cambridge Mass., 2001).

A second example is the Court's unwillingness to distinguish between invidious discrimination on the basis of race and purportedly benign discrimination. The Court has been concerned that decision-makers would too often create programs that actually imposed disadvantages on racial minorities but would then defend them as benign, and that courts evaluating those defenses would be unable reliably to sort the valid claims that the programs were benign from the invalid ones.[106] Note that this justification for refusing to distinguish between invidious and benign programs accepts the proposition that such a distinction is defensible as a matter of the constitutional principles of equality. Nonetheless, the Court refuses to enact such a distinction into law for reasons independent of the underlying constitutional principles.

The apportionment and affirmative action cases are united by a concern about implementation. The rules the Court articulates guide not simply the justices as they consider subsequent cases, but legislators and judges in lower courts as well. Simple rules provide guidance for other decision-makers, who might not be as competent at drawing fine distinctions as are the Supreme Court's justices themselves. Put another way: were all constitutional decisions to be made by the justices, they could invoke only principles derived directly from the Constitution. But, because others will make constitutional decisions that go unreviewed by the Supreme Court, the justices need to devise implementable rules that yield the best set of outcomes overall. Refusing to allow low-level decision-makers to defend affirmative action programs as benign will indeed lead to the invalidation of some programs that, as a matter of direct principle, ought to be upheld. But, allowing them to present such a defense will lead to the adoption of some programs that ought to be struck down but will not be because they never reach the courts. The Court's judgment is that the simple rule barring all discrimination on the basis of race provides, on balance, outcomes that track what the Constitution requires and permits more closely than would a rule allowing benign discrimination.

Justice Scalia has elevated these concerns about implementation into a comprehensive constitutional jurisprudence, in which clear rules are systematically preferred over more flexible standards.[107] According to Scalia J, a jurisprudence of rules provides more constraints on, and guidance to, decision-makers than does a jurisprudence of standards. This is clearly overstated, gaining its rhetorical force by focusing on the constraints that can be imposed by a single clear rule or a small set of clear rules. Once rule systems become more complex, decision-makers can navigate within them with almost the same degree of flexibility as they can in systems pervaded by standards instead of rules. Even so, considerations of administrability do play a significant role in the Supreme Court's constitutional rulings.

---

[106] The best expression of this concern is *Metro Broadcasting, Inc v FCC* 417 US 547, 635 (1990) (Kennedy J dissenting).

[107] A Scalia 'The Rule of Law as a Law of Rules' (1989) 56 U Chicago L Rev 1175.

(Moderately) Disfavoured Interpretive Methods

Presumptive interpretation

The Supreme Court briefly asserted that the First Amendment's protection of free speech held a 'preferred position' in constitutional law.[108] It continues to assert that legislation comes to it with a presumption of validity. These and similar claims about general presumptions regarding interpretation actually play a small role in the Court's interpretive practice. Indeed, the 'preferred position' doctrine was rejected within a decade of its initial articulation.

The small role given interpretive presumptions arises from the Constitution's overall structure. The Constitution enumerates the powers of the national government, and rests on the assumption that there are some limits to those powers. Without a specific limitations clause in the Constitution, interpretation focuses on identifying limits internal to the enumerations, such as limiting definitions of 'commerce among the several States.' Speaking of 'generous' interpretation in this context would eliminate whatever constraining force the enumeration has. A similar problem affects interpretation of the Constitution's rights-guaranteeing provisions. Again there is no general limitations clause such as appears in more modern constitutions, and yet all concede that governments must have some power to enact legislation that effectively limits the exercise of protected rights. Interpreting the rights provisions 'generously' without a countervailing text in a limitations clause would unduly restrict the ability of governments to enforce legislation that well-designed constitutions ought to allow.

Substantive constitutional doctrine, particular to specific provisions, takes the place of general interpretive presumptions. Some statutes imposing burdens differentially on different groups receive 'strict scrutiny' under the Equal Protection Clause, others do not, with the different treatment explained by the differences among the groups affected. An elaborate structure of free speech doctrine makes it difficult to challenge laws that regulate all speech even-handedly, without regard to its content but with regard only to its non-content-based effects, and easy to challenge laws that regulate speech because of its content. Capturing these complex doctrines in general interpretive presumptions is impossible.

Academic writing

Supreme Court opinions rarely invoke academic writing to support central interpretive conclusions.[109] In one of the Court's cases involving immunity from suit, Chief Justice Rehnquist disparagingly referred to the dissent's account of the origins

---

108 *Murdock v Pennsylvania* 319 US 105, 115 (1943).

109 Citations to academic work typically serve either to point to factual information provided in the cited work, or as decorations for conclusions already defended by using other interpretive techniques. The Supreme Court has cited the leading treatise on constitutional law, LH Tribe *American Constitutional Law* (Foundation Press, Mineola, 1976, 1988, 2000), 60 times, almost always for general and uncontroversial propositions.

of the immunity doctrines as 'disregard[ing] our case law in favor of a theory cobbled together from law review articles and its own version of historical events.'[110]

In the late 20th century legal academics began submitting briefs amicus curiae on their own behalf in major Supreme Court cases. Sometimes traces of those briefs can be found in the opinions. In an important case involving the rights of homosexuals, for example, five leading academics submitted an amicus brief describing the challenged enactment as 'a per se violation of the Equal Protection Clause' and stating, 'Never since the enactment of the Fourteenth Amendment has this Court confronted a measure quite like' the one at issue. The Court's opinion in the case echoed these points, calling the enactment 'unprecedented in our jurisprudence.'[111] Observers suggested that the opinion's structure was based on the law professors' brief, but the opinion itself did not cite the brief.

Non-United States law

Until the middle of the 20th century, Supreme Court opinions referred routinely to the laws of other nations, although only occasionally in support of constitutional interpretations.[112] Justice Felix Frankfurter argued that the traditions of Anglo-American jurisdictions should inform constitutional interpretation in determining which features of the adversary system were so fundamental as to be applicable in state court proceedings, pursuant to the Fourteenth Amendment's Due Process Clause. A 1958 decision dealing with the interpretation of the Eighth Amendment's ban on cruel and usual punishments said that the prohibition should be interpreted in light of 'evolving standards of decency,' and implied that in determining what those standards were the courts could look to practices outside the United States.[113] Beyond that, references to non-United States law were rare.

In the 1990s some justices began to refer to non-United States law. Sometimes the references were mere observations about what other constitutional (or human rights) systems did with respect to the issue the Court was considering. These observations had the rhetorical effect of demonstrating that the Court's actions were not out of line with the legal standards applied elsewhere, but they were not an integral component of the Court's interpretation of the US Constitution provision at issue. A footnote in an opinion holding it unconstitutional to impose the death penalty on people with mental retardation observed, '[W]ithin the world community, the imposition of the death penalty for crimes committed by mentally retarded offenders is overwhelmingly disapproved,' in a paragraph that began by asserting that the 'legislative judgment' of American states against such executions 'reflects a much broader social and professional consensus.'[114] The

---

[110] *Seminole Tribe v Florida* 517 US 44, 68 (1996).

[111] *Romer v Evans* 517 US 620, 633 (1996).

[112] For an overview, see VC Jackson 'Ambivalent Resistance and Comparative Constitutionalism: Opening Up the Conversation On "Proportionality," Rights and Federalism' (1999) 1 U Pennsylvania J Constitutional L 583, 584–93.   [113] *Trop v Dulles* 356 US 86 (1958).

[114] *Atkins v Virginia* 586 US 304, 316 n 21 (2002).

Court's opinion finding it unconstitutional to impose the death penalty on juvenile offenders contained a section stating that the majority's conclusion, based on domestic sources of constitutional interpretation, 'finds confirmation in the stark reality that the United States is the only country in the world that continues to give official sanction to the juvenile death penalty', but immediately added that that reality was 'not controlling'.[115]

Other recent references to non-United States law are slightly more substantive. The Court relied on a judgment of the European Court on Human Rights to counter the argument made by Chief Justice Warren Burger in an earlier case to support his conclusion that consensual homosexual sodomy had been condemned by law 'throughout the history of Western civilization.'[116] And, in one of the Court's anti-commandeering cases, Justice Stephen Breyer in dissent noted that other federal systems, such as Germany's, not only had no anti-commandeering principle but affirmatively relied on subnational governments to implement national laws, because in those systems it was thought that using subnational governments in that way respected their autonomy.[117]

These references to non-United States law, mild though they were, provoked a substantial critical response from some justices and commentators. As Justice Scalia put it, 'it is American conceptions of decency that are dispositive,' as he rejected the contention 'that the sentencing practices of other countries are relevant' to determining the constitutionality of imposing the death penalty on offenders who were aged 16 when they committed their crimes.[118] The critics had several concerns. First, they argued that the United States Constitution was a text that had been adopted by the people of the United States at a particular time, and lacked authoritative force unless it was interpreted only with reference to the understandings of the American people. Second, they believed that reference to non-United States law simply provided another resource for judges to use to overturn laws they disapproved of, when the other resources in US law failed to support that course of action. Finally, they noted that non-US law often arose in a particular institutional context that differed from the United States context in relevant ways, and that judges in the United States were unlikely to know enough about that context—or could spend their time more productively learning other things. Justice Breyer's reference to German federalism, for example, did not take into account the fact that the German länder had much more substantial representation in the German legislative process than American states do in the US national legislative process, a fact that plainly has some bearing on whether commandeering undermines or supports the autonomy of the subnational units.[119]

---

[115] *Roper v Simmons* 125 S Ct 1183 (2005).   [116] *Lawrence* (n 99) 2480.

[117] *Printz* (n 70) 976 (Breyer J dissenting).

[118] *Stanford v Kentucky* 492 US 361, 369 n 1 (1989).

[119] D Halberstam 'Comparative Federalism and the Issue of Commandeering' in K Nikolaïdis and R Howse (eds) *The Federal Vision: Legitimacy and Levels of Governance in the United States and the European Union* (Oxford University Press, 2001) 213.

Despite these strictures, it seems likely that references to non-US law will increase gradually, as United States judges continue to participate in conversations—both in person and through the exchange of opinions—with judges of constitutional courts in other nations.

Conclusion

The Supreme Court's repertoire of interpretive techniques is large. The eclecticism displayed in Marshall CJ's opinion in *McCulloch* has persisted in the Court's work. We can see some patterns, though.

Preferred interpretive techniques[120]

Taking the Court's work as a whole, we will find precedent-based interpretation predominating. Relying on precedents saves time and, by linking the decision at hand to earlier ones, allows the Court to draw on the public acceptance of the earlier decision to gain acceptance of this one. For similar reasons, considerations of administrability play a large role in defining the contours of the doctrines the Court articulates, although they are rarely mentioned as such.

It is difficult to distinguish in practice between text-based and originalist interpretation, because they so often go hand in hand. Together, text-based and originalist interpretation rank second in the hierarchy of the interpretive techniques the Court explicitly invokes. Structural concerns are less frequently mentioned, although the Court does advert to them in separation of powers and federalism cases, which of course involve the structures of government, and sometimes in individual rights cases, by describing the general goals of the constitutional order as including the preservation of liberty.

Explicit references to representation-reinforcing considerations, and to moral or political philosophy, are quite rare. Their relative absence can be misleading, though, because concern that constitutional interpretation be consistent with these considerations is quite pervasive. Sometimes the concern surfaces in rhetorical flourishes. So, for example, the joint opinion in *Casey* begins: 'Liberty finds no refuge in a jurisprudence of doubt,'[121] a proposition that, while not obviously meaningful in itself, drives the opinion's later analysis of precedent and overruling. Similarly, the Court's gay rights decision of 2003 opens with the sentence: 'Liberty protects the person from unwarranted government intrusions into a dwelling or other private places,' and continues: 'Liberty presumes an autonomy of self that includes freedom of thought, belief, expression, and certain intimate conduct.'[122] These are not well worked-out propositions in moral philosophy, but they animate the remainder of the opinion.

---

[120] For an insightful discussion of the Court's rankings of the techniques, see R Fallon 'A Constructivist Coherence Theory of Constitutional Interpretation' (1989) 100 Harvard L Rev 1189, 1243–46. [121] *Casey* (n 100) 843.
[122] *Lawrence* (n 99) 2475.

Eclecticism in practice

Not infrequently, the Court uses only one interpretive technique in an opinion. Even when it does, implicit questions of choice among techniques arise, and those questions can be brought into sharp focus by a dissenting opinion that suggests, for example, that the majority relies on precedent because text and original understanding point to a different result. Another frequent practice is to use several interpretive techniques and argue that all support the same conclusion. The opinion's rhetorical force is strengthened to the degree that it can appeal equally to those who think that original understanding matters most, for example, and to those who think that notions of justice matter most. It is weakened to the degree that readers might naturally be sceptical about claims that every way of approaching the interpretive problem leads to the same conclusion.

Opinions that openly acknowledge a conflict between the outcomes recommended by different interpretive approaches are rare indeed. Acknowledged conflicts are not resolved by some general hierarchical choice, in which, for example, the result recommended by original understanding necessarily prevails over the result recommended by the precedents. Instead, the opinions—which are, again, quite few—resolve the conflict by some sort of 'all things considered' balancing. In an interesting but not widely accepted analysis, Philip Bobbitt has argued that choice among techniques gives the Court's decisions their moral legitimacy, because it demonstrates that the justices are moral actors exercising the power to choose that defines a person as a moral actor.[123]

Techniques and subjects

There are no large differences between the Court's choices from its repertoire in cases involving the Constitution's structures of federalism and separation of powers, on the one hand, and its choices in individual rights cases.[124] Justiciability doctrines, and the Constitution's reliance on political bargaining between Congress and the president to resolve problems of the allocation of power between the branches, mean that there are relatively few precedents dealing with separation of powers. And, for the same reasons, the evidence from practice is rather substantial in that area. When separation of powers cases reach the courts, the justices invoke the text and practice, largely because that is almost all they have to go on.

When the Court enters an area anew, it almost necessarily starts with the text and what the Court recently has called 'first principles,'[125] by which it means original understandings and the political theory the present Court finds in the relevant texts. Which areas are new will of course vary over time. Areas can be new for either of two reasons. The Court simply may not have dealt with them before.

---

123 P Bobbitt *Constitutional Interpretation* (Blackwell, Cambridge, 1991).

124 Some constitutional provisions are so clear, or have raised so little controversy, that the Supreme Court has not interpreted them at all. Typically, these provisions deal with the Constitution's structural features, such as the guarantee of two Senators for each state. The existence of such provisions indicates that interpretation does have limits, but not what those limits are.

125 *United States v Lopez* (n 90) 552.

Or, more interesting, the present Court may not have dealt with issues that prior Courts did deal with, sometimes extensively, but in ways that today's justices think leads to wrong results. Obviously the Court cannot rely on (non-existent) precedents in the first category of new cases. In the second category, there are precedents, but the Court believes them to be erroneous. To displace the precedents, the Court must use one of the other interpretive techniques, and text and original understanding are the most obvious candidates.

These patterns are faint, and it would be a mistake to place them in the foreground. On the whole, the Court's eclecticism has been rather unstructured. The Court's practice appears to be to use whatever seems to work. What, then, does it mean for an interpretation to work?

Critical Evaluation

Constitutional interpretation in the United States is the means by which the Constitution is recurrently revised to accommodate the general values embodied in the Constitution with the realities of governance in a changing world. With a less cumbersome amendment process, constitutional amendments would perform that function. Yet, though constitutional interpretation in the United States may do some of what constitutional amendments do elsewhere, interpretation and amendment are obviously not equivalent along all dimensions. In particular, constitutional amendments have a more obvious warrant in the people's (current) views about constitutional values and the realities of governance than constitutional interpretation does.

In different versions, this concern has animated most of the modern critical discussion of constitutional interpretation. Alexander Bickel opened the conversation by describing judicial review as a 'deviant institution' in the US democratic system, posing what he called the 'countermajoritarian difficulty.'[126] That difficulty lay in the fact that some important questions about the content of public policy—both with respect to substantive law, such as abortion, and with respect to what Frank Michelman calls the 'law of law-making,'[127] such as the First Amendment—are resolved, not by the people themselves, but by unelected judges serving life terms and therefore responsive to the people only quite indirectly. Put in the starkest terms, the difficulty was that important questions of public policy could be answered by judges who, because they were not constrained by any other institution, might simply enact their personal preferences as the policy that governed everyone in the United States.

As noted earlier, the countermajoritarian difficulty supported the rhetoric of critics of judicial activism or creativity. Used as tools of analysis, those terms lack

---

[126] AM Bickel *The Least Dangerous Branch: The Supreme Court at the Bar of Politics* (Bobbs-Merrill, Indianapolis, 1962) 18.

[127] FI Michelman *Brennan and Democracy* (Princeton University Press, Princeton, 1999) 6.

the critical political content intended by most of those who use them. Decisions are 'activist' in the pejorative sense when the speaker disagrees with the results; they are 'creative' in an approving sense when the speaker agrees with the results. Discourse about constitutional law in the US has become so permeated by the political uses of the terms *activism* and *creativity* that it seems far too late to attempt to discipline them by stipulative definitions.

Constitutional interpretation entered the discussion of the countermajoritarian difficulty as a way of domesticating the judges' personal preferences. The argument was that although judges might not be constrained by other institutions, their work could be subject to the professional discipline imposed by the methods of constitutional interpretation. By adhering to those methods, judges would be barred from enacting their personal preferences into fundamental law.

This argument has a number of flaws, all variants on the theme that the interpretive methods in fact do not constrain. First, none of the interpretive methods actually does impose substantial constraints on a judge's decision-making. Each provides a structure for discussing the application of specific constitutional provisions to particular problems, but none forces the judge into especially narrow channels. Experience has demonstrated that talented judges who have *different* values and visions can deploy each interpretive method to promote their values and visions, each using the interpretive method well within the bounds set by standards of professional competence in using the method.

It would be unduly repetitive to demonstrate the point for each interpretive method discussed earlier.[128] Consider these sketches as an introduction.

(a) *Representation-reinforcing review* relies on discrimination against minorities as a reason for special judicial attention to some laws. Its defenders, usually political liberals, use it to explain why laws imposing disadvantages on racial minorities are constitutionally suspect. Yet, an enfranchised minority is in a position to strike deals with other groups to protect its interests. So, the argument must be that there are some impediments to that sort of bargaining. The most obvious impediment turns out to be difficulty in organizing the group for political action. And, as noted earlier, it is not America's racial minorities that are most difficult to organize, but its diffuse majorities. So, representation-reinforcing ideas can be used to attack the constitutionality of much modern regulation that imposes costs on diffuse majorities, and to defend against constitutional attack much regulation that adversely affects racial minorities.

(b) *Originalism* sometimes takes the Constitution's provisions to track what had been done in the common law and the system of government in Great Britain, and sometimes takes them to depart from what had been done there. More important, originalism contains within itself no resources to

---

[128] For my effort to develop the argument in the text in detail, for several interpretive methods, see M Tushnet *Red, White, and Blue: A Critical Analysis of Constitutional Law* (Harvard University Press, Cambridge Mass., 1988).

identify the level of generality at which the original understanding should be sought. An originalist can take a particular provision as a complete specification of the values the framers understood that provision to advance, or as an example of a broader set of values that the Constitution taken as a whole was understood to advance.

The general point here is that interpretive methods do not resolve the counter-majoritarian difficulty because none of the methods imposes a sufficiently powerful constraint on the mere policy preferences of interpreters.

Second, eclecticism exacerbates the problem. Even if a particular interpretive method could be sufficiently constraining, the fact that there are a number of such methods available to interpreters introduces another difficulty. Suppose a judge discovers that the text alone points against the result the judge wants to reach. Such a judge can look for some other interpretive method—precedent, or the moral values of the American people, for example—that he or she can invoke to support the preferred result. Then, the judge can simply ignore the textual argument, or say that, on balance, the other interpretive methods yield a better result than textualism does. And, importantly, all of this can be done within the bounds of what is professionally acceptable within the American judiciary.

Finally, there are no institutional mechanisms for committing judges to particular interpretive methods. Perhaps, as a matter of pure theory, someone could devise an interpretive method that does actually impose real constraints on judges, though no one appears to have done so as yet. The US constitutional system has no method of ensuring that those who are chosen as judges will use that method. The appointment process can be used to screen candidates for the judiciary to find out what their interpretive commitments are *at the time of appointment*. But, life tenure means that judges can change those commitments without facing any sanctions.[129]

Constitutional interpretation, then, does not dissolve the countermajoritarian difficulty. Is there some other democratic warrant for using interpretation as a substitute for amendment?

The first observation must be that, notwithstanding the difficulties associated with constitutional interpretation in the courts, no one questions that there *are* limits to interpretation. Constitutional claims that can be constructed in a theorist's imagination are never raised in court because the prospect of securing a favourable interpretation is non-existent. As noted earlier, litigants rarely offer creative interpretations of many of the Constitution's most important structural features in particular. Among the reasons for the existence on limits to interpretation is the clarity of some of the Constitution's terms. Weird hypothetical cases can be

---

[129] There might be no sanctions even in the internal forum of conscience, for a judge can rationalize a change between the views expressed at the time of nomination and the views held as a judge by referring to the impact of experience on the judge's understanding of the judicial role.

devised to bring into question what exactly the Constitution means when it says that each state shall have two Senators, but their very weirdness is a signal that the limits of interpretation are being breached.

A more controversial limit on interpretation is a pervasive ideology of individualism that, though not unchallenged in US constitutional history, remains a fundamental sub-strate on which specific constitutional interpretations are constructed. The expansiveness of the US approach to free expression illustrates the influence of individualist ideology on constitutional interpretation, as does the hostility to even the recognition of social and economic rights by most US constitutional theorists.

The general social, cultural, political, and economic surrounding also places limits on interpretation. Writing a 1957 article that has become a classic, political scientist Robert Dahl had an insight that has been quite productive in generating explanations for the persistence of judicial review in the face of the countermajoritarian difficulty.[130] As Dahl put it, 'the policy views dominant on the Court are never for long out of line with the policy views dominant among the lawmaking majorities of the United States.'[131] Dahl wrote at the outset of the Warren Court's transformation of constitutional law, and his insight, while remaining accurate, requires modification in detail in light of the experience over the succeeding decades. According to Lucas A Powe, the Warren Court's aggressive agenda had two items: the Court would find unconstitutional legislation that was an 'outlier,' that is, that was in force in no more than a handful of states, and it invalidated statutes that were expressions of the distinctive culture of the American South, a culture that was incompatible with that of much of the rest of the nation and, in particular, with the culture of the nation's legal elites.[132] *Griswold v Connecticut*,[133] the Connecticut anti-contraceptive case, is the best example of action against an outlier. In 1965, when the Warren Court found the statute to violate a constitutional guarantee of privacy, only Connecticut and Massachusetts outlawed the use of contraceptives. On Powe's analysis, then, the Warren Court was *not* countermajoritarian in a strong sense. It acted against outliers wherever it found them, and it acted against the American South, which it understood to be a minority region in the nation as a whole.

The pattern Powe identified has continued. Indeed, sometimes the Court relies on the fact that, as it sees things, the nation is already moving against a practice as a justification for pushing the movement along. An important theme in the Court's death penalty jurisprudence, for example, is an assessment of the degree to which a practice such as execution of those who committed their crimes while mentally retarded is approved of by the American people. Finding that most states had already eliminated persons with mental retardation from the class of those

[130] RA Dahl 'Decision-Making in a Democracy: The Supreme Court as a National Policy-Maker' (1957) 6 J Public L 279.   [131] ibid 285.
[132] LA Powe Jr *The Warren Court and American Politics* (Harvard University Press, Cambridge Mass., 2000).   [133] n 75.

eligible for capital punishment, the Supreme Court required all the remaining states to do so as well.[134] The Court's 2003 gay rights decision also relied on the fact that homosexual sodomy was not a crime in many states, and was rarely prosecuted even in states where the crime remained on the books, as a reason for finding such statutes to violate the Constitution.

Powe's analysis of the Warren Court and the American South points to another structural feature of judicial review—the role of formally extraconstitutional factors in making it seem appropriate for the courts to update the Constitution by interpretation. Bruce Ackerman divides American constitutional history into two groups of years, periods that he calls constitutional moments and those that are, in his terms, consumed by normal politics.[135] Ackerman's discussion of constitutional moments has attracted a great deal of scholarly attention, but for present purposes the periods of normal politics are more interesting. These are periods in which fundamental political arrangements are reasonably stable. Those arrangements consist of institutional structures and, important here, some basic substantive commitments that characterize the period, which we can call *regime principles*. The Warren Court's actions against the distinctive legislation of the American South advanced the regime principles characteristic of the long period between the early 1940s and the late 1970s. The Warren Court, that is, collaborated with the nation's political institutions in advancing the particular regime principles prevailing during that period.[136]

In disciplining outliers and in collaborating with the political branches to implement regime principles, the Supreme Court reduces the countermajoritarian difficulty. That reduction alleviates the corresponding anxieties about the fact that interpretive methods do not reduce that difficulty. The Court deploys its eclectic approach to constitutional interpretation so as to use and emphasize the modes of interpretation that advance the principles of the elites with which it is collaborating.

As suggested earlier, the appointment process is the mechanism by which the Court becomes collaborative. That process connects the judiciary to the political branches. Over time, the views held by federal judges are quite likely to correspond rather closely to the constitutional views the political branches would like federal judges to hold, although there may be periods when the political branches and the judiciary get somewhat disconnected, for example, when there are only a few Supreme Court appointments over quite a few years.[137] In those periods the Court might be seen as anti-collaborative, standing against the implementation of

---

[134] *Atkins v Virginia* (n 114).

[135] B Ackerman *We the People: Transformations* (Harvard University Press, Cambridge Mass., 2000) 6.

[136] Regime principles are different from what are more conventionally called constitutional values, in that regime principles change (in Ackerman's scheme, after constitutional moments have passed) and probably should be understood as the specification of constitutional values that has the deepest political appeal during a particular period of ordinary politics.

[137] As of this writing, the Supreme Court's composition has gone unchanged for a decade, a longer period than any since the early 1800s.

the constitutional principles pervasive in the political branches, or as pursuing a judgment reached independent of those principles.

Another aspect of the appointment process deserves mention as well. The process means that all who are appointed as justices will have respectable professional credentials. They will have been socialized into a professional culture that regards judicial wilfulness as particularly distasteful. Sharing that culture, judges are unlikely to be wilful in any interesting sense.[138] They will use the various interpretive techniques eclectically, true, but not to any strikingly novel—or countermajoritarian—conclusions.

Finally, it cannot go unremarked that the national courts in the United States have historically been, and remain today, among the most respected institutions of government in the nation. Particular decisions are sometimes controversial, but—with the exception of the Supreme Court's abortion decisions, and in the South the invalidation of segregation—the controversy usually dies down rather quickly, albeit sometimes because the Court modifies its decisions in light of an adverse public reaction. The American people have accepted judicial review as their method of updating the Constitution. That fact alone suggests that there really is no countermajoritarian difficulty.[139]

[138] For a defence of judicial review that relies on the combination of appointment by the political branches with the professional culture, see CL Eisgruber *Constitutional Self-Government* (Harvard University Press, Cambridge Mass., 2001).

[139] For a discussion connecting this fact to Jürgen Habermas's idea that modern pluralist nations require what he calls constitutional patriotism, see M Tushnet 'Forms of Judicial Review as Expressions of Constitutional Patriotism' (2003) 22 L & Philosophy 353.

2

Canada: From Privy Council to Supreme Court

Peter W. Hogg

Introduction to Canada's Constitution

Constitution Act 1867

Canada has no single document that is customarily described as 'the constitution'.[1] The closest approximation of such a document is the Constitution Act 1867, which was originally named the British North America Act 1867.[2] This is a statute of the United Kingdom Parliament that created the new Dominion of Canada by uniting three of the colonies of British North America and by providing the framework for the admission of all the other British North American colonies and territories.[3] This Act created a federal system by distributing legislative power between the newly created Parliament of Canada and the Legislatures of the provinces. Parliament's jurisdiction, while unlimited territorially, was limited by subject matter, primarily based on a list of federal powers set out in s 91. Each province had its own Legislature with powers limited both to the territory of the province and by subject matter, primarily based on a list of provincial powers set out in s 92.

The Constitution Act 1867 did not mark a break with the colonial past. Although the impulse to unite the British North American colonies came from the colonists themselves, and the basic terms of confederation (as Canadians usually refer to their federal system) were settled by the colonists themselves,[4]

---

[1] The sources of Canadian constitutional law are described in PW Hogg *Constitutional Law of Canada* (4th edn Carswell, Toronto 1997, annually supplemented in loose-leaf format) ch 1.

[2] Revised Statutes of Canada 1985 Appendix II no. 5. The name was changed by the Constitution Act 1982 (see n 5).

[3] The three colonies that united in 1867 were Canada (which became Ontario and Quebec), New Brunswick, and Nova Scotia. Canada thus started with only four provinces. Between 1867 and 1949, six more provinces joined (British Columbia, Prince Edward Island, and Newfoundland) or were created out of federal territories (Manitoba, Saskatchewan, and Alberta). Canada now has ten provinces and three federal territories (Yukon, Northwest Territories, and Nunavut).

[4] There were meetings of the principal colonial leaders at Charlottetown (1864) and Quebec City (1864), and the final details were negotiated in London with UK ministers as well (1866).

independence from the United Kingdom was neither desired nor even contemplated for the future. The new Dominion, although enjoying a considerable degree of self-government, remained a British colony. Of course, after 1867, there was an evolution to full independence, but it was a gradual process continuing well into the 20th century.

The Constitution Act 1867 did not follow the model of the Constitution of the United States in codifying all of the new nation's constitutional rules. On the contrary, it did no more than was necessary to accomplish confederation. The reason was stated in the preamble: the new nation was to have 'a constitution similar in principle to that of the United Kingdom'. Apart from the changes needed to establish the new federation, the British North Americans wanted the old rules to continue in both form and substance exactly as before.

Constitution Act 1982

A second document that rivals in importance the Constitution Act 1867 is the Constitution Act 1982. Like its 1867 predecessor, the Constitution Act 1982 was a statute of the Parliament of the United Kingdom. It filled two gaps in Canada's constitutional law. The first gap was the absence from the Constitution Act 1867 of any general provision for its own amendment. This meant that amendments had to be enacted by the Parliament of the United Kingdom, and that is how amendments were enacted until 1982 (although a convention developed that no amendment would be enacted except with the consent of Canada). The second gap was the absence from the Constitution Act 1867 of a charter of rights like the American Bill of Rights. The reason for the absence of a charter of rights was that the British model of parliamentary sovereignty appealed most to the framers.

The important developments of 1982 were actually carried out by two statutes of the United Kingdom Parliament. One was the Canada Act 1982,[5] which formally terminated the legislative authority of the United Kingdom over Canada. The other was the Constitution Act 1982,[6] which was technically a schedule to the Canada Act. Part V of the Constitution Act 1982 introduced new amending procedures that could be operated entirely within Canada. Part I of the Act introduced a new Charter of Rights that guaranteed various rights and liberties against legislative and executive action.

Amending Procedures

The amending procedures of Part V of the Constitution Act 1982 involve action by the Parliament of Canada and the Legislatures of the provinces in various combinations depending on the type of amendment.[7] Section 52 of the Act

---

[5] Statutes of the United Kingdom 1982 c 11.   [6] ibid Schedule B of Canada Act 1982.
[7] The complicated procedures are described in Hogg (n 1) ch 4.

defined the 'Constitution of Canada' for the first time. The definition includes the Constitution Act 1867, the Canada Act 1982, the Constitution Act 1982, and 29 other statutes, most of them amendments to the Constitution Act 1867. The Constitution of Canada comprises 'the supreme law of Canada'; any law that is inconsistent with the Constitution of Canada is 'of no force or effect'; and the Constitution of Canada can be amended only by the procedures stipulated in the Constitution Act 1982.[8] Since 1982, therefore, there has been no need (and indeed it is now impossible) to have recourse to the Parliament of the United Kingdom in order to make changes to the Constitution of Canada. The result of cutting the tie to the United Kingdom is generally described in Canada as the 'patriation' of the Constitution.

While it is obviously desirable for a sovereign state to have autonomous amending procedures, the procedures enacted by the Constitution Act 1982 are not an unmixed blessing. Most amendments require the so-called 7–50 formula, namely, the agreement of both houses of the Parliament of Canada and seven of the ten provincial legislative assemblies representing 50 per cent of the population. Some amendments require the unanimous agreement of all legislative bodies. These formulae have proved very difficult to operate, because there has been a tendency for each government to seek its own desired changes as the condition of agreeing to anything. A modest set of amendments, designed to correct grievances expressed by Quebec, was agreed to by all first ministers in the Meech Lake Accord of 1987, but strenuous opposition developed from groups whose constitutional objectives were not on the Meech Lake agenda, and it fell two provinces short of the unanimous ratification that was necessary.

There was criticism of the failure to hold a referendum on the Meech Lake Accord, and, although a referendum is not part of the formal amending procedures, there is now a widespread sense that significant amendments should be put to the people in a referendum. The Meech Lake Accord was followed by the Charlottetown Accord of 1992, which again proposed the same amendments as had been agreed to at Meech Lake, along with other changes desired by other constituencies (the western provinces, aboriginal people, for example). The manifold objectives of the Charlottetown Accord made it a long and complex document, which was far from ideal as the subject of a yes or no referendum. Nevertheless, it was put to a national referendum and the 'no' side easily prevailed. (There was something in the package to annoy just about everyone.) It was never presented to the legislative assemblies for ratification.

The failures of the Meech Lake Accord and the Charlottetown Accord have persuaded Canadian politicians that constitutional amendment is not a career-enhancing activity. One must conclude that significant amendments to the Constitution of Canada are, at least for the foreseeable future, impossible.[9]

---

[8] Constitution Act 1982 s 52.

[9] Since 1982, there have been eight amendments, but each affected either the Parliament of Canada alone or a single province. They are listed in Hogg (n 1) s 1.4.

Charter of Rights

The Charter of Rights was the other major new development contained in the Constitution Act 1982. Part I of the Act[10] consists of the Canadian Charter of Rights and Freedoms, which guarantees freedom of religion, expression, assembly and association, the right to vote, the right to move into, out of and within the country, the rights of criminal defendants to fair investigatory and trial procedures, equality rights, and French and English language rights. Aboriginal and treaty rights of the aboriginal peoples of Canada are also guaranteed.[11] These guarantees are all enforced by the sanction of nullification of any law or official act that is held to be in breach.[12] The result has been a massive increase in judicial review since 1982. Federalism cases, in which it is alleged that a law is in breach of the distribution of powers in the Constitution Act 1867, continue to come to the Supreme Court of Canada, but only at the rate of about two per year. Ten times as many Charter and Aboriginal rights cases, in which it is alleged that a law or official act is in breach of the guarantees in the Constitution Act 1982, now come to the Court.

Supreme Court of Canada

A striking omission from the Constitution Act 1867 was a national court of appeal. The Act gave authority for a general court of appeal to be established, but it did not establish one. The reason was that appeals already lay from the courts of the British North American colonies to the Judicial Committee of the Privy Council, and the framers were content to leave the supreme judicial authority in those safe British hands. However, pressures quickly developed for a Canadian court, and in 1875 the Supreme Court of Canada was established by federal statute. But the new Supreme Court was not the final court. There continued to be a right of appeal from the Supreme Court to the Privy Council. The appeal to the Privy Council was not abolished until 1949. The Supreme Court is still not entrenched in the constitution, but depends for its existence, composition and jurisdiction on an ordinary statute of the Parliament of Canada.[13]

The Supreme Court of Canada has nine judges. By statute, three of the judges must come from Quebec (with its distinctive civil law and French language), and the practice has been to appoint three from Ontario (the most populous province), two from the four western provinces, and one from the four eastern provinces. The judges are usually drawn from the ranks of the provincial appellate

---

10 Constitution Act 1982 ss 1–34.

11 Constitution Act 1982 s 35 (technically outside the Charter of Rights).

12 This is the consequence of the supremacy clause of s 52 of the Constitution Act 1982, described earlier. In addition, s 24 authorizes a court of competent jurisdiction to award an 'appropriate and just' remedy for a breach of the Charter of Rights.

13 The history of the Supreme Court of Canada is related in Hogg (n 1) ch 8.

courts, but occasionally a person is appointed directly from the practising bar. Most of the judges have a background in the private practice of law; some were academics before their appointment to a bench. The appointments are made by the Government of Canada. There is no requirement of legislative ratification or any other public process (although this lack of transparency is widely recognized as a deficiency that should be corrected). Fortunately, successive governments have evidently concluded that it is good politics to make good appointments, and the quality of appointments is generally agreed to be high. There has never been any serious suggestion that Canadian governments have attempted to 'pack' the court with judges of a particular approach or ideology.[14]

The Chief Justice decides which judges are to sit on each appeal. The quorum is five, and it used to be common for appeals, including appeals in constitutional cases, to be heard by less than a full bench. This is now uncommon. Most appeals, and certainly most constitutional appeals, are heard by a full bench of nine judges. The judges of the Court are free to write individual opinions, whether they are concurring in the result or dissenting, but in many cases a single unanimous opinion is written. Where the Court is divided, the majority judges usually manage to agree on a single opinion and the dissenting judges often achieve a similar consensus. However, more fragmented decisions are issued from time to time with several concurring and dissenting opinions.

The Supreme Court of Canada is a court of general appellate jurisdiction, standing at the top of the hierarchies of federal and provincial courts. It has jurisdiction over all kinds of cases, whether civil or criminal, private or public, and whether governed by provincial or federal or constitutional law. The Privy Council had a similar general jurisdiction before appeals were terminated in 1949. Apart from a limited category of appeals as of right, the Court controls its own docket, and the leave of the Court is required to bring an appeal to it from the Court of Appeal that exists in every province (or from the Federal Court of Appeal). In a typical year, the Court grants leave in about a hundred cases, of which about one third are constitutional cases.[15] The Court also has an original (non-appellate) jurisdiction to answer questions directed to it on a 'reference' by the Government of Canada. The answers are technically advisory opinions, although in practice they are treated as binding decisions. References are uncommon (one every two or three years), but some important constitutional cases have come to the Court in the form of a reference. The most recent example is *Re Same-Sex Marriage* (2004),[16] in which the Government of Canada asked the opinion of the Court as to whether Parliament had the power to legalize same-sex marriage.

---

[14] During the Privy Council period (1867–1949), Canadian governments had no control over the composition of the country's final court of appeal.

[15] There has been a recent tendency to reduce the number of appeals that are accepted for decision. In the 2003 calendar year, the Court handed down 81 judgments, of which 24 dealt with constitutional issues, divided into 17 Charter cases, 2 aboriginal rights cases, 4 federalism cases and 2 Canadian Bill of Rights cases.   [16] [2004] 3 SCR 698.

The Court said yes, the Government introduced a bill, and the Parliament of Canada enacted the amendment to the definition of marriage.[17]

Separation of Powers

The Constitution of Canada follows the British model in not having a rigid separation of powers between executive, legislative, and judicial powers. Indeed the relationship between the three branches of government is not directly addressed in the text of the Constitution.

As between the executive and the legislative branches, the relationship is governed by the unwritten 'conventions' of 'responsible government'. Those conventions govern the appointment of the Prime Minister and the formation of governments, both at the federal level of Canada and in each of the ten provinces (where the first minister is known as the Premier).[18] The conventions dictate that the Prime Minister (or Premier) is the leader of the party that commands a majority in the House of Commons (or provincial legislative assembly). In contrast to presidential systems, where the chief of state is elected independently of the legislative assembly, in a system of responsible government, the executive branch (headed by the Prime Minister and cabinet) possesses considerable control over the legislative branch. There is no rigid separation of powers between these two branches.

With respect to the judicial branch, the Constitution of Canada contains formal guarantees of independence for 'superior courts' and for all courts (superior or inferior) exercising criminal jurisdiction.[19] And the Supreme Court of Canada has supplemented these guarantees with a holding that there is an unwritten principle of judicial independence for all courts.[20] The Court has also imposed some restrictions on the conferral of 'judicial' functions on administrative tribunals.[21] But, subject to these limitations, Parliament and the Legislatures have the power to confer judicial functions on non-judicial bodies and to confer non-judicial functions on courts.

I have already mentioned that the Supreme Court Act confers on the Supreme Court of Canada a 'reference' jurisdiction, which requires the Court to give advisory opinions in answer to questions referred to the Court by the federal government. (Each provincial government also has the power to refer questions to the Court of Appeal of the province, from which there is a right of appeal to the Supreme Court of Canada.) The rendering of advisory opinions is usually seen as an executive function to be performed by the law officers of the government. For this reason, both the Supreme Court of the United States and the High Court of

---

17 Civil Marriage Act, Statutes of Canada 2005, c 33.
18 The rules of responsible government are described in Hogg (n 1) ch 9.
19 Constitution Act 1867 s 99; Constitution Act 1982 s 11(d).
20 *Re Remuneration of Judges* [1997] 3 SCR 3 (striking down reductions in judicial salaries).
21 This arcane jurisprudence is described in Hogg (n 1) s 7.3.

Australia have refused to accept a reference jurisdiction, reasoning that the judicial function is limited to the adjudication of genuine controversies. But the Privy Council refused to read any such limitation into Canada's constitutional law and upheld the grant of reference jurisdiction to the courts.[22] The Supreme Court of Canada has affirmed this ruling, saying that there is 'no constitutional bar to this Court's receipt of jurisdiction to undertake such an advisory role'.[23]

Problems of Interpretation

Interpretation of the Residuary Clause

From 1867 to 1982, the constitutional issues that reached the courts mostly concerned the interpretation of the federal division of powers in the Constitution Act 1982. It will be recalled that the Charter of Rights was not adopted until 1982 so that the interpretation of Charter rights was not an issue for the Canadian courts before 1982. What was adopted in 1867 was a federal system based on two lists of legislative powers. The legislative powers of the Parliament of Canada were defined primarily by s 91 of the Constitution Act 1867, which contained a list of 29 heads of power. The legislative powers of the Legislatures of the provinces were defined primarily by s 92 of the Constitution Act 1867, which contained a list of 16 heads of power.

In any federal system, the location of the residuary power is of utmost importance, since the residue will have to accommodate those topics of legislation that were not covered in the list (or in Canada's case, the lists) of legislative powers. In Canada, the drafting of the residuary power has given rise to considerable ambiguity and uncertainty. Indeed, the interpretive problems associated with the residuary power have been a central concern of the courts since confederation.

What appears to be the residuary power is contained in the opening words of s 91 of the Constitution Act 1867. Section 91 is the section that contains the list of 29 heads of legislative power that are allocated to the Parliament of Canada. That list is preceded by opening words that confer on the Parliament of Canada the power: 'to make laws for the peace, order, and good government of Canada, in relation to all matters not coming within the classes of subjects by this Act assigned exclusively to the Legislatures of the provinces'.

The conventional wisdom is that these words confer the residuary power on the Parliament of Canada. The point has not been entirely free of controversy. The power extends to 'all matters not coming within the classes of subjects assigned exclusively to the Legislatures of the provinces', which is obviously residuary in some sense. However, it is limited to 'laws for the peace, order, and good government of Canada', and it is matched in s 92(16) by a grant of power to the Legislatures of

[22] *A-G Ontario v A-G Canada* (Reference Appeal) [1912] AC 571 (PC).
[23] *Re Secession of Quebec* [1998] 2 SCR 217 [15].

the provinces over 'generally all matters of a merely local or private nature in the province'. That has led Albert S. Abel to argue that the residue is distributed between the two levels of government, depending on whether the unassigned matter of legislation is in relation to the peace, order, and good government of Canada (federal) or is a merely local or private matter (provincial).[24]

Section 92(16), even if it can in theory be regarded as one of two residuary powers, has proved to be quite unimportant in practice, because its work was done for it by another provincial head of power, s 92(13). Section 92(13), 'property and civil rights in the province', received an expansive interpretation at the hands of the Privy Council. The phrase 'property and civil rights' had a pre-confederation history in which it meant the private law of contract, tort, and property, that is, the law governing relationships between subject and subject.[25] (The term civil rights referred to proprietary, contractual, and tortious rights, not to civil liberties—the meaning later acquired in the United States.) When in the late 19th century the federal Parliament and provincial Legislatures moved to start regulating business[26] and labour relations,[27] the Privy Council held that, aside from certain industries specifically allocated to Parliament,[28] the power rested with the provinces under s 92(13). The regulation of business activity and labour relations were characterized as the regulation of property and civil rights in each province. Indeed, property and civil rights became the de facto residuary head of power in the Constitution of Canada.

The peace, order, and good government power of the Parliament of Canada, which appears to be the most obvious residuary power, was given a very narrow interpretation by the Privy Council. For the most part, new kinds of economic or social regulation were regarded as laws in relation to property and civil rights in the province, and were duly assigned to the provinces under s 92(13). The Privy Council was not moved by the national scope of large industries or the desirability of national regulation. A pattern was set under which Canada's federation became much more decentralised than that of the United States or Australia. The main lines of Privy Council interpretation were not disturbed by the Supreme Court of Canada after it became the final court of appeal in 1949.

---

[24] AS Abel 'What Peace, Order, and Good Government?' (1968) 7 Western Ontario L Rev 1; to the same effect, *A-G Ontario v A-G Canada* (Local Prohibition) [1896] AC 348, 365 (Lord Watson); K Lysyk 'Constitutional Reform and the Introductory Clause of Section 91' (1979) 57 Canadian Bar Rev 530, 541–543.

[25] Quebec Act 1774 (UK) s 8 (restoring French civil law to conquered colony of Quebec); Property and Civil Rights Act 1792 (Upper Canada) s 1 (restoring English law to the province of Upper Canada (now Ontario)).

[26] *Citizens Insurance Co of Canada v Parsons* [1881] 7 AC 96 (upholding provincial regulation of insurance industry).

[27] *Toronto Electric Comrs v Snider* [1925] AC 396 (striking down federal regulation of labour relations).

[28] The important exclusions from provincial power were 'navigation and shipping' (s 91(10)), 'banking' (s 91(15)), and interprovincial transportation and communication (s 91(29), read with s 92(10)(a)).

The Privy Council acknowledged a residuary role for the federal power over peace, order, and good government in filling gaps in the distribution of powers. One gap exists in the provision for the incorporation of companies. The provincial list includes a head of power over 'the incorporation of companies with provincial objects' (s 92(11)). But there is no matching power in the federal list. The Privy Council held that the power over the incorporation of companies with objects other than provincial must fall within the federal power over the peace, order, and good government of Canada, because of its residuary nature.[29]

The incorporation of companies was the only gap that the Privy Council ever found, although the treaty power seemed to be a rather clear example of another gap. Section 132 of the Constitution Act 1867 confers on the Parliament of Canada the power to enact laws for performing the obligations of Canada 'as part of the British Empire, towards foreign countries, arising under treaties between the Empire and such foreign countries.' The framers did not contemplate that Canada would eventually acquire the power to enter into treaties as a sovereign state in its own right, rather than as part of the British Empire. When Canada did acquire this power, the Privy Council initially held, in the *Radio Reference* (1932),[30] that the power to enact laws to perform Canadian, as opposed to imperial, treaties, came within the residuary power of peace, order, and good government because it was 'not mentioned explicitly in either s 91 or s 92'.[31] This reasoning appeared to be a faithful reading of the Constitution Act 1867.

The reasoning in the *Radio Reference* was later emphatically rejected by a differently-constituted Privy Council, speaking through Lord Atkin, in the *Labour Conventions* case (1937).[32] In that case, the Privy Council held that the federal Parliament had no power to implement Canada's obligations under multilateral treaties dealing with labour standards. Since s 132 applied only to Empire treaties, the power to implement Canadian treaties did not exist as a head of power, not even under the peace, order, and good government power. Instead, the power was distributed to whatever legislative body would have been competent if there were no treaty. On this basis, since labour standards came within the provincial authority over property and civil rights, only the provincial Legislatures could implement the treaty. As FR Scott commented: 'So long as Canada clung to the Imperial apron strings, her Parliament was all powerful in legislating on Empire treaties, and no doctrine of 'watertight compartments' existed; once she became a nation in her own right, impotence descended.'[33] This colourful language reflected the frustration of English-Canadian scholars at the Privy Council's relentless refusal to give significant content to the federal peace, order, and good government power whenever it came into potential conflict with the provincial power over property and civil rights.

---

[29] *Citizens Insurance Co v Parsons* (n 26).
[30] *Re Regulation and Control of Radio Communication in Canada* [1932] AC 304 (PC).
[31] ibid 312.   [32] *A-G Canada v A-G Ontario* (Labour Conventions) [1937] AC 326 (PC).
[33] FR Scott 'Labour Conventions Case' (1956) 34 Canadian Bar Rev 114, 115.

FR Scott's reference to 'watertight compartments' in the passage just quoted comes from Lord Atkin's opinion in the *Labour Conventions* case. In justifying his refusal to interpret the distribution of powers to accommodate a national treaty-making power that had developed after 1867, Lord Atkin had said: 'while the ship of state now sails on larger ventures and into foreign waters she still retains the watertight compartments which are an essential part of her original structure'.[34] For many critics, this dictum typified the narrow and technical approach that the Privy Council brought to the interpretation of the Constitution. Actually, the approach was not narrow and technical as applied to provincial powers. If property and civil rights was a 'watertight compartment', it was a large and flexible one, capable of accommodating much that could not have been contemplated in 1867. But peace, order, and good government was a small compartment, according to their lordships of the Privy Council.

Since the abolition of appeals to the Privy Council, the Supreme Court of Canada has generally accepted the main lines of interpretation laid down by the Privy Council. The *Labour Conventions* case has not been overruled, and continues to govern treaty-implementation practice in Canada—leading to great difficulty in implementing many multilateral treaties whose obligations call for changes in laws coming within the legislative competence of the provinces.

One office that the Privy Council did from the beginning acknowledge for the peace, order, and good government power was federal authority over emergencies. The Constitution Act 1867 made no mention of emergencies. Their lordships could have used their *Labour Conventions* reasoning to require even emergency legislation to conform to the distribution of legislative powers in ss 91 and 92 of the Constitution Act 1867. But in fact their lordships had no difficulty in deciding that a single plenary power over virtually all aspects of Canadian life was acquired by the Parliament of Canada during the first world war, and again during the second world war. For example, price control[35] and rent control,[36] both matters normally coming within property and civil rights in the provinces, were upheld as temporary wartime measures competent to the Parliament of Canada under the peace, order, and good government's emergency branch. The Privy Council was not, however, quick to recognize an emergency, and struck down the Parliament of Canada's 'Canadian New Deal' legislation (unemployment insurance, competition laws, minimum wages, natural products marketing scheme) on the basis that the depression of the 1930s was not an emergency.[37] Only a constitutional amendment enabled Parliament to enact a national scheme of unemployment

---

[34] *Labour Conventions* case (n 32) 350.

[35] *Fort Frances Pulp and Power Co v Manitoba Free Press Co* [1923] AC 695 (price of newsprint controlled by federal law during first world war).

[36] *Co-op Committee on Japanese Canadians v A-G Canada* [1947] AC 87 (deportation of Japanese Canadians during second world war); *Re Wartime Leasehold Regulations* [1950] SCR 124 (rent control during second world war).

[37] *Re Unemployment Insurance Reference* [1937] AC 355 (striking down federal unemployment insurance scheme).

insurance—in 1940, after the depression was over.[38] Parliament did persist in various attempts to enact a national competition law, and its persistence was eventually rewarded—but only after the abolition of appeals to the Privy Council. In an important departure from Privy Council precedent, the Supreme Court of Canada in 1989 upheld the competition law under the federal trade and commerce power.[39]

The Supreme Court of Canada, after the abolition of appeals, was more deferential to the legislative judgment as to the existence of an emergency, and was willing to accept the implausible proposition that double-digit inflation (a phenomenon that has recurred periodically throughout Canadian history) was an emergency; on that basis, the Court upheld temporary wage and price controls enacted by the Parliament of Canada.[40] This decision means that the Parliament has an emergency power that can be used at will, with only minimal judicial review of the factual basis for an emergency, but the Court has made clear that only temporary measures can be enacted under the emergency power.[41] It is not the answer to the shortfall in national legislative authority over the economy that is the major legacy of the Privy Council era.

The Supreme Court of Canada, after the abolition of appeals, developed another function for the peace, order, and good government power, and that was the 'national concern' branch of the power. Picking up on Privy Council suggestions that had never been fully explained or integrated into the jurisprudence, the Supreme Court of Canada held that the peace, order, and good government power not only extended to gaps and emergencies, but also to any matter that 'goes beyond local or provincial concern or interests and must from its inherent nature be the concern of the Dominion as a whole'.[42] Under this 'national concern' branch of the power, the Court has upheld federal jurisdiction over aviation,[43] over the national capital region (an area around Ottawa designated by federal legislation),[44] and over marine pollution.[45] While these decisions are obviously important, the Court has been careful not to permit the national concern branch to expand federal power too much. The Court has said:

For a matter to qualify as a matter of national concern . . . it must have a singleness, distinctiveness and indivisibility that clearly distinguishes it from matters of provincial concern and a scale of impact on provincial jurisdiction that is reconcilable with the fundamental distribution of legislative power under the Constitution.[46]

---

[38] Constitution Act 1940 (UK) adding new head 2A ('Unemployment insurance') to the federal list of powers in s 91 of the Constitution Act 1867.

[39] *General Motors v City National Leasing* [1989] 1 SCR 641.

[40] *Re Anti-Inflation Act* [1976] 2 SCR 373.   [41] ibid 427, 437, 461, 467.

[42] The quotation comes from a Privy Council judgment rendered shortly before the abolition of appeals: *A-G Ontario v Canada Temperance Federation* [1946] AC 193, 205.

[43] *Johannesson v West St Paul* [1952] 1 SCR 292.

[44] *Munro v National Capital Commission* [1966] SCR 663.

[45] *R v Crown Zellerbach* [1988] 1 SCR 401.   [46] ibid 438.

Federal wage and price controls, for example, although regarded by the Government of Canada in the 1970s as being necessary to control inflation (surely a matter of national concern in some sense), were not upheld under the national concern branch of peace, order, and good government, because inflation was too broad and diffuse a topic. Its acceptance as a head of federal power would confer on the Parliament of Canada jurisdiction over such a broad array of matters traditionally within provincial jurisdiction (under property and civil rights) that it would seriously disturb the existing balance of federal-provincial powers.[47] (The wage and price controls were in fact upheld, but under the emergency branch of peace, order, and good government, as temporary measures to combat the 'emergency' of double-digit inflation.)

The foregoing account does not begin to do justice to the manifold issues litigated and commented on about the meaning of the peace, order, and good government language of the Constitution Act 1867. It must be said that the problems were created by the language and were not invented by the courts. To place an apparent residuary clause at the beginning of a list of federal powers rather than at the end, to describe it in the language of peace, order, and good government rather than leaving it unqualified, and to accompany it with another apparent residuary clause at the end of the provincial list, was certainly calculated to create problems. The framers were experienced politicians, who included lawyers, and the final drafting was done in London with the benefit of the Westminster Parliament's parliamentary draftsmen. The ambiguity and uncertainty stemmed, I think, from the desire to create a federal system that met two conflicting desiderata. On the one hand, it was desired to create a strong central government. This was regarded as self-evidently desirable by the English Canadian politicians. Their centralizing impulse was reinforced in the aftermath of the American Civil War. One cause of that terrible conflict was widely held to be the granting of excessive powers to the states by the Constitution of the United States. But, on the other hand, the new federal system had to protect the French language and culture, including the civil code, of Quebec. Otherwise, it could not be acceptable to the French-Canadian minority, who were acutely aware that they would be a minority in the new Parliament of Canada, but would control the new Legislature of Quebec. Out of these conflicting goals came text that deliberately gave off conflicting signals, leaving the resulting ambiguities to be settled later, either by political practice or (as turned out to be the case) the courts.

Interpretation of the Two Lists

Another source of ambiguity and uncertainty in the structure of the Constitution Act 1867 was the two-list scheme of distribution of legislative powers. The earlier Constitution of the United States distributed legislative power in a single list of

---

[47] *Re Anti-Inflation Act* [1976] 2 SCR 373, 457–458.

enumerated powers that were conferred on the Congress of the United States; the states simply possessed the residue of legislative powers. The later Constitution of Australia followed a similar structure. In Canada, the framers constructed two lists of legislative powers, one federal (in s 91) and the other provincial (in s 92). Each list of powers was said to be exclusive to that level of government,[48] and, perhaps relying on the statement of exclusivity, no provision was made for conflict between federal and provincial laws. This structure led to many interpretative problems.

The most obvious problem was that the federal and provincial heads of power, although declared to be exclusive of each other, appeared to give rise to a good deal of duplication and overlapping. For example, the provincial power over 'property and civil rights in the province' (s 92(13)) appears apt to include 'the regulation of trade and commerce', which appears in the federal list of powers (s 91(2)). Trade and commerce is carried on by means of contracts that give rise to civil rights over property. (It will be noticed that the federal power over trade and commerce is not qualified in the same way as the federal commerce clause in the United States, which is expressly confined to international and interstate commerce.)[49] This issue quite quickly came before the Privy Council when both levels of government sought to regulate the insurance industry. The Privy Council held that the regula-tion of contracts of insurance came within property and civil rights in the province, and was accordingly within provincial jurisdiction.[50] The Privy Council read down the federal power over trade and commerce, holding that it should be interpreted as not including 'the power to regulate by legislation the contracts of a particular business or trade'.[51] The federal power was to be restricted to interna-tional and interprovincial trade and commerce, as well as a vague 'general regulation of trade affecting the whole dominion.'[52] By the same token, these topics were withdrawn from property and civil rights in the province.

Similar accommodations have been made between 'property and civil rights' and other heads of federal power, such as 'interest' (s 91(19)) and 'bankruptcy and insolvency' (s 91(21)). Another case of apparent overlapping is the federal head of power 'marriage and divorce' and the provincial head of power 'the solemnization of marriage in the province'. In all these cases, the courts have narrowed the meaning of the broader head of power in order to exclude the narrower one. By this process of 'mutual modification', the courts have attempted to eliminate the duplication and overlapping in the two lists. In that way, each head of power has been placed in its context as part of two mutually exclusive lists.

In order to determine into which exclusive head of power a contested law falls, the courts make a finding as to the 'pith and substance' of the law. This is an

---

[48] This is explicit in the opening language of ss 91 and 92. There are a few concurrent powers: over interprovincial export of natural resources (s 92A(3), old age pensions (s 94A) and agriculture and immigration (s 95)), but these are exceptional.

[49] Constitution of the United States art 1 s 3 ('to regulate commerce with foreign nations, and among the several states, and with the Indian tribes').

[50] *Citizens Insurance Co v Parsons* (n 26).   [51] ibid 113.   [52] ibid.

attempt to isolate the dominant characteristic of the law, which will then govern its classification for division-of-powers purposes. In the leading case of *Bank of Toronto v Lambe* (1887),[53] the Privy Council upheld a provincial law that imposed a tax on banks. The provinces have the power to levy 'direct taxation' (s 92(2)), but it is the Parliament of Canada that has the legislative authority over banks and banking (s 91(15)). As is the case with many laws, this one presented a provincial characteristic, namely, the tax, and a federal characteristic, namely, banking. The Privy Council held that the pith and substance of the law was the tax, which was intended to raise money and not to regulate or destroy the banks. Therefore, the law was valid despite its incidental effect on a federal head of power. As this case illustrates, each level of government, staying within its own exclusive list of legislative powers, can enact laws with substantial impact on matters outside its jurisdiction. Provided each law is in pith and substance within a head of power of the enacting body, any incidental effects on matters outside those heads of power will be valid. The exclusivity of the two lists has not been seen as preventing this kind of law. And indeed it would surely have been impracticable to decide that the laws of one level of government could have no effect on matters within the jurisdiction of the other level of government.[54] In any event, dozens of cases illustrate the courts' use of the distinction between 'pith and substance' and 'incidental effect' to allow Parliament or a Legislature to enact laws with effects that are outside its jurisdiction.[55]

The courts have even decided that some laws are open to both levels of government, despite the exclusivity of the two lists. These are laws that have a 'double aspect', meaning that they have a federal and a provincial characteristic that are equally significant. Neither can be singled out as the dominant 'pith and substance'. The best examples of the double aspect doctrine are the laws that regulate highway traffic. The Supreme Court of Canada has upheld provincial traffic offences of driving without due care and attention and failing to remain at the scene of an accident. These laws were within provincial power as regulation of the roads within the province (under property and civil rights in s 92(13)). At the same time, the Court has upheld very similar federal offences contained in the federal Criminal Code. They were within the federal authority over 'criminal law' (s 91(27)). Laws regulating conduct on the roads have a 'double aspect', and are therefore competent to both levels of government. In that field, legislative power is effectively concurrent, despite the exclusivity of the two lists of legislative powers.[56]

The double aspect doctrine obviously raises the possibility of conflicting federal and provincial laws. So does the pith and substance doctrine, since the incidental

---

[53] (1887) 12 AC 575.

[54] There is a doctrine of 'interjurisdictional immunity', which prohibits some kinds of relatively radical effects outside the jurisdiction of the enacting body: Hogg (n 1) s 15.8. This operates as an exception to the dominant doctrine of 'pith and substance', which is described in the text.

[55] An illustrative list is to be found in Hogg (n 1) s 15.5(a).

[56] Other examples are given in Hogg (n 1) s 15.5(c).

effects of the law of one level of government could conflict with a law of the other level of government. The framers made no provision for conflict between the laws of different jurisdictions, apparently assuming that the exclusivity of the two lists made conflict impossible. The rule adopted by the courts is that of federal paramountcy. Where there are conflicting federal and provincial laws, it is the federal law that prevails.[57] This is the same rule as in the United States (where it was inferred from the supremacy clause of the Constitution (article 6, clause 2)) and in Australia (where it is explicit in the Constitution (s 109)).

Interpretation of the Charter of Rights

As explained earlier, the Constitution Act 1867 did not contain a bill of rights. The Canadian Charter of Rights and Freedoms (Charter of Rights) was added to the Constitution of Canada in 1982, long after the Privy Council had ceased to be the final court of appeal for Canada. The Privy Council, therefore, never got the chance to work its magic on the Charter of Rights. The twenty-year life of the Charter has seen a heavy volume of cases, with the Supreme Court of Canada deciding about 20 per year. Most of the litigation is caused by the vagueness of the statements of the rights, which for the most part follow the traditional legal rights exemplified by the American Bill of Rights. For example, the Court has had to struggle with the meaning of freedom of religion (s 2(a)), freedom of expression (s 2(b)), freedom of assembly (s 2(c)), freedom of association (s 2(d)), the right to vote (s 3), rights to mobility (s 6), due process ('fundamental justice' in s 7), unreasonable search and seizure (s 8), arbitrary detention or imprisonment (s 9), the right to counsel (s 10(b)), rights of accused persons to speedy trial, non-compellability, presumption of innocence, jury trial, double jeopardy, and the like (s 11), equality rights (s 15), and language rights (ss 16–23). The application of these rights to the variety of legal and human interactions has given rise to the same difficulties of interpretation that are experienced by courts everywhere that have to apply constitutional guarantees of rights.

A unique Canadian feature of the Charter of Rights is the override clause of s 33, which authorises the Parliament or a Legislature to escape from the strictures of the Charter simply by inserting a 'notwithstanding clause' in a statute. The notwithstanding clause declares that the statute is to operate notwithstanding the Charter of Rights. The clause is effective for only five years, although it can be re-enacted at the end of each five-year period. The history of this provision is that it was a compromise reluctantly agreed to by Prime Minister Trudeau in 1981 as part of a package to make the new Charter acceptable to those provincial Premiers who were opposed to the entrenchment of a charter of rights. It has not turned out to be as important in practice as it is in theory, because it has been used rarely. The important issue of interpretation that is raised by s 33 is whether its use is subject

---

[57] The cases are described in Hogg (n 1) ch 16.

to judicial review. The Supreme Court of Canada has said no in a case that upheld a Quebec law that prohibited the use of any language but French on commercial signs in the province. The law contained a notwithstanding clause to protect the draconic measure from constitutional attack. The Court held that, if the law had no notwithstanding clause, the law would have been in conflict with the Charter guarantee of freedom of expression, but the notwithstanding clause was effective to insulate the law from judicial review.[58]

Another feature of the Charter of Rights that has no counterpart in the American Bill of Rights (although it does have counterparts in the international bills of rights) is the limitation clause of s 1. Under s 1, the guarantees of the Charter are subject 'to such reasonable limits prescribed by law as can be demonstrably justified in a free and democratic society'. This means that a law that infringes a Charter right will be upheld if it can be justified as a reasonable limit on the right and one that can be demonstrably justified in a free and democratic society. Section 1 is unlike s 33 (the override clause) in that it is the courts that must decide whether a law meets the standard of justification prescribed by s 1. Before a law can be struck down for conflict with the Charter, it is necessary to investigate whether the law can be justified under s 1. Section 1 is therefore an issue in nearly every case where a law is challenged on Charter grounds. The indeterminacy of s 1 is obvious on its face. What the Supreme Court of Canada has done[59] is to establish a series of four criteria that must be satisfied in order for a law to be justified under s 1. The criteria are: (1) a sufficiently important objective; (2) a rational connection to that objective; (3) minimum intrusion on the right; and (4) no disproportionately severe effects. These criteria involve an explicitly legislative role of weighing and balancing competing policies. These criteria have imposed a structure on the task of judicial review of s 1 justification, but of course every step of the way continues to be subject to contest by the parties and refinement by the Court, and outcomes are far from predictable.

The framers of the Charter sought to avoid the troublesome 'state action' jurisprudence of the United States by expressly providing (in s 32) that the Charter applied to the Parliament and government of Canada and to the Legislature and government of each province. The clear implication was that private action was not subject to the Charter, and the Supreme Court of Canada has so held.[60] But it turned out that the realm of the private is just as hard to define under s 32 as it has been in the United States, and so the Court has struggled with such issues as the application of the Charter to non-governmental agencies of various kinds, to delegated action of various kinds, to court orders, and to the common law.[61] So long as it is agreed that there is a private sphere into which state norms ought not to intrude, this kind of difficulty seems to be inherent in an entrenched bill of rights.

---

[58] *Ford v Quebec* [1988] 2 SCR 712, 740.   [59] *R v Oakes* [1986] 1 SCR 103, 138–139.
[60] *Retail, Wholesale and Department Store Union v Dolphin Delivery* [1986] 2 SCR 573.
[61] The jurisprudence is described in Hogg (n 1) ch 34.

The framers of the Charter also sought to avoid questions about the enforceability of the Charter's guarantees by two provisions of the Constitution Act 1982 (of which ss 1–34 are the Charter). One is the supremacy clause (of s 52), which expressly declares that laws inconsistent with the Constitution of Canada (which of course includes the Charter) are of no force and effect. The other is the remedy clause (of s 24), which expressly authorizes a court of competent jurisdiction to award an 'appropriate and just' remedy for breach of the Charter. But many questions arose to which these provisions provided no answer. Obviously, a court could, indeed must, hold that a law that violated the Charter was invalid. Could the court postpone the declaration of invalidity to leave time for the competent legislative body to repair the constitutional defect? Yes, said the Supreme Court of Canada.[62] Could the court itself repair the constitutional defect? Yes, said the Court, if that could be done by the judicious severance of a few words.[63] Could the court introduce ('read in') new language into the statute that had never been enacted? Yes, said the Court, even that radical measure was open to the judges, where there was a simple solution to the constitutional defect and no obvious alternative modes of repair.[64] In short, the Supreme Court of Canada has appropriated to itself extraordinarily broad remedial powers, which do not stop short of the direct redrafting of statutes that have been found to be in breach of the Charter of Rights.[65]

In applying the Charter of Rights, the Supreme Court of Canada has not adhered to those counsels of restraint that Alexander Bickel famously described as the 'passive virtues'.[66] The Court's aggressive approach to remedies has been described in the previous paragraph. A similar pattern of activism is evident everywhere else in the Court's practice. The Court has developed no doctrine of ripeness; mootness rarely defeats proceedings; lack of standing also rarely defeats proceedings (because of generous discretionary public-interest standing); public-interest intervenors are routinely admitted to appeals;[67] statutes are occasionally struck down on the basis of hypothetical facts that bear no relationship to the facts before the Court;[68] and sweeping constitutional rulings are occasionally issued as

---

[62] eg *R v Feeney* [1997] 2 SCR 13, postponing new requirement that police holding valid arrest warrant must obtain a second warrant to enter dwellinghouse to make the arrest.

[63] eg *R v Hess* [1990] 2 SCR 906, severing from the offence of statutory rape the language that made irrelevant the accused's belief that the victim was over the statutory age; this converted the offence into one of mens rea.

[64] eg *Vriend v Alberta* [1998] 1 SCR 493, inserting sexual orientation into the list of prohibited grounds of discrimination in Alberta's human rights legislation. (The Legislature had debated the point and deliberately chosen to omit that ground.)

[65] The jurisprudence is described in Hogg (n 1) ch 37.

[66] A Bickel *The Least Dangerous Branch* (2nd edn., Yale University Press, New Haven, 1986).

[67] The foregoing propositions are all elaborated in Hogg (n 1) ch 56.

[68] eg *R v Smith* [1987] 1 SCR 1045 (striking down minimum sentence for importing drugs, although the defendant had been given more than the minimum sentence); *R v Heywood* [1994] 3 SCR 761 (striking down prohibition on convicted sex offenders from loitering in playgrounds, because it might apply in situations where no children were at risk, although children were at risk on the facts before the Court).

obiter dicta.[69] Moreover, the number of statutes that have been struck down is striking. Figures compiled in 1996—after only 14 years of Charter litigation—showed that no less than 66 statutory provisions had been struck down on Charter grounds.[70] Of those 66, a surprisingly large number—43—were federal laws. And the number of 66 did not include the (much more numerous) cases where the actions of police officers or government officials were annulled and where a lesser remedy than the striking down of a law (such as the exclusion of evidence) was all that was required. The high rate of invalidation continues to this day.[71]

Interpretation of Aboriginal Rights

Section 35 of the Constitution Act 1982 provides that: 'The existing aboriginal and treaty rights of the aboriginal peoples of Canada are hereby recognized and affirmed.' Section 35 is outside the Charter of Rights, which ends at s 34 of the Act. The drafting of s 35 was highly contentious, and the resulting text is deliberately vague. It is not even clear whether aboriginal and treaty rights are guaranteed, since the words 'recognized and affirmed' seem to fall short of a constitutional guarantee (especially considering that the Charter rights are explicitly guaranteed in the opening words of s 1). Add to this the unclear effect of the word 'existing' (certainly included to reduce the rights), the uncertainty as to the effect of the inapplicability of the limitation clause in s 1 (because s 35 is outside the Charter of Rights), and the uncertainty as to the content of aboriginal rights (and even some of the older treaty rights). Indeed, s 35 was virtually meaningless at the time of its adoption. Meaning had to be breathed in by the Supreme Court of Canada.

In a series of cases from British Columbia, where no treaties exist, and from eastern Canada, where the treaties are very old and vague, the Supreme Court of Canada has approached with gusto the task of making s 35 meaningful. The Court has held that aboriginal and treaty rights are indeed guaranteed by s 35, and therefore prevail over inconsistent statutes. The word 'existing' does however exclude from constitutional protection those rights validly extinguished prior to 1982. Despite the inapplicability of s 1, aboriginal rights (and perhaps treaty rights) can be regulated in the service of compelling state objectives, for example, the conservation of resources or the protection of the environment. And the Court has provided some definition of aboriginal rights and aboriginal title, and laid down rules as to how they can be proved by aboriginal claimants, while at the same time exhorting aboriginal peoples and Canadian governments to negotiate

---

[69] eg *R v Brydges* [1990] 1 SCR 190 (instructing police officers to warn accused of availability of free duty counsel and legal aid).

[70] PW Hogg and AA Bushell 'The Charter Dialogue between Courts and Legislatures' (1997) 35 Osgoode Hall L J 76.

[71] In the volumes of the Supreme Court Reports for 1997 through 2002, for example, 11 provincial laws and 6 federal laws are struck down on Charter grounds, and many other cases found breaches of the Charter not involving the invalidity of a law.

the claims. Thanks to these decisions, the status of aboriginal and treaty rights has been greatly strengthened by s 35.[72]

One piece of unfinished business in the courts concerns the nature and scope of an aboriginal right of self-government.[73] This could lead to the recognition of a third order of government—First Nations' government—which would be constitutionally protected under s 35. As well, current treaty negotiations between First Nations and governments often cover rights of self-government, which, when successfully negotiated, would become part of a modern treaty. Self-government in a modern treaty would also be constitutionally protected under s 35.

Interpretation of Judicial Independence

The Constitution Act 1867, by s 99, following the language of the Act of Settlement 1701 in the United Kingdom, guarantees the tenure of the judges of the superior courts 'during good behaviour'. The Constitution Act 1982, by s 11(d), added that criminal trials must take place before 'an independent and impartial tribunal'. These are the provisions that explicitly guarantee the independence of the judiciary.

Before 1949 the Privy Council, and after 1949 the Supreme Court of Canada, raised obstacles to the creation of administrative tribunals by the provinces. If the effect of a new administrative tribunal was to take away some part of a jurisdiction traditionally exercised by a superior court, then the grant of jurisdiction to the tribunal was struck down. The basis for these decisions was ostensibly s 96 of the Constitution Act 1867, but s 96 was simply a power vested in the Governor General (that is, the Government of Canada) to appoint the judges of the superior courts of the provinces. In truth, the basis for the decisions was unclear or implausible, but they reflected a concern that judicial decision-making was being taken away from the superior courts, thereby denying the litigants the expertise and independence of the judges. Eventually, the Supreme Court of Canada came to see that there were significant advantages to a specialised tribunal in a regulated field, and it softened the rigidity of the old jurisprudence, but administrative tribunals exercising adjudicatory functions (and inferior courts) are still in jeopardy of being held to exercise superior court functions—in which case they are struck down.[74]

Judicial creativity in protecting the power and influence of judges has reached new heights in recent cases involving the remuneration of judges. The Supreme Court of Canada has held[75] that any reduction in judicial salaries, whether for

[72] The full story is told in Hogg (n 1) ch 27.

[73] For details, see Hogg (n 1) s 27.5(c).

[74] eg *Re Residential Tenancies Act* [1981] 1 SCR 714 (striking down rent tribunals with power to decide disputes between landlords and tenants); *MacMillan Bloedel v Simpson* [1995] 4 SCR 725 (striking down the contempt jurisdiction of youth courts).

[75] *Re Remuneration of Judges* (n 20).

superior or inferior judges, is a breach of judicial independence. The Court has struck down statutes reducing judicial salaries in Prince Edward Island, Alberta, and Manitoba, although in each case the judges' salaries had been reduced by a statute that applied across-the-board to all public sector salaries. How such a measure could be a threat to judicial independence was never explained. The Court invoked, not simply the guarantees of judicial independence that are explicit in the Constitution of Canada (ss 99 and 11(d), described two paragraphs above), but an 'unwritten constitutional principle' of judicial independence, which was broader than the carefully drafted language of the constitutional text.[76] What this unwritten principle required, the Court held, was that every province must establish a judicial compensation commission (whose members must include judges) to report regularly on the salaries of the judges. Any reduction in judicial salaries must be preceded by a report of the commission, and if a Legislature were to act inconsistently with the report of the commission, it would have to articulate what the Court described as 'a legitimate reason' for the departure.[77] All this was derived from an unwritten constitutional principle! Moreover, the penalty for non-compliance was the invalidity of statutes reducing judicial salaries. This was the outcome of the case, although the three provinces could hardly have complied with the ruling since it had not been announced at the time when they enacted their public sector salary measures, and (being based on a hitherto unknown unwritten principle) could not have been anticipated.[78]

The jurisprudence interpreting judicial independence is not based on any ambiguity or uncertainty in the text of the Constitution of Canada. Rather, the judges have constructed an elaborate edifice of doctrine with little or no basis in the text in order to protect the power, influence, salaries and perquisites of themselves and their colleagues.

Sources of Interpretation

Constitution as Statute

The Constitution Act 1867 provides no general rules or guidelines for its own interpretation. (Nor do any other instruments of the Constitution of Canada.)[79] The Constitution Act 1867 is, of course, literally a statute of the Parliament of the

---

[76] *Re Remuneration of Judges* [107].　　　[77] ibid [183].

[78] *Mackin v New Brunswick* [2002] 1 SCR 405 followed *Re Remuneration of Judges* (n 20), and arguably took it a step further by holding that even discretionary exemptions from a full workload for 'supernumerary judges' (who had qualified to retire but elected to stay on at full salary) could not be repealed, because the repealing statute had not been preceded by the report of a judicial compensation commission.

[79] An exception of limited scope is s 27 of the Constitution Act 1982, which provides that the Charter is to be interpreted 'in a manner consistent with the preservation and enhancement of the multicultural heritage of Canadians'.

United Kingdom. After confederation, there was some debate about whether it should be interpreted as a statute. In the Supreme Court of Canada, the sentiment was expressed that the British North America Act (as it then was) should be treated differently from other statutes:

Although an Imperial Act, to interpret it correctly reference may be had to the phraseology and nomenclature of pre-confederation Canadian legislation and jurisprudence, as well as the history of the union movement, and to the condition, sentiment and surroundings of the Canadian people at the time. In the British North America Act it was in a technical sense only that the Imperial Parliament spoke; it was there that in a real and substantial sense the Canadian people spoke, and it is to their language, as they understood it, that effect must be given.[80]

Pleas of this kind fell on deaf ears in the Privy Council, which took the view that the British North America Act should be interpreted as a statute.[81]

Since their Lordships of the Privy Council were interpreting a statute, they insisted on an absolute prohibition of any resort to legislative history in order to place the constitutional text in its context. That self-denying ordinance was a cardinal rule of statutory interpretation in the United Kingdom at that time.[82] This denied their lordships access to the records and debates that had preceded confederation in 1867, as well as the more general history of the union movement. This would have been unfortunate even for Canadian judges, who lived in Canada and (in the 19th century at least) had lived through confederation. It was doubly unfortunate for their Lordships of the Privy Council, who were quite ignorant of the history, geography and society of Canada, as numerous faux pas in their opinions demonstrate. Even Lords Watson and Haldane, who dominated the Privy Council in its Canadian appeals from 1880 to 1899 (Lord Watson) and from 1911 to 1928 (Lord Haldane), never visited Canada. They shared a preconceived notion of what a federal system should look like,[83] a notion that would have been contradicted by much of the legislative history.[84] Their decisions established precedents that elevated the provinces to coordinate status with the federal government, gave narrow interpretations to the principal federal powers

---

[80] *Re Prohibitory Liquor Laws* (1895) 24 SCR 170, 231 (Sedgwick J). Canadian courts typically took the view expressed in the quotation, relying on extrinsic aids to interpretation, especially the shared history: JT Saywell *The Lawmakers: Judicial Power and the Shaping of Canadian Federalism* (University Toronto Press, Toronto, 2002) 20–22.

[81] *Bank of Toronto v Lambe* (1887) 12 App Cas 575, 579. (Privy Council and other courts 'must treat the provisions of the Act in question [that is, the British North America Act] by the same methods of construction and exposition that they apply to other statutes.')

[82] This was a period of 'formalism' in English law, in which the law as seen as a science from whose principles one true answer could be obtained by a process of deduction. History, policy, morality and other extrinsic influences were suppressed in the consideration of legal questions. See PS Atiyah *The Rise and Fall of Freedom of Contract* (Clarendon Press Oxford 1979) 388.

[83] *A-G Australia v Colonial Sugar Refining Co* [1914] AC 237, 252, where, in an Australian appeal, Lord Haldane expounds on the nature of federalism in general and in Canada in particular.

[84] The definitive study of the Privy Council's role in interpreting the Canadian constitution is Saywell (n 80). It is a damning indictment of the quality of their work.

(over peace, order, and good government and over trade and commerce), and gave a wide interpretation to the principal provincial power (over property and civil rights).[85]

The decisions of the Privy Council—the 'wicked stepfathers of confederation', as they were wittily described—were much criticised in English Canada (although not in French Canada) for their provincial bias. In retrospect, however, the decisions of the Privy Council can be seen as consistent with other tendencies in Canada towards a less centralized federalism than that of either the United States or Australia. Pierre Trudeau famously remarked that 'if the law lords had not leaned in that [provincial] direction, Quebec separation might not be a threat today; it might be an accomplished fact'.[86] Recent appraisals of the work of the Privy Council have tended to recognize this, and have been much less critical.[87] In the end, then, and no doubt more by accident than design, Canada was on the whole not badly served by the Privy Council.

It must be acknowledged that their Lordships of the Privy Council, while eschewing all extrinsic aids to interpretation, were well aware that the statute they were interpreting was also the Constitution of Canada. It was an 'organic instrument' that was intended to 'cover the whole area of self-government within the whole area of Canada'.[88] And, by 1929, after the Watson-Haldane era, from time to time the Privy Council exhibited signs of abandoning its formalistic approach and taking a more generous and open-minded approach to the Constitution and to federal powers in particular.[89] The classic statement of this period came from Lord Sankey in 1929, when he said that: 'The British North America Act planted in Canada a living tree capable of growth and expansion within its natural limits'.[90]

After 1949, the Supreme Court of Canada, while not departing from the main lines of interpretation set by the Privy Council for the federal distribution of powers, began to cautiously develop the doctrine that allowed the main federal powers to expand. Peace, order, and good government,[91] trade and commerce,[92] and the criminal law power[93] were all expanded. Then in 1982, the Charter of Rights was adopted, and a whole new era of judicial review opened up. For this, the Court, now led by a scholarly and brilliant Chief Justice Dickson, was ready to

---

[85] I Binnie 'Constitutional Interpretation and Original Intent' (2004) 23 Supreme Court L Rev 345.

[86] PE Trudeau *Federalism and the French Canadians* (MacMillan of Canada, Toronto, 1968) 198.

[87] The best study is AC Cairns 'The Judicial Committee and its Critics' (1971) 4 Canadian J Political Science 301. KM Lysyk 'Reshaping Canadian Federalism' (1979) 13 U British Columbia L Rev 1, 5, citing Cairns, says that 'on the whole, the Privy Council did a creditable job of interpreting our Constitution in a way which preserved a balance in the Canadian federation'. Saywell (n 80) takes an unrepentantly critical approach, emphasizing their formalism, their ignorance of Canada, and their failure to understand the scheme that was established in 1867.

[88] *A-G Ontario v A-G Canada* [1912] AC 571, 581 (Earl Loreburn LC).

[89] Saywell (n 80) ch 8.   [90] *Edwards v A-G Canada* [1930] AC 124, 136.

[91] eg *R v Crown Zellerbach* (n 43) (upholding federal law prohibiting dumping at sea).

[92] eg *General Motors v City National Leasing* [1989] 1 SCR 641 (upholding federal competition law).

[93] eg *R v Hydro-Québec* [1997] 3 SCR 213 (upholding federal environmental protection law).

undertake the challenge of elaborating the vague guarantees of the Charter by an interpretative approach that was suitable to a constitution rather than a statute. Here is what the Court (speaking through Estey J) said in one of the early Charter cases:

The Charter comes from neither level of the legislative branches of government but from the Constitution itself. It is part of the fabric of Canadian law. Indeed, it is 'the supreme law of Canada': s 52, Constitution Act, 1982. It cannot be readily amended. The fine and constant adjustment process of these constitutional provisions is left by a tradition of necessity to the judicial branch. Flexibility must be balanced with certainty. The future must, to the extent foreseeably possible, be accommodated in the present. The Charter is designed and adopted to guide and serve the Canadian community for a long time. Narrow and technical interpretation, if not modulated by a sense of the unknowns of the future, can stunt the growth of the law and hence the community it serves. All this has long been with us in the process of developing the institutions of government under the B.N.A. Act, 1867 (now the Constitution Act, 1867). With the Constitution Act, 1982, comes a new dimension, a new yardstick of reconciliation between the individual and the community and their respective rights, a dimension which, like the balance of the Constitution, remains to be interpreted and applied by the court.[94]

And here is what the Court (speaking through Dickson J) said in another early Charter case:

The task of expounding a constitution is crucially different from that of construing a statute. A statute defines present rights and obligations. It is easily enacted and easily repealed. A constitution, by contrast, is drafted with an eye to the future. Its function is to provide a continuing framework for the legitimate exercise of government power and, when joined by a Bill or a Charter of Rights, for the unremitting protection of individual rights and liberties. Once enacted, its provisions cannot easily be repealed or amended. It must, therefore, be capable of growth and development over time to meet new social, political and historical realities often unimagined by its framers. The judiciary is the guardian of the constitution and must, in interpreting its provisions, bear these considerations in mind.[95]

Similar statements could be quoted from many other cases, and the practice of the Court has been true to its rhetoric. The concept of the Constitution as a statute is well and truly over.

Legislative History

The enactment of the Constitution Act 1867 (the British North America Act) was preceded by conferences at Charlottetown (1864), Quebec City (1864), and London, England (1866). No verbatim records were kept of the discussions at these conferences, although we do have the text of the 72 resolutions that were

---

[94] *Law Society of Upper Canada v Skapinker* [1984] 1 SCR 357, 365 (Estey J).
[95] *Hunter v Southam* [1984] 2 SCR 145, 155 (Dickson J).

agreed to at Quebec City and the 69 resolutions that were agreed to at London. The confederation debates in the legislative assembly of the united province of Canada (1865) are preserved in full, but of course these are not the debates of the drafters, but of the members of the legislative assembly of one of the three uniting provinces. (The united province of Canada emerged from confederation as Quebec and Ontario.) There were no debates in the legislative assemblies of the other two uniting provinces, namely, Nova Scotia and New Brunswick. The debate in the Parliament of the United Kingdom (1867) is available in the United Kingdom Hansard for 1867.[96]

As related in the previous section of this paper, the Privy Council held that the legislative history of the British North America Act was inadmissible on the ground that the legislative history of other statutes was inadmissible as an aid to their interpretation. This remained the orthodox position until some considerable time after the abolition of appeals in 1949. This rule did not entirely exclude extrinsic evidence of legislative intent. The 'mischief rule' allowed the courts to have regard to the 'mischief' for which the pre-existing law did not provide, and to advance the 'remedy' for which the legislation did provide.[97] In identifying the mischief and its remedy, the courts were allowed to consult the state of the pre-existing law, and to draw conclusions about the purpose of the change in the law. But they were not allowed to consult the best evidence of these matters, namely, the legislative history. In a series of constitutional cases starting in the 1970s, the Supreme Court of Canada reversed this position. The Court now routinely refers to the legislative history of the Constitution Act 1867 as an aid to the interpretation of the Act. The Quebec resolutions have been referred to in several cases,[98] as have the confederation debates[99] and (in one case) a speech in the United Kingdom Parliament.[100]

Unlike the relatively scanty records of the legislative history of the Constitution Act 1867, there are abundant records of the legislative history of the Constitution Act 1982 (which includes the Charter of Rights). We have the text of no less than seven versions of the Act, the minutes and proceedings of a legislative committee that considered a late version of the Act (with the benefit of testimony from those involved in its preparation), as well as the debates in the Parliament of Canada (which passed a resolution calling for enactment) and the United Kingdom Parliament (which enacted the law). This material is routinely referred to by the Supreme Court of Canada as an aid to the interpretation of the Act.[101]

While legislative history is now admissible as an aid to the interpretation of the various instruments comprising the Constitution of Canada, the Supreme Court

---

[96] The most comprehensive collection of confederation documents is in GP Browne *Documents on the Confederation of North America* (McClelland & Stewart, Toronto, 1969).

[97] *Heydon's Case* (1584) 3 Co Rep 7a; 76 ER 637.

[98] The most recent example is *MacDonald v City of Montreal* [1986] 1 SCR 460, 494.

[99] The most recent example is *A-G Canada v CN Transportation* [1983] 2 SCR 206, 226.

[100] *Di Iorio v Warden of Montreal Jail* [1978] 1 SCR 152, 200.

[101] eg *Re British Columbia Motor Vehicle Act* [1985] 2 SCR 486, 504–507.

of Canada does not regard itself as bound by even a clear indication of what the framers intended. Indeed, the Court gives little weight to legislative history. This is because 'originalism' has never gained a foothold in the jurisprudence of the Supreme Court of Canada. The Court, like the Privy Council before it, gives primary weight to its own interpretation of constitutional language. Although the Court informs itself of a wider context than the Privy Council was prepared to do, the legislative history is no more than a part of the context. It is a part that is less persuasive than the language and structure of the surrounding text. The text, after all, is what was enacted. This will be elaborated in the discussion of 'progressive interpretation', below.

Previous Decisions

The doctrine of precedent or stare decisis follows a similar history to that of legislative history. The Privy Council assumed that it should follow its own precedents in interpreting the Constitution Act 1867 in just the same way as it did in interpreting other statutes or the common law. Although the Privy Council (unlike the House of Lords) never actually stated that it was bound by its own previous decisions, it did state that 'on constitutional questions it must be seldom indeed that the Board would depart from a previous decision which it may be assumed will have been acted upon both by governments and subjects'.[102] The Privy Council never did expressly depart from a previous decision in a Canadian constitutional appeal, but there were many unacknowledged twists and turns in the jurisprudence from 1867 to 1949. It is unlikely that the apparently rigid adherence to stare decisis was as great a constraint on their lordships as one might have feared.

Before the abolition of appeals to the Privy Council in 1949, the Supreme Court of Canada was lower than the Privy Council in the judicial hierarchy, and was therefore bound by decisions of the Privy Council. During this period, the Supreme Court of Canada decided that it was also bound by its own prior decisions.[103] However, after the Court's accession to final appellate status, the Court gradually came to accept that, while it should normally adhere to its own prior decisions, it was not absolutely bound to do so. The Court has explicitly refused to follow a prior decision in several cases, some but not all of them constitutional cases.[104] The Court also gradually came to accept that the decisions of the Privy Council should have no more (and no less) binding force than its own decisions. The Court has explicitly refused to follow a Privy Council precedent in three constitutional cases.[105]

---

[102] *A-G Ontario v Canada Temperance Federation* [1946] AC 193, 206.
[103] *Stuart v Bank of Montreal* (1909) 41 SCR 516.
[104] eg *United States v Burns* [2001] 1 SCR 283.
[105] *Re Agricultural Products Marketing Act* [1978] 2 SCR 1198; *Re Bill 30 (Ontario Separate School Funding)* [1987] 1 SCR 1148; *Wells v Newfoundland* [1999] 3 SCR 199.

It is generally held that in constitutional cases a final court of appeal should be more willing to overrule prior decisions than in other kinds of cases. In non-constitutional cases, there is always a legislative remedy if the doctrine developed by the courts proves to be undesirable. The unwanted doctrine can simply be changed by the competent legislative body. This is not true of constitutional doctrine, which after its establishment by the final court can be altered only by the difficult process of constitutional amendment. It follows that there is greater need of judicial adaptation of constitutional law to keep the law abreast of new technology and new social and economic needs. This line of thought has not been articulated by the Supreme Court of Canada in loosening the bonds of precedent, and the Court has not explicitly, or in practice, drawn any distinction between constitutional cases and non-constitutional cases.

Academic Writings

So far as I can ascertain, the Privy Council never cited academic writing in any of its Canadian constitutional cases, and academic citation was very rare indeed in the Supreme Court of Canada as well. A change began to emerge in 1973, with the appointment of Bora Laskin as the Chief Justice of Canada. This was a remarkable appointment by the Government of Prime Minister Pierre Trudeau. Not only was Laskin the first Jew to be appointed to the Court, he was also the first appointee who had been a full-time law professor in his previous life; and, as a law professor, he had been a trenchant critic of the formalism of the Privy Council and the Supreme Court of Canada. In 1984, Laskin retired from the Court and was replaced as Chief Justice by Brian Dickson. Dickson CJ (although a corporate lawyer in his previous life) turned out to be even more scholarly in his approach than Laskin CJ. Moreover, Dickson's appointment coincided with the arrival in the Supreme Court of Canada of the first cases under the new Charter of Rights (which had been adopted in 1982). Also appearing at the same time was a flood of academic commentary speculating on the meaning of this fascinating new instrument of judicial review. Dickson CJ and his colleagues eagerly accepted the help that academic writing could provide, and citation of academic writings became very common indeed in the Court's opinions.[106] This has continued under Chief Justice Lamer (1990–2000) and Chief Justice McLachlin (2000-present).[107] It is not limited to constitutional cases.

Comparative and International Sources

In the early years of confederation, the Canadian courts often cited American constitutional cases, and discussed the similarities and differences between the

---

[106] Details are provided in V Black and N Richter 'Did She Mention My Name?': Citation of Academic Authority in the Supreme Court of Canada, 1985–1990' (1993) 16 Dalhousie L J 377.

[107] The writings of the present author have been cited 166 times by the Supreme Court of Canada: K Makin, 'Constitutional Expert a Major Influence', Globe and Mail newspaper, September 29, 2003, B16.

two constitutional systems.[108] But the Privy Council, true to its formalist approach to the interpretation of a statute, saw no relevance in the decisions of another constitutional system, and, so far as I can ascertain, never made any reference to American cases. After the Supreme Court of Canada became the final court of appeal in 1949, the interpretation of the Constitution Act 1867 had developed along such distinctive lines it really was not very useful to look to American and Australian cases (for example) in resolving new problems of interpretation. On federalism issues, the Supreme Court of Canada has accordingly continued to rely almost exclusively on Canadian cases.

The sea change occurred with the adoption of the Charter of Rights in 1982. As related above, the Supreme Court of Canada under Chief Justice Dickson was fully open to all sources that would help it to develop a new jurisprudence for a new era of judicial review. Many of the ideas and some of the language of the Charter had been taken from the American Bill of Rights, and the Canadian judges naturally looked across the border for help in deciding what they meant. Freedom of religion, freedom of expression, unreasonable search and seizure, right to counsel, cruel and unusual punishment, and equal protection were among the concepts for which the Court drew on the rich American case-law and commentary. Even when the language of the Charter was dissimilar, the American cases were useful sources of ideas and parallels. And the long experience of the Americans with their Bill of Rights had generated an extraordinarily rich academic commentary on rights issues and judicial review. These American sources, which are of course set against a familiar common law background and a social and economic milieu that is familiar to Canadians, are frequently referred to in Charter cases.[109]

Despite the obvious usefulness of American cases, their results have often not been followed in Canada. The different structure of the Charter, especially its limitation clause (s 1) and override clause (s 33), were formal encouragements to the Court to develop a distinctively Canadian jurisprudence. In any case, the Court certainly wanted to carve out its own road, exhorting itself to 'be wary of drawing too ready a parallel between constitutions born to different countries in different ages and in different circumstances.'[110] On most Charter issues the Canadian law now diverges significantly from the American law, even when the language of the two instruments is very similar. Generally, the Charter rights have been given a broader interpretation than their American counterparts.[111]

Canadian courts are accustomed to reading cases from the United Kingdom, Australia and New Zealand, English-speaking countries that share the same British Imperial history, the same common law, and similar social and economic conditions. But none of these countries has an entrenched bill of rights. The

---

108 Saywell (n 80) 22.
109 On the use by the Supreme Court of Canada of American cases, see Hogg (n 1) s 33.8(b).
110 *R v Keegstra* [1990] 3 SCR 697, 740.
111 The comparison is documented in R Harvie and H Foster 'Ties that Bind: the Supreme Court of Canada and American Jurisprudence' (1990) 28 Osgoode Hall LJ 729.

United Kingdom and New Zealand have unitary constitutions, so that they have no judicial review on federal grounds either. Australia has a federal constitution, but, for the reasons given above, the Privy Council and Supreme Court of Canada have tended to consider Canadian federal questions without reference to other countries' experiences.

Canada is a bilingual country (English and French) and a bijural country (Quebec has a civil code). But decisions from the countries of Europe (other than the United Kingdom) are almost never referred to in constitutional cases. The countries of Central and South America, Asia and Africa are also neglected. Even research libraries at university law schools will have minimal holdings of the law reports and journals from all these countries. Canadian lawyers and judges rarely even try and make use of these sources, assuming the material to be physically unavailable and intellectually inaccessible for reasons of language, culture or context.

Since the adoption of the Charter of Rights, the Supreme Court of Canada has made occasional reference to the International Covenant on Civil and Political Rights and to the decisions of the Human Rights Committee of the United Nations, which interprets the Covenant. The Covenant was one of the important influences on the drafting of the Charter. Canada has ratified the Covenant, and so its terms are relevant to the interpretation of the Charter by virtue of the rule that Canadian statutes and constitutional instruments should be interpreted into conformity with international law. The European Convention on Human Rights and the decisions of the European Court of Human Rights, which interprets the Convention, were also influences on the drafting of the Charter. Canada cannot be a party to the Convention, which is a regional treaty, but the Supreme Court of Canada does make occasional reference to the Convention, and cases thereunder, as aids to interpreting the Charter.[112]

Modes of Interpretation

Originalism

Originalism is the idea that the task of interpreting a constitution is to ascertain the 'original understanding'—the meaning intended by the original framers—and to give effect to that understanding. Fidelity to the original meaning will provide constant and consistent interpretation over time, despite changes in the composition of the final court. Fidelity to the original meaning will also provide an answer to the legitimacy of judicial review. If judicial review merely gives effect to the original understanding of the framers, then non-elected judges do not trespass on democratic values when they strike down a statute enacted by an

---

[112] On the use by the Supreme Court of Canada of international sources, see Hogg (n 1) s 33.8(c).

elected legislative body. As to the admitted necessity of adapting the constitution to new conditions and new values, the originalist argues that this should be accomplished by the constitutional amending process, not by the 'interpretations' of judges.

Originalism has never enjoyed any significant support in Canada.[113] As related in the earlier discussion of legislative history, their Lordships of the Privy Council were so indifferent to the original understanding that they refused even to look at any evidence of the intentions of the framers of the Constitution Act 1867 (other than the actual text).[114] While Americans debated whether the 'original under-standing' should be binding, Canadians debated whether evidence of the original understanding should even be disclosed to the Court! As related earlier, that debate has only recently been resolved by the full admissibility of legislative history as an aid to the interpretation of the Constitution of Canada. But admissibility is one thing, weight is another. And the indifference to the original understanding lingers on in the modern Supreme Court of Canada.

A critical issue of interpretation for the Supreme Court of Canada was the meaning of 'fundamental justice' in s 7 of the Charter of Rights. Section 7 guarantees 'the right to life, liberty and security of the person and the right not to be deprived thereof except in accordance with the principles of fundamental justice'. Before the legislative committee that reviewed the draft Charter of Rights, a parade of witnesses, including the Minister of Justice, who was responsible for the drafting, the officials who had actually prepared the drafts, and academic lawyers familiar with the jurisprudence of the United States, explained that the words 'fundamental justice' had been chosen in preference to 'due process' in order to avoid the substantive due process jurisprudence of the United States. While fundamental justice did not have a clear meaning in pre-Charter jurisprudence, it was a concept that was intended to cover procedural due process only, not substantive due process. The committee accepted this interpretation. The issue came to the Supreme Court of Canada for decision in the *British Columbia Motor Vehicle Reference*,[115] a case that reviewed a British Columbia law that imposed a term of imprisonment for an offence (driving without a licence) that lacked any element of mens rea. The Court examined the legislative history of s 7, and acknowledged that there was unanimity in the legislative history that fundamental justice meant procedural due process. But the Court held nevertheless, based on its reading of the language and structure of the constitutional text, that s 7 included substantive due process. The challenged offence created a substantive not a procedural injustice, the Court held, and was accordingly invalid for breach of s 7.

---

[113] One of the few cases where the original understanding was relied upon is *Re Eskimos* [1939] SCR 104, where the Court consulted contemporary documents to hold that the reference to 'Indians' in the Constitution Act 1867 must have been intended to include the Inuit.

[114] As related in the earlier discussion of legislative history, resort to the state of law before confedera-tion was not prohibited. In *Citizens Insurance Co v Parsons* (n 26) 111, the Privy Council relied on the pre-confederation meaning of 'property and civil rights' to give the phrase a broad meaning in the Constitution Act 1867. [115] *Re British Columbia Motor Vehicle Act* (n 101).

In the *British Columbia Motor Vehicle Reference*, Justice Lamer, who wrote for the majority of the Supreme Court of Canada, emphasized that the legislative history of the constitutional text, although admissible, was entitled to little weight. He pointed to the difficulty in assuming that the views of witnesses to a parliamentary committee were shared by the 'multiplicity of actors' who had negotiated, drafted and adopted the Charter. And, in direct contradiction of the originalist argument, he cautioned against the risk that adherence to legislative history would cause the meaning of the Charter to 'become frozen in time to the moment of adoption with little or no possibility of growth, development and adjustment to changing societal needs'. Such a result would 'stunt the growth' of the 'newly planted living tree that is the Charter.'[116]

It is, of course, rare that the legislative history of a constitutional text provides a clear answer to the very question before a reviewing court but that was the case in the *British Columbia Motor Vehicle Reference*. Not only were the various statements in the legislative history unanimous, they went to the fundamental question of why s 7 had been included in the Charter in the first place. For the Supreme Court of Canada to reject the original understanding in that case, illustrates in dramatic fashion how little weight the Court is prepared to give to legislative history. There are many other cases in which the Court has referred to the legislative history of a Charter provision. In none of the cases was the reference central to the Court's reasoning.[117]

Progressive Interpretation

The Privy Council gave no support to any doctrine like originalism, but of course their lordships were not in the habit of articulating their reflections on deep issues of constitutional interpretation. It was enough to say that the British North America Act was to be interpreted as a statute, albeit a statute that established a constitution for the British North American colonies. The fact that each decision of the Privy Council had to take the form of a single unanimous opinion, without any separate concurrences or dissents, also tended to produce short opinions without any superfluous discussion. Nonetheless, one might safely infer that their lordships would have been surprised by the notion that the interpretation of a constitution might change over time. Indeed, as late as 1937, in the *Labour Conventions* case, which was discussed earlier, Lord Atkin used his famous 'watertight compartments' metaphor in deciding that no federal power to implement treaties was to be inferred from Canada's accession in international law to sovereign statehood: 'while the ship of state now sails on larger ventures and into foreign waters she still retains the watertight compartments which are an essential part of her original structure'.[118]

---

[116] *Re British Columbia Motor Vehicle Act* (n 101) 507–509.
[117] The Court's use of legislative history is examined in Hogg (n 1) s 57.1.
[118] *Labour Conventions* case (n 32) 354.

Lord Haldane retired from the Privy Council in 1928, ending a period of 38 years that is often described as the Watson-Haldane era, when those two judges dominated the Privy Council and the principal doctrines of Canadian constitutional law were established. In 1929, an entirely new tone seemed to be set when the Privy Council decided the *Edwards* case.[119] That case held that women were 'persons' who were qualified to sit in Canada's Senate. The decision was a progressive one, and so was the 'living tree' metaphor by which Lord Sankey supported the decision: 'The British North America Act planted in Canada a living tree capable of growth and expansion within its natural limits'.[120]

Despite the formalism of the Privy Council's opinions, and despite the watertight compartments metaphor of Lord Atkin, during the Privy Council period as well as the modern Supreme Court period, the Constitution of Canada has adapted to the enormous social, economic, technological, and regulatory changes that have occurred since 1867. Agriculture has ceased to be the dominant activity. The population is now concentrated in large cities. Technological developments, including electricity, the internal combustion engine, the telephone, aviation, radio, television, and now the computer, have transformed the modes of communication and transportation, the appearance of the landscape, and the ways in which people live, work, and play. Governments have grown immensely, and the increasing acceptance of egalitarian, collectivist, and humanitarian values has required the regulation of industry to protect workers, consumers, investors, and the environment, the regulation of labour relations to permit collective bargaining, to impose labour standards, and protect against discrimination, and the creation of massive education, public health, and social security systems. While all this change was occurring, the nation had to endure the first world war, the great depression, the second world war, and periodic bouts of inflation. None of these developments were anticipated in 1867, as a glance at the two lists of legislative powers in the Constitution Act 1867 will confirm. All of these developments called for regulatory initiatives by Parliament and the Legislatures, and most of those initiatives were challenged in the courts. Some challenges succeeded and some failed, but the Privy Council and Supreme Court always managed to find a home in the Constitution for all the various new kinds of regulation.

During this time, the text of the Constitution of Canada changed very little, and only four small amendments were made to the division of powers.[121] Why was so little formal amendment needed? The answer is that the Privy Council was implicitly following a 'living tree' approach long before the metaphor was articulated by Lord Sankey in 1929. Since the abolition of appeals, the Supreme Court of Canada has acted on and frequently repeated the living tree dictum.[122] What

---

[119] *Edwards* case (n 90).   [120] ibid 136.

[121] Amendments were adopted dealing with unemployment insurance (1940), old age pensions (1951 and 1964) and natural resources (1982). The Charter of Rights, the guarantee of aboriginal rights, and the amending procedures, all of which were adopted in 1982, did not affect the distribution of legislative authority.

[122] eg *Re British Columbia Motor Vehicle Act* (n 101) 507–509, quoted in text accompanying n 116.

does it mean? It means that the language of the Constitution of Canada is not frozen in the sense that it would have been understood by its framers. For example, federal authority over 'undertakings connecting the provinces with any other or others of the provinces' (s 92(10)) includes an interprovincial telephone system, radio, television, a trucking line, a busline, and aviation, although none of these means of communication and transportation were known in 1867.[123] Federal authority over 'criminal law' (s 91(27)) 'is not confined to what was criminal by the law of England or any province in 1867'.[124] Federal authority over 'banking' (s 91(15)) is not confined to 'the extent and kind of business actually carried on by banks in Canada in 1867'.[125] On the contrary, the words of the constitutional text are to be given a 'progressive' or 'dynamic' interpretation, so that they are continuously adapted to new conditions and new ideas.[126]

Needless to say, the issue is not whether the original understanding should be investigated and (if it can be ascertained) taken into account. No one would argue that it should not be. Indeed, the historical context of a constitutional provision obviously places limits on the range of meanings that the provision will bear.[127] The issue is whether the original understanding is binding forever, which is the originalist position. The point of originalism is to deny that the courts may use their power of interpretation to adapt the text to new conditions and new ideas. For the originalist, adaptation can only come through the power of amendment.

A progressive interpretation of the constitutional text is inconsistent with originalism, because progressive interpretation concedes a power of adaptation to the courts. But it would be wrong to conclude that the principle of progressive interpretation is inconsistent with the intentions of the framers. What originalism ignores is the possibility that the framers were content to leave the interpretation of their text to the courts of the future, and approved of the possibility that the process of interpretation would apply the text in ways that were unanticipated at the time of the drafting.[128] In the case of the Constitution Act 1867, our records are too scanty to reach any kind of definite conclusion, but it is plausible to suppose that something like the doctrine of progressive interpretation was in the minds of the framers. They were sophisticated people who were familiar with the process of judicial review of laws (both from their own colonial experience as well as their knowledge of the United States). They knew that their handiwork would have to adapt to changes in their new country, and yet they did not seem to contemplate formal amendment as a frequent mode of adaptation, because they

---

[123] Hogg (n 1) ch 22.　　　[124] *P.A. T.A. v A-G Canada* [1931] AC 310, 324.

[125] *A-G Alberta v A-G Canada (Alberta Bill of Rights)* [1947] AC 503, 553.

[126] For modern formulations of progressive interpretation, see *Law Society of Upper Canada v Skapinker* (n 94) 365, quoted in text to n 94; *Hunter v Southam* (n 95), 155, quoted in text to note 95.

[127] In *R v Blais* [2003] 2 SCR 236, it was held that the word 'Indians' in the Natural Resource Transfer Agreements, which are scheduled to the Constitution Act 1930, did not include the Métis, because it was clear that in 1930 the intention was to exclude (and make separate provision for) the Métis. The Court ([39]–[41]) rejected an argument based on the living tree principle.

[128] This idea is articulated by Holmes J in *Missouri v Holland* 252 US 416, 433 (1920).

made no provision for amendment in the constitutional text, and amendment was in fact only possible by the agency of the Imperial Parliament of the United Kingdom. In the case of the Constitution Act 1982, our records are abundant, and the proceedings of the legislative committee that reviewed the text indicate clearly that the civil servants who drafted the text, and the ministers and members of Parliament who adopted it, assumed that the courts would not be bound by their views as to the meaning of the text, and would interpret the text in ways that could not then be predicted with certainty. Nor did anyone suggest that there was anything wrong with this prospect.[129]

In sum, the principle of progressive (or dynamic) interpretation, as articulated in the metaphor of the 'living tree', has become the dominant theory of interpretation in Canada. Under this theory, the language of the Constitution is applied to contemporary conditions and ideas without regard for the question whether the framers would have contemplated such an application. According to this approach, legislative history is a relevant 'starting point' in the process of interpretation, but it cannot be conclusive in interpreting provisions that are 'essentially dynamic'.[130] Moreover, the weight of legislative history diminishes with the passage of time, as the views of the framers become less and less relevant to contemporary conditions.

Generous Interpretation

For Lord Sankey in the *Edwards* case, the primary implication of his 'living tree' metaphor was that a constitution should receive a generous interpretation. He went on to say that the provisions of the Constitution Act 1867 should not be 'cut down' by a 'narrow and technical construction', but should rather be given 'a large and liberal interpretation'.[131] This case decided that women were 'persons' and accordingly eligible to be appointed to the Senate. The case did not concern the federal division of powers, and of course the support for generous interpretation was quite inconsistent with the narrow interpretations that the Privy Council had placed on federal (but not provincial) legislative powers during the Watson-Haldane period (1890–1928). But the dictum was taken up in later cases that did concern the federal distribution of powers.[132] The later cases emphasized that a large and liberal interpretation of the provisions of the Constitution that allocate powers to the Parliament of Canada and the Legislatures of the provinces has the effect of conferring the 'widest amplitude' of power on those bodies. In the context of federalism,

---

[129] PJ Monahan *Politics and the Constitution* (Carswell, Toronto, 1987) 78–82, draws this conclusion from his analysis of the proceedings of the committee. I agree with the analysis.

[130] *Martin Service Station v Minister of National Revenue* [1977] 2 SCR 996, 1006.

[131] *Edwards* case (n 90) 136.

[132] *British Coal Corp v The King* [1935] AC 500, 518; *A-G Ontario v A-G Canada (Privy Council Appeals)* [1947] AC 127, 154 (both cases giving a generous interpretation to s 101 of the Constitution Act 1867, which empowers Parliament to establish a general court of appeal for Canada).

the large and liberal interpretation is the course of judicial restraint; it tends to uphold challenged legislation, reinforcing a presumption of constitutionality. Generally speaking, this has been the approach of the Supreme Court of Canada into the modern period. The Court is reluctant to strike down statutes on division of powers grounds, and not many have been struck down.

The Charter of Rights does not confer power on the Parliament or Legislatures. On the contrary, it denies power to the Parliament and Legislatures. A generous interpretation of the Charter of Rights cannot be justified as increasing the powers of the legislative bodies, because it will reduce their powers. It is the course of judicial activism, because it will lead to more invalidations of laws than would a narrow interpretation of the Charter. The justification for a generous interpretation of the Charter is that it will give full effect to the rights guaranteed by the Charter. Even before the Charter was adopted, the Supreme Court of Canada had held that the language rights in s 133 of the Constitution Act 1867 (one of the few bill-of-rights provisions in that Act) were to be interpreted generously.[133] With respect to the Charter, the Court has taken the same approach: the Charter calls for 'a generous interpretation . . . suitable to give to individuals the full measure of the fundamental rights and freedoms referred to'.[134]

The Supreme Court of Canada's generous interpretation of the Charter of Rights is not merely rhetoric. The Charter of Rights has in most of its provisions been given a broader interpretation than comparable provisions in the American Bill of Rights.[135] Because of the limitation clause (s 1) of the Charter, which was described earlier, a broad interpretation of a guaranteed right will not always result in the invalidation of the challenged law; the law can still be upheld as a 'reasonable limit' on the right. But, despite this way out, and setting aside the many cases where police or other sub-legislative action has been struck down, a study published in 1997 showed that the Supreme Court of Canada had struck down 66 laws on Charter grounds since the adoption of the Charter in 1982; 43 of the invalid laws were federal, and 23 were provincial.[136] A similar rate of invalidation has continued since then.[137] Canada is a tolerant, sophisticated, liberal society with a flourishing democracy. For so many of its laws to be found in conflict with Charter guarantees can only be explained by activism on the part of the Supreme Court of Canada.

Purposive Interpretation

At the same time as the Supreme Court of Canada insists on a 'generous' approach to the interpretation of the constitutional text, it also claims to follow a 'purposive' approach.[138] In the context of the Charter of Rights, what is involved in a purposive

---

[133] *A-G Quebec v Blaikie* [1979] 2 SCR 1016, 1029.

[134] eg *Hunter v Southam* (n 93), 156. The quotation has been repeated in many other cases.

[135] Harvie and Foster (n 111).   [136] Hogg and Bushell (n 70).

[137] The figures for the 1997–2002 period are 17 invalidations, of which 6 were federal and 11 were provincial: (n 71).

[138] eg *Hunter v Southam* [1984] 2 SCR 145, 156; *R v Big M Drug Mart* [1985] 1 SCR 295, 344.

interpretation is an attempt to ascertain the purpose of each Charter right, and then to interpret the right so as to include activity that comes within the purpose and exclude activity that does not. Of course, this can never be anything more than a very general approach to interpretation. The original purpose of a right (which is what is relevant) is usually unknown, and so the Court has a good deal of discretion in deciding what the purpose is, and at what level of generality it should be expressed. The Court (speaking through Justice Dickson) has expressed the search for purpose in these terms:

In my view, this [purposive] analysis is to be undertaken, and the purpose of the right or free-dom in question is to be sought by reference to the character and the larger objects of the Charter itself, to the language chosen to articulate the specific right or freedom, to the historical origins of the concepts enshrined, and where applicable, to the meaning and purpose of the other specific rights and freedoms with which it is associated within the text of the Charter.[139]

Thus, guidance can be obtained from the language in which the right is expressed, from the implications to be drawn from the context of the surrounding text, from the pre-Charter history of the right, and from the legislative history of the right. Moreover, as a body of caselaw develops on the meaning of a particular right, the core of the definition tends to become settled.[140]

In the context of the Charter of Rights, the Court has usually assumed that a generous approach and a purposive approach are one and the same thing—or at least are not inconsistent. Indeed, statements of the purposive approach have nearly always been accompanied, often in the same sentence, by statements of the generous approach.[141] In the case of some rights, that is correct: a purposive inter-pretation will yield a broad scope for the right. For example, if the purpose of the guarantee against unreasonable search and seizure (s 8) is to protect a right of privacy (as the Court has held), then search and seizure cuts a wide swathe indeed, including (as the Court has held) electronic surveillance, inspection of computer records and demands for the production of documents, as well as the more obvious invasions of property rights.[142]

In the case of most rights, however, a generous approach is not the same as a pur-posive approach. The widest possible interpretation of the language, which is the most generous interpretation, will 'overshoot' the purpose of the right by including behaviour that is outside the purpose and unworthy of constitutional protection. For example, the guarantee of equality (s 15), although expressed in wide general terms, could hardly be read as condemning all legislative distinctions. If its purpose is to protect human dignity (as the Court has held), then only distinctions based on immutable personal characteristics offend the guarantee.[143] The reference to the

---

[139] *R v Big M Drug Mart* (n 138) 344 (Dickson J).

[140] For an analysis of purposive interpretation, see SR Peck 'An Analytical Framework for the Application of the Charter' (1987) 25 Osgoode Hall L J 1, 6–31.

[141] In earlier notes I have cited *Hunter v Southam* [1984] 2 SCR 145, 156 as authority for both approaches.   [142] The broad interpretation of s 8 is described in Hogg (n 1) ch 45.

[143] The narrow interpretation of s 15 is described in Hogg (n 1) ch 52.

purpose of s 15 results in a narrowing of the right. Indeed, that will often be the effect of purposive interpretation.[144] Generosity is a helpful idea only if it is subordinate to purpose. Obviously, in interpreting a constitutional text, the Court should avoid narrow, legalistic interpretations that might be suitable to a detailed statute. But, if the goal of generosity were set free from the limiting framework of purpose, the results of a generous interpretation of rights would often be inconsistent with the results of a purposive approach.

The practice of the Supreme Court of Canada is to apply a purposive approach to the Charter of Rights, and this does inevitably diminish the generosity or breadth of the rights. However, as noted in the previous section of this paper, the Court has still given a broad interpretation to the rights in comparison with the interpretations of the American Bill of Rights by the Supreme Court of the United States, and the Court has found that a considerable number of federal and provincial statutes are invalid for breach of the Charter.

Unwritten Constitutional Principles

The interpretation of a constitutional text over a long period of time will result in an accumulation of precedents that may come to assume more importance than the original text. Indeed, the judicial exegesis may come to bear only a tenuous resemblance to the text that it purportedly interprets. The earlier section of this paper on 'Progressive interpretation' has explained the phenomenon of the accommodation of the text to changes in the economy, technology, living patterns and ideas about the role of government. Obviously, the judges have played a creative role in that accommodation. But, even if the world remained the same, the courts would still have to apply the text to unpredictable human and institutional behaviour, and a superstructure of judge-made law would become encrusted onto the text. There is nothing strange about this process. Cases come before the courts that were not foreseen when the text was drafted, and the courts see implications in the text that were not obvious when it was drafted. Each new case becomes a precedent, and before long there is a lot of detailed doctrine to supplement some brief phrase in the general language of the constitutional text. In this sense, no one doubts that judges make new law.

An entirely different order of judicial law-making is the discovery (meaning invention) by the courts of 'unwritten constitutional principles', the word 'unwritten' being a frank acknowledgment that the 'principles' are not to be found in the written constitutional text, and cannot be derived from the text by normal processes of interpretation. Now it goes without saying that the Constitution of Canada is constructed on a set of unwritten foundational principles that have profoundly influenced the drafting of the text and that continue to inform

---

[144] eg *Law Society of Upper Canada v Skapinker* (n 94) (s 6 does not confer a freestanding right to work—its purpose is to protect mobility).

its interpretation. Democracy, responsible government, the rule of law, the independence of the judiciary, the protection of civil liberties and federalism are among those principles. Any capsule description of the Constitution of Canada would normally make use of these ideas. But the normal assumption of Canadian lawyers is that only the actual text of the Constitution—a text that is admittedly subject to interpretation—creates enforceable rights and obligations. There are, however, a number of cases in which the Supreme Court of Canada has found an 'unwritten constitutional principle' in the Constitution that is enforceable in exactly the same way as if it were an express term. When an unwritten constitutional principle is enforced in that fashion, it is hard to avoid the conclusion that the Constitution has been amended by judicial fiat in defiance of the procedure laid down by the Constitution for its amendment.

In a later section of this chapter, 'Crisis Management by the Court', we will see that the Supreme Court of Canada in the *Manitoba Language Reference* (1985)[145] found that the 'rule of law' was an unwritten constitutional principle. The Court invoked the principle to solve the crisis that would have resulted from the Court's holding that all of the laws of Manitoba enacted since 1890 were invalid. They had been enacted in English only in defiance of a constitutional requirement to enact the laws in English and French. The rule of law required that the Manitoba Legislature must follow the law of the Constitution, which in turn required the Court to hold the laws to be invalid. But another aspect of the rule of law called for a community regulated by law, which would be violated if Manitoba were left with a vacuum of law. The solution to these conflicting aspects of the rule of law was to hold the laws enacted in English to be invalid, but to also hold that the laws were to remain in force for a temporary period stipulated by the Court while the existing laws were translated and re-enacted. By virtue of the unwritten constitutional principle of the rule of law, the people of Manitoba continued to be governed temporarily by a body of law that had been invalidly enacted, and that owed its force solely to the fiat of the Court.

In 1990, the Supreme Court of Canada invoked an unwritten constitutional principle of federalism to find an unwritten 'full faith and credit' rule in the Constitution, requiring each province to recognize judicial judgments of the other provinces.[146] Such a rule is of course explicit in the constitutions of the United States and Australia, but it is not explicit in the Constitution of Canada.

In the earlier section of this paper on 'Interpretation of Judicial Independence', we noticed that the Supreme Court of Canada had in 1997 found an 'unwritten constitutional principle' of judicial independence. The only text that the Court

---

[145] *Re Manitoba Language Rights* [1985] 1 SCR 721, 757.
[146] *De Savoye v Morguard Investments* [1990] 3 SCR 1077. Whether this was just a rule of the conflict of laws or was one of constitutional law was not perfectly clear until *Hunt v T & N* [1993] 4 SCR 289, which held that a Quebec statute could not bar the removal of documents from the province when the court of another province had ordered their production. This made clear that the unwritten principle was a rule of constitutional law that would invalidate an inconsistent statute.

was able to invoke was a reference in the preamble to the Constitution Act 1867 to 'a constitution similar in principle to that of the United Kingdom'. This reference seems rather to point against the unwritten principle. The only guarantee of judicial independence in the United Kingdom is in the Act of Settlement 1701, and its provisions were essentially reproduced in s 99 of the Constitution Act 1867. No broader principle, of the kind found by the Canadian Court, has ever been accepted in the United Kingdom. Canada's unwritten principle applied to courts that had been deliberately left out of the express guarantees of judicial independence in s 99 and in s 11(d) of the Charter of Rights. Moreover, and again in defiance of United Kingdom doctrine, the unwritten principle caused the invalidity of statutes enacted in breach of its requirements. What the unwritten principle required (on pain of invalidity) was that elaborate procedures (designed by the Court) be established by statute and followed in order to reduce judicial salaries or perquisites. The Court has not shrunk from applying the unwritten guarantee to strike down three provincial statutes that reduced judicial salaries in tandem with all other public sector salaries,[147] and another provincial statute that imposed full workloads on judges who were eligible for retirement but instead chose 'supernumerary' status on full salary.[148] These measures all offended the unwritten constitutional principle. As I commented earlier, these cases seem to be blatant exercises of power by judges for the purpose of protecting their own salaries and perquisites. It is hard to muster nostalgia for the appeal to the Privy Council, but it is surely unfortunate that there is no corrective appeal for these cases.

In the later section of this paper on 'Crisis Management by the Court', we will see that the Supreme Court of Canada in the *Secession Reference* (1998),[149] invoked unwritten constitutional principles of 'federalism' and 'democracy' to hold that, if Quebec were to hold a referendum on a clear question in favour of secession, and if there was a clear majority in favour of secession, then the rest of Canada would come under a legal duty to negotiate in good faith the terms of the secession. This duty to negotiate was an entirely new idea in the constitutional law of Canada, but it stemmed from unwritten constitutional principles. Its exact nature has never had to be tested, since no referendum on secession has been held in the province of Quebec since the decision, and Quebec now has a federalist government that is not interested in secession.

Unwritten constitutional principles are no doubt available to accommodate virtually any grievance about governmental policy. Fortunately, lower courts have maintained a wise reluctance to invalidate government initiatives on the basis of unwritten constitutional principles, and the Supreme Court of Canada shows some sign of reigning in its creative impulses. The Court in a recent case[150] refused to invalidate a federal law that restricted access to cabinet documents in litigation. The challengers invoked three unwritten principles, namely, the rule of

---

[147] *Re Remuneration of Judges* (n 20).   [148] *Mackin v New Brunswick* [2002] 1 SCR 405.
[149] *Secession Reference* (n 23).   [150] *Babcock v Canada* [2002] 3 SCR 3.

law, the separation of powers and the independence of the judiciary. But Chief Justice McLachlin for the unanimous Court refused to strike down the federal law, and she said that 'the unwritten principles must be balanced against the principle of parliamentary sovereignty',[151] a salutary caution notably absent from the judicial independence cases.

The principal cases that apply unwritten constitutional principles are very recent, having been decided in the last 20 years. However, the phenomenon has some roots in dicta from earlier periods. Starting in 1938,[152] some of the judges of the Supreme Court of Canada began to articulate an 'implied bill of rights' for the Constitution of Canada. The theory was that the Constitution, although lacking an express bill of rights (a deliberate choice of the framers in 1867), should nevertheless be interpreted as forbidding the provincial Legislatures and perhaps the Parliament of Canada from restricting freedom of expression and other fundamental freedoms. This theory never attracted a majority of the Court, and, with the adoption of the explicit Charter of Rights in 1982, it has now lost its rationale. But the implied bill of rights is at least a nascent example of an unwritten constitutional principle.

Influences on Interpretation

Bilingual and Bicultural Country

The unique characteristic of Canada, in comparison with other former British colonies, is the presence of a large French-speaking minority. Moreover, that French-speaking minority forms a majority in the second largest province, Quebec. Indeed, the major driver of confederation in 1867 was the conflict between French and English in the united province of Canada, which combined the predominantly French-speaking, Catholic communities in the lower part of the St Lawrence valley with the rapidly growing English-speaking, Protestant communities in the upper part of the valley. Confederation offered to the English (who by 1867 were more populous than the French) representation by population in a new national Parliament, as well as their own separate province (Ontario). Confederation offered to the French a separate province (Quebec) which would be controlled by a French-speaking, Catholic majority, and which would have jurisdiction over education, language, culture and most private law (property and civil rights). These were the keys, although economic and military considerations also argued for the inclusion of the Atlantic provinces to the east of Quebec, and for the opening up and settlement of the vast territories to the west of Ontario. Now, of course, the country stretches across North America without a break from the Atlantic to the Pacific Ocean. But Ontario and Quebec, with more than half

---

[151] *Babcock v Canada* [55].
[152] *Re Alberta Statutes* [1938] SCR 100; and see Hogg (n 1) s 31.4(c), for the history.

of the country's population, continue to dominate the country's politics in ways that cannot but influence all Canadian institutions, including the courts.

Federalism in Canada was bound to take a more decentralized form than in the United States (the only real precedent in 1867) or in Australia (which federated in 1900). Since the majority of French Canadians live in Quebec (although there are substantial numbers in Ontario and New Brunswick and small minorities in each of the other provinces), their concern to protect their language and culture has taken the form of an insistence on provincial rights, a demand that Quebeckers be masters in their own house. Contrast this attitude with that of a minority that is dispersed across the country, like the African Americans in the United States, or the aboriginal people of Canada and other countries. Such minorities are typically unsympathetic to the rights of states or provinces. They typically look to the institutions of the federal government for redress of their grievances, both in the form of legislation and judicial decisions. They accordingly reinforce the economic and social forces that tend to favour the growth of central power in countries with modern, national economies, high personal mobility, and efficient national communication and transportation systems.

The economic and social forces that in all modern economies are increasing the power of national governments in relation to regional governments are present in Canada as well, of course, but they do meet continuous resistance from Quebec. And Quebec cannot be ignored. It has nearly 25 per cent of Canada's population (7.5 million of 32 million) and when it does not elect a separatist government it elects a government with strong 'nationalist' (meaning provincialist) ambitions.[153] These governments, aided and abetted by the French-language media, keep the federal government highly sensitive to the province's concerns. In all federations, there is a high volume of rhetoric about states' rights (or similar such ideas). But in Canada these ideas are not just rhetoric. The threat of Quebec's secession gives the provinces more leverage in federal-provincial relations than is possessed by the states in the United States or Australia. And, of course, within Canada, Quebec's concerns are taken more seriously than those of the other provinces, because the other provinces (notwithstanding the occasional western separatist movement) are certainly here to stay. Canadians will often complain about what is seen as too many demands by Quebec, but virtually all would regard the secession of Quebec as a tragedy. No one wants a large hole in the middle of the country, dividing the Atlantic provinces from Ontario and the western provinces. More importantly, Quebec's secession would leave a large hole in the image that Canadians hold of their country; French Canada is an important part

---

[153] If there is an exception, it is the current Liberal government of Premier Charest, which was elected in 2003 following two terms of Parti Québécois government, which had included a 1995 referendum on separation. The new government obviously believes there should be some respite from the divisive politics of the previous government, but it is safe to speculate that the new government will not behave much differently from its predecessors when issues arise that are seen as important to Quebec's autonomy.

of Canadians' self-image. No serious politician outside Quebec ever expresses indifference to (let alone support for) 'breaking up the country'.

Canada's two largest provinces are larger in relation to the population as a whole than are any of the American states. Ontario has more than a third of the population of the country (12 million of 32 million) and Quebec (7.5 million) has nearly a quarter of the population of the country. Together they form a densely populated manufacturing and service economy. The other provinces, or small groups of them, namely, the four Atlantic provinces, the three prairie provinces and British Columbia, come much closer to representing distinct economic regions of the country than do the American states or the Australian states. The Canadian provincial governments thus become the natural advocates of regional interests, further reinforcing the credibility and power of the provinces.

As noted above, the Privy Council, whose members never visited Canada and whose constitutional decisions often seemed ill-informed about Canada, somehow perceived some part of the dynamic of federal-provincial relations in Canada. I have already described the decisions of the Privy Council that, according to its many critics, exhibited a provincial bias. Certainly, the extent of the provincial power over property and civil rights, and the limitations on the federal trade and commerce power, mean that much social and economic regulation that is federal in the United States and Australia is provincial in Canada. In a highly integrated economy, it makes little economic sense to regulate labour relations and business primarily at the provincial level. But in a federal country such as Canada efficiency is far from the only value that has to be taken into account. As Pierre Trudeau commented in the passage I quoted earlier, the Privy Council's provincial bias may have been what was needed to head off an incipient French-Canadian nationalism. Since the abolition of appeals to the Privy Council, as noted earlier, the Supreme Court of Canada has cautiously ratified modest expansions of the trade and commerce power and the other principal federal powers, but the Court has shown no disposition to reject the lines of interpretation laid down by the Privy Council, no doubt in part because Canada's governments have accommodated themselves to those lines of interpretation.

Aboriginal Peoples

When the French and English first arrived in North America, the land was populated by indigenous people. Indian peoples had been living there from time immemorial. In the barren northern regions, the Inuit ('Eskimo') people lived. And the French-Canadian men who journeyed inland to purchase furs from the Indians (the 'voyageurs') married Indian women, whose children and their successors formed in the west a *Métis* ('half-breed') people. As European settlement proceeded, the settlers discovered that the Indians exhibited considerable military prowess, and this (more than common honesty and morality) meant that taking their land usually involved entering into treaties with them that reserved lands for their exclusive use as well as guaranteeing hunting and fishing rights to them. But many of these treaties seem to have been imperfectly explained to the Indian signatories. Many treaties were blatantly unfair. Many treaty promises, for example, to set aside a reserve, were simply never carried out. In some regions (including the whole of British Columbia), settlement of Indian lands proceeded without treaties. After confederation, the aboriginal peoples derived some protection from s 91(24) of the Constitution Act 1867, which conferred on the Parliament of Canada the power to legislate in relation to 'Indians, and lands reserved for the Indians'. This was not much, but it did restrict the power of the local legislative assemblies over aboriginal peoples and their lands by conferring the power on the more distant level of government.

Aboriginal and treaty rights were poorly recognized by the law that was 'received' by Canada. The extent to which aboriginal law survived the process of settlement was by no means clear and even the status of the treaties was unclear. Eventually, some degree of recognition was accorded by Canadian courts to aboriginal and treaty rights. However, they still suffered from the important infirmity that they could be extinguished by legislation. They were not constitutionally protected. That changed with the adoption of the Constitution Act 1982, which, by s 35, declared that: 'The existing aboriginal and treaty rights of the aboriginal peoples of Canada are hereby recognized and affirmed'. As related earlier in this chapter, 'Interpretation of aboriginal rights', this ambiguously worded provision has been turned into an unambiguous guarantee of aboriginal and treaty rights by the Supreme Court of Canada. The recognition and enforcement of aboriginal and treaty rights has become an important part of the Court's caseload (typically two or three cases per year).

Crisis Management by the Court

The 'reference' jurisdiction of the Supreme Court of Canada has been described in the earlier section of this chapter on 'Supreme Court of Canada'. The Government of Canada has a statutory power to refer questions to the Court for an advisory opinion. The normal requirement of a real case or controversy does not exist, and the end result of a reference is an advisory opinion by the Court. The reference power is not used frequently, and the most common occasion is when the Government would like to secure an authoritative ruling on the constitutionality of proposed (or recently enacted) legislation. The reference is a speedy way to resolve the constitutional doubt. There have been some occasions, however, all of them in the modern era, when a government has sought a reference as a way of defusing a political or legal crisis. In each case, the Court came up with a solution that arguably exceeded the normal limits of judicial power, but the solution was a clever one that defused the crisis.

In the *Manitoba Language Reference* (1985),[154] the Supreme Court of Canada had to deal with the wholesale invalidity of the laws and institutions of Manitoba.

[154] (n 145).

The Manitoba Act 1870, which is the constitution of the province of Manitoba, requires that Manitoba statutes are to be enacted in English and French. In 1890, the province enacted the Official Language Act, which purported to provide that enactment in English only was sufficient. This was an attempt to alter a constitutional requirement by ordinary legislation, but it was not until 1979 that the Supreme Court of Canada ruled that the 1890 Act was invalid for conflict with the Manitoba Act.[155] This caused a serious problem. Ever since 1890, Manitoba had been enacting its statutes in English only. Manitoba had not even been preparing unofficial French translations of the statutes. The task of translation and re-enactment was huge. After cases started to enter the court system challenging the validity of Manitoba's unilingual statutes, the Government directed a reference to the Supreme Court of Canada for an opinion on the validity of all of Manitoba's statutes that had been enacted in English only.

The Supreme Court of Canada in the *Manitoba Language Reference* rejected the argument that the constitutional requirement of bilingual enactment was 'directory' only, and held that the consequence of unilingual enactment was invalidity. If the Court had stopped there, it would have followed that all of the laws enacted since 1890 in English only were invalid, along with the courts, municipal institutions, school boards, and all the other institutions that had been established or changed by provincial law since 1890. Even the legislative assembly of the province would be invalid. Although the legislative assembly was established in 1870 by the Manitoba Act, it had been radically changed in composition by laws enacted in English only, including, for example, the law granting women the right to vote and be a member. This meant that even future laws could not be enacted in both languages. Even a remedial constitutional amendment would be unavailable, because the amending procedure of the Constitution Act 1982 required a resolution of the legislative assembly of Manitoba. If Manitoba lacked a lawful legislative assembly, it could not pass the requisite resolution.

The Court's solution to the vacuum of law in Manitoba was to hold that the laws enacted in English only were invalid, but to hold as well that the laws were 'deemed to have temporary force and effect for the minimum period necessary for their translation, re-enactment, printing and publication'. This latter holding protected the existing body of Manitoba laws, and all things done on the basis of past laws. Future laws, that is, the laws enacted after the date of the Court's opinion (June 13, 1985), had to comply with the constitutional requirements and did not benefit from any period of temporary validity. At a later hearing, the Court stipulated the date by which the process of translation, re-enactment, printing, and publication was to be completed, allowing a period of three years for important current laws and a period of five years for the remainder.[156] In the result, the people of Manitoba were bound for several years by laws that had never been

---

[155] *A-G Manitoba v Forest* [1979] 2 SCR 1032.
[156] *Re Manitoba Language Rights Order No. 1* [1985] 2 SCR 347; the periods were subsequently extended on application by the Government of Manitoba.

constitutionally enacted. The laws derived their force exclusively from the order of the Supreme Court of Canada—an order that had been issued in an advisory opinion.

The Supreme Court of Canada justified its ruling in the *Manitoba Language Reference* by recourse to the 'rule of law', which, it said, had 'constitutional status', because it was referred to in the preamble to the Constitution Act 1982, and because it was 'implicit in the very nature of a Constitution'.[157] The Court noted two aspects of the rule of law that, on the facts of this case, contradicted each other. One aspect required that the Manitoba Legislature must abide by the law of the constitution by enacting all laws in English and French as the constitution stipulated. The other aspect of the rule of law required simply that a community be governed by law. The latter aspect recognized that 'law and order are indispensable elements of civilized life'.[158] It was the latter aspect that justified the order of temporary validity that preserved Manitoba's de facto legal system. It is hard to criticize the Court's ruling, since the Court could hardly allow the Manitoba Legislature to ignore its constitutional obligations, and could hardly leave Manitoba with a vacuum of law. Unwritten constitutional principles become attractive in such situations.

Another example of a crisis intervention by the Supreme Court of Canada is the *Patriation Reference* (1981).[159] This was part of the history of the Constitution Act 1982. Prime Minister Trudeau had proposed to 'patriate' the Constitution with an earlier version of the Act under which the United Kingdom Parliament would act one last time for Canada, relinquishing its authority over Canada for the future, enacting amending procedures that could be operated entirely within Canada, and adding a charter of rights. Eight of the ten provinces were opposed to the federal initiative, opposition focusing on the amending procedures and the charter of rights, which of course directly affected the provinces. Despite this opposition, Prime Minister Trudeau proposed to send his bill to the United Kingdom for enactment. Three of the eight provinces that were opposed to the measure directed references to their Courts of Appeal asking whether there was a requirement of provincial consent before a radical constitutional change was proposed by the Government of Canada for enactment by the United Kingdom Parliament.[160] The Supreme Court of Canada, on appeal from the three decisions of the Courts of Appeal, held that there was no requirement of *law* that prior provincial consent be obtained. But the Court went on to hold in answer to a second question that there was a requirement of *convention* that a 'substantial degree' of provincial consent be obtained before an important constitutional initiative was taken to the

---

[157] (n 145) 750.   [158] ibid 749.

[159] *Re Resolution to Amend the Constitution* [1981] 1 SCR 753.

[160] The provincial governments have the same reference power as the federal government, except that the provincial reference questions go initially to the Court of Appeal of the province, not directly to the Supreme Court of Canada. There is however an appeal as of right from the decision of the provincial Court of Appeal to the Supreme Court of Canada.

United Kingdom for enactment into law. The Court's answer to the legal question was widely expected and clearly correct. But the Court's answer to the convention question was unexpected. In the first place, the orthodox constitutional law was that the 'conventions' of the Constitution (although widely obeyed as a matter of custom) were not cognizable in the courts. In the second place, there was no evidence of consistent past practice of a kind that would support the convention articulated by the Court.

The decision in the *Patriation Reference* had the effect of stopping the unilateral action of the Prime Minister. Faced with the ruling, he felt politically obliged to go back to the provincial Premiers to try and reach the agreement that had hitherto eluded them. They met again, and this time the Prime Minister agreed to amending procedures favoured by the dissenting provinces and agreed to the insertion in the proposed charter of rights of an override clause. The new package of amendments was agreed to by nine of the ten provinces, was passed in a joint address of the House of Commons and Senate, was sent to London and was enacted by the United Kingdom Parliament as the Canada Act 1982, which included as a schedule the Constitution Act 1982. The Court's unprecedented ruling on the existence of a convention thus had a profound effect on the bargaining power of the provinces. It blocked the unilateral initiative of the Prime Minister and led to a substantial degree of agreement on a markedly different constitutional package.[161] Whether it was a 'better' package than the Prime Minister's preferred option is doubtful. The amending procedures have turned out to be largely unworkable, and the override clause of the Charter of Rights is still highly controversial.[162]

The third and last example of an intervention by the Supreme Court of Canada in a constitutional crisis is the *Secession Reference* (1998).[163] In that case, the Government of Canada used its reference power to ask the Supreme Court of Canada if a province (Quebec) had a right to unilaterally secede from Canada. The reference came in the aftermath of a referendum in Quebec in 1995 in which the (separatist) Parti Québécois government of the province proposed that the province secede from Canada. The referendum was only defeated by the narrow margin of 50.4 per cent to 49.4 per cent. The referendum had proceeded on the assumption that a unilateral declaration of independence by Quebec would be legally effective to remove Quebec, with its present boundaries, from Canada, without the need for any amendment to the Constitution of Canada, and regardless

---

[161] The one province that was not part of the agreement was Quebec, then under the separatist Parti Québécois government of Premier Levesque. Quebec brought a reference to ask whether without Quebec there was a 'substantial degree' of provincial consent, as required by the convention. The Supreme Court of Canada, again choosing to answer a question about a convention, held that 9 out of 10 was a substantial degree of provincial consent: *Re Objection by Quebec to Resolution to Amend the Constitution* [1982] 2 SCR 793.

[162] This is because most people assume that a 'strong form' of judicial review is preferable to a 'weak form', where the decision of the courts can be overridden by inserting a notwithstanding clause in a corrective statute. In fact, because of its controversial character, the override clause has rarely been used.

[163] *Secession Reference* (n 23).

of whether the terms of separation were acceptable to the rest of the country.[164] This extraordinary claim was never challenged by the federal government of Prime Minister Chrétien before or during the referendum campaign. However, after nearly losing the referendum, and facing the prospect that there would be another referendum in the future, the Chrétien government directed a reference to the Supreme Court of Canada for a ruling on the question whether a province could indeed secede unilaterally. The Court replied that secession could not be accomplished unilaterally. The rule of law could not be displaced by a popular vote. Quebec's secession would have to take place in compliance with the amending procedures of the Constitution of Canada,[165] which would involve the participation of the other governments, and which would therefore require a negotiation of terms with the other governments.[166]

The ruling in the *Secession Reference* that provinces could not depart the country at will, but that the amending procedures were available to authorize the secession of a province, was orthodox constitutional law that had long been recognized by most constitutional lawyers in Canada. As a practical matter, it was also obvious that the operation of the amending procedures would only be possible if the seceding province successfully negotiated terms of separation with the rest of the country. But the Supreme Court of Canada here introduced a new idea that had never been publicly suggested before and had not even been argued by counsel in the case. The Court held that, if a province voted to secede, the rest of Canada would come under a legal obligation to negotiate the terms of secession with that province. Where did this obligation come from? It came from the unwritten principles of the Constitution, specifically unwritten principles of 'federalism' and 'democracy'. This ruling made the decision much more palatable to sovereigntists in the province of Quebec. However, since there has been no subsequent vote to secede, the meaning and implications of the ruling remain unknown.

Conclusions on Interpretation

Dialogue between the Court and Legislatures

Ever since the publication in 1997 of what I like to describe as a ground-breaking study of judicial review under the Charter of Rights,[167] the Supreme Court of

---

[164] An earlier referendum in Quebec in 1980 had proposed merely a mandate to negotiate a 'sovereignty-association agreement' with Canada, with the outcome to be approved by a second referendum. The 1980 referendum was defeated by the federal government of Prime Minister Trudeau by a margin of 59.5 per cent to 40.5 per cent.

[165] The Court did not say, and it is not entirely clear, which of the amending procedures was the appropriate one. It is either the 'unanimity' procedure, which would require the assents of both houses of the Parliament of Canada and the legislative assemblies of all ten provinces, or the '7–50' procedure, which would require the assents of both houses of the Parliament of Canada and the legislative assemblies of seven provinces representing 50 per cent of the population of all the provinces.

[166] The Court also recognized that a de facto secession that took place without the required amendment might eventually become successful.   [167] Hogg and Bushell (n 70).

Canada and academic commentators have become intrigued by the notion of a 'dialogue' between the Court and the Legislatures. The study, by Allison Bushell and me, was entitled 'The Charter Dialogue between Courts and Legislatures', and it investigated the legislative sequels to all of the cases in which laws had been struck down by the Supreme Court of Canada on Charter grounds. There were 66 such cases, and all but 13 had elicited some response from the competent legislative body. In seven cases, the response was simply to repeal the offending law, but in the remaining 46 cases (more than two-thirds of the total) a new law was substituted for the old one. The data illustrated that the decisions of the Court usually leave room for a legislative response, and they usually get a legislative response. In the end, if the democratic will is there, the legislative objective can usually be accomplished, albeit with some new safeguards to protect individual rights. The override clause of s 33 accounted for only one of the 46 sequels; in most cases a more carefully drafted law was available as a 'reasonable limit' under the limitation clause of s 1. We concluded that judicial review did not typically impose a veto on a desired legislative policy, but rather began a dialogue with the competent legislative body as to how to accommodate the policy to the competing Charter right.

The Hogg-Bushell study demonstrated that the Charter of Rights led to a weaker form of judicial review than existed in the United States (although I know of no similar study in that country) and than had commonly been supposed to exist in Canada (where commentators had tended to assume that the Charter was no different in principle than the American Bill of Rights). Since the publication of the study, the concept of a dialogue between the Supreme Court of Canada and the legislative bodies has attracted much academic writing and has been referred to in several cases in the Supreme Court of Canada.[168] Although the study was largely empirical and did not seek to draw normative conclusions, it has fundamentally changed the debate in Canada about the legitimacy of judicial review under the Charter of Rights. It may not answer the majoritarian objection to judicial review (since unelected courts influence the final outcomes), but it robs the objection of much of its force: weak-form judicial review does not conflict with majoritarian desires as much as strong-form judicial review. In the Supreme Court of Canada, the dialogue theory has been invoked to reinforce the Court's practice of suspending declarations of invalidity to give time for the drafting and enactment of corrective legislation,[169] and to justify a more deferential approach to judicial review of the corrective legislation when it is enacted.[170]

No study has been done of the legislative sequels to cases where laws have been struck down on federalism grounds. But the federal distribution of powers cannot be overcome by an override clause or a limitation clause. A decision that a law is invalid on federalism grounds means that laws of that kind cannot be enacted by that level of government. Of course, by the same token, it means that laws of that kind can be enacted by the other level of government, and sometimes that is

---

[168] The references are collected in Hogg (n 1) s 33.4(e).
[169] eg *Corbiere v Canada* [1999] 2 SCR 203.   [170] eg *R v Mills* [1999] 3 SCR 668.

exactly what happens. But the original level of government cannot pass the corrective law. The most obvious kind of corrective measure has been forbidden: the Supreme Court of Canada has held that a power withheld from the provincial Legislatures cannot be delegated to them by the Parliament of Canada, and nor can gaps in the Parliament's powers be filled by delegation from the provincial Legislatures.[171] However, a few cooperative legislative schemes have managed to survive the rule against legislative inter-delegation.[172] And, of course, there are some cases where a redesign of an invalid law changes its classification for division-of-powers purposes and brings it within the power of the legislative body previously held to be incompetent.[173]

Presumption of Constitutionality

A study of sequels to the federalism cases would be interesting, and might disclose more 'dialogue' than now meets the eye. But, on the face of it, the concept of dialogue has much less purchase in that context than it does in the Charter context. What the Supreme Court of Canada generally does do in federalism cases is to apply a 'presumption of constitutionality', meaning that it exercises restraint in judicial review.[174] The general idea is that a burden of demonstration lies upon those who would challenge the validity of a law that has emerged from the democratic political process. There are three doctrines that support the presumption. First, where there is more than one plausible way of classifying the law, the Court will normally choose the one that supports the validity of the law. Secondly, where the validity of a law depends on a finding of fact, for example, the existence of an emergency, the government is not put to strict proof of the required fact; it is enough to show a 'rational basis' for the fact. And, thirdly, where a law is open to a wide and a narrow interpretation, and under the wide interpretation the law would extend beyond the powers of the enacting body, the Court will normally 'read down' the law so as to confine it to applications that are within the powers of the enacting body. As a result of these doctrines, laws are challenged infrequently on federalism grounds (two or three cases per year typically reach the Supreme Court of Canada), and the challenges are usually unsuccessful.

The 'reading down' doctrine described in the previous paragraph is also applied in Charter cases. Where a law can be interpreted into compliance with the Charter of Rights by selecting a plausible interpretation that does not infringe a Charter right, then that interpretation will be selected. But other determinations of law and fact in Charter cases are subject to their own distinctive rules, and those rules are not compatible with a presumption of constitutionality. A presumption of

---

[171] *A-G Nova Scotia v A-G Canada (Nova Scotia Inter-delegation)* [1951] SCR 31.

[172] eg *Coughlin v Ontario Highway Transport Board* [1968] SCR 569.

[173] eg after Sunday closing laws were held incompetent to the provinces (as criminal laws), the provinces redrafted them as labour standards laws and they were upheld on that basis in *R v Edwards Books and Art* [1986] 2 SCR 713.   [174] The presumption is discussed in Hogg (n 1) s 15.5(h).

constitutionality is rightly seen as inappropriate where individual rights are at stake. Moreover, even regarding the issue from the point of view of the government propounding the law, since Charter review is a weaker form of judicial review than federalism review, the presumption of constitutionality is less necessary.

Formalism and Creativity

The adoption of the Charter of Rights in 1982 required the Supreme Court of Canada (and lower courts) to interpret a new constitutional instrument. The earlier section of this chapter on 'Interpretation of the Charter of Rights' has described the radical new role that the Charter thrust onto the Court. The Charter used vague language that was unfamiliar to Canadian judges, requiring them to look at a wider range of sources than the Court was accustomed to consult. If the Charter had called for no more than the interpretation of the new guaranteed rights, it would have been a considerable new enterprise. But the limitation clause (s 1) of the Charter authorized Parliament and the Legislatures to enact laws that infringed the Charter, provided the law was a 'reasonable' limit that could be 'demonstrably justified in a free and democratic society'. This limitation clause is relied on by government in nearly every case where the Court finds an infringement of a Charter right by legislation. The Court developed a structure for assessing justification under the limitation clause, and that structure inevitably called for the weighing of the importance of the statute's objective against the Charter right that was infringed, the consideration of other legislative instruments that could achieve the same objective by less drastic means, and a determination of whether the Charter right could be displaced. The Court had never before had such an explicitly legislative role to weigh and balance competing policies. As has been related earlier, the Court approached its new role with surprising enthusiasm, and with no regard for the 'passive virtues' of judicial restraint. As a result, no less than 66 statutes were struck down on Charter grounds in the first 14 years of the Charter (1982 to 1996) and this active judicial review continues to this day.

The constitutional law of federalism did not undergo an upheaval in 1982, when the Charter of Rights was adopted. To be sure, the Constitution Act 1982 introduced new amending procedures that were to be operated by the various legislative bodies acting in stipulated combinations; and the Act made one change to the federal distribution of legislative powers. But these new provisions did not affect the role of the courts in interpreting the various heads of legislative power that are conferred on the federal and provincial legislative bodies. In that department, the most important event is still the abolition of appeals to the Privy Council, which occurred in 1949. The Privy Council had drawn very narrow boundaries around the three principal powers of the Parliament of Canada, which are the powers over peace, order, and good government, trade and commerce and criminal law. The Supreme Court of Canada has expanded those powers somewhat, the most important effects of which are to allow the Parliament a role in the regulation of the environment[175] and the regulation of competition.[176] These are hardly surprising or revolutionary outcomes.[177] On the whole, balance has been the watchword of the Court's federalism cases, and balance means preserving the main elements of the judicial interpretation of the federal division of powers that were inherited in 1949.

The Supreme Court of Canada is still capable of extraordinary law-making in federalism cases—provided it is in the service of balance. The *Patriation Reference* (1981)[178] invented a new constitutional convention to regulate the amendment of the Constitution in order to give a role to the provinces that was (before the Constitution Act 1981) denied them by law. And the *Secession Reference* (1998)[179] invented a constitutional duty to negotiate with a province that had voted to secede in order to soften the ruling that Quebec had no right to secede unilaterally. Both of these cases established new rules to govern the federation in times of crisis. The first ruling forced the federal government of Prime Minister Trudeau to negotiate a compromise with the provinces that were opposed to his 'patriation' plan. The second ruling has not yet been put to the test, because no referendum on secession has been held since the ruling; but, if Quebec ever were to vote in favour of secession, the ruling would drastically limit the options legally open to the Government of Canada.

The formalism of the Privy Council period (1867–1949) simply reflected the rhetorical style that was current in the courts of the United Kingdom during that period. As related earlier, a substantial disadvantage of the style was that it excluded consultation of the legislative history of the British North America Act and of the context of the federalism movement in Canada—matters upon which their Lordships of the Privy Council were profoundly ignorant. But in terms of actual outcomes, it would be wrong to assume that the formalist style was inconsistent with creative law-making. As Saywell's study[180] demonstrates, the Privy Council remade the federal system of Canada into a less centralized model than had been planned by the framers. The formalist style robs us of information as to why their Lordships took this tack. But, as related above, the less centralized model is probably the right model for a federal country that includes Quebec. No radical change has occurred since the abolition of appeals to the Privy Council in 1949, and none is likely. Indeed, the two most dramatic federalism cases of the Supreme Court period, namely the *Patriation Reference* and the *Secession Reference*, described in the previous paragraph, were cases in which the Court granted new powers to the provinces in situations of crisis.

---

[175] *R v Crown Zellerbach* (n 45) (peace, order, and good government); *R v Hydro-Québec* (n 93) (criminal law power).

[176] *General Motors v City National Leasing* [1989] 1 SCR 641 (trade and commerce).

[177] Perhaps the most innovative of the federalism decisions is *De Savoye v Morguard Investments* [1990] 3 SCR 1077, which (as related above) requires provinces to give full faith and credit to the judicial decisions of other provinces. Dicta in the case may also presage a larger federal role in guaranteeing mobility of persons and economic factors throughout the country.

[178] *Patriation Reference* (n 159).   [179] *Secession Reference* (n 23).   [180] Saywell (n 80).

The hold of formalism on the Supreme Court of Canada had loosened markedly by 1982, but the adoption of the Charter of Rights in that year profoundly changed the style of judicial opinion-writing. The decision of Charter cases required the explicit weighing of legislative objectives, the explicit consideration of alternative legislative instruments to achieve those objectives, and generally called for a creative interpretation of the vague guarantees of the Charter. The Court proved only too willing to undertake the policy-laden tasks that were involved, and became explicit—indeed long-winded—in articulating its reasoning processes. A symposium held on the 125th anniversary of the Court revealed that the new style of decision-making, including a willingness to explicitly change outmoded rules, had spread throughout the Court's jurisdiction, affecting administrative law, evidence, criminal law and procedure, and even private law areas where the Charter was irrelevant such as tort and family law.[181] The Court now frankly acknowledges a law-making role in all of its work, certainly including constitutional law.

[181] The conclusions of the symposium are briefly summarized in PW Hogg 'The Law-Making Role of the Supreme Court of Canada: Rapporteur's Synthesis' (2001) 80 Canadian Bar Rev 171. The symposium papers are published in the same volume 80 of the Canadian Bar Review.

3

Australia: Devotion to Legalism

*Jeffrey Goldsworthy**

The Constitution's Origins and Structure

The Constitution

The Commonwealth of Australia is a federation of six states, whose Constitution was enacted by the United Kingdom Parliament in 1900, when Australia was part of the British Empire.[1] The six states had previously been separate British colonies, each with its own constitution that continued in force after 1900, although subject to the new federal Constitution. The authority of the United Kingdom Parliament to change Australian law was not formally terminated until 1986, when the Australia Act was passed by both the United Kingdom and the Commonwealth Parliaments.[2] The fundamental documents of Australian constitutional law therefore comprise the federal Constitution, the Australia Act, and the six state constitutions.[3] This chapter will be confined to judicial interpretation of the federal Constitution, which will be referred to simply as 'the Constitution'.

The Constitution was drafted in Australia by representatives of the six colonies at constitutional conventions during the 1890s, and subsequently approved by voters in separate referenda in each colony.[4] To make it binding, it was enacted, with very few changes, by the United Kingdom Parliament. The Preamble to The Commonwealth of Australia Constitution Act 1900 (Imp) begins with the words '[w]hereas the people of New South Wales, Victoria [*et cetera*] . . . have agreed to unite in one indissoluble Federal Commonwealth'. Given this history and these words, it was accepted from the beginning that, although its legal authority derived solely from the sovereignty of the United Kingdom Parliament, its political authority and legitimacy were equally due to its having been agreed upon by

---

* I thank Sir Daryl Dawson and Dr Greg Taylor for helpful comments on an earlier draft.
[1] The Constitution is set out in s 9 of the Commonwealth of Australia Constitution Act 1900 (Imp) 63 & 64 Vic, c. 12.
[2] Australia Act 1986 (UK), and Australia Act 1986 (Cth), the substantive provisions of which are almost identical.
[3] Australia's two mainland territories enjoy self-government under Commonwealth statutes.
[4] The right to vote at that time was, of course, restricted.

representatives, and assented to by a majority of the voters, of each colony.[5] In many early cases, the High Court accepted the idea that the Constitution is not only a statute, but a compact between the peoples of the states.[6] Any suggestion that it was a compact between sovereign states was emphatically rejected in the influential *Engineers'* case (1920),[7] yet the majority of the High Court still affirmed that it was 'the political compact of the whole of the people of Australia, enacted into binding law by the Imperial Parliament'.[8] Such language has continued to be used, although in recent years some judges have gone further, and suggested that the authority of the Constitution now rests on the continuing assent, and therefore the 'sovereignty', of the people.[9] Whether this debatable suggestion makes any difference to the way in which the Constitution should be interpreted will be considered below.[10]

No constitutional recognition is currently given to aboriginal sovereignty, or to any agreements or treaties between the British government or settlers and the original aboriginal inhabitants. Although the High Court recently recognised native title to land as a matter of common law, it expressly declined to disturb the basic legal premise that the British Crown acquired full sovereignty over the land and its inhabitants.[11] Aboriginal Australians possess no special status, or rights, under the Constitution.

Australia is a constitutional monarchy, whose Queen is also (in a separate capacity) Queen of the United Kingdom. At the Commonwealth level, she is represented by a Governor-General. Constitutional convention requires that the powers of the Crown (including that of appointment of the Governor-General) be exercised on the advice of the elected government, controlled by Cabinet and headed by the Prime Minister.[12] The Constitution combines the Westminster system of 'responsible government', in which government Ministers are members of Parliament, and regarded as responsible to it, with an American-style federal

[5] eg J Quick and RR Garran *The Annotated Constitution of the Australian Commonwealth* (Angus & Robertson Sydney 1901) 285; Commonwealth of Australia *Parliamentary Debates* House of Representatives 18 March 1902, 10967 (A Deakin); Commonwealth of Australia *Parliamentary Debates* House of Representatives 11 June 1903, 805–6 (E Barton); TC Brennan *Interpreting the Constitution* (Melbourne University Press, Melbourne, 1935) 13.

[6] *Tasmania v Commonwealth* [1904] HCA 11; (1904) 1 CLR 329, 340. There are similar statements in many cases before 1920.

[7] *Amalgamated Society of Engineers v Adelaide Steamship Co Ltd (Engineers')* [1920] HCA 54; (1920) 28 CLR 129.

[8] ibid 142; see also ibid 160; *Victoria v Commonwealth* [1971] HCA 16; (1971) 122 CLR 353, 370 (Barwick CJ), 395–96 (Windeyer J); V Windeyer *Some Aspects of Australian Constitutional Law* (1972), 28–9; The Right Hon. Sir J Latham 'Interpretation of the Constitution' in The Hon. Mr Justice Else-Mitchell (ed) *Essays on the Australian Constitution* (2nd edn., Law Book Co of Australasia Pty Ltd, Melbourne, 1961).

[9] See cases cited in S Evans 'Why is the Constitution Binding? Authority, Obligation and the Role of the People' (2004) 25 Adelaide L Rev 103, Section III.   [10] Text to nn 131–132.

[11] T Blackshield and F Dominello 'Sovereignty' in T Blackshield, M Coper and G Williams (eds) *The Oxford Companion to the High Court of Australia* (Oxford University Press, Melbourne, 2001) 632.

[12] In some exceptional circumstances the Governor-General may act independently.

system that distributes legislative, executive and judicial powers between the state and federal levels. Its federal elements are based much more on the American than the Canadian model, which was thought to grant excessive power to the national parliament and government.[13] But ironically, the Constitution, as interpreted by the High Court, has proved in practice to be much more centralist than Canada's. In preferring the American to the Canadian method of dividing legislative powers between the national and the state parliaments, the Australian founders made the wrong strategic choice.

As in Britain, responsible government depends heavily on compliance with unwritten, judicially unenforceable conventions, and on common law principles. Consequently, the provisions in Chapter II of the Constitution, dealing with the structure and powers of the executive government, are so terse and elliptical as to be positively misleading. By contrast, the provisions in Chapter I dealing with the structure and powers of the Commonwealth Parliament (which I will refer to simply as 'Parliament') are detailed and comprehensive. They specify the composition, respective powers, and procedures of the two Houses, including a Senate in which all the states are equally represented (although senators are elected by the voters of each state rather than appointed by state governments). They follow the American method of allocating legislative powers, by listing Parliament's legislative powers, but saying little about state parliaments, which continue to possess general legislative power under their own constitutions, except in rare cases where the Constitution withdraws a specific power from them.[14] Most of Parliament's powers are not withdrawn from state parliaments, and are therefore described as 'concurrent' rather than exclusive.

Chapter III deals with the structure, powers, and independence of the federal judicature. It vests federal judicial power in the High Court, other federal courts that Parliament may create, and state courts that Parliament may vest with federal jurisdiction. This has been interpreted as impliedly prohibiting both the vesting of federal judicial power in any non-judicial body, and the vesting of non-judicial power in federal courts.[15] The High Court (unlike the American Supreme Court) has jurisdiction to hear appeals from state as well as lower federal courts, in matters of both state and federal law.[16]

The remaining sections of the Constitution concern finance and trade, including a crucial provision guaranteeing free trade among the states; the relationship between the Commonwealth and the states, including the supremacy of Commonwealth laws over inconsistent state laws; territories; the seat of government; and constitutional amendment.

The Constitution may only be amended by a law passed by Parliament, and then approved by a majority of voters both nation-wide, and in a majority

---

[13] JA La Nauze *The Making of the Australian Constitution* (Melbourne University Press, Melbourne, 1972) 27–28, 274; EM Hunt *American Precedents in Australian Federation* (AMS Press, New York, 1930) 15–16, 19, 49, 53–54, 251–53.   [14] s 107.

[15] Text to n 157.   [16] The Constitution ss 71–80.

of states.[17] Amendment has proved difficult to achieve in practice, with only eight out of forty-four proposals having been passed. Unsuccessful proposals have usually failed to attract a majority of votes nation-wide: only three that were approved by a national majority were not approved in a majority of states. Various explanations of this discouraging record have been offered. Some applaud the supposed common-sense of the electorate, in rejecting proposals that would mostly have expanded Commonwealth power; some lament the supposed inherent conservatism or timidity of the electorate; and others criticise the proponents of reform for failing to secure bipartisan support in advance.

The Constitution is not a lengthy document: it comprises 128 sections, many of them very brief. It is 'a prosaic document expressed in lawyer's language',[18] and does not include grand declarations of national values or aspirations. It includes a number of provisions designed to suppress regional favouritism, but no Bill of Rights.[19] Despite borrowing heavily from the United States in designing the federal system, the framers included only a few scattered provisions that protect individual rights. Section 41 provides that persons entitled to vote in state elections cannot be prevented from voting in Commonwealth elections, but judicial interpretation has made this a dead letter.[20] The Commonwealth, but not the states, is not permitted to compulsorily acquire property without just compensation, remove trial by jury for indictable offences, or violate freedom of religion.[21] The states are not permitted to discriminate against the residents of other states.[22]

With respect to rights, the framers were influenced more by the British than the American constitutional tradition. Australian federation resulted not from armed rebellion against perceived tyranny, but from calm, pragmatic reform by colonial politicians encouraged and assisted by the Imperial government. Utilitarianism had replaced natural rights as the main currency of British political thought, and Australia has been described as a paradigmatically utilitarian society.[23] In general, the framers deemed it both unnecessary and unwise to fetter their parliaments. Given the progress of liberal ideas under British institutions, democratically elected parliaments seemed to them the best possible guardians of liberty. The harsh Australian environment was still being settled by Europeans, who wanted strong government to underwrite enterprise, provide necessary infrastructure, and enact social regulation. The framers feared that judicial interpretations of abstract rights could have unpredictable and undesirable consequences. For one thing,

---

[17] If certain vital interests of a particular state are concerned, a majority of voters in that state must also approve the amendment.

[18] The Honourable Sir A Mason 'The Australian Constitution in Retrospect and Prospect' in R French G Lindell and C Saunders (eds) *Reflections on the Australian Constitution* (The Federation Press, Sydney, 2003) 8.   [19] ss 51(1), 51(2), 92, 99, 117 discussed at pp 141–143 of text.

[20] See p 123 of text.

[21] ibid ss 51(31), 80, and 116 respectively. In 1946, a guarantee against conscription in the provision of medical or dental services was added, as a proviso to a new federal power to legislate with respect to such services (s 51(23A)).   [22] ibid s 117.

[23] H Collins 'Political Ideology in Australia: The Distinctiveness of a Benthamite Society' (1985) Winter 114 Daedalus 147.

they did not want to be prevented from discriminating against people of other races in order to protect the racial and cultural homogeneity of their communities.[24]

It was necessary to arm an independent federal judiciary with power to enforce the terms of the federal compact. But, with a few minor exceptions, the traditional British doctrine of parliamentary sovereignty was disturbed only to that extent. Provided they were acting within their respective spheres of responsibility, and not violating either paramount Imperial laws or constitutional limits, Australian parliaments were deemed to exercise powers as plenary and ample—as sovereign— as that of the United Kingdom Parliament itself.[25]

Australians remain wary of constitutionally entrenched rights. In 1988, a proposal to amend the Constitution by extending to the states the existing guarantees of religious freedom, jury trial, and just terms for the expropriation of property, suffered the worst defeat of any amendment ever proposed, being approved by less than 31 per cent of the electorate. Since then, there has been no significant political impetus towards strengthening the protection of rights in the Constitution, although the popularity of the idea among younger Australians ensures that it will be revived.

Judicial Review

The Constitution does not explicitly confer on the courts the power of judicial review, that is, the power to restrain or remedy unconstitutional acts of the other branches of government. But the framers clearly assumed that the courts would possess it. Courts throughout the Empire had regularly invalidated colonial legislation inconsistent with local constitutions and other Imperial legislation. Discussion in the Convention Debates reveals that the power was taken for granted.[26] Moreover, some provisions of the Constitution plainly assume it. The highest court of appeal from colonial courts was the Judicial Committee of the Privy Council, which sat in London. Section 74 of the Constitution provides that the High Court has power to decide 'the limits *inter se* of the Constitutional powers of the Commonwealth and those of any State', and that appeals from such decisions can be taken to the Privy Council only with the High Court's consent. Section 76 authorises Parliament to confer original jurisdiction on the High Court in any matter 'arising under this Constitution, or involving its interpretation', which it did in 1903.[27] Judicial review was therefore treated from the beginning as 'axiomatic'.[28]

---

[24] J Goldsworthy 'The Constitutional Protection of Rights in Australia' in G Craven (ed) *Australian Federation Towards the Second Century* (Melbourne University Press, Melbourne, 1992) 151, 152–54.

[25] *The Annotated Constitution of the Australian Commonwealth* (n 5) 509–10; *D'Emden v Pedder* [1904] HCA 1; (1904) 1 CLR 91, 110 (Griffith CJ); *Nelungaloo Pty Ltd v Commonwealth* (1948) 75 CLR 495 (HCA) 503–4 (Williams J).

[26] B Galligan *Politics of the High Court* (University of Queensland Press, Melbourne, 1987) ch 2.

[27] Judiciary Act 1903 (Cth) s 30(a).

[28] *Australian Communist Party v Commonwealth* [1951] HCA 5; (1951) 83 CLR 1, 262 (Fullagar J).

Section 74 (the *inter se* provision) embodies a compromise between the British determination to retain Privy Council appeals from all corners of the Empire, and a prevalent Australian fear (due partly to Canadian experience) that British judges would lack an adequate understanding of both written federal constitutions and local Australian conditions. Because the Privy Council's subsequent performance in several Australian appeals was held to vindicate that fear, the High Court permitted an appeal on an '*inter se*' question only once, in 1913.[29] But appeals from the High Court on other constitutional questions continued to be taken to the Privy Council until 1968, when Parliament abolished them.[30] To prevent the High Court being by-passed, Parliament legislated in 1907 to prevent any constitutional question being referred directly from state courts to the Privy Council.[31] Moreover, constitutional issues are often removed from lower courts into the High Court at a preliminary stage for speedier resolution.[32] Since 1907, therefore, the High Court has been the immediate, and since 1968 the final, court of appeal in all constitutional cases. The Privy Council became involved only intermittently, in the small minority of cases that did not involve '*inter se*' questions, and even then it often merely affirmed the views of either the majority or minority in the High Court. It therefore had a much less substantial impact on the development of Australian constitutional law than on that of Canada. Consequently, this chapter mainly concerns constitutional interpretation by the High Court, which will be referred to simply as 'the Court'.

Until 1984, many appeals could be taken to the Court as of right, and it did not have the ability of its American counterpart to evade constitutional disputes on essentially prudential grounds.[33] In 1984, Parliament abolished appeals to the Court as of right, and authorised it to grant special leave to appeal only in cases raising difficult issues of national importance.[34] Because it is unlikely to select 'easy' cases in which the law is well settled and uncontroversial, its decisions are now more likely to involve some element of judicial creativity, and the Court to appear more 'activist', than previously.[35]

The Court held at an early stage that it could not provide advisory opinions: the 'matters' over which it has jurisdiction must involve a real disagreement as to legal rights or duties. It requires that parties have standing, although it has been more generous on this score than the American Supreme Court, especially in permitting states to challenge federal legislation.[36] In addition, constitutional questions must

---

[29] G Sawer *Australian Federalism in the Courts* (Melbourne University Press, Melbourne, 1967) 29–30.

[30] Exercising a power conferred by s 74. See T Blackshield, M Coper and J Goldring 'Privy Council, Judicial Committee of the' in *The Oxford Companion to the High Court of Australia* (n 11) 560–64; Australia Act 1986 (Cth) s 11.

[31] The complex provisions inserted into the Judiciary Act 1903 (Cth) are succinctly explained in Sawer (n 29) 24–27.   [32] Pursuant to the Judiciary Act 1903 (Cth) s 40.

[33] SH Kadish 'Judicial Review in the High Court and in the United States Supreme Court Part I' 2 (1959) Melbourne U L Rev 4, 31–34.   [34] Judiciary Amendment Act (No. 2) 1984 (Cth).

[35] M Gleeson *The Rule of Law and the Constitution* (ABC Books, Sydney, 2000) 78.

[36] H Burmester 'Limitations on Federal Adjudication' in B Opeskin and F Wheeler *The Australian Federal Judicial System* (Melbourne University Press, Melbourne, 2000) 248, 252–53; Kadish (n 33) 23–25.

be justiciable, although the Court has not adopted the broad American 'political questions' doctrine. The requirement of justiciability has had little operation in constitutional cases, being invoked mainly in relation to internal parliamentary proceedings and foreign affairs.[37] The Court has also not adopted the American Court's method of interpreting legislation so as to avoid raising constitutional issues.[38] It is sometimes speculated that because the Constitution lacks a Bill of Rights, it has generated less politically contentious 'public interest' litigation of the kind that the American Court has sometimes preferred to duck.[39]

The Judges

High Court judges are appointed by the Commonwealth government, which since 1979 has been required by statute to consult with state governments, although it is not bound by their views.[40] In practice it consults, on an informal and discretionary basis, members of the judiciary and legal profession. There is no requirement, as there is in the United States, of parliamentary ratification.[41] Although a few appointments suspected of being based more on political than legal criteria have aroused controversy in the legal profession, the process has usually been uneventful. Appointees have generally achieved eminence as barristers— lawyers who represent clients in court—and many have previously served as judges in lower state or federal courts.[42] Until 1975, many also had a background in politics, but almost all of these had also enjoyed high standing as barristers.[43] Most of them had appeared as counsel before the High Court itself on numerous occasions.[44] No academics have been appointed directly to the Court.

Since barristers have tended to come from relatively privileged social and educational backgrounds, most appointees have been middle-aged, white, male, and educated at private rather than government schools followed by university.[45] Only one woman has served on the High Court to date, although more will undoubtedly be appointed as women advance in greater numbers through the profession.[46] Most judges previously practiced at the Sydney or Melbourne Bars, known for their political and legal conservatism, which has reinforced the social

[37] H Burmester 'Limitations on Federal Adjudication' in *The Australian Federal Judicial System* (n 36) 254–61; Kadish (n 33) 29–31.   [38] Kadish (n 33) 27–29.

[39] Burmester (n 36) 261–62.   [40] High Court of Australia Act 1979 (Cth) s 6.

[41] E Campbell and HP Lee *The Australian Judiciary* (Cambridge University Press, Cambridge, 2001) 75–76.

[42] F Dominello and E Neumann 'Background of Justices' in *The Oxford Companion to the High Court of Australia* (n 11) 49.

[43] Since 1975 no appointee has had direct involvement in politics.

[44] T Blackshield, M Coper, G Fricke and T Simpson 'Counsel, notable' in *The Oxford Companion to the High Court of Australia* (n 11) 164–65.

[45] A Goldsmith 'A Profile of the Federal Judiciary' in *The Australian Federal Judicial System* (n 36) 365, 397; see also F Dominello and E Neumann 'Background of Justices' in *The Oxford Companion to the High Court of Australia* (n 11) 48–50.

[46] Justice Mary Gaudron was a member of the Court from 1987–2003.

and intellectual homogeneity of the Bench.[47] As one commentator observed, because most eminent barristers acquire considerable wealth by attending to the affairs of affluent people and businesses in commercial and property cases, they are usually politically conservative or moderate.[48] They also have an ingrained professional commitment to using technical methods of analysis to resolve legal, including constitutional, problems. One former Chief Justice expressed pride that major constitutional cases can be conducted by 'dry legal argument', whose lack of political rhetoric makes them indistinguishable from 'a minor contest between citizens.'[49]

The preference of governments to appoint eminent barristers or serving judges to the Court is partly due to the nature of its work. Until 1977, the Court was often required to conduct trials of law and fact as part of its original jurisdiction.[50] Because it is the highest court of appeal from state and federal courts, in matters of private as well as public law, including criminal law, the number of constitutional cases rarely exceeds 10 percent of its workload.[51] The judges must possess the technical legal knowledge and skills needed to resolve the complex questions that arise in commercial and criminal cases. It is not surprising that they have applied the same techniques and habits of thought in constitutional cases. Moreover, because the Constitution does not include a Bill of Rights, the kinds of constitutional questions that have arisen have tended—or at least, have seemed—to be more susceptible to technical legal analysis than the broad questions of political philosophy that other constitutional courts have so often had to resolve.[52]

Once appointed, High Court and other federal judges enjoy constitutionally guaranteed independence. Section 72 of the Constitution currently provides that they must be appointed until the age of 70 (until it was amended in 1977, they were appointed for life). They may not be removed from office except at the request of both Houses of Parliament on the ground of proved misbehaviour or incapacity, and their salaries may not be diminished during their term in office.

The High Court consisted of three judges until 1906, then five until 1912, and since then seven, except between 1931 and 1947 when there were only six. Decisions affecting Commonwealth powers are required by statute to be supported by not less than three judges, and in practice, constitutional cases are usually heard by all available Justices.[53] Until 1998, the Court did not hold regular conferences in which cases are discussed before judgments are written, as is the practice of the

---

[47] 36 out of 44 have come from New South Wales or Victoria, six from Queensland, and two from Western Australia. No judges have been appointed from South Australia or Tasmania.

[48] Sawer (n 29) 64.

[49] Sir G Barwick *A Radical Tory* (Federation Press, Sydney, 1994) 66.

[50] In 1977 the Federal Court of Australia was established to relieve the High Court of this work.

[51] The Full Court has lately decided an average of about five substantial constitutional cases each year: High Court of Australia *Annual Report 1999–2000* 69, Table 14.

[52] Sawer (n 29) 53–56 emphasised these factors; see also The Right Hon Sir O Dixon 'Two Constitutions Compared' *Jesting Pilate* (The Law Book Company Ltd, Sydney, 1965) 104.

[53] Judiciary Act 1903 (Cth) s 23(1); A Robertson 'Procedure' in *The Oxford Companion to the High Court of Australia* (n 11) 565.

American Supreme Court.[54] Unanimous judgments are rare. Although joint judgments of two or more judges are common, multiple concurring as well as dissenting judgments are routine. Judgments are also often very long. As a result, it is sometimes difficult to discern what, if any, general principle has been authoritatively decided.

Problems and Methods of Interpretation

Causes of Interpretive Difficulties

Many of the difficulties that have arisen in interpreting the Constitution were inevitable, in that they were inherent in the use of very general language to govern practical affairs over a long period of unpredictable social and technological change. The language has often proved ambiguous or vague. An example is the way in which the Parliament is empowered to make laws 'with respect to' the 40 subject-matters enumerated in s 51. In addition to the difficulty of interpreting each of the subject-matters themselves (eg what are 'external affairs'? what are 'trading corporations'?), it is far from clear how one should decide what subject-matter or matters a law is 'with respect to'. There are countless other examples of ambiguous or vague terminology.

Other problems inherent in the interpretation of any constitution have resulted from changes over time in the meanings of words, and in external circumstances and social values. Such problems have multiplied as the Constitution has aged. For example, the Court has had to decide whether in 1972 the word 'adult' still meant '21 years of age or more', as it did in 1900,[55] whether radio and television broadcasts are 'telephonic, telegraphic and other like services',[56] and whether Britons have become 'aliens' as a result of Australian independence.[57] In the near future, the Court may have to decide whether Parliament's power to make laws with respect to 'marriage', which for the founders must have meant the union of a man and a woman, can extend to same-sex unions.

Attempts to resolve such problems by recourse to the purposes underlying the text have sometimes been hampered by those purposes themselves being obscure, ambiguous, vague, or arguably outdated and inappropriate in the modern world.

In addition to these inevitable problems, some unnecessary difficulties have resulted from deficiencies in drafting. Although very experienced and eminent lawyers prepared the initial draft of the Constitution, they did so hurriedly.[58] A federal system was a novelty in Australian constitutional thinking, and raised problems that were not always anticipated and provided for.[59] Most important

---

[54] On the practice since 1998, see The Hon. Murray Gleeson 'The State of the Judicature' (2000) 74 Australian L J 147, 157.   [55] *King v Jones* [1972] HCA 44; (1972) 128 CLR 221.
[56] *The King v Brislan; ex p Williams* [1935] HCA 78; (1935) 54 CLR 262.
[57] *Sue v Hill* [1999] HCA 30; (1999) 199 CLR 462.   [58] Sawer (n 29) 9–13.
[59] 'Marshall and the Australian Constitution' in Dixon (n 52) 167.

issues were resolved in principle, but inadequate attention was sometimes given to details. Consequently, some provisions have proven to be elliptical, or to require implications that expand or qualify their literal meaning. An example is section 92, a crucial provision requiring that trade, commerce and intercourse among the states shall be 'absolutely free'. The framers were aware that these elliptical words (absolutely free *from what?*) were 'a little bit of layman's language'—in effect a political slogan—but failed to foresee the interpretive perplexities and excessive litigation they would generate.[60]

When the language of a provision has seemed incapable of fully achieving its apparent purpose, or potentially harmful to some other constitutional objective, the Court has had to decide whether it should be expanded or qualified by implication.[61] This is problematic, because if the Court is too willing to supplement the language to give effect to underlying objectives, it might end up rewriting the Constitution, which is a legislative rather than judicial function. Moreover, in doing so the judges might give effect to what they believe the Constitution's objectives ought to be, rather than what they actually are. Judges are sometimes tempted to change a constitution under the guise of interpretation to correct what they perceive to be undesirable government practices.

Sources of Interpretive Principles

The Constitution itself says nothing about how it should be interpreted. In choosing principles of interpretation, the Court initially had two traditions to draw upon: first, the way in which courts in Britain and other British colonies had interpreted statutes, including colonial constitutions such as Canada's; and second, the way in which the American Supreme Court had interpreted the United States Constitution. Since the Australian Constitution was enacted in a British statute, and combines the Westminster system of responsible government with an American-style federal system, it was appropriate that the Court seek guidance from both traditions. But by 1900 they were arguably quite different: British courts tended towards literalism and formalism, whereas the American Supreme Court was widely believed to have adopted a more purposive or even creative approach. The interpretive principles that have predominated in Australia since 1920 emerged from a contest between these two traditions.

Many of the Australian framers were aware of the potential for considerable judicial creativity in constitutional interpretation, but did not agree about its desirability. Some had studied James Bryce's *The American Commonwealth* (1889)—once called the 'bible' of the Australian framers—in which he applauded the creative development of the American constitution by the Supreme Court.[62]

[60] Text between n 141 and n 147.

[61] s 96 is an example: see text between n 205 and n 212.

[62] (2nd edn., Macmillan, London, 1889), especially 267–68, 363–68, 373–75. For its influence on the Australian framers, see *The Making of the Australian Constitution* (n 13) 18–19. For 'bible' see JA La Nauze 'The Name of the Commonwealth of Australia' (1971) 15 *Historical Studies* 59.

In the Constitutional Conventions, and subsequently, some framers and lawyers expressed admiration for the work of the American court, and criticised the more literal approach of the Privy Council in interpreting the Canadian constitution.[63] One of them summed up the difference by arguing that because constitutions laid down broad, general principles, a court must be guided 'by a far higher and broader apprehension than the mere lawyer who is dealing with an ordinary Act of Parliament'—in short, it must adopt a 'statesmanlike' approach.[64] But many others criticised American judicial creativity for being political rather than legal, and supported the idea that the Constitution should be interpreted strictly, as a British statute.[65] They insisted that the Constitution should be changed only by formal amendment, and not by creative judicial interpretation.[66]

The first High Court consisted of three judges—Chief Justice Griffith, Justices Barton and O'Connor—who were all eminent lawyers, but also experienced politicians who had been actively involved in framing the Constitution. Many early cases involved claims of intergovernmental immunity: that is, immunity of government or its instrumentalities at one level of the federal system (Commonwealth or state) from legislation passed at the other level. The Constitution is deficient in not including express provisions dealing generally or comprehensively with the issue.[67]

The Court initially adopted the doctrine of intergovernmental immunity previously developed in American cases such as *McCulloch v Maryland* (1819) and *Collector v Day* (1871).[68] In *D'Emden v Pedder* (1904), the Court relied partly on the presumption that when words are enacted that have previously been judicially interpreted, the law-maker intends the words to bear the meaning attributed to them. It maintained that 'some, if not all' of the framers of the Constitution (including, presumably, themselves) were familiar with the American constitution, and 'intended that like provisions should receive like interpretation.'[69] But in reality, the relevant provisions of the two constitutions were far from the same.[70] Moreover, like its American counterpart, the Court was not really concerned with specific provisions, but with inferences from unexpressed premises on which the whole federal system was supposedly based.[71] It held that the Commonwealth and the states were all intended to possess sovereignty in exercising their respective powers; that 'sovereignty subject to extrinsic control is a contradiction in terms'; and therefore that each was entitled to exercise its powers without any interference or control from the others.[72]

---

[63] G Craven 'Heresy as Orthodoxy: Were the Founders Progressivists?' (2003) 31 Federal L Rev 87, especially 104, 116–17, 108–9, 113–15 and 117–18.   [64] Quoted in ibid 117.
[65] ibid 107–8, 117–21.   [66] ibid.
[67] There are only a few relevant provisions that deal with particular aspects of the issue, some granting immunity, and others excluding it. Compare ss 51(13) and 51(14) and s 114 with s 51(31) and s 98.
[68] *McCulloch v State of Maryland* 17 US 316 (1819); *Collector v Day* 78 US 113 (1871).
[69] *D'Emden* (n 25) 113. See also *Municipal Council of Sydney v Commonwealth* (1904) 1 CLR 208 (HCA) 239–40 (O'Connor J).   [70] Sawer (n 29) 121–22.
[71] Comments of the Privy Council in *Webb v Outtrim* [1906] HCA 76; (1906) 4 CLR 356 (PC) 359.
[72] *D'Emden* (n 25) 110, plus later cases extending the same doctrine to protect the states.

This American doctrine was a prime example of the kind of purposive, or perhaps creative, judicial approach that some Australian lawyers admired, but others disapproved of.[73] The Privy Council was believed to have discouraged its adoption in Canada, and the Court, therefore, to have preferred American to British authority.[74] Its endorsement of the American immunities doctrine encouraged hopes that it would favour similar reasoning in other contexts. In the third constitutional case to arise, one party argued that '[t]he Constitution is only a declaration of principles for guidance',[75] and that the Court should 'look beyond the letter of the Constitution', identify principles of 'inter-State ethics', and interpret the text accordingly.[76]

But in this case the judges rejected the proposal that the Constitution should be governed by special rules of interpretation.[77] Ordinary principles of statutory interpretation, which they expounded with copious quotations from British precedents, had to be applied. These principles required a statute to be interpreted according to the intent of the legislature, but if its words—understood in their ordinary and natural sense—were not ambiguous, they constituted the best evidence of that intent.[78] Only if the words were ambiguous, could the legislature's intention be 'gathered from the other provisions of the Statute aided by a consideration of surrounding circumstances', namely, 'the history of the law', consisting of 'previous legislation . . . [and] the historical facts surrounding the bringing of the law into existence.'[79] One of the judges was a little more flexible, holding that the 'spirit and intention' of the legislature, to be gathered from the Act itself, might be 'so plain and cogent as to shake, and, perhaps, control, the otherwise plain meaning of the words themselves.'[80] But he was adamant that principles of abstract justice, equity, or public policy should not be used in this way, absent clear evidence within the Act itself that the legislature intended to implement them.[81]

These judges denied that there was any difference between British and American principles of interpretation.[82] They argued that ordinary principles of statutory interpretation themselves required the special nature of a constitution to be taken into account. They frequently quoted Chief Justice Marshall's statement in *McCulloch v Maryland* that 'we must never forget, that it is *a Constitution* we are expounding'.[83] The Constitution was special in that it was not a detailed code,

---

[73] Views of Higgins J noted in *Commissioners of Taxation (NSW) v Baxter* (1907) 4 CLR 1087 (HCA) 1164.

[74] *Re Income Tax Acts (No 4); Deakin's and Lyne's Cases* (1904) 29 VLR 748 (VSC) 763–64.

[75] *Tasmania v Commonwealth* (n 6) 335.   [76] ibid 338, 359.

[77] ibid 338 (Griffith CJ), 358–59 (O'Connor J) and clearly assumed by Barton J. See also *Federated Sawmill Timberyard & General Woodworkers Employees Association of Australasia v James Moore & Sons Pty Ltd* [1909] HCA 43; (1909) 8 CLR 465, 486, 501.

[78] *Tasmania v Commonwealth* (n 6) 338–39 (Griffith CJ).

[79] ibid 359 (O'Connor J). For an example of the practical application of this approach, see *Municipal Council of Sydney v Commonwealth* (n 69) 239–40 (O'Connor J). See also *Deakin v Webb* (1904) 1 CLR 585 (HCA) 630.   [80] *Tasmania v Commonwealth* (n 6) 348–49.

[81] ibid 347–50.   [82] *Municipal Council of Sydney v Commonwealth* (1904) (n 69) 237–38.

[83] eg *Attorney-General (NSW) v Brewery Employees Union of NSW* (1908) 6 CLR 469 (HCA) 612.

and so many powers and rights were conferred by implication rather than expressly.[84] *McCulloch v Maryland* was influential in the development of the doctrine that, by implication, every express legislative power includes an implied power over matters that are 'incidental and ancillary' to the principal subject-matter.[85]

The Court in these early years held another doctrine, of 'reserved state powers', to be implicit in the federal system. The Constitution confers legislative powers only on Parliament. As for state parliaments, section 107 merely provides that they continue to possess their pre-existing powers, except for powers specifically withdrawn from them or given exclusively to the Commonwealth. These continuing state powers are not 'reserved' exclusively for the states, because they include powers given to Parliament concurrently rather than exclusively.[86] Nevertheless, the Court held that the Constitution implicitly reserved for the states power over certain internal matters, such as trade and commerce, and industrial relations, within each state. These reservations were thought to follow from the way that particular Commonwealth powers were deliberately limited. Section 51 gives Parliament power with respect to inter-state, not intra-state, trade and commerce, and with respect to the prevention and settlement of industrial disputes only if they cross state borders.[87] The inherent limits of these powers were regarded as controlling, by implication, the scope of every other power as well. Consequently, Parliament was not permitted to use its power with respect to taxation, or corporations, to control trade and commerce, or industrial relations, within a state.[88] This doctrine also found some support in American cases concerning the trade and commerce power.[89]

The Court was wrong to regard the doctrine of intergovernmental immunities as consistent with orthodox British interpretive principles. The Constitution expressly confers supremacy on federal law, grants some exclusive powers to the Commonwealth, exempts the states from some Commonwealth powers, and exempts the property of both the states and Commonwealth from one another's taxes. The maxim *expressio unius exclusio alterius* suggests that no further immunities were thought necessary. After all, the Commonwealth is able to protect itself from state interference by enacting overriding legislation, and the framers expected the states to protect themselves through their representation in the Senate. In this regard they have been proved wrong: in practice, the Senate has operated as a party rather than as a states' house.[90] Nevertheless, this was their expectation. And there is no evidence whatsoever that a significant number of the framers had any knowledge of the American doctrine of intergovernmental immunities, let alone that

---

[84] *Tasmania v Commonwealth* (n 6) 338 (Griffith CJ); *Baxter* (n 73) 1105; *Jumbunna Coal Mine, No Liability v Victorian Coal Miners' Association* (1908) 6 CLR 309 (HCA) 343, 356.

[85] Sawer (n 29) 101.

[86] Contrast G de Q Walker 'The Seven Pillars of Centralism: Engineers' Case Federalism' (2002) 76 Australian L J 678 esp 682.　　　　　　　　　　　　　　　　　[87] sub-ss 51(1), (35).

[88] *Huddart, Parker and Co Pty Ltd v Moorehead* [1909] HCA 36; (1909) 8 CLR 330.

[89] *United States v Dewitt* (1869) 9 Wall. 41 is cited in *Huddart, Parker* (n 88) 350, 363.

[90] S Bach *Platypus and Parliament* (The Department of the Senate Parliament House, Canberra, 2003) 143–45.

they intended—without expressly providing—that it be part of the Constitution. Indeed, there is no reference to the doctrine in the Convention Debates, which there surely would be if they really had such an important doctrine in mind.[91] In reality, the judges relied on their own, *post hoc*, understanding of what kind of federation a majority of the framers had wanted to establish, and what was necessary for it to function effectively. But some of the framers subsequently disagreed with them,[92] and since the matter was not discussed, it is impossible to know what a majority would have intended. In any event, the judges' *post hoc* understanding was not manifested in the words of the Constitution itself: in effect, they were correcting what they regarded as a major oversight in its drafting.[93] Whether or not this was justified, it was an exercise of creative statesmanship that went well beyond the application of ordinary interpretive principles.[94]

The doctrine of reserved state powers was more consistent with orthodoxy. The evidence of the framers' intentions on which it was based consisted of the wording of particular provisions, which conferred carefully limited powers on the Commonwealth. In interpreting a statutory provision, it has always been proper to consider the context provided by related provisions of the same statute.[95]

When a case was appealed from a state court directly to the Privy Council, it rejected the doctrine of intergovernmental immunities, criticising the Court's suppositions about what the framers had in mind as an 'expansion' of orthodox interpretive principles, and upholding the *expressio unius* argument.[96] But its reasoning was marred by a failure to grasp some consequences of written constitutionalism. In a scathing response, the Court disparaged the quality of the Privy Council's interpretation of the Canadian constitution—'the subject of much criticism'—by quoting James Bryce's quip that the United States would never have achieved greatness had its Constitution been interpreted in a similar manner.[97]

But in the end, the opinion of the Privy Council prevailed. In 1906, two new Justices—Isaacs and Higgins JJ—were appointed to the Court. They, too, had been active participants in the Constitutional Conventions, but did not accept the doctrines of intergovernmental immunities and reserved state powers. Applying the same interpretive principles as the Privy Council, Isaacs J insisted that the Court should be guided by the Constitution's language alone, rather than 'wander at large upon a sea of speculation searching for a suitable intent by the misty and uncertain light of what is sometimes called the spirit of the document, for that is largely fashioned subjectively by the preconceptions of the individual observer.'[98] Justice

---

[91] Even the better informed framers seem to have had little knowledge of American case law: in 1898, Barton himself acknowledged that he had not heard of *Marbury v Madison*: see J Williams 'The Emergence of the Commonwealth Constitution' in HP Lee and G Winterton (eds) *Australian Constitutional Landmarks* (Cambridge University Press, Cambridge, 2003) 23–24.

[92] See the views of Isaacs and Higgins JJ (text following n 97).

[93] Many of these points are made in G Sawer 'Implication and the Constitution Part II' (1948–1950) 4 *Res Judicatae* 85, 88–90.   [94] Sawer (n 29) 200.

[95] ibid 199–200.   [96] *Webb v Outtrim* (n 71) 359–61.

[97] *Baxter* (n 73) 1110; see also 1111.

[98] *Huddart, Parker* (n 88) 388. Also *Federated Sawmill* (n 77) 536–37.

Higgins described Marshall CJ's judgment in *McCulloch v Maryland* as 'the utterance rather of the statesman than of the lawyer,'[99] and disapproved of uncritical reliance on American cases, which often overlooked crucial differences between the two constitutions.[100] He denied that the Court had a duty to ensure that the intention behind the Constitution was not defeated: 'Our function is to construe the [Constitution], not to improve it, or to alter it on the ground of probable intention'.[101]

By 1920, the original three judges had departed, and three out of four new judges joined Isaacs and Higgins JJ to over-rule the doctrines of implied intergovernmental immunities and reserved state powers.[102] In the celebrated *Engineers'* case, the majority affirmed that British rather than American interpretive principles should be applied. The Court's duty was 'faithfully to expound and give effect to [the Constitution] according to its own terms, finding the intention from the words of the compact, and upholding it throughout precisely as framed', 'clear of any qualifications which the people of the Commonwealth or, at their request, the Imperial Parliament have not thought fit to express'.[103] Orthodox principles did permit the recognition of 'necessary' implications.[104] But the rejected doctrines were necessary only in a political, and not a legal, sense. They were 'based on distrust, lest powers, if once conceded to the least degree, might be abused to the point of destruction. But possible abuse of powers is no reason in British law for limiting the natural force of the language creating them.'[105]

Here, the majority was strongly influenced by the British tradition of parliamentary sovereignty, which was antithetical to American distrust of government, and relied on political rather than legal control of government. In British law,

the extravagant use of the granted powers in the actual working of the *Constitution* is a matter to be guarded against by the constituencies and not by the Courts . . . . If it be conceivable that the representatives of the people of Australia as a whole would ever proceed to use their national powers to injure the people of Australia considered sectionally, it is certainly within the power of the people themselves to resent and reverse what may be done. No protection of this Court in such a case is necessary or proper.[106]

The rejected implications were also condemned as 'referable to no more definite standard than the personal opinion of the Judge who declares it', based on 'a vague, individual conception of the spirit of the compact'.[107] They were too subjective and contentious to provide a proper basis for legal judgment.

It is often alleged that Isaacs and Higgins JJ were motivated less by interpretive orthodoxy than by policy considerations, which led them to favour an expansion of Commonwealth power. This is debatable,[108] but in any event, there is no

---

[99] *Baxter* (n 73) 1164. Also HB Higgins 'McCulloch v Maryland in Australia' 18 (1905) Harvard L Rev 559.   [100] *Huddart, Parker* (n 88).
[101] *Baxter* (n 73) 1169–70.   [102] *Engineers'* (n 7).   [103] ibid 142 and 160 respectively.
[104] ibid 155.   [105] ibid 151.   [106] ibid 151–52.
[107] ibid 142 and 145 respectively.
[108] J Goldring 'The Path to *Engineers'* in M Coper and G Williams (eds) *How Many Cheers for Engineers?* (Federation Press, Sydney, 1997) 39.

evidence that the new judges concurred with them for such ulterior motives.[109] These three judges had been distinguished barristers with no political experience or involvement in framing the Constitution. They approached the issues as lawyers interpreting the constitutional text without preconceptions, based on personal experience, concerning the nature of the federation it was intended to establish.

The reasoning in the *Engineers'* case did not put an end to disagreement about the proper approach to constitutional interpretation. In 1937, the Court was criticised for rejecting the 'thoroughly relevant learning' of American precedents 'in favour of the crabbed English rules of statutory interpretation, which are one of the sorriest features of English law and are . . . particularly unsuited to the interpretation of a rigid constitution'.[110] But in 1936 another commentator criticised American precedents for paying excessive regard 'to considerations of policy, necessity, and other vague notions which can have no place in a statutory constitution',[111] and praised the Court for being 'as jealous of the written word as the Privy Council, if not more so'.[112] Both views continue to be advocated to this day.

It is often claimed that the Court in *Engineers'* laid down interpretive principles that have been applied ever since. This is only partly true. Those principles had always been endorsed by the Court. What was novel in *Engineers'* was the insistence that they had not previously been strictly applied. As for whether they have been applied ever since, that is true only in general. The Court continues to interpret the Constitution as a statute, albeit of a special kind. This is true even of Justice Kirby, the current most 'activist' judge.[113] The doctrine of reserved state powers has never been revived, and is still regarded as 'heresy'. But the Court subsequently developed a new doctrine of implied intergovernmental immunities, admittedly much narrower than the original one, for reasons not dissimilar to those which the Court rejected in *Engineers'*.[114]

Current Interpretive Methodology

Words

The principles of statutory interpretation that the Court affirmed in *Engineers'* require courts to start from, and always adhere closely to, the words of the statute in question. They also require that, until the words are amended, they continue to mean what they meant when they were first enacted. At least until recently, the

---

[109] Sawer (n 29) 128; Galligan (n 26) 97, 102.

[110] RTE Latham *The Law and the Commonwealth* (Oxford University Press, London, 1949) 563 (first published in 1937); see also 56, 567.

[111] W Anstey Wynes *Legislative and Executive Powers in Australia* (Law Book Co of Australiasia Ltd, Sydney, 1936) 20; see also 23. [112] ibid 76; see also 14, 42–43.

[113] *Abebe v Commonwealth* [1999] HCA 14 [203] (Kirby J); (1999) 197 CLR 510, 581. See also *McGinty v Western Australia* [1995] HCA 46; (1996) 186 CLR 140, 230 (McHugh J).

[114] G Sawer 'Implication and the Constitution Part I' 4 (1949–1950) *Res Judicatae* 15; Sawer (n 93).

Court has always accepted that, unless formally amended, the words of the Constitution continue to mean what they meant in 1900.[115] As Barton J explained, '[t]o attempt to give [the words] a larger meaning is to attempt to alter the Constitution', which can only be legitimately achieved by referendum.[116]

On the other hand, the judges have often agreed that where there is a choice, the words should generally be understood broadly rather than narrowly, at least where Commonwealth powers are concerned. According to one frequently quoted dictum,

> it must always be remembered that we are interpreting a Constitution broad and general in its terms, intended to apply to the varying conditions which the development of our community must involve. For that reason, where the question is whether the Constitution has used an expression in the wider or in the narrower sense, the Court should, in my opinion, always lean to the broader interpretation unless there is something in the context or in the rest of the Constitution to indicate that the narrower interpretation will best carry out its object and purpose.[117]

The judges have always acknowledged that new developments, unanticipated in 1900, may fall within the meaning of general constitutional terms: 'if the language of a Statute includes a whole genus, a species of that genus, unknown when the Act was passed and only afterwards coming into existence, is still within the language.'[118] In other words, the meaning of a constitutional provision cannot change without formal amendment, but it can be applied to new objects that the framers may not have anticipated.[119] The Court later borrowed, from John Stuart Mill, the terms 'connotation' and 'denotation' to designate, respectively, the meaning of a word, and the objects to which it applies. The distinction is useful in explaining many High Court decisions. For example, in 1900 Britons were not subject to Parliament's power with respect to 'aliens', but at some indeterminate point in Australia's transition to independence, their status changed. While the connotation of 'aliens' did not change, its denotation did. Nevertheless, the distinction raises difficulties that will be discussed later.[120]

The words of the Constitution are given their ordinary meaning unless there are grounds for thinking that a technical legal meaning was intended.[121] An

---

[115] *Brewery Employees Union of NSW* (n 83) 469, 501, 521. See also *R v Barger* [1908] HCA 43; (1908) 6 CLR 41, 68, 116; *Federated Sawmill* (n 77) 487, 521; *R v Coldham, ex p Australian Social Welfare Union* [1983] HCA 19; (1983) 153 CLR 297, 313.

[116] *Brewery Employees Union of NSW* (n 83) 521.

[117] *Jumbunna Coal Mine, No Liability v Victorian Coal Miners' Association* (1908) 6 CLR 309 (HCA) 367–68. See also Dixon J in *Australian National Airways v Commonwealth* [1945] HCA 41; (1945) 71 CLR 29, 81.

[118] *Brewery Employees Union of NSW* (n 83) 521–22 (Barton J); see also 501.

[119] For a very clear statement, see Sir G Barwick, 'Foreword' to PH Lane *Lane's Commentary on the Australian Constitution* (Law Book Co, Sydney, 1986) vii.   [120] Text to nn 281–292.

[121] See *R v Coldham* (n 115) 312–13 for an example of words—'industrial dispute'—treated as having their 'popular meaning—what they convey to the man in the street [as at 1900]. And that is essentially a question of fact.'

example of the latter are the words used in conferring Parliament's powers: it is given power to make laws 'for the peace, order and good government' of the Commonwealth with respect to the various subject-matters enumerated. This phrase, in ordinary parlance, might suggest that Parliament's powers are subject to a general but vague limitation, requiring courts to invalidate legislation that does not, in their opinion, contribute to 'peace, order and good government'. But it is merely a stock phrase, routinely used in conferring legislative power on colonial legislatures, which the Privy Council in the late 19th century held did not impose any substantive limits on that power.[122] It was, on the contrary, understood to confer absolute or plenary power, of the same sovereign nature as that of the United Kingdom Parliament itself.[123] The High Court has always held that the words were used in this special legal sense in the Constitution.[124]

Context

The Court also examines the meaning of the same or similar words used elsewhere in the Constitution, and the relationship between apparently related provisions. A vivid example is the Court's interpretation of s 41, whose literal meaning is that no adult person with a right to vote in a state election may be prevented from voting in a Commonwealth election. In *Pearson's* case (1983), the Court held that the scope of this guarantee was limited by its original purpose, revealed partly by reading it together with s 30. That section provides that until the Commonwealth enacts its own electoral laws (which happened in 1902), the right to vote in Commonwealth elections shall be governed by state laws. According to the Court, the purpose of s 41 was merely to ensure that no right to vote in Commonwealth elections acquired under s 30 could be taken away by Commonwealth legislation. This was to ensure that women who had acquired the right to vote in South Australia, and could there-fore vote in the referendum on whether the Constitution should be enacted, would not reject it for fear that the new Parliament might not allow them to vote in Commonwealth elections. The upshot was that s 41 applied only to people who acquired a right to vote before 1902, so that by 1983 it was a dead letter.[125] But there is no hint of this restricted purpose and scope in the words of s 41 itself. Moreover, even its dependence on s 30 would not be apparent to anyone who did not consult extrinsic evidence of the framers' intentions, which is the next factor to be considered.

Extrinsic evidence of framers' intentions and purposes

British courts traditionally held that in interpreting a statute, the pre-existing state of the law, and the historical context in which it was enacted, could be taken into

---

[122] 'Substantive' as distinct from 'territorial': the words were held to require some connection with the particular colony in question.

[123] Privy Council cases *R v Burah* (1878) 3 AC 889; *Hodge v The Queen* (1883) 9 AC 117; *Powell v Apollo Candle Co* (1885) 10 AC 282; *Riel v The Queen* (1885) 10 AC 675 in T Blackshield and G Williams *Australian Constitutional Law & Theory* (2nd edn., Sydney, The Federation Press, 1988) 380.   [124] Text to n 25.

[125] *R v Pearson, ex p Sipka* [1983] HCA 6; (1983) 152 CLR 254, 261, 271.

account, but parliamentary debates could not. The High Court adopted similar principles in interpreting the Constitution. It was prepared to take into account the state of the law, and general historical facts, at the time the Constitution was drafted and enacted, as part of the context informing the likely meaning of its provisions. It was also willing to consider earlier drafts of the Constitution, which might suggest reasons for the arrangement or wording of the final text, but not the published verbatim records of what was said by members of the Constitutional Conventions.[126] This rule against directly consulting the Convention Debates continued until 1988, although it was occasionally breached before then, as in *Pearson's* case.[127] But paradoxically, the Court was willing to consult an authoritative early text, *The Annotated Constitution of the Australian Commonwealth* (1901), which analysed the meaning and purpose of every provision of the Constitution seriatim, by reference to historical antecedents, drafting history, and the Convention Debates.[128]

At an early stage, the Court scoffed at the idea that the Constitution should be interpreted 'merely by the aid of a dictionary, as by an astral intelligence, and as a mere decree of the Imperial Parliament without reference to history.'[129] The judges referred to the intention of the legislature, but also to what was in 'the minds of the framers' and of 'the people'.[130] They do not seem to have thought that these alternatives made much difference, since the apparent intention to be gathered from the text, in the light of its historical context, could be attributed to all three—the Imperial Parliament's intention having been to enact the scheme of government that the framers had proposed, and the people approved, in Australia.[131] Even if, as some judges have recently suggested, the authority of the Constitution now rests exclusively on its continued acceptance by the Australian people, who possess ultimate 'sovereignty', it is hard to see why this would entail any change in interpretive method. The Court from the beginning often said that the Constitution was both an Imperial statute and an expression of the will of the Australian people. It repeated this in the *Engineers'* case, and argued that close adherence to ordinary principles of statutory interpretation would best ensure that the will of both Parliament and people would be faithfully executed, rather than distorted by judicial creativity.[132]

---

[126] *Tasmania v Commonwealth* (n 6) 333. In a previous case the Court had been more amenable to consulting the Convention Debates: *Municipal Council of Sydney v Commonwealth* (n 69) 213–14.

[127] *R v Pearson, ex p Sipka* (n 125).

[128] *The Annotated Constitution of the Australian Commonwealth* (n 5). See Chief Justice Latham 's reference to *The Annotated Constitution of the Australian Commonwealth* in *R v Federal Court of Bankruptcy, ex p Lowenstein* [1938] HCA 10; (1938) 59 CLR 556, 570.

[129] *Baxter* (n 73) 1109.

[130] *Tasmania v Commonwealth* (n 6) 343–44 (Griffith CJ), 348 and 351–52 (Barton J), 360 (O'Connor J). See also *Deakin v Webb* (1904) 1 CLR 585, 630–31 (O'Connor J); *Baxter* (n 73) 1109, 1112.

[131] Statement of the Secretary of State for the Colonies, Mr Chamberlain, on introducing the Constitution in the House of Commons: *Commonwealth of Australia Constitution Bill, Reprint of the Debates in Parliament, the official correspondence with the Australian delegates, and other papers* (Wyman & sons Ltd, London, 1900) 12. The exception concerned Privy Council appeals, which the British believed to affect the Empire as a whole: see text between n 26 and n 29.   [132] Text to n 103.

In an early case dealing with the meaning of 'duties of excise', the Court was influenced by the facts 'that the Constitution was framed in Australia by Australians, and for the use of the Australian people, and that the word 'excise' had a distinct meaning in the popular mind, and that there were in the States many laws in force dealing with the subject'.[133] The Court preferred the Australian to the broader English meaning of the word.[134] In another early case, it determined the meaning of the term 'trade marks' by examining late 19th century statutes that would have been 'in the minds of' the framers.[135] Since then, the Court has 'frequently grubbed around the historical roots of a constitutional term in order to unearth its content.'[136]

But the role of historical considerations should not be exaggerated. In many—probably most—cases, they have played little role. Until 1988, the Court was able to infer the framers' intentions and purposes only from a very limited range of material. It often preferred not to gloss the ordinary or natural meaning of the text, especially when interpreting Commonwealth powers.[137] Sometimes the attribution of a purpose to a provision was little more than dogmatic assertion, reflecting a judge's view of what purpose it ought to be regarded as serving.[138]

It is unfortunate that the Court refused for so long to consult the Convention Debates, because doing so could have prevented some major interpretive errors that had unfortunate consequences. For example, sections 101–103 of the Constitution provided that 'there shall be an Interstate Commission, with such powers of adjudication and administration as the Parliament deems necessary' to execute other provisions relating to trade and commerce. These include s 92, which requires that inter-state trade and commerce shall be 'absolutely free'. In the *Wheat* case (1915), the Court held that 'powers of adjudication' in s 101 could not include judicial powers, on the ground that s 71 of the Constitution requires that 'the judicial power of the Commonwealth' may be vested only in a court, and the Commission was not a court. 'Powers of adjudication' were, instead, confined to adjudication of factual disputes that were ancillary and incidental to the Commission's exercise of administrative powers.[139]

Not only was this decision at odds with the ordinary meaning of the words of s 101, and the implications of related provisions, but the Convention Debates make it clear that the framers did intend that the Commission could be vested

[133] *Peterswald v Bartley* [1904] HCA 21; (1904) 1 CLR 497, 509.
[134] ibid. See also *Brewery Employees Union of NSW* (n 83) 535.
[135] *Brewery Employees Union of NSW* (n 83) 522 (Barton J). See also *Federated Sawmill* (n 77) 503–4.
[136] PH Lane *The Australian Federal System* (2nd edn., The Law Book Co Ltd, Sydney, 1979) 1110. For other examples, see J Goldsworthy 'Originalism in Constitutional Interpretation' 25 (1997) Federal L Rev 12, section 2.
[137] Lane (n 136) 1113–14. In *R v Trade Practices Tribunal, ex p St George CC* [1974] HCA 7; (1974) 130 CLR 533 it gave short shrift to evidence about the historical meaning of 'trading corporations'.
[138] eg Chief Justice Dixon's assertion of the purpose behind s 90, and Chief Justice Barwick's regarding s 92: L Zines *The High Court and the Constitution* (4th edn., Butterworths, Sydney, 1997) 450–51.
[139] *New South Wales v Commonwealth* ('the *Wheat* case') [1915] HCA 17; (1915) 20 CLR 54, 61.

with judicial powers. Indeed, Mr Isaacs expressly acknowledged this during the Debates, although he either forgot or ignored this when, as a judge, he joined the majority in the *Wheat* case.[140] By ignoring this evidence, the Court was able to rewrite s 101 to protect a principle that it plainly regarded as paramount: that judicial power should be exercised only by independent courts. But the framers had taken care to avoid the dangers of departing from that principle: s 103 provided the Interstate Commission with independence from political interference similar to that enjoyed by the federal judiciary, and s 73(iii) provided for appeals to the High Court from all 'judgments, decrees, orders, and sentences' of the Interstate Commission on questions of law.

The Interstate Commission was so emasculated by the Court's decision that the government decided to abolish it. As a result, the Court assumed sole responsibility for interpreting and enforcing s 92, one of the most important provisions in the Constitution, and made a thorough botch of it. The Court was disadvantaged by lacking the expertise, and the flexible powers of fact-finding and decision-making, that the Commission could have developed had it survived.[141] But once again, the Court's problems were partly due to its refusal to consult the Convention Debates and other historical evidence of the intended meaning of the elliptical words of that section ('absolutely free' from what?). At one stage, Isaacs J persuaded the Court to adopt a broad interpretation that he himself had earlier, during the Convention Debates, warned might be adopted by someone ignorant of its intended meaning![142] Unwilling to admit extrinsic evidence of intended meaning, the Court 'embarked on an abstract exercise of giving an almost context-free meaning to the words of the section.'[143] It turned s 92 into a partial guarantee of laissez-faire, rather than the much more limited prohibition of state protectionism that the framers had intended. The result was that s 92 became the most litigated section of the Constitution, an obstacle to the democratic regulation of commerce by all political parties, a source of bitter political controversy, and the subject of continuous judicial disagreement, uncertainty, and changes of mind.[144]

This unsatisfactory state of affairs lasted until 1988, when the Court in *Cole v Whitfield* returned to the historically intended meaning of the section.[145] In order to do so, it reversed its long-standing refusal to consult the Convention Debates and other historical evidence. It was no doubt influenced by recent legislation

---

[140] JM Finnis 'The Separation of Powers in the Australian Constitution' (1968) 3 Adelaide L Rev 159, 172–75.

[141] A Bell 'Inter-State Commission' in *The Oxford Companion to the High Court of Australia* (n 11) 354.

[142] J Goldsworthy 'Realism about the High Court' (1989) 18 Federal L Rev 27, 34 n 66. Note that in exempting the Commonwealth from scope of s 92 he also apparently relied on an implication from s 51(1)—it's contrary to the literal meaning of the text!

[143] M Coper 'Interstate trade and commerce, freedom of' in *The Oxford Companion to the High Court of Australia* (n 11) 356.   [144] See Zines (n 138), chs 6, 7 and 8.

[145] *Cole v Whitfield* [1988] HCA 18; (1988) 165 CLR 360.

requiring the courts to consult parliamentary debates when interpreting ordinary statutes.[146] But the Court attempted to limit the use made of such material:

Reference to the history of s 92 may be made, not for the purpose of substituting for the meaning of the words used the scope and effect—if such could be established—which the founding fathers subjectively intended the section to have, but for the purpose of identifying the contemporary meaning of language used, the subject to which that language was directed and the nature and objectives of the movement towards federation from which the compact of the Constitution finally emerged.[147]

These distinctions, repeated in later judgments, are not completely clear.[148] The Court is apparently interested in what the Constitution's words were generally understood to mean, and what their basic purposes were thought to be, at the time they were enacted, whether or not individual framers intended, expected, or would have approved of, particular applications of them. This is consistent with earlier dicta. Dixon J once rejected an argument for 'confus[ing] the unexpressed assumptions upon which the framers of the instrument supposedly proceeded with the expressed meaning of the power.'[149] In a later case, Justice Mason observed that 'mere expectations held in 1900 could not form a satisfactory basis for departing from the natural interpretation of words used in the Constitution.'[150] In recent cases judges have emphasised that the meaning of the Constitution is an objective, rather than subjective, matter. Chief Justice Gleeson and Justice McHugh recently stated that:

An understanding of the context in which an instrument was written is ordinarily useful, and sometimes essential, for an understanding of its meaning. To recognise that is not to treat the subjective understanding of the framers, if it is possible to find any such common understanding, as the determining factor in a dispute about interpretation. It is simply to accept the historical context in which an instrument was written, which such an understanding may reflect, as potentially relevant to a question about the meaning of the instrument.[151]

The decision in *Cole v Whitfield* has led to a substantial increase in judicial references to the framers' intentions, and to the Convention Debates. Nevertheless, it must be acknowledged that on many, and possibly most, contentious issues, historical evidence remains of little assistance, because either the framers did not discuss the issue, or what they said is itself unclear or divided.

---

[146] Acts Interpretation Act 1901 (Cth) ss 15AA, 15AB.

[147] *Cole v Whitfield* (n 145) 385.

[148] *Eastman v R* [2000] HCA 17 [146]; (2000) 203 CLR 1, 46. See also *Cheng v R* [2000] HCA 53 [218]; (2000) 203 CLR 248, 321 (Kirby J); *Re Governor, Goulburn CC, ex p Eastman* [1999] HCA 44 [87]; (1999) 200 CLR 322, 355 (Kirby J); *Singh v Commonwealth* [2004] HCA 43, [19], [52], [159], [247] and [295].

[149] *Australian National Airways v Commonwealth* (n 117) 81.

[150] *Commonwealth v Tasmania* ('*Tasmanian Dam* case') [1983] HCA 21; (1983) 158 CLR 1, 127.

[151] *Brownlee v R* [2001] HCA 36 [8]; (2001) 207 CLR 278, 285.

'Structural' principles and implications

The Court has traditionally been wary of 'top-down' reasoning that deduces conclusions from abstract principles rather than concrete provisions.[152] Chief Justice Barwick once asserted that constitutional disputes are 'not to be solved by resort to slogans or to political catch-cries or to vague and imprecise expressions of political philosophy', but instead, 'by the meaning of the relevant text of the Constitution having regard to the historical setting in which the Constitution was created'.[153] Nevertheless, the Court has often been guided by broad principles that it regards as underlying parts of the Constitution. Even Isaacs J, who wrote the majority judgment in *Engineers'*, referred in another case to 'the silent operation of constitutional principles.'[154] The most important are federalism, the separation of powers, responsible government, representative government, nationhood, and the rule of law. Some judges have recently added the sovereignty of the people to this list.

These principles have frequently been used both to interpret specific provisions, and to derive implications from the Constitution. In cases of ambiguity or vagueness, they have sometimes helped fill the vacuum created by the Court's previous refusal to consult extrinsic evidence of the framers' purposes. Their use in the derivation of implications has been more controversial, given the Court's disapproval in *Engineers'* of implications not firmly based on 'legal', as opposed to 'political', necessity. But as Dixon J later insisted, a rule completely excluding implications 'would defeat the intention of any instrument, but of all instruments a written constitution seems the last to which it could be applied.'[155] This must be true, given that the courts' power of judicial review itself depends largely on implication. Justice Windeyer later added the qualification that 'I would prefer not to say "making implications", because our avowed task is simply the revealing or uncovering of implications that are already there.'[156]

The way in which the first three Chapters of the Constitution follow the American pattern of dealing separately with legislative, executive and judicial powers, and vesting each in a different branch of government, was regarded as powerful evidence that the Constitution embodies the doctrine of the separation of powers, modified by the system of responsible government and considerations of practical convenience. That inference is debatable, since the Convention Debates offer little evidence that the framers had any such intention, although

---

[152] *McGinty* case (n 113) n 427 (McHugh J), quoting R Posner 'Legal Reasoning From the Top Down and From the Bottom Up: The Question of Unenumerated Constitutional Rights' 59 (1992) U Chicago L Rev 433.

[153] *Attorney-General (Cth) (Ex rel McKinlay) v Commonwealth (McKinlay's* case) [1975] HCA 53; (1975) 135 CLR 1, 17.

[154] *Commonwealth v Kreglinger & Fernau Ltd and Bardsley* [1926] HCA 8; (1926) 37 CLR 393, 413.

[155] *West v Commissioner of Taxation (NSW)* [1937] HCA 26; (1937) 56 CLR 657, 681.

[156] *Victoria v Commonwealth* (n 8) 402, approved in *McGinty* (n 113) 168–70 (Chief Justice Brennan), 184 (Dawson J), 202 (Toohey J).

they clearly wanted to protect the independence of the federal judiciary.[157] Nevertheless, the Court has established a fairly strict separation of judicial and non-judicial powers, but not of legislative and executive powers. In developing this doctrine, as we have seen, the Court unnecessarily eviscerated the Interstate Commission, whose exercise of judicial power could have been treated as a special exception to the general principle.[158] The Court subsequently felt obliged by historical and practical considerations to recognise a few other exceptions, such as military tribunals, which exercise judicial power under federal laws even though they are not courts.

The *Engineers'* case spelt the end of reserved state powers, but not of implied intergovernmental immunities. Led by Dixon J, a dominant intellectual force from the 1930s until the 1960s, the Court gradually developed new doctrines, which are still being refined. These prohibit both the Commonwealth and the states from both (1) passing laws that impose discriminatory disabilities or burdens on one another; and (2) interfering in certain ways with one another's 'capacities' as independent governments.[159] The precise rationale of these immunities remains unclear. The judges relied on reasoning not dissimilar to that which was rejected in the *Engineers'* case, and American decisions were once again extensively cited.[160] These immunities are apparently regarded as practically necessary to ensure the minimal degree of autonomy that is required by governments in any genuine federation. They have been distinguished from the pre-*Engineers'* immunities on the ground that they are exceptional rather than typical.[161] They have had little practical impact, and the states would have been better off had the doctrine of reserved state powers been revived instead.

Several cases have supported the idea that the Commonwealth possesses an 'implied nationhood power', comprised of the inherent requirements of any national government, but excluding powers that are either coercive or likely to be claimed by the states.[162]

Judicial reasoning based on underlying structural principles became more common in the late 1980s.[163] As we will see, the principle of representative democracy helped to persuade the Court in 1992 that the Constitution includes an implied freedom of political communication.

---

[157] Finnis (n 140); F Wheeler 'Original Intent and the Doctrine of the Separation of Powers in Australia' (1996) 7 Public L Rev 96; Sawer (n 29) 152–53.　　　　　　　　　[158] See n 139, above.

[159] This abstract summary necessarily glosses over various complications, and possible differences, in the way that the states and the Commonwealth are protected.

[160] Sawer (n 114); Sawer (n 93).

[161] M Coper *Encounters With The Australian Constitution* (CCH Australia Ltd, New South Wales, 1988) 177.

[162] *Victoria v Commonwealth* ('*AAP* case') [1975] HCA 52; (1975) 134 CLR 338; *Davis v Commonwealth* [1988] HCA 63; (1988) 166 CLR 79.

[163] JJ Doyle 'Constitutional Law: "At The Eye of the Storm" ' 23 (1993) U Western Australia L Rev 15, 20–21, 27.

Precedent

The judges devote considerable attention to the decisions, reasoning, and dicta of previous cases, provided that they were not based on principles that the Court subsequently rejected. It has never regarded itself as strictly bound by its own previous decisions, and in constitutional cases the principle of stare decisis has probably been of less weight than usual, because judicial errors cannot be corrected by Parliament, and fidelity to the Constitution is regarded as paramount. Two dramatic over-rulings of long-standing doctrines, in *Engineers'* and *Cole v Whitfield*, have already been mentioned, and there have been many others.[164] But the Court is reluctant to reverse itself. It has adopted a rule of practice that counsel must obtain its permission in order to challenge the correctness of one of its previous decisions.[165] And it will uphold such a challenge only after weighing up factors such as the number of previous decisions affected, the extent to which earlier judges were in agreement, and the consequences in terms of unsettled expectations and public inconvenience.[166]

The Court does not engage in 'prospective over-ruling', because it refuses to concede that overruling involves altering legal rights as opposed to declaring what they have always been. It regards the alteration of legal rights as inconsistent with the exercise of 'judicial power' under the Constitution.[167] This view is in tension with many extra-judicial acknowledgements that judges often do make law, and that the old declaratory theory of the judicial function is a 'fairy tale'.

Deference to other branches

The Court does not defer to the constitutional interpretations apparently adopted by other branches of government, or apply any general presumption of constitutional validity to their acts.[168] In the *Boilermakers'* case (1956), the Court said that a 30-year governmental practice of vesting non-judicial powers in a federal court, based on legislation whose validity has never been previously challenged, could raise a presumption of validity, but it could not be decisive, and the Court had a duty to decide the question for itself.[169] In *Re Wakim* (1999), Kirby J argued that a long-standing and rare agreement between the Commonwealth, and all state and Territory, governments and legislatures was a strong reason for the Court to

---

[164] Text following n 102 discussing *Engineers'* (n 7) and text following n 145 discussing *Cole v Whitfield* (n 145).

[165] *Evda Nominees Pty Ltd v Victoria* [1984] HCA 18; (1984) 154 CLR 311.

[166] Zines (n 138) 442.

[167] *South Australia v Commonwealth* [1942] HCA 14; (1942) 65 CLR 373, 408 (Latham CJ); *Ha v New South Wales* [1997] HCA 37; (1997) 189 CLR 465, 504. See Lane (n 136) 1144.

[168] H Burmester 'The Presumption of Constitutionality' (1983) 13 Federal L Rev 277; Sawer (n 29) 118–19. Dicta apparently to the contrary (see, eg W Anstey Wynes *Legislative, Executive and Judicial Powers in Australia* (5th edn., The Law Book Co Ltd, Sydney, 1976) 35 n 26) usually concern the presumption that legislation should, if possible, be construed so as to ensure its validity.

[169] *R v Kirby, ex p Boilermakers' Society of Australia (Boilermakers'* case) [1956] HCA 10; (1956) 94 CLR 254, 296.

uphold the validity of a scheme cross-vesting jurisdiction between federal and state courts.[170] But the majority denied that this was a criterion of constitutional validity, and proceeded to hold the scheme invalid.

In rejecting arguments that legislative powers are subject to implied constitutional limitations, the Court has sometimes invoked the British tradition of parliamentary supremacy, based partly on trust that an elected legislature will not abuse its powers.[171] But it does not defer to parliaments when deciding whether or not they have exceeded constitutional powers or violated limitations that are expressed or otherwise well established. The Court regards itself as the principal guardian of the Constitution, not only authorized, but obligated, to interpret and enforce it when constitutional questions are properly raised.[172] This is partly because in a federal system, where the powers of one legislature may affect those of another, a policy of deference to one may adversely affect the other.[173] For example, in deciding whether Commonwealth legislation exceeded its power with respect to interstate trade and commerce, the Court resolutely resisted calls for it to adopt the more deferential and accommodating approach of the American Supreme Court, which virtually abandoned the attempt to limit Congress's commerce power on the ground that interstate and intrastate commerce had become inseparably 'commingled'. The Court insisted that, because the framers deliberately limited the power to interstate trade and commerce, so as not to intrude any further than necessary into the internal affairs of the states, it had a duty to enforce the limit regardless of any deleterious effects on the implementation of Commonwealth regulatory policies.[174]

On the other hand, the Court has interpreted most Commonwealth powers very generously, in ways that some critics regard as detrimental to the states, and they might allege that in practice this has amounted to a kind of deference to the national Parliament.[175]

Policy considerations

Isaacs J once claimed that 'no considerations of expediency or desirability springing from any source whatever' should influence the Court in determining the limits of a constitutional power: 'It is a mere question of dry law . . . to be determined on ordinary legal principles.'[176] In reality, given the ambiguity and vagueness of much of the Constitution's language, even after historical evidence of intended meaning has been consulted, the judges must often resort to 'policy' considerations, such as justice, utility, and good government.[177] These include whether a particular interpretation can be translated into a judicially manageable test of validity.[178] But policy considerations have generally been couched, not in

---

[170] *Re Wakim, ex p McNally* [1999] HCA 27; (1999) 198 CLR 511. See text to n 184.
[171] Text to n 25.
[172] *Victoria v Commonwealth (PMA case)* [1975] HCA 39; (1975) 134 CLR 81.
[173] Zines (n 138) 484.   [174] Text to n 189.   [175] pp 136–141 of text.
[176] *Brewery Employees Union of NSW* (n 83) 559.   [177] Zines (n 138), ch 17.
[178] Coper (n 161) 374.

terms of what the judges themselves regard as desirable, but in terms of what, because it is desirable, was probably intended.[179] For example, Gleeson CJ and McHugh J recently argued that one interpretation of Parliament's power to confer federal jurisdiction 'would create immense practical problems for the administration of federal law which the makers of the Constitution can hardly have intended.'[180]

Recall *Pearson's* case, concerning s 41, which provides that people entitled to vote in state elections must be permitted to vote in Commonwealth elections. The Court held that this provision was implicitly limited to the protection of voting rights acquired before 1902.[181] The decision was based not only on contextual and historical evidence of the section's purpose, but also on the desirability of a uniform Commonwealth franchise, unaffected by disparate state electoral laws. There are many other examples of the Court taking practical consequences into account. For example, it refused to apply the doctrine of separation of powers in a rigid fashion, so as to forbid the delegation of law-making power to the executive branch, largely because that would have been inconsistent with the practical necessities of modern government.[182] Other more limited exceptions to that doctrine, permitting federal courts to delegate minor judicial powers to non-judicial officers, and military tribunals to exercise judicial power, also owe their existence partly to considerations of practicality.[183]

But the Court is not always swayed by such considerations, and will refuse to relax a constitutional requirement that it regards as clear, in order to avoid practical inconvenience. *Re Wakim* (1999) is an example.[184] In order to minimise the inconvenience, expense, and delays caused by parties having to litigate separately in federal and state courts, where their disputes involve matters arising in both federal and state jurisdiction, all nine Australian governments—Commonwealth, State, and Territory—had enacted co-operative legislation to establish a cross-vesting scheme. State courts were vested with federal jurisdiction, where appropriate, and two federal courts (but not the High Court) with state jurisdiction. This enabled whichever court was best placed to deal with a dispute in its entirety to exercise both federal and state jurisdiction.

The scheme operated for over ten years and was generally regarded as a success, until the Court by a majority of six to one held that it was invalid on the ground that federal courts could only exercise federal jurisdiction as specified in Chapter III of the Constitution: they could not be invested with state jurisdiction, even

---

[179] Coper (n 161) 47.

[180] *Abebe v Commonwealth* (n 113) [41]; 531.   [181] *Pearson's* case (n 125).

[182] *Victorian Stevedoring and General Contracting Co Pty Ltd v Dignan* (*Dignan's* case) [1931] HCA 34; (1931) 46 CLR 73. Both Evatt and Dixon JJ (extra-judicially) admitted this.

[183] See Toohey J's reference to pragmatism in upholding the constitutionality of defence force magistrates exercising judicial power (see Zines (n 138) 457). Also *Harris v Caladine* [1991] HCA 9; (1991) 172 CLR 84 (see Brennan J's dissenting complaint about the Constitution not bending to exigencies of a budget).   [184] *Re Wakim* (n 170).

with Parliament's consent.[185] The decision has been widely criticised, because it was based not on any express provision, but on a putative implication that is not necessary to protect any important constitutional principle. As one eminent critic put it, the cross-vesting scheme posed no threat to the separation of powers, the position of the High Court in the judicial hierarchy, the rule of law, common law rights, or state rights and independence. '[T]he practical demands of government gave way to a doctrinal form of reasoning that . . . seemed to have no obvious constitutional object.'[186]

The majority was unmoved by arguments based on the practical utility of the scheme. Justices Gummow and Hayne disapproved of using 'perceived convenience as a criterion of constitutional validity instead of legal analysis and the application of accepted constitutional doctrine.'[187]

The Court is entrusted with the preservation and application of constitutional distinctions. Were the Court to discard those distinctions, on the ground that at a particular time and to some minds they appear inconvenient or otherwise unsatisfactory, the Court not only would fail in its task but would exceed its authority.[188]

Many years before, the Court took the same view of the distinction between interstate and intrastate trade and commerce. Justice Kitto said that the Court had a duty to maintain constitutional distinctions 'however out of touch with practical conceptions or with modern conditions they may appear to be in some or all of their applications.'[189]

Formal and conceptual analysis

A former characteristic of the Court's methodology that contributed to its reputation for excessive legalism was a tendency to prefer formal, abstract, and conceptual analysis, to substantive factual or evaluative reasoning. For example, in applying several provisions that prohibit discrimination against states or their residents, the Court consistently adopted a formal rather than substantive conception of discrimination, preferring to look no further than the terms of the law in question, rather than at its practical effects in the particular circumstances of the people it affected. Again, in deciding whether or not a law was 'with respect to' a subject-matter within Commonwealth power, or violated a limitation on power, the Court often preferred to confine its enquiry to the terms of the law—its 'direct legal operation' or 'criteria of operation'—rather than examine its practical effects.

---

[185] This is a little inexact: they can also exercise so-called 'accrued' jurisdiction over matters of state jurisdiction that the Court regards as inseverable from matters of federal jurisdiction. Note that s 77 of the Constitution expressly authorises the Parliament to vest federal jurisdiction in state courts.

[186] L Zines 'The Present State of Constitutional Interpretation' in A Stone and G Williams (eds) *The High Court at the Crossroads: essays in Constitutional Law* (Federation Press, Sydney, 2000) 224, 234–35.   [187] *Re Wakim* (n 170) [126]; 581.

[188] ibid [94]; 569.

[189] *Airlines of NSW Pty Ltd v New South Wales (No. 2)* [1965] HCA 3; (1965) 113 CLR 54, 115.

A prime example is the Court's former treatment of s 92, which provides that interstate trade and commerce shall be 'absolutely free'. Having rejected the view that it was only intended to forbid discriminatory state protectionism, the Court had to find some other way of qualifying the words 'absolutely free', because interstate trade and commerce could obviously not enjoy total immunity from legal control. Taking its lead from the Privy Council, the Court held that only 'unreasonable' burdens that 'directly' affected interstate trade and commerce were prohibited. It then attempted to finesse the difficult question of degree raised by the concept of directness by abstruse conceptual means:

If a law takes a fact or an event or a thing itself forming part of trade commerce or intercourse, or forming an essential attribute of that conception, essential in the sense that without it you cannot bring into being that particular example of trade commerce or intercourse among the states, and the law proceeds, by reference thereto or in consequence thereof, to impose a restriction, a burden or a liability, then that appears . . . to be direct or immediate in its operation[190]

The Court also tried to clarify the notion of 'reasonable' regulation by conceptual means, distinguishing between the 'essence' and the 'incidents' of interstate trade and commerce, and holding that laws governing the latter would usually (but not necessarily) amount to reasonable regulation.[191] The gradual breakdown of this artificial conceptual approach eventually persuaded the Court in *Cole v Whitfield* to reconsider its interpretation of s 92, and adopt a protectionist rather than laissez-faire reading, including a substantive rather than formal approach to protectionism.

A highly formal approach was also taken by many judges in deciding whether or not a state law violated s 90 of the Constitution by imposing an excise tax, which was interpreted as a tax imposed 'directly' on goods. They held that the question depended on the terms of the challenged law—on the precise legal criteria of liability to pay the tax—rather than its practical effects. As one critic observed, the strict application of this approach led to results that were 'inconsistent with any rational, social or economic purpose that can be discerned.'[192] It enabled the states to raise substantial revenue from so-called 'fees' for the purchase or renewal of licences required to sell goods such as alcohol, tobacco and petrol, even when the amount of the fee depended on the value of goods sold in a previous period. These were held to be fees for the right to sell goods, rather than taxes imposed directly on the goods themselves. This was because, as for goods sold previously, a licence might not be renewed, in which case no fee would be payable, and as for goods to be sold in the future, someone might purchase or renew a licence but not proceed to actually sell anything!

---

[190] *Hospital Provident Fund Pty Ltd v Victoria* [1953] HCA 8; (1953) 87 CLR 1, 18.
[191] P Hanks *Australian Constitutional Law* (3rd edn., Butterworths, Sydney, 1985) 695.
[192] Zines (n 138) 446.

It should be added in the Court's defence that in relation to both s 92 and s 90, these highly formalistic tests had the benefit of limiting the practical impact of prohibitions that had arguably been interpreted too broadly.[193]

Comparative and international law

As we have seen, the Court from its inception relied heavily on British and American cases, and to a much smaller extent on Canadian ones, and it continued to do so even after the repudiation of American doctrines in the *Engineers'* case. Even Isaacs J, who wrote the majority judgment in *Engineers'*, subsequently acknowledged that he found American cases on the commerce power of great assistance.[194] But this reliance steadily declined as the accumulation of local precedents made it less necessary, and Australians' sense of independence grew stronger.

From 1900–1980 Australian constitutional law seemed to be evolving into 'a self-referential system of jurisprudence.'[195] But since 1980, this trend has been reversed, and there has been a marked increase in citations of foreign judgments, although the numbers are still small compared with the early years of federation. British and American cases are still by far the most frequently cited, in that order, followed by South African, Canadian, New Zealand and Indian cases. This latest trend is a consequence of 'globalisation', including easier access to foreign materials through the internet, and increased interaction among judges at international conferences.[196]

Recently, Kirby J has argued that when the Constitution is ambiguous, the Court should adopt whatever interpretation best conforms with principles of international law.[197] To date, no other judge has agreed with this, and McHugh J has strongly disagreed. He acknowledges that rules of international law in existence in 1900 might illuminate the Constitution's meaning; but if rules created subsequently were to affect its meaning, it would be illegitimately amended. A Constitution whose meaning could be changed by changes in international law would be a 'loose-leaf' Constitution.[198] It is not clear what Kirby J means by 'ambiguous'. If he regards the Constitution as ambiguous whenever its words, read literally, are unclear, then principles of international law could supplant or trump other factors that help determine meaning, such as context and historical evidence of original meaning. Since Kirby J, as we will see, regards original meanings as of little relevance, and believes that the Constitution should be interpreted in the light of contemporary Australian needs and values, he would probably welcome that result.

---

[193] L Zines 'Characterisation of Commonwealth Laws' in HP Lee and G Winterton (eds) *Australian Constitutional Perspectives* (The Law Book Co Ltd, Sydney, 1992) 41.

[194] *Commonwealth and Commonwealth Oil Refineries Ltd v South Australia* (1926) 38 CLR 408 (HCA) 428.

[195] B Opeskin 'Australian Constitutional Law in a Global Era' in *Reflections on the Australian Constitution* (n 18) 184.   [196] ibid 187.

[197] *Newcrest Mining (WA) Ltd v Commonwealth* [1997] HCA 38; (1997) 190 CLR 513, 657.

[198] *Al-Kateb v Godwin* [2004] HCA 37, paras 62, 68 and 73.

Academic writings

For many years the Court seldom referred to academic writings, other than a few 'classics' such as Quick and Garran's *The Annotated Constitution of the Australian Commonwealth* (1901). But it has done so much more often in recent years.

Weighing the Factors

The Court has not adopted any formula or rank ordering of the various interpretive factors just described, and their relative influence varies from case to case. Judges may strike a different balance in different cases between plain meaning, context, historical evidence, apparent purpose, structural principles, and policy considerations, depending on how they assess their respective weight in each case.

This does not necessarily make the Court's reasoning unprincipled or chaotic. There are two main reasons why no general formula or rank ordering is possible. First, the Court has traditionally regarded its task as being to ascertain what the admissible evidence, as a whole, suggests was the intended meaning of the provision in question.[199] The admissible evidence includes all the factors previously mentioned. In any single case, different items of evidence of intended meaning can point in different directions, and no formula can dictate what weight each item should be given in the particular circumstances. The second reason is that this evidence as a whole is often inconclusive, leaving the judges no alternative but to make a decision on policy grounds, even if they are loathe to admit it. The role of policy can therefore vary, from evidence of intended meaning ('surely the framers could not have intended *that*'), to grounds for the exercise of judicial discretion.

On the other hand, it is possible to discern general patterns in the Court's reasoning. Since *Engineers'*, the Court has usually placed considerable emphasis on the ordinary or technical meaning of the Constitution's words, and has been reluctant to limit or supplement it by implications based on their apparent purpose. It has usually required that any such implication be either logically or practically 'necessary', although it has tended to use these terms rather loosely.

Application of Interpretive Methodology

Grants of powers

Orthodox principles of interpretation have always been regarded as accommodating the special nature of a constitution as 'an instrument of government meant to endure and conferring powers expressed in general propositions wide enough to be capable of flexible application to changing circumstances.'[200] For this reason the Court has adopted a rebuttable presumption that Parliament's powers should

---

[199] Conceded by Sir A Mason 'Trends in Constitutional Interpretation' (1995) 18 U NSW L J 237, 237.   [200] *Australian National Airways v Commonwealth* (n 117) 81.

be broadly construed. Since the doctrine of reserved state powers was overturned in the *Engineers'* case, those powers have been interpreted broadly, subject to any express limitation, regardless of any potential impact on the states.[201]

The words 'with respect to', used in granting these powers, were also interpreted broadly. The process of deciding what subject-matter or matters a law is 'with respect to' is known as characterisation, because it concerns the character of the law. The Court has been generous in two respects. First, if the statute can reasonably be described as a law with respect to a subject matter within Commonwealth power, it is irrelevant that it can also be described as a law with respect to one or more other subject-matters outside Commonwealth power. Once the Court held that the Constitution does not reserve any powers exclusively for the states, it became unnecessary to insist that a choice must be made between alternative characterisations of Commonwealth laws. The Court therefore rejected the Canadian 'pith and substance' test that aims to uncover the one true 'essence' of a statute.

Secondly, in most cases characterisation depends on the 'direct legal operation' of the law—'the nature of the rights, duties, powers and privileges which it changes, regulates or abolishes'—even if it is obvious that both its purpose and practical effect is to control other subject-matters that the Commonwealth may not directly regulate.[202] For example, the Commonwealth can use its power to impose taxation to encourage or discourage any behaviour it chooses, and its power to regulate overseas trade and commerce to prohibit the export of commodities for any reason, such as environmental protection at the stage of mining or manufacture (which is not itself a subject matter of Commonwealth power). In other words, a law whose 'direct legal operation' is the imposition of a tax, or the prohibition of an export, is within the relevant power, even though its purpose and effect is to control behaviour that the Commonwealth could not directly regulate.

This is often cited as an example of the Court's legalistic approach, emphasising legal form rather than purpose and practical effect. But it has been defended on policy grounds, in that it allows maximum scope for legislative policy-making, and eliminates the need for the Court to make invidious value judgments about what policy objectives the Parliament may or may not pursue in exercising its powers.[203] This is consistent with the well-established principle that if a law is within a head of power, the justice and wisdom of its objectives, and the degree to which the means it adopts are necessary or desirable, are entirely matters for legislative discretion.[204]

---

[201] An example of the latter is the power that is limited to interstate trade and commerce, mentioned in text to n 189.

[202] The quote is from *Fairfax v Commissioner of Taxation* [1965] HCA 64; (1965) 114 CLR 1, 7 (Kitto J).   [203] Zines (n 138) 32–33.

[204] *Grain Pool of Western Australia v Commonwealth* [2000] HCA 14 [16]; 202 CLR 479, 492; *Nationwide News Pty Ltd v Wills* [1992] HCA 46; (1992) 177 CLR 1, 44 (Brennan J).

The Commonwealth has therefore benefited from (a) the abandonment of the doctrine of reserved state powers, (b) a presumption that favours broad interpretations of its powers, and (c) a legalistic approach to the characterisation of laws that mostly ignores their purposes and effects. In combination, these factors have contributed to a massive expansion of Commonwealth powers since 1920.[205] The most dramatic examples of their effects are the Commonwealth's monopolisation of income taxation in the 1940s, and its use of the external affairs power since 1983.

During the Second World War, in order to maximise and streamline revenue raising, the Commonwealth enacted several statutes whose combined operation forced the states to abandon income taxation. One statute imposed income taxes at extremely high rates, designed to raise as much revenue as all Commonwealth and state income taxes had raised in the previous year. A second statute offered to each state a grant of financial assistance equivalent to the amount of income tax it would otherwise have collected itself, subject to the condition that it not levy income tax. A third statute required tax-payers to pay any income tax owed to the Commonwealth before paying any income tax owed to a state.[206]

The combined effect of these statutes was to make it politically impossible for the states to continue to collect income taxation. Had they attempted to do so, they would have incurred most of the political backlash from angry taxpayers. This was the Commonwealth's obvious purpose, and was freely admitted by the Court when the validity of the statutes was challenged by four states in the *First Uniform Tax* case (1942).[207] Nevertheless, the Court rejected their principal complaint, that the statutes constituted a scheme whose purpose and effect was to do indirectly what the Commonwealth had no power to do directly: namely, to compel them not to exercise their constitutional power to levy income taxation.

The decision might be explained partly as a response to a national crisis: at the time, Australia was threatened with invasion by Japan. But it was reached without any need to bend or stretch legal doctrine. The Court applied standard principles of characterization, examining the 'direct legal operation' of each statute rather than its purpose and effect. The first statute imposed a liability to pay income tax, and the third concerned the discharge of the liability: both were plainly laws with respect to taxation (s 51(2)). The second statute merely offered a grant of financial assistance to the states, subject to a condition that they were legally free to reject. It therefore came within the grants power (s 96), which provides that 'the Parliament

---

[205] To a large extent, however, that expansion was probably inevitable, given the structure and wording of the Constitution that the framers' adopted: G Winterton 'The High Court and Federalism: A Centenary Evaluation' in P Cane (ed) *Centenary Essays for the High Court of Australia* (LexisNexis Butterworths, Brisbane, 2004).

[206] A fourth statute compulsorily acquired all state offices, furniture, records, and personnel used in the collection of income tax. This can be ignored for present purposes. It was based on the defence power, and was held valid only because of the extraordinary exigencies of the War.

[207] *South Australia v Commonwealth (First Uniform Tax* case) [1942] HCA 14; (1942) 65 CLR 373, 411–12.

may grant financial assistance to any State on such terms and conditions as the Parliament thinks fit.' The states were subject to political, not legal, compulsion, which the Court found itself unable to remedy. Latham CJ said:

[T]he controversy before the Court is a legal controversy, not a political controversy. It is not for this or any court to prescribe policy or to seek to give effect to any views or opinions upon policy. We have nothing to do with the wisdom or expediency of legislation. Such questions are for Parliaments and the people.[208]

It is perhaps not out of place to point out that the scheme which the Commonwealth has applied to income tax of imposing rates so high as practically to exclude State taxation could be applied to other taxes so as to make the States almost completely dependent, financially and therefore generally, upon the Commonwealth.... [I]f the Commonwealth Parliament were prepared to pass such legislation, all State powers would be controlled by the Commonwealth—a result which would mean the end of the political independence of the States. Such a result cannot be prevented by any legal decision. The determination of the propriety of any such policy must rest with the Commonwealth Parliament and ultimately with the people. The remedy for alleged abuse of power or for the use of power to promote what are thought to be improper objects is to be found in the political arena and not in the Courts.[209]

This is a remarkable admission of the inability of strict legalism to prevent the abuse of constitutional powers. And the case is a remarkable demonstration of the way in which such powers can be used, in combination, in unexpected ways. But it is not easy to show how the Court could have prevented this. It could not invent a limit on the amount of taxation the Commonwealth could impose. It is equally difficult to see how the express words of s 96, conferring an apparently unlimited discretion to impose terms and conditions on financial assistance granted to the states, could be limited by implication. Dixon CJ, who was absent in the *First Uniform Tax* case, later suggested that the original purpose of this apparently innocuous provision was to enable the Commonwealth to make *ad hoc* grants to help states cope with particular, special needs, and to impose conditions relevant to the occasion calling for the assistance.[210] But how could the Court convert that vague and unexpressed purpose into a justiciable implication limiting the discretion deliberately conferred on Parliament? Moreover, the Commonwealth could evade any such limit simply by imposing conditions informally, without referring to them in any legal instrument.[211] The problem is ultimately political, and requires a political solution. The framers thought they had provided such a solution, but the Senate has not fulfilled its intended role of protecting the states from abuses of Commonwealth power. In effect, the Court declined to act as a surrogate Senate.

The case was decided under the continuing influence of the decision in *Engineers'*, and before the Court developed the modern doctrine of intergovernmental immunities, which prohibits the Commonwealth from threatening the capacity of

---

[208] ibid 409.   [209] ibid 429.
[210] *Victoria v Commonwealth* [1957] HCA 54; (1957) 99 CLR 575, 609.
[211] As Latham CJ pointed out: *First Uniform Tax* case (n 207) 429.

the states to function as independent governments. That doctrine could possibly be used to prevent the federation being destroyed in the manner imagined by Latham CJ, but surely not to invalidate the uniform income tax scheme itself. It has, after all, continued ever since 1943, yet the states still exist and function with a considerable degree of independence.[212] Admittedly, though, that independence has been compromised by the financial dominance of the Commonwealth, which under s 96 often imposes detailed conditions on expenditure of the financial assistance that constitutes 40 per cent or more of the states' annual budgets. This has enabled the Commonwealth indirectly to control many areas of public policy over which it has no legislative power, such as education, housing, hospitals, and roads.

The second example of the expansion of Commonwealth power is its power with respect to 'external affairs'. In 1983 the Court, by a majority of four to three, held that this enables Parliament to give effect within Australia to the terms of any international treaty that the executive government has entered into, even if its subject-matter would otherwise be a purely domestic matter that only the states could regulate. The dissenting judges objected that this decision threatened the constitutional division of legislative powers, and therefore the federal system itself. The majority judges dismissed the objection as an attempt to revive the 'heresy' of reserved state powers, and reiterated the presumption that Commonwealth powers should be broadly construed. They explained the expansion of the power beyond anything that the framers could have anticipated in terms of its denotation, rather than its connotation, having changed.[213] But they also invoked policy arguments, maintaining that the Commonwealth would be severely hampered in the conduct of international affairs if it lacked the ability to discharge its treaty obligations; and that it was impossible to formulate justiciable legal criteria to distinguish treaties that warrant domestic implementation from those that do not.

The external affairs power has been used to enact legislation protecting human rights and the environment. To rub salt into the states' wounds, that legislation is binding on them, and has been used to override their laws.[214] The Court has also held valid, on this ground, Commonwealth legislation regulating industrial relations, despite the fact that its only express power over that subject-matter is limited to the prevention or settlement of industrial disputes extending beyond one state, and despite the failure of five previous attempts to expand that power by formal constitutional amendment.[215]

These are just two examples of the way in which the Court's interpretive principles have benefited Commonwealth powers, but many others could be given. The corporations and industrial relations powers, for example, have

---

[212] Sawer (n 29) 145–46.

[213] *Koowarta v Bjelke-Peterson* [1982] HCA 27; (1982) 153 CLR 168, 254 (Brennan J), 228 (Mason J). On this distinction, see pp 122 and 150–152 of text.

[214] *Tasmanian Dam* case (n 150), *Mabo v Queensland (No. 1)* [1988] HCA 69; (1988) 166 CLR 186.

[215] *Victoria v Commonwealth* [1995] HCA 45; (1996) 187 CLR 416, 565 (Justice Dawson).

expanded in ways that probably go far beyond anything the framers either intended, or would have approved of. Whenever dissenting judges complained that such developments upset the 'federal balance' between Commonwealth and state powers, they were criticised for attempting to revive the 'heresy' of reserved state powers. In fact, when interpreting specific Commonwealth powers, the Court could have taken into account the context provided by the distribution of powers as a whole, without reviving the idea that some powers were 'reserved' to the states.

Limitations on power, including rights

Until 1988, the Court also took a legalistic approach to constitutional guarantees, including the few that protect rights. The Court tended to interpret them literally, but for the most part, without any presumption that they should be interpreted broadly.[216] Indeed, it was occasionally suggested that they should be interpreted narrowly, out of respect for legislative supremacy, but that view did not prevail.[217] Nevertheless, literal interpretations have usually led to rights being interpreted narrowly, and in the few cases in which a purposive rather than literal interpretation was adopted, the result was the same.

Section 80 provides that '[t]he trial on indictment of any offence against any law of the Commonwealth shall be by jury'. The Court has consistently interpreted these words literally, so as to require trial by jury only if the Commonwealth has provided for the charge to be brought by indictment. It can therefore avoid a jury trial, even for a serious offence punishable by imprisonment, merely by authorizing some other mode of prosecution. This interpretation was initially adopted with little analysis, as if it were obviously correct.[218] But it has been adhered to in subsequent cases, partly for reasons of stare decisis, notwithstanding several impassioned dissents complaining that it makes a mockery of the provision's supposed purpose.[219] Defenders of the literal interpretation have recently responded by quoting passages in the Convention Debates in which the framers were clearly warned that the wording of the provision would allow Parliament to legislate so as to avoid jury trials. Indeed, McHugh J has argued that the literal interpretation gives effect not only to the provision's plain meaning, but also to its purpose, which was precisely to enable the Commonwealth to do so.[220] In his opinion, to interpret s 80 as a fundamental guarantee of jury trial for 'serious offences' would lead to uncertainty and inconvenience, and would 'be

---

[216] s 51(31) was an exception.

[217] *Attorney-General (Vic) (Ex rel Black) v Commonwealth (the DOGS case)* (1981) 146 CLR 559.

[218] *R v Archdall and Roskruge, ex p Carrigan and Brown* [1928] HCA 18; (1928) 41 CLR 128, 136; see also 139–40.

[219] *Katsuno v R* [1999] HCA 50 [49], [52]; (1999) 199 CLR 40, 63–64, 65; *Re Colina; ex p Torney* [1999] HCA 57; (1999) 200 CLR 386; *Cheng v R* (n 148) [174]–[175]; 306–7; *Cheung v R* [2001] HCA 67 [114]–[117]; (2001) 209 CLR 1, 38–39 (Kirby J).

[220] *Cheng v R* (n 148) [129]–[143]; 292–95 (McHugh J); see also [53]–[56]; 268–69 (Gleeson CJ, Gummow and Hayne JJ).

crossing the admittedly often uncertain line between constitutional interpretation and constitutional amendment and amending the Constitution by giving effect to my own values or beliefs.'[221] To these arguments, Kirby J replied that the framers' 'subjective expectations, wishes or hopes' could not override what the Constitution requires, when it is read by the present generation of Australians as a constitutional charter of government.[222] Disagreement between McHugh and Kirby JJ over the relevance of the framers' intentions has been a persistent theme in many recent cases.[223]

Section 116 provides, inter alia, that 'the Commonwealth shall not make any law for establishing any religion, . . . or for prohibiting the free exercise of any religion'. A majority of the Court recently reaffirmed the literal interpretation that to infringe these prohibitions, a law must have been passed 'for' establishing a religion or prohibiting its free exercise, in the sense of having either of these as one of its purposes. If they are merely among its consequences, and not its purposes, the law is valid.[224] The Court has also rejected the American doctrine of the separation of church and state, by holding that Parliament may grant financial assistance to religious schools, at least if it does so in a non-discriminatory fashion. The Court preferred the view that 'establishing' a religion, in the late 19th century sense of the word, involves making a particular religion or church the official state religion or church.[225] The Court has also applied the 'free exercise' clause narrowly, refusing to exempt a person from compulsory military service on the ground of religious objection, or to exempt the Jehovah's Witnesses from a prohibition on activities deemed prejudicial to the war effort in the 1940s.[226]

Several provisions of the Constitution prohibit discrimination against states or residents of states: ss 51(2) and 99 forbid Commonwealth laws with respect to taxation or trade and commerce from discriminating between states or parts of states, and s 117 prohibits the states from discriminating against the residents of other states. For decades the Court conceived of discrimination in a formal rather than a substantive sense. In an extraordinarily narrow and formalistic series of decisions, it held that s 117 was not infringed by: (a) a law that discriminated on the basis of domicile as well as residence, despite the close relationship between the two concepts;[227] (b) a law that discriminated on the basis of former rather than current residence;[228] and (c) a law that discriminated on the basis of temporary rather than permanent residence.[229] Justice Gibbs said that the precise nature of s 117 'must depend not upon general theories as to the broad purposes of the

---

[221] *Cheng v R* (n 148) [125]; 291 and [144]–[150]; 295–99.   [222] ibid [218]; 321–322.
[223] See pp 150–152 of text.
[224] *Kruger v Commonwealth (Stolen Generation case)* [1997] HCA 27; (1996) 190 CLR 1.
[225] *DOGS* case (n 217).
[226] *Krygger v Williams* [1912] HCA 65; (1912) 15 CLR 366; *Adelaide Company of Jehovah's Witnesses Inc v Commonwealth* [1943] HCA 12; (1943) 67 CLR 116.
[227] *Davies and Jones v Western Australia* [1904] HCA 46; (1904) 2 CLR 29.
[228] *Lee Fay v Vincent* [1908] HCA 70; (1908) 7 CLR 389.
[229] *Henry v Boehm* [1973] HCA 32; (1973) 128 CLR 482.

provision, but upon the actual language of the section itself.'[230] In *Street v Queensland Bar Association* (1988)[231], the Court breathed new life into s 117, by holding that discrimination would henceforth be understood in a substantive rather than a formal sense.

As we have seen, in *Pearson's* case (1983) s 41 was interpreted purposively, not literally, but the result yet again was to narrow the scope of the guarantee—in that case, to vanishing point. As one commentator observed:

In the case of section 80, the superficial meaning of the words 'trial on indictment' was permitted to prevail over the achievement of a substantive guarantee of rights. In the case of section 41, the achievement of a substantive guarantee of rights was defeated not by insistence on but by repudiation of the superficial meaning of the words. Is there some animus against constitutionally entrenched rights?[232]

On the other hand, the Court has favoured broad interpretations of constitutional limitations that protect the practice of medicine from 'civil conscription', private property from compulsory acquisition, and interstate trade and commerce from interference of an unspecified kind.[233] This might lead one to suspect that the Court, before 1988, systematically favoured the rights of upper-middle-class professionals, property owners, and businesses. But that would be unfair.

While the judges' social backgrounds have undoubtedly influenced their attitudes toward rights, their particular brand of legalism has probably had a greater influence. The most important civil liberties case in Australia's history was decided in favour of unpopular Communists at the height of the Cold War, by the application of orthodox legal principles. In 1950, Parliament enacted draconian legislation that proscribed the Communist Party and affiliated organisations, confiscated their property without compensation, and excluded persons deemed dangerous to national security from certain kinds of employment in government and industry. The legislation also violated some traditional elements of due process, such as by reversing the onus of proof, and restricting judicial review of government decision-making. It had been central to the platform on which the government had been enacted in December 1949, and was generally supported by the newspapers and, according to an opinion poll, 80 per cent of the electorate.[234]

The Court, by a majority of six to one, held the legislation invalid on standard characterization, rather than civil liberties, grounds. The validity of the legislation depended on whether it was a law with respect to defence. The Court said that this was a question that only it could authoritatively decide. This was fundamental to judicial review under a written constitution, and the underlying principle of the rule of law. Parliament could not authoritatively declare that its own legislation was a valid law with respect to defence. But this is what Parliament, in effect, had

---

[230] ibid 495.   [231] [1988] HCA 37; (1989) 168 CLR 461.
[232] Coper (n 161) 313.   [233] ss 51 (23A), 51(31), and 92 respectively.
[234] This account is based on G Winterton 'The *Communist Party* Case' in *Australian Constitutional Landmarks* (n 91) 108.

attempted to do. The legislation commenced with a lengthy preamble that purported to justify itself by describing the subversive aims and activities of the Communists, and asserting that its provisions were necessary for the security and defence of the nation. This was analogous to a Bill of Attainder that simply declares a person to be guilty of an offence, and imposes punishment on him, without any proof being provided to a court.

Strictly speaking, the *Communist Party* case involved the characterisation of legislation as exceeding a power, rather than the enforcement of a limitation on power. But the majority was clearly influenced by civil liberties concerns, and the importance of maintaining the rule of law.[235] It was able to protect the rights of an unpopular minority through orthodox legalism.

For unelected judges to invalidate legislation enacted unanimously, and for which the government had a clear electoral 'mandate', would itself demonstrate judicial independence of a high order. To do so at a time of national hysteria against an 'enemy' . . . whose supposed overseas allies were fighting and killing Australian troops [in Korea], is surely a remarkable, virtually unique, achievement.[236]

Changes Over Time: Recent Debates

It is generally agreed that in the late 1980s, the Court took a new direction, adopting a more purposive and even creative approach in constitutional and other cases. In extra-judicial speeches, some members of the Court expressed the view that it had been too formalistic in the past. They advocated a more purposive approach to constitutional interpretation, and a more frank disclosure of the policy grounds that inevitably influence decisions.[237]

It became apparent that Australian judges were increasingly influenced by the global trend of expanding judicial power to protect rights, either by the adoption of bills of rights, or by creative interpretation of their existing powers. Previously, Australian judges had tended to express scepticism about the desirability of a bill of rights, partly because they did not feel well qualified to make the inherently political judgments that it would require of them.[238] But the balance of judicial opinion began to shift. An increasing number of judges appeared to be losing faith in parliamentary supremacy, partly because of the extent to which parliaments seemed to be dominated by executive governments.[239] These judges seemed less content with their subordinate, and generally passive, role in protecting rights.

The new emphasis on purposive interpretation inspired the broader interpretation of s 117, which prohibits the states from discriminating against residents of other

---

[235] *Australian Constitutional Landmarks* (n 91) 132.   [236] ibid.

[237] eg Sir A Mason 'The Role of a Constitutional Court in a Federation: A Comparison of the Australian and the United States Experience' (1986) 16 Federal L Rev 1.

[238] eg Barwick (n 49) 24.

[239] HP Lee 'The Implied Freedom of Political Communication' in *Australian Constitutional Landmarks* (n 91) 391.

states, adopted in *Street's* case.[240] It also contributed to the revolution in the interpretation of s 92 in *Cole v Whitfield*, where the Court for the first time officially permitted recourse to the Convention Debates.[241]

Implied rights

In another landmark decision, the Court in 1992 purported to discover in the Constitution an implied freedom of political communication.[242] The judges disagreed as to its basis. Some held that it was implied by a few specific provisions requiring that members of Parliament be 'directly chosen by the people'. Others argued that it was implicit in the principle of representative democracy, which underlies numerous provisions dealing with Parliament, the executive, and constitutional amendment. Some judges also suggested that, with Australian independence from the United Kingdom, the Constitution had come to rest on the sovereignty of the people, an even deeper principle than that of representative democracy.

The judges held that the people would be unable to make a genuine electoral choice, or that true representative government or popular sovereignty would be impossible, in the absence of freedom of political communication. The freedom was therefore a necessary implication in that it was practically necessary for the Constitution to achieve some of its most fundamental purposes. On these grounds, the Court invalidated legislation that prohibited political advertising on radio and television stations during election campaigns, and in lieu thereof, required stations to provide free time for the broadcast of political messages.[243] The declared purposes of the legislation were to reduce the dependence of politicians on the donors of the vast funds needed for political advertising, with its associated risks of undue influence or even corruption; to reduce inequality, due solely to variable economic resources, in the ability of citizens to influence public opinion; and to improve the quality of public political debate.

In a subsequent case, *Theophanous v Herald and Weekly Times Ltd*, the Court held that the common law of defamation was inconsistent with the implied freedom of political communication, because it had a 'chilling effect' on investigative journalism and public criticism of political figures.[244] The Court was influenced by American cases such as *New York Times v Sullivan*,[245] although it created a less sweeping constitutional defence to defamation actions.

These decisions gave rise to the hope, or fear, that the Court would go much further, and find other rights implicit in the principles of representative democracy or popular sovereignty. One of the more activist judges said in a speech that the

---

[240] Discussed text to n 231.   [241] (n 145) 402.

[242] *Australian Capital Television v Commonthwealth (ACTV)* [1992] HCA 1; (1992) 177 CLR 106; *Nationwide News* (n 204).

[243] The legislation did not affect the discussion of political issues on news, current affairs, or talk-back programs, or political advertising in the other mass media.

[244] [1994] HCA 46; (1994) 182 CLR 104.   [245] 376 US 254; 84 S Ct 710 (1964).

gradual development of an implied bill of rights was a possibility,[246] and in *Leeth v Commonwealth*, he and another judge held that the Constitution contained an implied right to equality.[247] A new era of bold judicial creativity was widely anticipated.[248]

These developments provoked a vigorous theoretical and critical commentary. In addition, they aroused heated disagreement within the Court itself, between those who derived the implied freedom of political communication from specific provisions, and those who derived it from broader principles. In the *Theophanous* case, McHugh J, in dissent, objected that judges who treated the principle of representative democracy as if it were part of the Constitution independently of specific provisions, 'unintentionally depart from the method of constitutional interpretation that has existed in this country since the time of the *Engineers' Case*.'[249] Another dissenter, Dawson J, insisted that implications must be 'necessary or obvious having regard to the express provisions of the Constitution itself. To draw an implication from extrinsic sources . . . would be to take a giant leap away from the *Engineers' Case*, guided only by personal preconceptions of what the Constitution should, rather than does, contain.'[250]

In the *McGinty* case (1996), it was argued that either the words 'directly chosen by the people', or the principle of representative democracy, required that Commonwealth elections conform to the principle of 'one vote, one value', and therefore that the number of voters in electorates be as equal as possible. But the composition of the Court had changed, and those who had dissented in the *Theophanous* case found themselves in the majority. McHugh J repeated his complaint that representative democracy should not be treated as an independent or 'free-standing' constitutional principle,[251] and added that insofar as they so treated it, the previous decisions were 'fundamentally wrong and . . . an alteration of the Constitution without the authority of the people under s 128'.[252] One of the new judges, Gummow J, agreed that the earlier cases were inconsistent with orthodox interpretive principles and should be reconsidered.[253]

The *McGinty* case also raised questions about the relevance of the framers' intentions. The majority rejected the claim that the Constitution guarantees the principle of 'one vote, one value', largely on the ground that the principle was not widely recognised in 1900.[254] McHugh J reiterated the familiar principle that the Constitution should be interpreted as a statute, 'according to the ordinary and natural meaning of its text, read in the light of its history.'[255] Justice Toohey, in dissent, insisted that democracy is a 'dynamic phenomenon' that 'cannot be frozen by reference to the year 1900': '[t]he Constitution must be construed as a living

---

[246] Justice J Toohey 'Government of Laws, and Not of Men?' 4 (1993) Public L Rev 158, 170.
[247] [1992] HCA 29; (1991) 174 CLR 455.
[248] Doyle (n 163) 15; The Hon Mr Justice M Kirby 'Courts and Policy: The Exciting Australian Scene' (1993) 19 Commonwealth L Bulletin 1794.   [249] *Theophanous* case (n 244) 202.
[250] ibid 194.   [251] *McGinty* case (n 113) 232.   [252] ibid 235–35.
[253] ibid 289.   [254] ibid.   [255] ibid 230.

force and the court must take account of political, social and economic developments since that time.'[256] Gummow J replied that legislation was the intended and proper means by which the system of representative government should be kept in tune with contemporary values, the Constitution in this respect being explicitly based on trust in Parliament.[257]

The *McGinty* case suggested that a majority of the Court was unwilling to develop implied rights in the creative fashion that many had hoped for, and others had feared. The judges then attempted to resolve their interpretive disagreements. In the *Lange* case (1997) they delivered a unanimous judgment, which was a remarkable achievement, given their previous passionate disagreements. The implied freedom of political communication was held to be based on 'the text and structure of the Constitution', rather than on representative democracy as an independent principle.[258] This appeared to concede the main objection of McHugh and Dawson JJ. But they, too, were required to compromise. McHugh J had previously insisted that the implied freedom operated only during federal election campaigns, but this was rejected in the *Lange* case. As for Dawson J, he had not previously conceded that there was an implied freedom of political communication at all. The decision left the implied freedom intact, but by rejecting the broader of the two grounds on which it had previously been based, appeared to reduce the likelihood that further implied rights would be recognised. In the *Kruger* case (1997), a majority rejected the previously suggested implied right to equality, but left open the possibility of an implied freedom of movement and association.[259]

Doubts remain about the consistency of the implied freedom of political communication with interpretive orthodoxy. Its recognition made a substantial change to Australia's system of government, which to many, seemed more like a constitutional amendment than the discovery of a genuine implication. It signified a change in judicial approach to implications. When the very activist Justice Murphy suggested, in 1986, that the Constitution included an implied right to free speech, his brethren treated the suggestion with disdain.[260] In 1975, Barwick CJ said

It is very noticeable that no Bill of Rights is attached to the Constitution of Australia and that there are few guarantees . . . .[U]nlike the case of the American Constitution, the Australian Constitution is built upon confidence in a system of parliamentary Government with ministerial responsibility. The contrast in constitutional approach is that, in the case of the American Constitution, restriction on legislative power is sought and readily implied whereas, where confidence in the parliament prevails, express words are regarded as necessary to warrant a limitation of otherwise plenary powers.[261]

[256] ibid 200; see also 216. Gaudron J agreed, ibid 222.
[257] ibid 280–81 and 284.
[258] *Lange v Australian Broadcasting Corporation* [1997] HCA 25; (1987) 189 CLR 520.
[259] *Kruger* case (n 224).
[260] *Miller v TCN Channel Nine Pty Ltd* [1986] HCA 60; (1986) 161 CLR 556, 569 (Gibbs CJ), 579 (Mason J), 636 (Dawson J).   [261] *McKinlay's* case (n 153) 23–24.

By deciding against a bill of rights, the framers entrusted to parliaments, not courts, the responsibility for striking the necessary balances between competing rights, and between rights and other community interests, balances that require political rather than legal judgment. The implied freedom had escaped the notice of Australian lawyers and judges (other than Murphy J) for the previous ninety years, despite cases such as *Communist Party* (1950) in which it might have proved decisive.[262] Moreover, this in itself suggests that the implied freedom is not necessary, either for the existence of representative government, or for the people to make genuine electoral choices. The fact is that Australia had such a government, and the people were able to make such choices, throughout those ninety years. It would undoubtedly be legitimate for the Court, in enforcing express provisions requiring that the people directly choose their representatives, to invalidate legislation restricting political communication so severely that it prevents them from doing so. But the Court has gone one step further, and derived from those provisions an implied freedom that it then applies largely independently of them, invalidating laws deemed to infringe the freedom whether or not they prevent genuine electoral choices.[263] In other words, the implied freedom is vulnerable to the same kind of objection that McHugh J raised, to representative democracy being treated as a free-standing principle, independent of the constitutional provisions from which it is inferred, and which give it only partial effect.[264]

Separation of powers

One free-standing implied principle that the Court has enthusiastically enforced is that of the separation of powers, or at least, the separation of judicial power. It has always been zealous in protecting the exclusivity and independent exercise of federal judicial power. We previously saw how the Court undermined the Interstate Commission, by holding that it could not be vested with judicial power, contrary to both the Constitution's plain words and the framers' intentions. This is the area in which judges have most frequently succumbed to the temptation to stray beyond the limits of orthodox *Engineers'* legalism, and engage in 'doctrinal basket weaving'.[265] It is the most likely launching pad for future judicial activism in the cause of protecting rights.

The principle of separation of powers was recently held to prohibit the appointment of federal judges, as individuals rather than in their official capacity

---

[262] *Australian Communist Party* (n 28).

[263] For example, neither the political advertising legislation invalidated in *ACTV* (n 242), nor the common law of defamation overridden in *Theophanous* (n 244), could seriously be argued to have made it impossible for the people to make genuine electoral choices, whether or not they infringed free speech to some extent (which is debatable).

[264] On the other hand, the Court after *Lange* (n 258) is likely to require a closer connection between the political communication in question, and Commonwealth (as opposed to state) governmental and electoral decision-making.

[265] L Zines 'The Present State of Constitutional Interpretation' in *The High Court at the Crossroads: essays in Constitutional Law* (n 186) 231.

as judges, to part-time or temporary positions involving the exercise of non-judicial powers that might jeopardise their reputation for strict judicial independence. This was an issue previously left to the discretion of the judges.[266]

In *Kable v Director of Public Prosecutions for NSW*, the Court stretched the principle of the separation of federal judicial power far beyond the provisions from which it was originally inferred.[267] These concern federal jurisdiction only. They allow Parliament to vest state courts with federal jurisdiction, but say nothing about their exercise of state jurisdiction. Nevertheless, the Court held that no state court vested with federal jurisdiction may exercise, even in cases of state jurisdiction, any non-judicial power that might jeopardise its reputation for independence from the political branches of the state government. This was supposedly because damage to that reputation might also taint its exercise of federal jurisdiction. The decision was inconsistent with previous authority holding that, although Parliament may choose to vest federal jurisdiction in a state court, it cannot interfere with that court's existing constitution and character: it must accept the court 'as it is'. Since Parliament may choose not to vest federal jurisdiction in state courts, and state governments cannot interfere with its exercise anyway, it is difficult to argue that the implication found in the *Kable* case is 'necessary' to protect its independent exercise, and the majority judgements did not seriously attempt to make such an argument. This was particularly surprising given that McHugh J, the stern critic of 'free-standing principles' abstracted from specific provisions, was a member of the majority.

It has been accepted in many recent judgments that certain procedural principles, of impartiality and procedural fairness, are essential to the exercise of judicial power.[268] In other words, the separation of judicial and non-judicial powers implicitly guarantees some degree of 'procedural due process' in the exercise of federal judicial power. Future cases are certain to develop this idea, which 'allows much discretion for the court to determine what common law rules of procedure, pleading and evidence are so fundamental that to abolish or alter them would amount to the court trying cases by reference to methods that are not judicial.'[269]

The idea might even be expanded to require some kinds of 'substantive due process'.[270] That possibility was raised in *Polyukhovich v Commonwealth* (1991), in which the Court evenly divided over whether or not a retrospective criminal law violates the independent exercise of judicial power.[271] Several judges held that it does, on the ground that it requires courts to find that the law at some previous

---

[266] *Wilson v Minister for Aboriginal and Torres Strait Islander Affairs* [1996] HCA 18; (1996) 189 CLR 1.   [267] [1996] HCA 24; (1996) 189 CLR 51.

[268] F Wheeler 'Federal Judges as Holder of Non-judicial Office' in *The Australian Federal Judicial System* (n 36) 442.

[269] L Zines 'Judicial Activism and the Rule of Law in Australia' in T Campbell and J Goldsworthy *Judicial Power, Democracy and Legal Positivism* (Ashgate Dartmouth, Aldershot, 2000) 394.

[270] G Winterton, 'The Separation of Judicial Power as an Implied Bill of Rights', in G Lindell (ed) *Future Directions in Australian Constitutional Law* (Federation Press, Sydney, 1994) 185.

[271] [1991] HCA 32; (1991) 172 CLR 501.

time was something other than it was in reality. This is contrary to the established principle, which these judges did not reject, that in general, the plenary nature of Parliament's legislative powers enables it to legislate retrospectively. If that is so, then it makes little sense to say that retrospective legislation requires the courts to decide contrary to what the law was in reality, because the legislation determines the legal reality. These judges declined, illogically, to extend their reasoning to retrospective civil laws, which affect the judicial function in exactly the same way. This makes it clear that their real concern was not the judicial function as such, but individual rights. But the question remains unresolved.

Original meaning and framers' intent

A major issue that has aroused spirited debate on the Bench in many recent cases is the continued relevance of the Constitution's original meaning, and the framers' intentions. McHugh J has strongly defended the Court's traditional, moderately 'originalist' position, while Kirby J has advocated a radically 'non-originalist' one. In the most recent case dealing with the question, the other five judges—Gleeson and Callinan JJ most forcefully—sided with McHugh J.[272]

As previously observed, the Court has often insisted that until they are changed by amendment, the Constitution's words continue to mean what they meant in 1900, although their application or 'denotation' can change. It has also frequently taken into account the state of the law, and general historical facts at the time the Constitution was created, to illuminate the original meanings, and purposes, of constitutional expressions.[273]

Until the mid-1990s, these interpretive methods were seldom questioned.[274] Deane and Toohey JJ then began to refer to the Constitution as a 'living instrument' or 'living force', which should not be constrained by the dead hands of the framers.[275] Since then, Kirby J has mounted a sustained attack on the principle that the contemporary meaning of the Constitution is the same as its original meaning, and partly dependent on the framers' intentions or purposes.[276] According to him, its original meaning, and the framers' intentions, are of little relevance.[277] '[T]he *Constitution* is to be read according to contemporary understandings of its meaning, to meet, so far as the text allows, the governmental needs of the Australian people.'[278]

---

[272] *Singh v Commonwealth* (n 148).
[273] For many examples and other references, see Goldsworthy (n 136) 12–18. See also *Singh v Commonwealth* (n 148) [12–27] per Gleeson CJ, [49–55] per McHugh J, [159] per Gummow, Hayne and Heydon JJ, and [293–296] per Callinan J.
[274] One exception was Windeyer J: see *Victoria v Commonwealth* (n 8), and Windeyer (n 8) 36–38.
[275] Goldsworthy (n 136) 16–17.
[276] eg *Re Wakim* (n 170) [186]–[187]; 599–600; *Re Colina* (n 219) [96]–[99]; 422–425; *Grain Pool* (n 204) [90]; 515; The Hon Justice M Kirby 'Constitutional Interpretation and Original Intent: A Form of Ancestor Worship?' Melbourne U L Rev 24 (2000) 1.
[277] *Eastman v R* [2000] HCA 29 [241]; (2000) 203 CLR 1, 79. But in *Singh v Commonwealth* (n 148) at [248], Kirby J modified this stance, acknowledging that these matters are relevant but not determinative.   [278] ibid [242]; 80.

The other judges have resisted his arguments. According to Gummow J, 'it would be to pervert the purpose of the judicial power if, without recourse to the mechanism provided by s 128 and entrusted to the Parliament and the electors [constitutional amendment by referendum], the *Constitution* meant no more than what it appears to mean from time to time to successive judges'.[279] McHugh J has been the most forthright defender of orthodoxy, insisting that

the judiciary has no power to amend or modernise the *Constitution* to give effect to what the judges think is in the public interest. The function of the judiciary, including the func-tion of this Court, is to give effect to the intention of the makers of the *Constitution* as evinced by the terms in which they expressed that intention. That necessarily means that decisions, taken almost a century ago by people long dead, bind the people of Australia today even in cases where most people agree that those decisions are out of touch with the present needs of Australian society . . . .Change to the terms and structure of the Constitution can be carried out only with the approval of the people in accordance with the procedures laid down in s 128 of the *Constitution*.[280]

Kirby J rightly insists that the words of the Constitution must often be applied in ways that the framers could not have anticipated. Moreover, he has challenged the soundness of the thesis that the meaning or 'connotation' of those words cannot change, but their application or 'denotation' can. As previously noted, the distinction does help explain many High Court decisions.[281] But in other cases it is far from straightforward. It is tempting to think that a word's 'connotation' can be expressed by a list of criteria that are necessary and sufficient for the word to be correctly applied.[282] But many words cannot in principle be defined so precisely. Moreover, unexpected developments can change our understanding of what we mean by a word, revealing that a characteristic previously associated with it was never really essential (as when the discovery of black swans showed that swans need not be white). Therefore, when a word enacted in 1900 must be applied, many decades later, to circumstances not envisaged by the framers, it is often difficult if not impossible to know what criteria they themselves—if they had envisaged those circumstances—would have regarded as essential for its correct application.[283]

McHugh J has suggested that connotations should usually be regarded as very general concepts, which do not change, rather than particular conceptions of those concepts, which can change.[284] This may be merely another way of expressing the well-established principle that, unless the context suggests otherwise, the Court should favour broad rather than narrow meanings. The problem of how to

[280] *Re Wakim* (n 170) [35]–[39]; 549–50. See also *Singh v Commonwealth* (n 148), [6] per Gleeson CJ and [295] per Callinan J.   [281] Text following n 119.
[282] In examining contemporary legislation to illuminate the intended meaning of a subject-matter, the Court had to separate the 'essential' meaning of the term from mere 'incidentals'.
[283] L Zines 'Characterisation of Commonwealth Laws' in *Australian Constitutional Perspectives* (n 193) 35.
[284] *Re Wakim* (1999) 198 CLR 511, 552; see also *Eastman v R* (2000) 172 ALR 39, 72–3.

identify the general concepts remains. The solution seems to lie in the framers' apparent purpose in using the word in question. For example, in deciding whether or not modern reforms to the jury system are consistent with the constitutional requirement of 'trial . . . by jury', the majority has recognised that although the requirement 'is referable to that institution as understood at common law at the time of federation', its 'essential features are to be discerned with regard to the purpose which [it] was intended to serve'.[285] The word 'jury', a philosopher might say, is a 'functional term'.[286]

In examining the current meaning of the term 'patents of invention', Kirby J also sought its 'essential characteristics',[287] which are 'universally attach[ed] to the idea in all circumstances' and therefore 'more fundamental and enduring' than the particular characteristics associated with it in 1900.[288] These words suggest that the term's essential characteristics cannot have changed since 1900, but he denied this by asserting that they 'may grow and expand, or may contract over time.'[289] In discussing the requirement of jury trial he, like the majority, adopted a 'functional approach' aimed at identifying the 'essential characteristics' of the term. But again, he said that the function of the jury is not determined historically, but by reference to 'the way in which that institution had evolved and operates for constitutional purposes . . . today.'[290] Most recently, he has referred to 'the unchanging, essential elements of the word "aliens".'[291] These remarks leave the method of identifying 'essential characteristics' obscure. Gleeson CJ and McHugh J replied tellingly that Kirby J's approach should make it difficult to invalidate recently enacted legislation, which is more likely to reflect contemporary standards and understandings than the opinions of any judge. If contemporary standards expressed in current legislation are to be held inconsistent with constitutional requirements, the latter must enshrine more permanent objectives and values.[292]

A majority of the Court is likely to maintain its moderately originalist methodology, which attempts to reconcile permanence with adaptability to changed circumstances by taking a purposive approach, and construing the Constitution's words in broad, general terms consistent with original understandings.

The Balance Between Legitimate and Illegitimate Creativity

On his appointment as Chief Justice, Sir Owen Dixon famously asserted that the only safe guide to judicial decisions in constitutional cases is 'a strict and complete

---

[285] *Ng v R* [2003] HCA 20 [9]. See also *Brownlee v R* (n 151) [54]; 298 (Gaudron, Gummow and Hayne JJ).
[286] M Moore 'Law as a Functional Kind', in R George *Natural Law Theory, Contemporary Essays* (Clarendon Press, Oxford, 1992) 188 esp 206–8.
[287] *Grain Pool* case (n 204) [103]; 519; [123]; 527–8; [135]–[136]; 532–33.
[288] ibid [129]; 530 and [123]; 527 respectively.   [289] ibid [129]; 530
[290] *Brownlee v R* (n 151) [145]; 329.   [291] *Singh v Commonwealth* (n 148), [253].
[292] *Brownlee v R* (n 151) [4]–[6]; 284 and [11]–[12]; 286. See also *Singh v Commonwealth* (n 148) [5] per Gleeson CJ.

legalism'.[293] By 'complete', he presumably meant that legal argument should be completely exhausted before judges resort to policy considerations, rather than that legal argument can resolve every case completely, without any need for policy. He previously said that, compared with problems that arise under a Bill of Rights, questions concerning the federal demarcation of powers 'lend themselves, if not entirely, at least in a higher degree, to a purely legal treatment.'[294]

Dixon's insistence on strict legalism is one of many, almost ritual, judicial declarations that the judges' duty is to interpret and apply the Constitution as it stands, rather than change it according to their own political philosophies.[295] But not even the most legalist judges accepted the 'slot machine' theory of judicial decision-making. For example, Justice Kitto acknowledged that the Constitution 'lays down broad lines for application by courts and therefore by logical and imaginative judicial reasoning. As an inevitable consequence, cleavages of opinion will appear from time to time, for men's minds are not made to a pattern'.[296] Justice Menzies acknowledged that the language of the Constitution could leave two courses open to the Court, the choice between them depending on a practical assessment of good governance.[297]

The judges have not generally denied the existence of judicial choice.[298] What they have emphatically denied is that they do or should act 'pragmatically', by balancing legal considerations against, and sometimes finding them outweighed by, considerations of justice or public policy. In one case, when counsel asked the Court to take commercial realities into account, he received the reply: 'Not in disregard of legal realities.'[299] As Justice Wilson later observed, when discussing the concept of excise taxation, 'one is not justified . . . in looking beyond the Constitution in order to mould the concept to fit subjective understandings of desirable contemporary economic or political goals'.[300]

Until the early 1990s, the Court's decision-making was widely thought to justify the reputation for strict legalism that it cultivated. Its traditional methodology has

---

[293] 'Upon Taking the Oath of Office as Chief Justice' in Dixon (n 52) 247.

[294] 'Two Constitutions Compared' in Dixon (n 52) 104. See also 'Concerning Judicial Method' in Dixon (n 52) 156–157.

[295] *R v Barger* (n 115) 64; *Brewery Employees Union of NSW* (n 83) 500, 559; *Federated Sawmill* (n 77) 492, 539–40; *Australian Boot Trade Employes Federation v Whybrow & Co.* [1910] HCA 8; (1910) 10 CLR 266, 280. See also Latham CJ, quoted by Zines (n 138) 427.

[296] *Western Australia v Hammersley Iron Pty Ltd (No. 1)* [1969] HCA 42; (1969) 120 CLR 74, 84.

[297] Sir D Menzies 'Australia and the Judicial Committee of the Privy Council' (1968) 42 Australian L J 79, 86.

[298] Barwick CJ may have been an exception: he said that '[i]n deciding, the Court educes what was always present, though perhaps latent, in the constitutional text': 'Foreword' to Lane (n 119) viii. See also Sir G Barwick 'Book Review' (1981) 4 U NSW L Rev 131, 134.

[299] Lane (n 136) 1185 n 39 (quoting transcript of argument in *Beal v Marrickville Margarine* [1966] HCA 9; (1966) 114 CLR 283.).

[300] *Gosford Meats Pty Ltd v New South Wales* [1985] HCA 5; (1984) 155 CLR 368, 402. See also *Western Australia v Commonwealth* [1975] HCA 46; (1975) 134 CLR 201, 249 (Gibbs J): 'the function of this Court is to consider not what the Constitution might best provide but what, upon its proper construction, it does provide.' See also *McKinlay's* case (n 153) 43–44 (Gibbs J), and V Windeyer (n 8) 3.

been described as 'literalistic' and 'positivistic', but 'legalistic' is more accurate.[301] The judges never claimed to be able to resolve constitutional uncertainties simply by consulting a dictionary. They were always willing to take into account considerations of history, purpose, and policy, both in disambiguating express provisions and in revealing implications. But they did so within a relatively narrow compass, severely restricting the admissibility of historical evidence of original meaning and purpose, and insisting both that non-textual considerations must help to illuminate, or at least be consistent with, the meaning of the text, and that any implications must be 'necessary' to fulfil its intended purposes.

In particular, the Court generally resisted any temptation to abstract general principles from, and apply them independently of, express provisions. Menzies J once replied to criticism that the Court had cramped the development of constitutional law by giving insufficient weight to changing economic, social and political ideas. His words would have been endorsed by most of the judges who have served on the Court.

It is true, of course, that neither the Privy Council nor the High Court has been filled with crusading zeal and each has emphasized that its role is to decide cases according to the Constitution as it stands and to develop the law step by step rather than seize every opportunity of enunciating some pregnant generality which will set the law upon a new course depending on the current winds of economic, social and political thought. It is likely, however, that the decision of cases upon what may seem to have been narrow grounds has provided the stability which the bolder spirits of the Supreme Court of the United States have failed to achieve . . . For my own part I do not believe that judges, in the exercise of their judicial power, have any need to play the part of legislators, and when they do, the result is often unfortunate.[302]

Brennan J recently described the balance that must be struck between fidelity and change in constitutional interpretation in a passage that accurately summarises the Court's traditional stance:

[I]t is clear that judicial development of the common law is a function different from judicial interpretation of statutes and of the *Constitution*. . . . The Court, owing its existence and its jurisdiction ultimately to the *Constitution*, can do no more than interpret and apply its text, uncovering implications where they exist. The Court has no jurisdiction to fill in what might be thought to be lacunae left by the *Constitution*. . . . Under the Constitution, this Court does not have nor can it be given nor, a fortiori, can it assume a power to attribute to the Constitution an operation which is not required by its text construed in the light of its history, the common law and the circumstances or subject matter to which the text applies. The notion of "developing" the law of the *Constitution* is inconsistent with

---

[301] G Craven 'The Crisis of Constitutional Literalism in Australia' in *Australian Constitutional Perspectives* (n 193), E McWhinney *Judicial Review in the English-Speaking World* (2nd edn., University of Toronto Press, USA, 1960) ch 5; G Evans 'The High Court and the Constitution in a Changing Society' in AD Hambly and JL Goldring (eds) *Australian Lawyers and Social Change* (The Law Book Co Ltd, Sydney, 1976); Lane (n 136) 1177–79, 1196.

[302] Sir D Menzies 'Australia and the Judicial Committee of the Privy Council' (1968) 42 Australian L J 79, 81.

the judicial power it confers. Clearly the Court cannot change the *Constitution*, nor can it convert constitutional silence into a legal rule with constitutional force. I do not mean that, in changing conditions, the *Constitution* does not have a changing effect, that the denotation of its terms does not change, that the course of judicial interpretation does not reveal that a past constitutional doctrine is untenable or that new situations do not reveal new doctrines inherent in the constitutional text. The *Constitution* speaks continually to the present and it operates in and upon contemporary conditions.[303]

Institutional and Cultural Factors

The Court's legalism is rooted in British legal traditions imbibed by Australian lawyers educated in the late 19th and early 20th centuries. As Atiyah and Summers have shown, these traditions are much more formal than those of the United States. British lawyers have traditionally preferred rules to principles, formal to substantive reasoning, and 'interpretive formality' that gives more weight to plain meaning than to purpose. British courts have played a much narrower law-making role than American ones. All this is reflected in the predominant positivism of British legal theory, compared with the natural law and instrumentalist thinking that has been more influential in America.[304] These tendencies were at their height in the late nineteenth century. The importance of legal education is confirmed by evidence that the Court's change of direction in the late 1980s was partly due to several of its members having been exposed to more pragmatic, consequentialist legal theories at Sydney University in the 1950s.[305]

While the Constitution's federal elements were based extensively on the American model, it does not include a Bill of Rights. Its few express guarantees of rights do not include such broad, vague phrases as 'due process' or 'equal protection', whose interpretation is widely thought to have contributed to the more substantive and evaluative reasoning of American judges. This made it easier for the Court to assume that British principles of statutory interpretation could be applied to the interpretation of the Constitution. It was, after all, enacted in a British statute, even though it was also held to express the will of the Australian people.

British legal traditions were regarded with particular veneration in the conservative Bars of Sydney and Melbourne, where most members of the Court practiced before accepting judicial appointment. Moreover, the Court has appellate jurisdiction from state and federal courts in all fields of law, private as well as public. Both the barristers appearing before them, and the judges themselves, were naturally inclined to apply the same methods of analysis in all these fields.

[303] *Theophanous* case (n 244) 143–44.
[304] PS Atiyah and RS Summers *Form and Substance in Anglo-American Law* (Clarendon Press, Oxford, 1987), summarised at 408–15.
[305] H Patapan *Judging Democracy* (Cambridge University Press, Cambridge, 2000) 20–22.

Judicial review was in tension with one fundamental element of the British constitutional tradition: the doctrine of parliamentary sovereignty. But it was required by another equally fundamental element: the rule of law.[306] The Court had to strike a balance between these two basal principles. It has rarely shown reluctance to review or invalidate the acts of the other branches of government. Indeed, it has confidently proclaimed its duty to do so as the appointed guardian of the Constitution.[307] On the other hand, it has also frequently acknowledged that, subject only to constitutional limits, the powers of Australian parliaments are as ample and plenary as those of the United Kingdom Parliament. The balance struck between the rule of law, and parliamentary sovereignty, depended on distinguishing legal from political considerations, the former being the domain of the courts, and the latter of parliaments. In interpreting constitutional limits to legislative authority, the Court therefore attempted to minimise the need to make controversial judgments of political morality or policy. As an American observer observed, if a court believes that matching legislation to heads of power is 'a problem of strict legal characterization entailing no value judgments or appeals to general principles of government or policy, then there is no occasion for a self-conscious and halting undertaking of the Court's function.'[308]

The Court's legalism has enabled central power to steadily expand, without hindrance from implied limits based on the framers' unexpressed assumptions about the proper balance of power between the Commonwealth and the states. Some critics allege that legalism was motivated partly by a majority of judges positively favouring expansive Commonwealth power.[309] It has also been suggested that this was not entirely accidental, given that the judges are appointed by the Commonwealth.[310] At the very least, the judges must have been influenced by intellectual fashions that have increasingly favoured the exercise of national rather than state authority as the solution to social problems.[311] There may be some truth in this. In 1971, Windeyer J speculated that the decision in the *Engineers' Case* was based partly on 'a growing realization that Australians were now one people and Australia one country and that national laws might meet national needs.'[312] And in 1995, a recently retired Chief Justice admitted that this sentiment 'unquestionably played a part' in the adoption of a broad interpretation of the external affairs power.[313] It is worth noting that Australia is a much more

[306] AV Dicey *Introduction to the Study of the Law of the Constitution* (10th edn., MacMillan & Co Ltd, London, 1964) 184.   [307] eg *PMA* case (n 172) 117–18 (Barwick CJ) 181–82 (Mason J).
[308] Kadish (n 33) 19.
[309] G Craven 'The Crisis of Constitutional Literalism in Australia' in *Australian Constitutional Perspectives* (n 193) 7; but see Barwick's emphatic denial of this in his 'Foreword' Lane (n 119) vii-viii.
[310] LJM Cooray and S Ratnapala 'The High Court and the Constitution—Literalism and Beyond' in G Craven (ed) *Official Record of the Debates of the Australian Federal Constitution* (Legal Books, Sydney, 1986) vol 6, 208; Coper (n 161) 116.
[311] G Craven 'The Crisis of Constitutional Literalism in Australia' in *Australian Constitutional Perspectives* (n 301) 8.   [312] *Victoria v Commonwealth* (n 8) 396.
[313] Mason (n 199) 243.

culturally homogeneous federation than either Canada or the United States. That might partly explain the failure of the Senate to function as a genuine states' house, despite the states being equally represented in it, as well as the Court's lack of sympathy (since 1920) for 'states rights' arguments.

Politicians and the general public have generally, at least until recently, accepted the Court's decisions with equanimity. Although the Court has at different times invalidated cherished legislation of all the major political parties, the general pattern has been one of 'bold assertion followed by popular acceptance'.[314] Rather than attacking the Court, politicians unhappy with its decisions have sometimes attempted to amend the Constitution, although rarely with success.[315] It has often been suggested that this acquiescence is largely attributable to the Court's profession of strict, apolitical legalism.[316]

This may have been especially important because political debate in Australia has long been polarised by struggle between the conservative parties and the Labor Party. Labor has advocated democratic socialist policies, including the provision of generous social welfare, extensive regulation of business and the economy, and in the 1940s, government monopolies and the nationalisation of banking. This required centralised power, to implement planning and control on a national scale, which was often thwarted by the federal distribution of powers. It was also strenuously opposed by the conservative parties and business interests, who mounted many successful challenges to the validity of Labor's legislation. According to one political scientist, the Court operated in a more difficult political environment than its American counterpart, because Australia 'lacked the dominant liberal consensus that anchors the American constitution in the political culture of the nation . . . In Australia, in contrast to America, the constitution did not preside over political conflicts; rather it was itself one of the points of conflict.'[317] This comparison is debatable, given the ferocious clashes between political movements and constitutional doctrines in the United States in periods such as the 1930s. But the point remains that legalism has been defended by Australian judges, including two Chief Justices, explicitly on the ground that it offers the best way of maintaining the confidence of all parties in the judicial resolution of constitutional disputes.[318] The Court thereby avoided entanglement in the fiercely partisan debates that characterise Australian politics.

The hypothesis that the acquiescence of politicians and their constituencies depends partly on their faith in the Court's apolitical legalism is corroborated by events in the 1990s, when it was subjected to criticism unprecedented in quantity

---

[314] SH Kadish 'Judicial Review in the High Court and the United States Supreme Court Part II' Melbourne U L Rev 2 (1959) 157; see also 156–57. On acquiescence of the ALP in the 1940s, see Galligan (n 26) 119, 144–46, 153. See also KH Bailey 'Fifty Years of the Australian Constitution' (1951) 25 Australian L J 314, 333.   [315] Kadish (n 314) 157–58.
[316] ibid 161; Galligan (n 26) passim.   [317] Galligan (n 26) 39–40.
[318] ibid 31, 40–41, quoting Dixon CJ and Barwick CJ.

and vehemence. This was provoked more by controversial common law decisions recognising native title to land, than by constitutional decisions. The
native title decisions in the *Mabo*[319] and *Wik*[320] cases were passionately opposed
by farmers, miners, and conservative politicians, who attacked the Court in
intemperate terms.[321] But the constitutional decisions that first recognised
an implied freedom of political communication were also subjected to severe
criticism—this time on the Labor rather than the conservative side of politics—
which may have been exacerbated by their being handed down shortly after
Mabo, when the Court was perceived by many to have embarked on a path of
judicial activism.[322] After *Wik*, the Deputy Prime Minister called for the
appointment of 'Capital C conservative' judges,[323] and indeed, the government
proceeded to fill a series of vacancies with judges believed to subscribe to more
traditional, legalistic methods. Shortly before his appointment, one of them
publicly accused the Court under Chief Justice Mason (1987–1995) of undermining the rule of law, by departing from the strict legalism of Sir Owen Dixon.[324]
Kirby J has since responded by portraying such criticism as a misguided and
dangerous attempt to revive the old 'fairy tale' that judges only declare, and
never make, law.[325]

The external political environment in which the Court operates has thus reinforced a legal culture and judicial ethos that already favoured legalism, and the
government has demonstrated its ability to use judicial appointments to 'correct'
a perceived departure from it.

Critical Evaluation

Not surprisingly, assessments of the Court's overall performance have varied.
While it has often been accused of excessive legalism, it has also been credited with
imparting some breadth and flexibility to the Constitution, at least with respect to
Commonwealth powers.[326]

Critics have objected to the Court's legalism for different reasons. Until the
1970s, notwithstanding the steady expansion of Commonwealth powers, it
was sometimes criticised for inhibiting an even greater expansion, assumed by

---

[319] *Mabo v Queensland (No 2)* (1992) 175 CLR 1.
[320] *Wik Peoples v Queensland* (1996) 187 CLR 1.   [321] Campbell and Lee (n 41) 58.
[322] For the criticisms, see HP Lee 'The Implied Freedom of Political Communication' in
Australian Constitutional Landmarks (n 91) 392.   [323] Campbell and Lee (n 41) 62.
[324] D Heydon 'Judicial Activism and the Death of the Rule of Law' (2003) 47 Quadrant 9.
[325] M Kirby 'Beyond the Judicial Fairy Tales' (2004) 48 Quadrant 26.
[326] On legalism, G Evans 'The High Court and the Constitution in a Changing Society' *Australian
Lawyers and Social Change* (n 301) especially 38; McWhinney (n 301); Lane (n 136) 1177–88; on flexibility, Lane (n 136) 1188–96; LF Crisp *Australian National Government* (5th edn., Longman,
Melbourne, 1983) 82; AR Blackshield 'The Courts and Judicial Review' in S Encel, D Horne and
E Thompson (eds) *Change the Rules!* (Penguin Books Ltd, Harmondsworth, 1977) 133, 137–38.

the critics to be in the national interest.[327] That complaint evaporated with the subsequent adoption of broad interpretations of the corporations, industrial relations, and external affairs powers. But for that very reason, more recent critics have made the opposite complaint, that the Court's legalism has severely eroded the powers and autonomy of the states, and thereby undermined the federal system itself.[328] In addition, human rights advocates have often objected to legalism for having stunted the few express provisions that protect rights, although they have been mollified by recent developments including the 'discovery' of the implied freedom of political communication.

This variety of complaints indicates that even if the Court had been less legalistic, it would still have had to choose between very different approaches, based on different understandings of the function of the Constitution and of judicial review. Its traditional style of legalism emphasised textual meaning, severely limited extraneous evidence of original intent, minimised implications, and downplayed the role of policy considerations. This can be contrasted with:

(a) a predominantly textual approach that is more open to extraneous evidence of the text's original meaning and purposes, and more candid about the need for judicial discretion on policy grounds when that evidence is indeterminate. The Court shifted to this approach in 1988, and is unlikely to reverse itself. The question is whether it will and should go further, and adopt one of the following approaches.

(b) a predominantly purposive approach that is more open to extraneous evidence of the framers' purposes, and more willing to give effect to them, if necessary by qualifying or supplementing the text. Champions of 'states rights' in effect advocate this approach, on the assumption that one of the framers' main objectives was to establish a national polity of strictly limited powers, with most domestic policy-making remaining in the hands of the states. They regret the decision in *Engineers'*, and favour the revival of something like the doctrine of reserved state powers.[329] But it is unlikely that the Court will move far in that direction, which would violate interpretive principles, and upset governmental arrangements, of long standing.

(c) a more creative approach, also less wedded to the text, which eschews both original meanings and original purposes in favour of what the judges take to be contemporary values and governmental needs. Using this method, anything that is necessary to fulfil these values and needs, and is consistent with the bare text, could possibly be 'implied'. Some advocates of greater national power have advocated a creative approach, no doubt because they realised that their cause

---

[327] G Evans 'The High Court and the Constitution in a Changing Society' *Australian Lawyers and Social Change* (n 301) 72; Sawer (n 29) 89.

[328] G Craven 'The High Court of Australia: a Study in the Abuse of Power' (1999) 22 U New South Wales L J 216; Cooray and Ratnapala (n 310); Walker (n 86).

[329] Cooray and Ratnapala (n 310); Walker (n 86).

would not be served by greater emphasis on the framers' purposes.[330] Human rights activists, who urge an expansive interpretation of express rights, and the 'discovery' of more implied rights, implicitly favour the same approach, because their agenda is also a modern one that finds little support in the framers' objectives.

The implied freedom of political speech, ostensibly justified on purposive grounds, is best justified on this basis, and in the early 1990s, some observers perceived the Court to be moving towards a more creative approach.[331] But that movement seems to have been halted, at least for the time being. Kirby J is the only judge to have unequivocally advocated a creative approach, and his brethren seem unlikely to join him. They are likely to remit demands for enhanced constitutional protection of rights to the political arena, where constitutional amendment properly belongs. They will probably persist with a predominantly textual approach that is more open to historical and purposive considerations, and more candid about the need for policy considerations to resolve stubborn ambiguities, which brings an element of legitimate creativity to their task. But no doubt they will occasionally succumb to temptation, and indulge in furtive creativity of a more radical kind, in order to invalidate legislation that egregiously violates their vision of justice or good government.[332] As in the past, this is most likely in order to protect the independent, fair, and authoritative exercise of judicial power, which the Court has always held particularly close to its heart.

[330] G Evans 'The High Court and the Constitution in a Changing Society' *Australian Lawyers and Social Change* (n 301).
[331] Doyle (n 163) 31–32.
[332] *Kable* case (n 267) comes to mind.

4

Germany: Balancing Rights and Duties

*Donald P. Kommers**

Introduction

Germany's constitutional charter, adopted in 1949, is entitled the Basic Law.[1] Under the circumstances of a divided nation, the founders decided, pending Germany's reunification, to write a 'basic law' (*Grundgesetz*) rather than a 'constitution' (*Verfassung*). Similarly, they chose to call the assembly charged with framing the Basic Law a parliamentary council (*Parlamentarischer Rat*) instead of a constitutional convention (*verfassunggebende Versammlung*). Symbolically, the terminology was important. A 'constitution' in the traditional German understanding is a framework for the permanent organization of a nation-state. By contrast, the Basic Law was adopted as a provisional charter for the governance of a 'mere fragment of a state,' as one of the framers described the western half of Germany. But within the space of 40 years, the Basic Law had demonstrated its durability, resulting in a general acceptance of its legitimacy.[2] During these years, it had also evolved into one of the world's most admired constitutions, even rivaling that of the United States in influence and prestige

* For their comments on an earlier version of this essay, I would like to thank Professors Winfried Brugger, Helmut Steinberger, Jochen Frowein, and Walter Murphy. The essay was also the subject of a Northwestern University Law School colloquium in constitutional theory co-directed by Steven Calabresi and Andrew Koppelman. I am grateful for their participation and the comments of their students.

[1] *Grundgesetz für die Bundesrepublik Deutschland* [The Basic Law of the Federal Republic of Germany], Promulgated by the Parliamentary Council on 23 May 1949 (hereafter cited as GG).

[2] Even if a new Constitution had been adopted on the eve of Germany's reunification, it would probably have been largely a duplicate of the Basic Law. After 40 years of peace and prosperity, the Basic Law had rooted itself in Germany's civic culture as well as in the consciousness of the German legal community. By 1990, the Federal Constitutional Court had decided nearly 80,000 cases under the Basic Law, approximately 95 per cent of which had been filed by individual citizens in the form of constitutional complaints. By then the published opinions of the Court had been reported in 83 volumes of *Entscheidungen des Bundesverfassungsgerichts* [Decisions of the Federal Constitutional Court] (JCB Mohr [P Siebeck], Tübingen) (hereafter cited as BVerfGE). Thousands of essays and articles commenting on the Court's work had also appeared in numberless books, periodicals, and newspapers. See for example J Mackert and F Schneider (eds) *Bibliographie zur Verfassungsgerichtsbarkeit des Bundes and der Länder* (JCB Mohr [P Siebeck], Tübingen, 1971).

around the world.[3] So when the day of unity finally arrived in 1990, East and West Germany merged under the imprint of the Basic Law itself. Today, in both structure and substance, although frequently amended, it remains *the* constitutional text of reunited Germany. Accordingly, the terms ' basic law' and 'constitution'— ie, the constitutional *text*—are used interchangeably in this chapter.

Genesis

The Basic Law of the Federal Republic of Germany (FRG) was a product of the Cold War. In mid-1948, responding to the Soviet Union's refusal to implement the terms of the Potsdam Agreement regarding Germany's economic and political unification, the Allied Powers—France, Great Britain, and the United States— resolved to combine their respective zones of occupation into a separate state. Accordingly, they offered West Germans an opportunity to remake themselves politically under a new charter. The machinery for organizing a constituent assembly was already in place. As early as 1946, regional territories or states (*Länder*) had been established in the three zones.[4] All had parliamentary governments chosen in free elections, all were committed to democracy, and all were presided over by prime ministers who commanded the trust of the Military Governors. In cooperation with their *Land* legislatures, the prime ministers were the principal players in laying the groundwork for the new constitution. The Governors had authorized them to convene a constituent assembly by September 1, 1948. They received instructions to establish a federal form of government, to protect the rights of the states, and to provide for a central authority capable of safeguarding individual rights and freedoms.[5] Within these broad guidelines, Germans were free to craft a constitution of their own choosing, subject of course to Allied approval.

[3] For a discussion of the Basic Law's global influence, see J Kokott, 'From Reception and Transplantation to Convergence of Constitutional Models in the Age of Globalization—With Particular Reference to the German Basic Law' in C Starck (ed) *Constitutionalism, Universalism and Democracy—A Comparative Analysis* (Nomos Verlagsgesellschaft, Baden-Baden, 1999) 71–134.

[4] The original states were comprised of Baden, Bavaria, Bremen, Hamburg, Hesse, Lower Saxony, North Rhine-Westphalia, Rhineland-Palatinate, Schleswig-Holstein, Württemberg-Baden, and Württemberg-Hohenzollern. In 1951, the three Southwest states of Baden, Württemberg-Baden, and Württemberg-Hohenzollern were consolidated into the single state of Baden-Württemberg and in 1957 the Saarland, having been occupied by France, was returned to Germany. In 1990, finally, pursuant to the Unification Treaty, the existing ten states were joined by the former East German states of Berlin, Brandenburg, Mecklenburg-Western Pomerania, Saxony, Saxony-Anhalt, and Thuringia.

[5] These guidelines were broad and vague. They failed to specify the kind of democracy or federal state contemplated by the Allies or the nature and scope of the rights to be protected. The imprecision was deliberate, and for two reasons: It helped to deflect criticism that a new Versailles-like betrayal of German interests was in the making; and it helped to conceal substantial differences among the Occupying Powers over the details of Germany's political reconstruction. More than anything else, however, as the Cold War heated up, the pressure of time and the need for immediate German cooperation prompted the Allies to soften their differences and empower the Germans to proceed with the business at hand.

After agreeing to convene the assembly by the suggested date, the prime ministers appointed a 25-member committee to prepare a draft constitution for the consideration of the forthcoming assembly.[6] The committee included one delegate for each of the 11 *Länder* and 14 advisors, most of whom were constitutional experts or high ministerial officials in their respective governments. All but two of the official delegates were affiliated with a political party; most were Christian and Social Democrats. The Herrenchiemsee Convention,[7] as it was called, finished its work in two weeks (August 10–23) of around-the-clock negotiations. Its members produced a draft constitution consisting, *inter alia*, of a bill of rights, a two-house national legislature, a strong chancellor, a mostly ceremonial president, an independent judiciary, including a constitutional court, and a federation (*Bund*) of independent *Land* (ie, state) governments empowered to administer federal law, share tax revenue with the national government, and exercise significant power over education, police affairs, and local government.[8]

Constitutive assembly

The fast work of the Herrenchiemsee Convention allowed the Parliamentary Council to convene, as planned, on September 1, in Bonn—the city chosen as West Germany's capital. Each state's delegation, as with the Philadelphia Convention of 1787, was elected by its respective parliament or legislature. (Unlike the United States Constitution, however, the Basic Law was ratified by these same legislative bodies.) The Council consisted of 65 delegates. Collectively, they represented West Germany's political elite. Nearly all were experienced politicians. Forty delegates had been politically active in the Weimar Republic; 18 had served in zonal advisory councils; and 13 had participated in their *Land* constitutional assemblies. Fifty-two were members of their respective parliaments, several of whom held high ministerial positions in their *Land* cabinets. All were affiliated with political parties approved or licensed by the Occupying Powers.[9]

---

[6] This method of drafting a constitution was not unusual for Germany. *Land* (state) governments had traditionally authorized ministerial officials to propose draft constitutions which would then be submitted to a constituent assembly. Such was the case with the Imperial Constitution of 1871 and the Constitution of 1919. See K Pinson *Modern Germany* (2nd edn., New York, Macmillan Company, 1966) 156–157, 339.

[7] At the invitation of Hans Ehard, Bavaria's Prime Minister, the delegates met in a resplendent medieval castle, built by Bavaria's popular King Louis II, on an island in Lake Herrenchiemsee.

[8] *Bericht über den Verfassungskonvent auf Herrenchiemsee vom 10. bis 23. August* (Richard Pflaum, Munich, 1948). For other treatments of the personalities and decisions of the Herrenchiemsee conference see K Stern *Das Staatsrecht der Bundesrepublik Deutschland* (CH Beck'sche Verlagsbuchhandlung, Munich, 2000) V 1244–1270; P März and H Oberreuter (eds) *Weichenstellung für Deutschland: Der Verfassungskonvent von Herrenchiemsee* (Olzog Verlag GmbH, Munich, 1999); W Benz 'Der Verfassungskonvent von Herrenchiemsee' in *Aus Politik und Zeitgeschichte* 31 July 1998 13–19.

[9] These parties included the Social Democratic Party (SPD), the Christian Democratic Union (CDU) and its Bavarian affiliate, the Christian Social Union (CSU), the Free Democratic Party (FDP), the Center Party (Z), the German Party (DP), and the Communist Party of Germany (KPD). These abbreviations will be used hereafter. The Center or Catholic Party, a prominent actor on the

Social and Christian Democrats each claimed 27 members; the remaining delegates consisted of five Free Democrats and two members each of the Center, German, and Communist Parties.[10]

The delegates were also distinguished by their age, occupation, and religious affiliation. As their political backgrounds suggest, an older generation of Germans framed the Basic Law. The framers (61 men and four women) were mainly democrats exiled, imprisoned, or dismissed from office during the Nazi period. Fifty-five was their median age; 23 were over 60; only three were in their 30s. Occupationally, lawyers and high civil servants were the most numerous, especially within the CDU/CSU and FDP, whereas teachers, journalists, and trade union leaders had a larger presence within the SPD. (No fewer than 51 of the 65 delegates were university graduates.) As for religion, Roman Catholics were heavily represented among Christian and Center Party delegates. Free and Social Democrats, by contrast, were identified mainly as Protestant or religiously unaffiliated. Like the Council's political divisions, these differences would produce a number of cleavages on cultural and church-state issues.

The Council remained in session for nearly ten months, far longer than the Allies or the Germans had hoped. More time than anticipated was needed to work through disagreements separating the Germans from the Allies and the German political parties from each other. Social, Free, and Christian Democrats in particular strove to compose their differences, the most crucial having been the allocation of power between federal and *Land* governments. The delegates felt the proposed constitution's ratification in the federal *Land* parliaments would depend on an overwhelmingly favorable vote in the Council. This favorable result was finally achieved on May 8, 1949. By May 22, all the *Länder* except Bavaria followed suit, ratifying the Basic Law by resounding majorities. (Bavaria signed on shortly thereafter.) The decision not to submit the Basic Law to a popular referendum for ratification was deliberate. With the experience of Weimar in mind, the framers were deeply suspicious of any form of direct democracy, a mistrust reflected in the Basic Law itself.[11] They also believed that its legitimacy depended less on its submission to a popular vote than on its objective content and compatibility with the spirit of the German people.

The Basic Law incorporated most of the provisions of the Herrenchiemsee draft, although in substantially reordered form. The document entering into force on May 23, 1949 consisted of a preamble and 146 articles, including five articles

political stage during the Weimar Republic, dissolved early on in the Federal Republic. Most of its members joined the CDU or the CSU.

[10] These and the following statistical data have been drawn from W Sörgel *Konsens und Interessen* (Stuttgart, Ernst Klett Verlag, 1969) 261; *Documents on the Creation of the German Federal Constitution* (Civil Administration Division: Office of Military Government for Germany [US] 1 September 1949) 50–61; and various editions of *Wer ist Wer? Das Deutsche Who's Who* (Verlags Grünewald, Berlin).

[11] Especially GG art 20(2). Commentary by I Münch and P Kunig *Grundgesetz-Kommentar* (4th edn., CH Beck'sche Verlagsbuchhandlung, Munich, 1992) 1054–1055.

of the Weimar Constitution on church-state relations incorporated into the Basic Law's article 140. No fewer than 60 articles dealt directly or indirectly with *Bund-Länder* relations, many of which were lengthy and layered with details, a result owing as much to the Allied insistence on constitutionalizing the rights of the *Länder* in the fields of tax policy and public administration as to any German penchant for precision and thoroughness. Since 1949, however, the Basic Law's text has been formally amended on numerous occasions. (The amendatory process is described below in section 2.) It includes 39 new articles, all of which have been woven into one of the constitution's original sections.[12]

Although influenced by the Occupying Powers, the Bonn Constitution, as it came to be known, was a home-grown product. The framers relied mainly on the structures, usages, and traditions found in the national constitutions of 1849, 1871, and 1919, not to mention their presence in several postwar *Land* constitutions. The Weimar Constitution (1919) was their main model. Like the Herrenchiemsee draft, the Basic Law adopted most of the institutions and practices of the Weimar Republic save for those crippling defects alleged to have facilitated Hitler's rise to power. In borrowing so heavily from the Weimar Constitution, the Basic Law was largely a work of political restoration. But it also broke new ground. In short, Bonn's *constitutional* democracy had replaced the *popular* democracy of the Weimar Republic, emphasizing, as it did, substantive limits on the exercise of political power and constraints on majoritarian political institutions.

Constituent power and reunification

Given Germany's division and occupation, it was crucially important at the outset to identify the source of constituent power and the people for whom the Basic Law was being crafted. Much of the debate in the Council's opening sessions centered on these preambulatory issues. After undergoing several revisions over as many weeks, the Council adopted the following version of the preamble:

'Conscious of their responsibility before God and men, animated by the resolve to preserve their national and political unity and to serve the peace of the world as an equal partner in a united Europe, the German people in the [various] *Länder*..., desiring to give a new order to political life for a transitional period, have enacted, by virtue of their constituent power, this Basic Law of the Federal Republic of Germany.'

By convening—and speaking—in the name of the 'German people' as represented in the eleven original *Länder*, the founders rejected Bavaria's proposal to place

---

12 For example the new art 16a (composed of five lengthy paragraphs), which qualifies the right to asylum, follows the original art 16, which simply declares that the 'politically persecuted enjoy the right to asylum.' As of December 31, 2003, the Basic Law included the preamble and 13 major sections, namely, Basic Rights (I arts 1–19); Federation and *Länder* (II arts 20–37); Federal Parliament (III arts 38–49); Federal Council (IV arts 50–53); Joint Committee (IVa art 53a); Federal President (V arts 54–61); Federal Government (VI arts 62–69); Legislative Powers of Federation (VII arts 70–82); Federal Administration (VIII, arts 83–91b); Judiciary (IX arts 92–104); Finance (X arts 104a–115); State of Defense (Xa arts 115a–115l); and Transitional Provisions (XI arts 116–146).

constituent power in the separate federal states as corporate entities (reminding Americans of the 'league of friendship' into which the states had entered under the Articles of Confederation). The preamble also stipulated that the framers were 'acting on behalf of those [East] Germans to whom participation was denied.'

The preamble's reference to a transitional political order anticipated Germany's eventual reunification, as did Art 146, declaring that the Basic Law would cease to be in force on the day when *all* Germans freely adopt a new constitution. Article 23, on the other hand, provided that the Basic Law would apply to 'other [German] territories on their accession.' When pursuant to this provision, Saarland acceded to the Federal Republic in 1959, its territory succumbed forthwith to the rule of the Basic Law. But could the Federal Republic incorporate the German Democratic Republic (GDR) under the procedure of Art 23? Or did the promise of the preamble in tandem with Art 146 require reunited Germany to adopt a new constitution? That German leaders agreed to reunify under the relatively painless procedure of Art 23, instead of Art 146, was a momentous act of constitutional interpretation in its own right. By providing for the GDR's accession to the FRG, millions of East Germans had no opportunity to vote for or against the Basic Law.[13] When unity finally arrived on October 3, 1990, the GDR ceased to exist.

The Basic Law, however, did not survive reunification unchanged. To account for new social and political realities, the Unity Treaty itself amended the document in several respects. First, it crafted a new article providing for temporary deviations from the Basic Law's structure of federal-state relations and certain measures related to basic liberties.[14] Second, the treaty repealed Art 23, effectively freezing Germany's present borders with Poland at the Oder-Neisse line. Third, and importantly, the preamble was rewritten to delete all references to the goal of reunification and to provide for the incorporation of five new *Länder*.[15] The revised preamble simply decrees: 'The German people have adopted, by virtue of their constituent power, this Basic Law.' It concludes by asserting that 'Germans,' now represented in 16 *Länder*, 'have achieved the unity and freedom of Germany in free self-determination,' reaffirming that '[t]his Basic Law is thus valid for the entire German people.'[16]

---

[13] Reunification pursuant to art 146 would have meant (1) the dissolution of both East and West German governments, (2) the framing of a new constitution, presumably by an elected constitutional convention, (3) ratification by the electorate or perhaps by the *Land* legislatures, and (4) the election and formation of a new government under the terms of the new constitution. The process may not have occurred precisely in this sequence, but it would surely have been a long and cumbersome affair, not to mention the divisiveness that would have been caused by reopening constitutional issues resolved when the Basic Law was drafted forty years earlier.

[14] See GG art 143, replacing the old art 143 repealed in 1968. For alterations in the preamble, the repeal of art 23, and other changes in the Basic Law, see *Einigungsvertrag* (Unity Treaty) 31 August 1990 art 4.   [15] See n 4.

[16] To assuage the unease of East and many West Germans who wanted substantial constitutional change, the Unity Treaty urged the new all-German parliament to consider additional amendments to the Basic Law in the light of reunification. The parliament made good on this promise by establishing a 64-person Commission on Constitutional Revision. The Commission held hearings

The new preamble, finally, retains the language of Germany's responsibility 'before God and men,' a phrase with important interpretive implications. This direct reference to the deity in the original preamble italicized Germany's return to religious values in the aftermath of its Nazi allegiance. But the reference also expressed the widespread belief, especially among Christian Democrats, in the existence of a law higher than the will of the people or even the positive law of the constitution. The SPD and FDP, on the other hand, maintained that human dignity and freedom could be acknowledged and realized in the absence of any belief in or reference to God. They might also have pointed out that the Herrenchiemsee draft omitted any such reference. But they yielded, reluctantly, to the strong view of the Christian and Catholic parties that 'a godless political and social order,' as the Bavarian Constitution proclaimed, had brought Germany to ruin.[17] It is uncertain whether this language would have been retained had East Germans been given the chance to participate in the making of a fresh all-German constitution.

The Basic Law: General Features

The Basic Law includes many code-like provisions affecting such matters as the administration of federal law, apportionment of expenditures and tax revenue between Federation and *Länder*, and rules the various branches of government must follow in the event of an armed attack on the Federal Republic. Even the section on fundamental rights includes detailed provisions on public education, compulsory military service, and the right of asylum. Although far from unimportant, these provisions will not be taken up here. The following treatment confines itself to the Basic Law's main principles, structures, and values. It also highlights particular clauses, phrases, and concepts the open-ended nature of which poses challenging questions of constitutional interpretation.

Supremacy of the Constitution

As already noted the Basic Law borrows heavily from the practices and procedures of previous constitutions in Germany's democratic tradition. What is new about the Basic Law is the ringing affirmation of its supremacy. Crowned by the principles of liberty and human dignity, it creates a normative legal order binding on all

for most of 1992 and 1993, receiving hundreds of recommendations from as many persons and groups. It rejected nearly all the proposals before it, including calls for the introduction of national initiatives and referenda, and only a few minor changes it did favor won parliamentary approval. The Commission's work and the fate of its proposals is discussed in DP Kommers 'The Basic Law Under Strain: Constitutional Dilemmas and Challenges' in C Anderson (et al) *The Domestic Politics of German Reunification* (Rienner Publishers Lynne 1993) 135–154.

[17] The phrase, 'conscious of their responsibility before God,' was actually lifted from the preamble of Rhineland-Palatinate's 1947 constitution, which defined God as the 'source of right and the creator of human society.' In fact, five of the seven existing *Länder* constitutional documents invoked God's assistance in reconstructing Germany's political order.

state agencies and governmental officials. Articles 1 and 20 constitute the heart of this normative order. Article 1 proclaims the inviolability of human dignity, obligates the state to respect and protect it, and declares that specified guaranteed rights 'shall bind the legislature, the executive, and the judiciary as directly applicable law.'[18] Article 20, by contrast, identifies the constituent principles of the new constitutional order, requires the legislature to observe this order, subjects the executive and the judiciary to 'law and justice' (*Gesetz und Recht*), and creates a constitutional court to enforce these and all other rules and principles of the Basic Law. Two other provisions reinforce the document's supremacy. The first bans any interference with 'the essence of a basic right,'[19] whereas the second limits the amending power by disallowing any constitutional amendment that would erode the value of human dignity anointed by Art 1 or the bedrock principles of the political system ordained by Art 20.[20] The 'eternity clause,' as it has been dubbed, expressed the founders' conviction that human dignity and democracy could be realized in perpetuity only by freezing certain principles of governance into the constitutional order itself.

The constitutional structure

The Constitution defines Germany as 'a democratic and social federal state' and proclaims that 'all state authority is derived from the people.'[21] Like the United States Constitution, the Basic Law establishes a system of separated and divided powers, except that the system is parliamentary rather than presidential. Executive authority continues to be shared by a president, a chancellor, and a cabinet of federal ministers, except that now the role of the federal president is largely ceremonial. The key official in the executive branch is the chancellor, and his position is far more secure than it was during the Weimar Republic. He no longer competes with a popularly elected president and parliament may dismiss him only by simultaneously electing a successor, an innovation known as the 'constructive vote of no confidence.'[22] The Basic Law maintains Weimar's commitment to democracy, but it establishes an indirect democracy that bars the use of popular initiatives and referenda at the federal level. Still another innovation is the Basic Law's recognition of political parties, describing them as major participants 'in forming the political will of the people.'[23] According to the Federal Constitutional Court, Germany is no less than a *Parteienstaat* (political party state),[24] possessing an authoritative status equal to that of the *Sozialstaat* (social welfare state) and the *Rechtsstaat* (law state). By a 'law state,' the Germans mean one rooted in the principles of liberty, equality, and human dignity.

[18] Grundgesetz art 1(1). Hereafter cited as GG.   [19] GG art 19(2).
[20] GG art 79(3). These principles include federalism, democracy, republican representation, separation of powers, rule of law, popular sovereignty, and the social welfare state.
[21] GG art 20(1) and (2).   [22] GG art 67.   [23] GG art 21(1).
[24] Judgment of 30 May 1961, *Entscheidungen des Bundesverfassungsgerichts* [Decisions of the Federal Constitutional Court] (JCB Mohr [P Siebeck], Tübingen, 1963) Vol 13 1 16. Hereafter cited as 13 BVerfGE 1 16 (1961).

Germany is also a *Bundesstaat* (federal state), but it differs markedly from American federalism. Whereas the latter embraces dual executive and judicial institutions, with legislatures, courts, and administrative agencies serving each level of government, German federalism confers the bulk of *legislative* power on the national government, with the *Länder* being responsible mainly for the *administration* of both state and federal law. Powers reserved exclusively to the *Länder* include education, law enforcement, and cultural policy, including regulation of the press. Nevertheless, the *Länder* enjoy an important role in the enactment of national law through a *Bundesrat* (Federal Council) vested with formidable powers of suspension and consent. Each state is entitled to three to six votes, depending on its population. The chamber's 68 members are appointed by their respective *Land* government, and each may appoint as many members as it has votes; the votes of each *Land* must be cast as a unit and only by the members present.[25] The *Bundestag*, on the other hand, is the popular branch of the national parliament. Its 598 members are elected for terms of four years unless the house is dissolved in accordance with the prescribed procedures of Articles 67 or 68. Elections to the *Bundestag* are dominated by political parties whose 'internal organization must conform to democratic principles.'[26] Indeed, the Basic Law prohibits parties seeking to undermine or abolish democracy, prompting commentators to characterize the German 'party state' as a militant democracy (*streitbare Demokratie*).[27]

The Basic Law, finally, unlike previous written constitutions, commits the FRG to internationalism. The post-unity preamble expresses Germany's 'determination to promote world peace as an equal partner in a united Europe.' A new Art 23, passed in 1992, spells out the details of the nation's participation in the European Union. In addition, the Basic Law contains articles incorporating the general rules of international law into federal law, banning actions that disturb 'the peaceful relations between nations,' and permitting the FRG, 'for the maintenance of peace,' to enter into systems of collective security. As noted later in this essay, the Basic Law's frequent references to 'peace' would raise significant questions of interpretation.

Rights, duties, and institutional guarantees

Articles 1 through 19 lay down an impressive list of guaranteed rights. Article 1 elevates human dignity to first place among the Basic Law's values, and obligates the state to respect and protect it. The remaining articles embrace most of the liberties associated with western constitutionalism, including freedoms of speech, assembly, association, and religion as well as the rights to property and equality before the law.[28] Buttressing these rights are the general liberty clauses of Art 2: they

---

[25] GG art 51.   [26] GG art 21(1).

[27] For example HD Jarass and B Pieroth *Grundgesetz für die Bundesrepublik Deutschland* (5th edn., CH Beck'sche Verlagsbuchhandlung, Munich, 2000) 526.

[28] The Basic Law frames most of these rights as universal but several rights are reserved for Germans. These include the rights of assembly (art 8), association (art 9), and movement (art 11),

declare 'the freedom of the person' to be inviolable, while protecting the rights to 'life and physical integrity' and the 'free development of [one's] personality.'[29] Like 'human dignity,' these open-ended words and phrases are not self-defining; each presents difficult problems of constitutional interpretation, as we shall see.

The bill of rights, however, covers more than *individual* liberties. It also protects collective rights known as institutional guarantees enjoyed by such entities as the press, broadcasting stations, private schools, and marriage and the family. Relatedly, it protects the right of parents to decide whether their children shall receive religious instruction in the public schools. Institutional guarantees found outside the bill of rights include local governments and the civil service, not to mention the protection extended to the corporate rights of religious communities.[30] According to the Federal Constitutional Court, these institutions implicate individual rights, for they constitute the seedbeds of personal growth and dignity. The state is thus duty-bound to see that these institutions flourish in the interest of the developing human personality.[31]

Two other features distinguish the bill of rights. First, the Basic Law speaks in the language of duties as well as rights As already noted, the state is charged with respecting and promoting human dignity. Recent amendments also require parliament to adopt affirmative action plans to eliminate disadvantages women have sustained because of past discrimination and, mindful of future generations, to take steps needed to 'protect the natural bases of life. . .in accordance with law and justice.'[32] Duties also extend to individuals: Parents are charged with the primary duty of caring for their children; mandatory military service is constitutionally required of all young men; and teachers have the duty of loyalty to the Constitution. According to Art 14, property too 'imposes duties;' in declaring that its use 'shall serve the public good,' Germans are reminded of the principle of solidarity implicit in the concept of the social welfare state.

The second feature attaches limitation clauses to particular rights and liberties. For example, the right to the development of one's personality must accord with the demands of the 'constitutional order' and the 'moral law.' Similarly, free speech finds one of its limits 'in the right to respect for personal honor.' Other fundamental rights may be restricted if used to combat or undermine the free democratic basic order. The right of association may even be prohibited if 'directed against . . . the concept of international understanding.' And rights such as asylum, privacy, and occupational choice may be restricted or prohibited under other specified circumstances. On the other hand, there are limits to the abridgment of

together with the right to choose one's trade or profession (art 12) and the right of a citizen not to be extradited to a foreign country (art 16).

[29] GG art 2(1) and (2).

[30] The Federal Constitutional Court has supported all of these guarantees. For example, the guarantees of broadcasting, marriage and family, private schools, and associations were affirmed, respectively, in the following cases: 12 BVerfGE 205, 259 (1961), 10 BVerfGE 59, 66 (1959), 6 BVerfGE 309, 355 (1957), and 50 BVerfGE 290 (354 (1979).   [31] 35 BVerfGE 79, 114–116.

[32] GG art 20a.

rights. First, a basic right can be restricted pursuant only to a general statute that specifies the right affected and the article that protects it; second, the framers bolted rights to the command that 'in no case may the essence of a basic right be encroached upon,'[33] leaving interpreters with the task of defining this *essence* when a right is statutorily limited.

Finally, it might be noted that the Basic Law's guaranteed rights contain ingredients from Germany's socialist, liberal, and Christian intellectual traditions. These traditions of political thought were represented, respectively, by the three dominant parties in the Parliamentary Council, namely, the SPD, FDP, and CDU/CSU.[34] To achieve the consensus these parties thought necessary to pass and ratify the Basic Law, their respective members, in a remarkable display of concord, drew willingly from the humanistic content of each tradition to create a document that combines the important values of each in a seemingly workable, if not always easy, alliance. The working out of the tension among these values would predictably fall to the Federal Constitutional Court.

The amending process

Constitutional transformation in Germany has often occurred in step with the Basic Law's formally prescribed amending procedures. In the last ten years alone (since 1994), amending acts have deleted, added, or modified provisions affecting no fewer than 25 articles and 44 clauses. In the United States, by contrast, the main instrument of constitutional change has been judicial interpretation. Plainly, Germany's highest tribunal has been as adept as the Supreme Court in adjusting the Basic Law to social and political realities. In the early 1960s, for example, the Court sustained gender classifications based on the dominant German view that woman's place was in the home. Much later, in 1979, the Court rejected this view in holding that a *Land* law entitling working women, but not men, to a day off per month to take care of household duties violated the principle of equality.[35] Even so, Germans amended their Constitution in 1994 to make it indisputably clear that the state was empowered to remove existing inequalities between men and women.[36] As this amendment might suggest, the Basic Law's complicated structure of separated and divided powers, its many code-like provisions on fiscal affairs and emergency powers, and its detailed list of rights and duties, and the qualifications thereof, make the formal procedure of amendment a principal mode of constitutional change. From a German perspective, any judicially imposed remodeling of the Basic Law—enduring and binding changes in particular—would diminish the clarity, precision, and predictability required of the constitutional *Rechtsstaat*.

Article 79 specifies the procedures for amending the Constitution. First, the Basic Law can be amended only by a statute that 'expressly amends or supplements

---

[33] GG art 19(2).   [34] See n 9 for the full titles of these parties.
[35] 52 BVerfGE 369 (1979).   [36] GG art 3(2).

its text.' Second, an amendatory statute requires the consent of two thirds of the members and votes, respectively, of the *Bundestag* and *Bundesrat*. (Such extraordinary majorities are difficult to achieve without a consensus across party lines or between federal and state governments.) Finally, Art 79(3) limits the amending power itself by disallowing any constitutional amendment that would affect the federal system or erode the principles laid down in Articles 1 and 20. This so-called 'eternity clause' expressed the founders' conviction that human dignity and democracy could be realized in perpetuity only by freezing certain principles of governance into the constitutional order itself. In the leading opinion interpreting the clause, the Federal Constitutional Court affirmed its readiness to declare any amendment contrary to these principles unconstitutional.[37]

Given Germany's penchant for textual precision in constitution-making, it is no surprise to learn that many—not all—of the most important changes in the constitutional order over the years have taken place under the procedures of Art 79. These alterations include amendments endorsing West Germany's remilitarization, adopting procedures for the exercise of emergency powers, and adjusting the Basic Law to Germany's reunification. The changes occurred, respectively, in the years 1954–56, 1968–69, and 1990–92. Challenges were even mounted against the validity of the reunification amendments because they were accomplished by treaty instead of by *statute* in strict accordance with the formal amending procedure.

The Federal Constitutional Court

One of the great innovations of the Basic Law is the creation of the Federal Constitutional Court (FCC). Unlike the United States Supreme Court, which is a court of general appellate review charged with hearing cases and controversies arising under federal law, including the law of the Constitution, the FCC is a specialized court of constitutional review organized apart from and independent of the regular judicial establishment. As the only tribunal in Germany empowered to declare statutes and other governmental actions unconstitutional, its status as a major guardian of the Constitution is firmly anchored in the Basic Law. The FCC is also the only tribunal whose composition is constitutionally specified.

Its members are to consist of 'federal judges and other members,' half of whom are to be elected by the *Bundestag* and the other half by the *Bundesrat*, but in no case may a judge of the FCC serve simultaneously in either parliamentary house, in the Federal Government, or in any corresponding *Land* body.[38] All other

---

[37] *Article 10 Case*, 30 BVerfGE 1, 24–26. The case challenged an amendment to the provision in the bill of rights preserving the secrecy of the mail and telecommunications. The amendment qualified this right to protect democracy and curtailed the power of the judiciary to adjudicate interferences with it. Even as it sustained the validity of the amendment, the Constitutional Court held that any fundamental substantive change in the existing constitutional order is absolutely forbidden. Ibid 24.

[38] GG art 94(1).

details of organization and procedure, together with the number, tenure, and qualifications of the court's members, are to be regulated by law. The statute incorporating these details is officially known as the Federal Constitutional Court Act (FCCA).[39]

Organization and composition

FCCA describes the FCC as a 'court of justice independent of all other constitutional organs.'[40] Yet, in the beginning , the Court was subject administratively to the supervisory authority of the Federal Ministry of Justice. Finding the insecurity of this arrangement intolerable, even arguing that it was unconstitutional, the Justices themselves mounted a campaign to break free of ministerial supervision. By the mid-1950s, they had achieved their objective. Over the opposition of the Ministry of Justice, parliament enacted legislation giving the Court total control over its budget and all other internal administrative matters, thus granting it a status coordinate with the *Bundestag*, *Bundesrat*, Federal President, and Federal Government (ie, the Chancellor and his cabinet).[41] This development underscored the Court's role as a major player in Germany's constitutional system. In fact, when the Basic Law was amended in 1968 to provide for emergency powers, one of its provisions forbade any impairment of the FCC's status or functions during an emergency.[42]

Structurally, the FCC is divided into two panels, called senates—the First and Second Senates—each of which is presently composed of eight justices chosen for a single non-renewable term of 12 years.[43] Half the judges of each senate are chosen by the *Bundestag's* 12-member Judicial Selection Committee, a body consisting of legislators elected in numbers proportionate to each party's overall parliamentary strength. The *Bundesrat*, in which the *Land* governments are represented, select the remaining judges. Two-thirds of all votes are required in both electoral organs. These procedures, together with the informal practice of having the *Bundestag* and *Bundesrat* alternate in the selection of the court's president and vice-president, usually means that judicial appointments are the subject of intensive bargaining

[39] The original version of the statute was passed on 12 March 1951 (*Gesetz über das Bundesverfassungsgericht* [Law on the Federal Constitutional Court]), *Bundesgesetzblatt* (Federal Gazette) I (1951) 243, hereafter cited as FCCA.   [40] FCCA art 1.
[41] For a description of the Court's campaign to change its status see DP Kommers *Judicial Politics in Germany* (Sage Publications, Beverly Hills, 1976) 83–86.   [42] GG art 115g.
[43] The twin senate idea was proposed originally to deal with two different categories of jurisdiction. The First Senate was assigned jurisdiction over cases arising out of ordinary litigation, largely constitutional complaints and concrete judicial review proceedings, whereas the Second Senate was assigned the so-called 'political' cases, namely those involving direct conflicts between branches and levels of government, including cases submitted to the Court on abstract judicial review. (These categories are discussed in the next subsection.) Ninety-five per cent of the Court's increasingly heavy workload fell within the jurisdiction of the First Senate. Consequently, FCCA was amended to shift certain constitutional complaints and concrete review cases—mainly in the area of criminal law—over to the Second Senate, which largely equalized the workload of the two senates. Each senate exercises mutually exclusive jurisdiction, but any doctrinal or jurisdictional conflict that arises between the senates must be resolved by the *plenum* (both senates sitting together).

among the two major parliamentary parties—SPD and CDU-CSU—and often between the *Bundesrat* and *Bundestag*. No one of these parties has been strong enough to make appointments over the objection of the other. Thus, the Court's membership has reflected fairly well the balance of forces in parliament as a whole. Owing to the extraordinary majorities required to elect judges, the 16 seats have been evenly distributed over the years between Social and Christian Democrats.[44] Occasionally, however, a minor party has received a seat on the FCC as a reward for joining one of the major parties in forming a governing coalition.

By 2004, no fewer than 90 justices had been elected to the FCC. They are required to be 40 years of age, eligible for election to the *Bundestag*, and qualified to serve as a judge.[45] The partisan distribution of seats, facilitated by the limited tenure of the justices and the two-thirds vote required to elect them, has resulted in a selection process marked by settled expectations. Ideological wrangling of the American variety seldom takes place. On the whole, the justices have been middle-class, university educated, law-trained men and women who, before taking their seats, had been prominent in party politics, government service, the judiciary, or the legal academy. Several have been national political figures, often SPD or CDU leaders with strong cross-party appeal. In recent years, however, justices have been recruited mainly from the universities and the judiciary. In 2004, 14 of the 16 justices had careers mainly as judges or law professors, although several also served in ministerial or related capacities at the national or state level. Only one had been a member of the national parliament. Still, the system has worked well, producing technically competent and politically moderate justices no less independent than the members of the United States Supreme Court.[46]

Authority and jurisdiction

The United States constitutional text contains no express reference to any judicial power to pass upon the validity of legislative or executive actions. The Basic Law, by contrast, confers sweeping powers of constitutional review upon the FCC.[47] Its main business falls into five jurisdictional categories: disputes between high state organs (ie, separation of powers conflicts), federal-*Land* conflicts, abstract judicial review, concrete judicial review, and constitutional complaints, each of which underscores the distinctive role the FCC plays in Germany's political order. First, all of its jurisdiction is compulsory. Unlike the United States Supreme Court, it

---

[44] This process of judicial recruitment is discussed in Kommers n 41, ch 4.

[45] FCCA art 3 (1) and (2).

[46] See DP Kommers 'Autonomy versus Accountability: The German Judiciary' in PH Russell and DM O'Brien (eds) *Judicial Independence in the Age of Democracy* (University Press of Virginia, Charlottesville, 2001) 131–154.

[47] These powers are set forth in 13 separate articles of the Basic Law. See especially GG arts 18, 21(2), 41(2), 61, 84(4), 93, 98(2), 99, 100, 126, and 137(2). They include the express power to rule on the constitutionality of political parties, to review the validity of election results, the impeachment of the federal president, the forced removal of federal judges, and even the decision of a *Land* constitutional court to deviate from an FCC ruling.

has no discretionary authority to reject cases when filed by the properly authorized petitioners. Second, when duly filed, a case may not be withdrawn on a motion by the petitioners. In the German understanding of constitutional jurisdiction, a properly filed case presents an issue in the public interest, and only the Court has the discretion to drop a case when the initiating party is no longer interested in its judicial resolution. In short, the Court is supposed to represent the national interest in the resolution of duly presented constitutional conflicts, particularly when brought by national and *Land* political leaders.

What most distinguishes the FCC from the Supreme Court is abstract judicial review. Whereas the latter limits itself to actual 'cases and controversies,' the FCC is empowered, at the request of a *Land* government, the Federal Government, or one-third of the *Bundestag's* members, to resolve 'differences of opinion and doubts' about the constitutionality of state or federal law or the compatibility of the former with the latter. Moreover, these decisions, which number no more than two or three per year, carry the binding force of statutory law.[48] Concrete review, on the other hand, arises out of an actual lawsuit, but may be initiated only by a lower court, not by the parties before it. (Lower courts are not empowered to declare post-1949 statutes unconstitutional.) Similarly, access to the FCC in constitutional conflicts between governments or among their branches is limited to these political units. Again, the purpose of judicial review in Germany's *Rechtsstaat* is to resolve constitutional doubts about laws and the operations of government, not to consign them to the limbo of non-justiciability or to reject them because they present a 'political question' unfit for judicial resolution. Constitutional complaints, about which more will be said below, may be filed by individuals or local governments: by individuals when claiming that the state has violated one or more of their guaranteed rights; by local governments when claiming an invasion of their guaranteed autonomy.[49]

Workload and decisional procedures

From 1951 to 2005, the FCC had disposed of an astounding 149,442 cases, 96.2 percent of which were constitutional complaints.[50] Individual citizens in particular have relied heavily on the Court for vindication of rights that the state has allegedly violated. In recent years, these complaints have averaged around 4700 per year, about equal to the number of *certiorari* petitions filed in the Supreme Court. In the 1960s, to ease the workload of the Court, FCCA was amended to allow each senate to establish committees of three justices each, now called 'chambers,' to determine a complaint's admissibility.[51] Later on, the chambers were empowered to decide a complaint on its merits, but only unanimously and only when the decision conformed to the Court's existing jurisprudence. If, however, two of the three justices 'are of the opinion that a decision in the matter would

---

[48] GG art 31(2).   [49] GG art 92(1).

[50] http://www.bverfg.de/cgi-bin/link.pl?entscheidungen. Filing a constitutional complaint is a relatively costless and painless affair; it may even take the form of a handwritten letter to the FCC. Many are prepared without legal assistance.   [51] FCCA s 15a.

clarify an important constitutional issue,' the complaint must be forwarded to the full senate for resolution.[52] If, in turn, three of eight justices find the complaint admissible, the full senate must decide the case.

Unless rejected on procedural grounds, each complaint is considered on its merits. Most, however, are found to be lacking in merit for reasons ranging from their triviality to the unlikelihood of their success. Roughly, only some 2.5 per cent of all constitutional complaints are accepted by a full senate, and these cases make up the bulk of the FCC's published opinions. Abstract judicial review cases, on the other hand, have been few in number but, like federal-state and inter-branch conflicts, they have had a substantial impact on Germany's political system.[53] In these cases, the Court's exposure to politics is immediate and direct. Abstract review permits a parliamentary minority, if equal to one-third of the *Bundestag's* members, to transpose a legislative fight into a legal proceeding by petitioning the Court to resolve its doubts about the enacted law's constitutionality. Little wonder these petitions have resulted in the Court's most controversial decisions.[54] Concrete review cases, finally, constitute the second largest number of the FCC's published opinions, numbering roughly between 10 and 20 per year.

Specialization, as in much of German public life, marks the FCC's decision-making process. First, the two senates are assigned—by law—specified categories of jurisdiction. Second, there is further specialization among the justices themselves. Before the start of a business year, each senate establishes the ground rules for the assignment of cases. By mutual agreement, and in consultation with a senate's presiding officer, each judge agrees to serve as the rapporteur (*Berichterstatter*) in cases related to his or her particular expertise.[55] The rapporteur's task is to prepare a document, called a *votum*, for the consideration of his colleagues. With the assistance of his clerks—they are not, as in the United States, recent law school graduates but experienced legal professionals chosen from the judiciary, the civil service, or university law faculties—he or she prepares a *votum*, often meticulously researched, on all aspects of the case, including detailed statements of the arguments on both sides of the dispute. Only when finished—and the final work-product may take months to prepare—is the *votum* submitted to the collective deliberation of the full senate.

---

[52] In recent years, the chambers have been empowered to decide concrete review cases under similar procedures unless the reference originates in a *Land* constitutional court or in one of the high federal courts. See FCCA ss 80(1) and 81a.

[53] See DP Kommers 'Constitutional Politics in Germany' (1994) 26 *Comparative Political Studies* 470–491.

[54] Examples of these decisions are Abortion Case I, *Entscheidungen des Bundesverfassungsgerichts* Vol 39 (JCB Mohr [P Siebeck], Tübingen, 1975) 1 hereafter cited as 39 BVerfGE 1 (1971), Abortion Case II, 88 BVerfGE 203 (1993); Party Finance Case I, 8 BVerfGE 51 (1958); Inter-German Basic Treaty Case, 83 BVerfGE 238 (1973); Television Case I, 12 BVerfGE 205 (1961); Geriatric Nursing Case, 106 BVerfGE 62 (2002); and the recent Immigration Case, 106 BVerfGE 310 (2002).

[55] In addition to scaling the bar of political acceptability as well as meeting an impressively high standard of professional competence, judges are often chosen for their individual specialties. So if a judge whose term expires is an authority in international law, his replacement—whether chosen by the SPD or the CDU/CSU—will in all probability be another person who has a demonstrated interest in this field.

The Court's published opinions are largely based on the rapporteur's *votum* and his or her recommendations. But the rapporteur does not always prevail. Known for their independence, the justices are unlikely to accept a *votum* unless well researched and persuasively argued. Final drafts of judicial opinions are collective work-products and take the form of unsigned institutional opinions. Personalized dissenting opinions, although permitted since 1971, are infrequent. The Court's published opinions tend to be lengthy, averaging around 26 printed pages, the equivalent of a 10,000 word essay.

Problems of Interpretation

There are no interpretive provisions in the Basic Law analogous to the Ninth Amendment of the United States Constitution or Section 27 of the Canadian Charter of Rights and Freedoms. The former instructs readers that enumerated rights are 'not to be construed to deny or disparage others retained by the people,' the latter that the Charter is to be read 'in a manner consistent with the preservation and enhancement of the multicultural heritage of Canadians.' What the Basic Law does do is identify its principal interpreter, namely, the Federal Constitutional Court, and the interpretive problems it faces are substantial. As explained earlier, the Basic Law creates a delicate balance between competing powers, principles, and rights. We have seen that some guaranteed rights may be limited by law and various public interests. Relatedly, the Basic Law reflects deep tensions between democracy and constitutionalism, between freedom and order, between law's authority and its rectitude, between personal rights and institutional guarantees, and between the liberal individualism of the *Rechtsstaat* and the principle of solidarity found in the concept of the *Sozialstaat*. Second, some provisions of the Basic Law seem antagonistic to one another. An example is the provision that subjects only men to compulsory military service,[56] yet Art 3(2) extends equal rights to 'men and women.' Finally, we have pointed to the imprecision of general concepts such as human dignity, free development of personality, freedom of the person, freedom of conscience, the free democratic basic order, international understanding, and the constitutional ban on any interference with the 'essence' of a fundamental right. A great deal of creative imagination would be needed to reconcile the Basic Law's tensions and opposites and, as well, to concretize its majestic generalities.

Conception of the Constitution

As noted, the Basic Law is an elaborate and often inconsistent framework of rules, powers, and principles. Notwithstanding its repeated reference to the need for

[56] GG 12a(1).

balancing rights and duties, the Federal Constitutional Court tends to define its interpretive role as one of harmonizing inconsistencies and carving order out of uncertainty and paradox. From the beginning, the FCC has insisted on the Basic Law's fundamental underlying unity. The Court has even described the document as a 'logical-teleological' entity,[57] a concept traceable to Rudolf Smend's 'integration' theory of the constitution.[58] More recently, the Court has referred to the 'constitutional order as a holistic unity of meaning.'[59] This notion of the constitution as a substantive unity has good pedigree in Germany's tradition of *Begriffsjurisprudenz* (conceptual jurisprudence), a tradition that envisions law as a self-contained, internally coherent, system of rules and norms. Yet constitutional law transcends the boundaries of positive law. Social context, political morality, and cultural norms play an important role in constitutional interpretation. An important interpretive canon postulates the interdependence of the constitutional order and the broader community. The nature of the community—ie, the German people—defines and refines the constitutional order, just as the latter defines and refines the existential reality of the community.[60] It is in this sense that constitutional normativity and constitutional reality—terms frequently encountered in the scholarly literature—converge. Any divergence between the two would threaten the unity of the Constitution if not the rule of law itself.

Yet the unity the FCC has found in the Constitution does not imply a single grand theory of the polity that pervades the Basic Law as a whole. The German state's constitutional design is multi-faceted; as noted earlier, the Basic Law defines the political system as federal, social, and democratic, just as Germany's democracy has been judicially characterized as a liberal and militant party state. The liberalism and militancy of German democracy has in turn been linked to the Basic Law's principle of human dignity. The interpretive problem is to keep each

---

[57] Church Construction Case, 19 BVerfGE 206, 220 (1965). This concept can be traced to Rudolp Smend's 'integration' theory of the Constitution. See his *Verfassung und Verfassungsrecht* (1928) 188–189.

[58] See *Verfassung und Verfassungsrecht* (Duncker & Humblot, Munich, 1928) 188–189. Smend, along with Heinrich Triepel, Hugo Preuss, and Gerhardt Anschütz, was a leading commentator on the Weimar Constitution. He argued that a constitution should serve as a unifying force, just as its interpretation should lead to an integrated community of common values. These values are more than procedural. They are the substantive values that define the community, clarify its will, enrich the human personality, and bind individual persons to the community.

[59] 34 BVerfGE 269, 287 (1973). 'Holistic unity of meaning' is a liberal rendition of the italicized words in the following sentence: Gegenüber den positiven Satzungen der Staatsgewalt kann unter Umständen ein Mehr an Recht bestehen, das seine Quelle in der *verfassungsmäßigen Rechtsordnung als einem Sinnganzen besitzt* und dem geschriebenen Gesetz gegenüber als Korrektive zu wirken vermag.'

[60] German constitutionalism, influenced by 'integration' theory, has strong communitarian underpinnings. While personal autonomy ranks high as a constitutional value, as it must in any liberal constitutional regime, it does not descend—or rise, depending on one's point of view—into an ideology of autonomous individualism that pervades many decisions of the American Supreme Court. For an excellent discussion of communitarianism in German constitutional law see W Brugger 'Kommunitarismus als Verfassungstheorie des Grundgesetzes' 123 *Archiv des öffentliches Rechts* (1998) 337. See also W Brugger 'Liberalismus, Pluralismus, Kommunitarismus' 83 *Kritische Vierteljahresschrift für Gesetzbegung und Rechtswissenschaft* (2000) 153.

of these visions of the state—federal, democratic, militant, social, liberal, and party-directed—alive and in some kind of creative balance, so that a judicial emphasis on any one dimension within a particular context does not result in the erosion or neglect of another in some other context.

In Germany as in the United States, judicial interpretation is a creative enterprise. Yet the German theory of interpretation is not precisely the same as the one Chief Justice John Marshall advanced in *McCulloch v Maryland*. The nature of a constitution, Marshall intoned, 'requires, that only its great outlines should be marked, its important objects designed, and the minor ingredients [omitted].' After all, he went on to say, 'it is a *constitution* we are expounding.' But few German interpreters would concede that the Basic Law is any less a constitution for the minor ingredients it contains, if indeed minor ingredients can be distinguished from important objects. Marshall's statement envisions a constitution as a living instrument subject to change by interpretation. Most Germans would accept the 'living instrument' conception of the Basic Law, but they would be less inclined, as suggested earlier, to admit to leaving major change—transformative change if you will—to interpretation. Taking the constitution seriously in Germany implies heavy reliance on the formal amendatory process when political or social realities begin to diverge from the original handiwork of the Basic Law's framers.

This thesis should not be driven too far, however, if only because judicial discretion is intrinsic to constitutional decision making. Some justices, of course, have insisted that the judicial task is one of discovering rather than making law and that there are objective ways to accomplish this task.[61] But, as the following sections make clear, the FCC sees its task as one of weighing and balancing conflicting values, and most justices would agree that there is no slide rule to calculate how much weight to assign these values. Dieter Grimm, a member of the Court from 1987 to 1999, recently wrote that the exercise of judicial review 'is not one of principle but of pragmatics.'[62] Still other justices envision the FCC as a political referee, enabling the government to function democratically as well as justly.[63] Most would concede that the FCC's role is inevitably and invariably political, especially when deciding major controversies among branches and levels of government.

An objective order of values

The FCC's jurisprudence may not embody a single overarching theory of the Constitution, but it incorporates what the Court has often described as an 'objective

[61] See H Simon 'Verfassungsgerichtsbarkeit' in Ernst Benda *et al* (ed) *Handbuch des Verfassungsrechts* (Walter de Gruyter, Berlin, 1984) 1282. Professor Konrad Hesse, on the other hand, a former member of the First Senate (1975–1987) and the author of a leading treatise on constitutional law, rejected the view that the judicial function could be seen as an objective process of discovery upon the application of a given methodology. See his 'Grundrechtstheorie und Grundrechtsinterpretation' (1974) 27 *Neue Juristische Wochenschrift* 1530–38.

[62] 'Constitutional Adjudication and Democracy' (1999) 33 *Israel Law Review* 201.

[63] In an interview with the author, former Justice Kirchhof compared himself to a soccer referee whose job it is to throw red and yellow flags in accordance with the official rules of the game.

order of values.' These objective values presumably inform the interpretation and application of guaranteed rights and indeed all of the Basic Law's provisions. The notion of an objective value order rings strange to the ears of a common lawyer. Its origin may be traced to the postwar effort to reaffirm moral values after the experience of the Third Reich. Several philosophical currents converged to produce the 'objective values' doctrine; they include the anti-positivism of Gustav Radbruch, Rudolf Smend's integralism, the neo-Thomist revival of natural law, and Kantian moral theory.[64] Günter Dürig, an original co-author of the leading commentary on the Basic Law,[65] was among the first to describe the human dignity clause of Article 1 as a 'norm of objective law' that infuses and inspires the meaning of the human personality as well as all other guaranteed rights. As advanced by Dürig, the concept of an objective value order is rooted in a theory of Christian personalism.[66] Shortly thereafter, in the famous *Lüth Case* (1958),[67] the FCC imported the concept into its case law. Since then, the Basic Law's value order has become a benchmark of German constitutional interpretation, except that it is no longer tied to Dürig's religious ontology.[68]

According to this imaginative concept, the Constitution includes the framers' 'basic value decisions,' the most basic of which is the principle of human dignity. Institutionally, these value decisions include the framers' choice of a free democratic basic order, that is, a liberal, representative, federal, parliamentary democracy. They are objective because in the FCC's view they are said to have an independent reality under the Constitution,[69] imposing on all organs of government an affirmative duty to see that they are realized in practice. The nature of this objective order may be stated in another way. Every constitutional right, from freedom of speech and press all the way over to the right to choose one's profession or occupation, has a corresponding value. The value is attached to, or evolves out of, a specified right.[70] In short, a basic right is a negative right against the state, but this

---

[64] Radbruch was famous for his defense of legal positivism in the 1920s but renounced the theory in the light of the Nazi regime. See *Der Mensch in Recht* (Vandenhoeck and Ruprecht, Göttingen, 1957)105ff. Smend, on the other hand, strongly advocated an integral, communitarian conception of the Basic Law, a theory that has had a major influence on the development of German constitutional law. For a treatment of Smend—in English—see AJ Jacobson and B Schlink (eds) *Weimar: A Jurisprudence of Crisis* (University of California Press, Berkeley, 2000) 207–248.

[65] T Maunz, G Dürig, *et al Kommentar zum Grundgesetz*, published in the form of a continually updated loose-leaf edition.

[66] See 'Die Menschenauffassung der Grundgesetzes' (1952) 7 *Juristische Rundschau* 260.

[67] 7 BVerfGE 198 (1958). *Lüth* is discussed below under the section on negative and positive rights.

[68] For a recent discussion of the objective value theory see H Dreier *Grundgesetz Kommentar* (Mohr Siebeck, Tübingen, 1996) 66–67.   [69] See n 79.

[70] 'Objective values' in German constitutional law are not the same as 'fundamental values' often proclaimed by the American Supreme Court. An objective value is one specified by the constitutional text as informed, *inter alia*, by history and which the state, apart from any individual claim, must foster and protect. A fundamental value, on the other hand, such as marital privacy—vindicated in *Griswold v Connecticut* 381 US 479 (1965)—is a subjective, defensive right of the individual rooted not so much in a particular text or in its original understanding or in the structure of the text as a whole, but rather in precedential reasoning or what might be called 'common law' justification. See in this regard DA Strauss 'Common Law, Common Ground, and Jefferson's Principle' (2003) 112 *Yale Law Journal* 1717.

right also incorporates a 'value' and, as a value, it imposes an obligation on the state to insure that it becomes an integral part of the general legal order.[71] For example, the right to freedom of the press protects broadcasters against any state policy that would encroach upon their independence, but as an objective value applicable to the polity as a whole the state is duty-bound to regulate broadcasting—and the press—in the interest of democracy and the multiplicity of views it represents. In the recent *Broadcast Fee-Setting Case* (1994) overturning Bavaria's procedures for setting public broadcasting user fees, the FCC remarked: 'Public broadcasting may not be abandoned either to the state or to any social group. The fundamental right of broadcasting freedom calls for a positive legal order that insures that public broadcasters take up and communicate the variety of topics and opinions that play a role in society.'[72]

In addition, the objective values of the Basic Law, according to the FCC, have been ordered hierarchically. The hierarchy is crowned by the principle of human dignity, the norm that informs the ultimate meaning of all rights. Following close behind in the hierarchy are the values of human life and the free development of one's personality. The interpretive problem is whether to give preference to the right or the value. In some situations, as the example of the free press shows, a value may override a right. Other examples are readily available. In the famous *Abortion Case I* (1975), the FCC invoked the principle (ie, the value) of human dignity to strike down a statute that effectively decriminalized any abortion procured during the first twelve weeks of pregnancy. As a matter of constitutional principle, declared the Court (in an abstract review proceeding), the value of life, when informed by the supreme value of dignity, takes precedence over the right to the development of the human personality. In a nuanced balancing process, however, the Court did not wholly reject the dignity or personality rights of pregnant women, for the FCC ruled that in verified hardship cases the state may be required, out of regard for the dignity and personality *rights* of pregnant women, to provide statutorily for the decriminalization of abortion.[73] So, in such situations, the subjective right would trump the objective value.

Still another example of the clash of values and rights is the well-known *Lebach Case* (1973) in which the FCC enjoined the broadcasting of a television play about a notorious and widely publicized crime that had taken place years earlier.[74] Long after the publicity had died down, and with the defendant about to be released from prison, a TV station planned to reenact the crime while disclosing the convict's name, displaying his picture, and divulging the details of his personal

---

[71] P Quint puts it this way: 'These [objective] values are not only specified rights of individuals but are also part of the general legal order, benefiting not only individuals who may be in a certain relationship with the state but possessing relevance for all legal relationships in 'Free Speech and Private Law in German Constitutional Theory' (1989) 48 *Maryland Law Review* 261.

[72] 90 BVerfGE 60, 88 (1994). See also *Television Case I*, 12 BVerfGE 205 (1961) in which the FCC declared that 'broadcasting companies. . .must be so organized so that binding guidelines ensure that programs contain a minimum of balance, objectivity, and reciprocal respect' 262–63.

[73] 39 BVerfGE 1 (1975).   [74] See 35 BVerfGE 202 (1973).

life. The FCC noted that the press and public once had a valid interest in knowing the details of the complainant's life and crime. But with the passage of time, said the Court, the public's interest in the person of the convict recedes, whereas his personal, private interest in living within the community and entering into fulfilling relations with other persons increases. 'The pre-eminent importance of the right to the free development and respect of personality,' said the Court, 'which follows from its close connection with the supreme value enshrined in the Constitution, ie, human dignity, demands that any intrusion of the right to personality which may appear necessary to protect such interest, must always be balanced against the protective rule [ie, the value] laid down in Art 2(1) in conjunction with Art 1(1) of the Constitution.' This 'balancing' process, as the Court described its process of reasoning, resulted in a victory for the complainant. Dignity prevailed over the freedom to broadcast a long-ago event eminently newsworthy at the time of its occurrence. In the United States, by contrast, as *Time Inc. v Hill* (1967) would suggest,[75] liberty—ie, the right to publish a public event involving a private person, no matter how long ago it occurred—would have prevailed over dignity.

It might be noted that not all the justices—or constitutional scholars—are comfortable with the value theory of constitutional interpretation. Wolfgang Zeidler, a former President of the FCC, strongly criticized the Court's tendency 'to superimpose "a higher order of values" on the positive constitutional order.'[76] In his opinion, the notion of a basic value order—a 'tyranny of values' according to some commentators[77]—was often used as a tool to incorporate religious and philosophical views into the meaning of the Constitution.[78] By advancing the notion of an objective value order, the Court seems to have rejected, at least in its earlier years, the legal positivism (*Rechtspositivismus*) and moral relativism presumed to have been at the basis of Weimar's constitutional order. In recent years, however, the exact source of the Basic Law's objective values has been a disputed subject on and off the Court. Those who would describe themselves as legal positivists—the dominant perspective today among judges and constitutional scholars—find these values anchored in the Basic Law itself or, perhaps

[75] 385 US 374 (1967). *Hill* vindicated the right to publish a newsworthy event even though the private persons involuntarily caught up in the event were presented in a 'false light.'

[76] W Zeidler 'Grundrechte und Grundentscheidungen der Verfassung im Widerstreit' Festvortrag anlässlich des 53. Deutschen Juristentages in Berlin am Dienstag, 16 September, 1980 3.

[77] Carl Schmitt, the Weimar Republic's renowned, conservative critic of liberal constitutionalism, was the first to describe the objective value theory in these terms. See 'Die Tyrannei der Werte' in *Säkularisation und Utopie: Ebracher Studien* 1967 37–57.

[78] On other occasions, however, President Zeidler wrote as if he too were subscribing to value theory. 'Far from being some vague spirit hovering over the land,' he noted, '[basic] values can be discerned by a careful reading of the Basic Law.' Zeidler note 76, 4. The values he specifically mentioned, perhaps betraying his Social Democratic background, were those of equality, social justice, the welfare state, the rule of law, and militant democracy. These values, he said, constitute the 'objective contents' of the Basic Law and are equal in rank to any and all guaranteed basic rights. Like German constitutional commentators generally, he distinguished basic rights from basic values, and appeared as willing as other justices to use values for the purpose of overriding rights.

more precisely, in the intent of the Constitution's framers. Others find them embedded in the history or traditions of the German people; that is, in customs, habits, practices, or virtues that define a way of life to which Germans, as a people, are committed and which drive the interpretation of law. Here the task of interpretation is no less than creating and maintaining a nation of shared values. Still others, finally, continue to speak in the language of universal values or ethical principles that transcend society, tradition, or the written Constitution.[79]

Negative and positive rights

German constitutional theory posits the dual character of basic rights. These rights are both negative and positive as well as subjective and objective.[80] A negative right is a subjective right to liberty. It protects individuals against the state, vindicating their right to freedom and personal autonomy. A positive right, on the other hand, represents a claim the individual has on the state and, more generally, on society. In the German understanding, positive rights embrace not only a right to certain social needs but also a right to the *effective* realization of personal freedoms and autonomy. Yet, as we have seen in the discussion of objective values, personal freedom and autonomy are limited by the requirements of human dignity—which the state is duty-bound to foster and respect—and the common good, a principle found to exist in the Basic Law's 'social state' clause as well as in Art 14(2), requiring that property be used for the 'public good.' Another way of describing the German perspective is to suggest that the Basic Law embodies a 'facilitative' model of freedom as opposed to the American 'privatizing' model deeply rooted in Lockean political theory. The facilitative model, as W. Cole Durham defines it, '[reflects] a tradition in which freedom tends to be seen not as the polar opposite of community, but as a value that must be achieved in synthesis with community.' In this setting, Durham continues, 'it is natural for the state to assume a more affirmative role in actualizing specific constitutional rights.'[81]

Although closely related, a positive right is not the same as an objective value. An objective value imposes a duty upon the state. The state must create and maintain an environment conducive to the realization of basic values. In short, objective values speak to the organization of the state and society as a whole. A positive right, on the other hand, is an *individual* right or, perhaps more accurately, an entitlement that the individual may claim *from* the state. Reference to the positivity of rights implicates the particular situation of an individual, one who may need the state's help to enjoy a basic right effectively, such as, for example, the right to

[79] These are the senses in which objective values are said to have an independent reality under the Basic Law. For extensive treatments of these perspectives see J Ispen *Staatsrecht II: Grundrechte* (8th edn., Luchterhand Verlag, Berlin, 2005) 30–37 and C Starck *Das Bonner Grundgesetz* (4th edn., Verlag Franz Vahlen, Munich, 1999) 120–125.

[80] See D Currie 'Positive and Negative Grundrechte' (1986) 111 *Archiv des Öffentlichen Rechts* 230–52.

[81] WC Durham 'General Assessment of the Basic Law—An American View' in P Kirchhof and DP Kommers (eds) *Germany and Its Basic Law* (Nomos Verlagsgesellschaft, Baden-Baden, 1993) 45.

the development of one's personality. In this respect, the notion of a right under the Basic Law is broader than the concept of a right under the United States Constitution. A right in the German constitutionalist view embraces not only the right to be left alone, free of state interference, but also a claim to assistance in the enjoyment of the right.

It is not always clear, however, whether the positivity of a right prevails over its negativity. In the famous *School Prayer Case* (1979), for example, the positive right to confess one's belief in public—here in an interdenominational state school— trumped the negative right of certain parents and students opposed to school prayer. In a closely reasoned opinion, the Court carefully weighed all the arguments involved on both sides of this issue, finding that the voluntary nature of the prayer supported the exercise of positive freedom, in part out of respect for the constitutional right of parents to direct the religious education of their children. (Perhaps the decision is better understood in the light of the constitutional provision that makes religious instruction a normal part of the regular curriculum in state schools.) But the Court did not regard this as a zero-sum game. It warned that the negative right might have been violated in the presence of discrimination or ostracism. The accommodation in the special context of this case 'provided the teacher with an excellent opportunity to teach the importance of tolerance and mutual respect.'[82] On the other hand, in the highly controversial *Classroom Crucifix Case II* (1995), in which non-Christian parents objected to the prominent display of a crucifix in classrooms assigned to their children, the negative freedom of religion prevailed over the corresponding positive right.[83] Once again, the German analytical perspective is one of balancing or adjusting rights, not one of abstract or categorical interpretation, as seems so often the case in the United States.

The horizontality of rights

The famous *Lüth Case* (1958) resolved an interpretive issue that judges and scholars debated at length in the early 1950s, which was whether guaranteed rights constituted only defensive rights against the state or whether these rights were equally applicable to third persons whose complaints arise out of employment contracts, tortious conduct, or other private legal transactions or relationships.[84] In *Lüth*, Veit Harlan, a popular film director under the Nazi regime and the producer of a notoriously antisemitic film, sued Erich Lüth, Hamburg's director of information, for publicly advocating a boycott of his new film. An active member of an organization of Christians and Jews, Lüth was outraged by Harlan's recrudescence in film making after the War. In response, Harlan sued Lüth under Article 826 of the Civil Code, obligating any person causing 'damage to another

---

[82] 52 BverfGE 223, 249–50 (1979). The United States Supreme Court reached the opposite conclusion in the case of *Engel v Vitale*, 370 US 421 (1962).   [83] 93 BVerfGE 1 (1995).
[84] 7 BVerfGE 198 (1958).

person intentionally and in a manner offensive to good morals' to compensate that person for the damage.

Lüth, a seminal free speech case, formalizes much of what has already been said about the FCC's interpretive perspective. First, the case emphasizes the importance of the personal and social dimensions of speech. Second, the FCC speaks of the negative and positive character of basic rights. (Its negativity protects the individual against official restraints on speech; its positivity obliges the state and its agents to establish conditions necessary for the effective exercise of speech rights.) Third, and most importantly for present purposes, *Lüth* solidifies the canonical status of the Basic Law as a hierarchy of objective values. The case also acknowledges that basic rights are indeed fundamentally negative rights against the state, suggesting that constitutional rights normally prevail over any countervailing public law. But the Court goes on to say that the Constitution's objective values 'reinforce the effective power of these rights,' extending their reach *indirectly* into the domain of private law (the so-called *Drittwirkung*, literally 'third-party effect'). Thus, constitutional law interacts with—or, as the FCC occasionally puts it, has a 'radiating effect' upon—private law, requiring the latter to be interpreted in conformity with the former. Here constitutional law seldom overrides private law but rather transforms it or, more precisely, *influences* its interpretation. This teaching has resulted in the virtual constitutionalization of private law, effectively giving rise to a 'constitutional tort' when a private legal relationship arguably interferes with a basic right.

After ruling that s 826 constitutes a 'general statute' within the meaning of Art 5(2),[85] the FCC held that a general statute in the field of private law must be read in the light of the Constitution's values. When constitutional rights—here freedom of speech—conflict with valid social interests protected by ordinary civil or criminal law, the lower courts, declared the FCC, are under an obligation to weigh the significance of the constitutional value against the importance of the statutorily protected social interest. The FCC insisted that it is not an appellate tribunal (a *Revisionsgericht*); it refused to assess facts *de novo* or to review the correctness of lower court judgments; it claimed merely to be engaged in determining whether lower courts have attached the proper weight to constitutional values in the application of statutory law. *Lüth* held that the lower court, by focusing on Harlan's private interests to the exclusion of any meaningful consideration of the significance of Lüth's free speech rights, had failed to engage in the necessary weighing or balancing process. Lüth won the case largely because of the public educational importance of his message. The lower court's focus on Harlan's private interest as a film-maker—a mere economic interest—was unacceptable in

---

[85] The provision reads: 'These [speech] rights find their limits in the provisions of general statutes, in statutory provisions for the protection of young persons, and in the right to respect for personal honor.' According to *Lüth*, statutes protective of valid public interests or the common good are 'general statutes' within the meaning of art 5(2). Excluded from the category of such statutes are laws that seek directly to suppress a particular message or viewpoint.

view of the purity of Lüth's motives and the overriding public interest in the reasons for the boycott.

In still another leading case, decided in 1969,[86] a small pro-communist newspaper, *Blinkfür*, which published the text of radio programs from East Berlin, sued a powerful conservative publisher in West Berlin for advising its dealers to boycott *Blinkfür* and for threatening to withhold its products from them if they refused. The newspaper sued for damages under the Civil Code, but the Federal Supreme Court held for the publisher on free speech grounds. The FCC reversed, vindicating *Blinkfür's* claim on an alternative free speech rationale, namely, the right to disseminate information on radio programs in East Berlin. As one commentator has suggested, this case seems to 'require the judiciary to create what is in effect a constitutional cause of action that will allow private individuals to enforce their constitutional interests against other private individuals.'[87]

Lüth's doctrine of 'horizontal effect' has lost none of its vitality over the years. The most prominent, recent example of the horizontal extension of constitutional rights is the recent *Marital Agreement Case* (2001).[88] It involved a signed agreement between a pregnant woman—the mother of a five-year old child from her first marriage—and her new husband. The agreement specified that in the event of a divorce, she would not sue her husband for alimony, although he in turn agreed to pay her a monthly sum of $80 for the support of the child she was carrying. Several years later they divorced, and she sued him for additional support in the light of his superior financial situation. The woman filed a constitutional complaint against a lower court judgment sustaining the validity of the original agreement. Citing *Lüth*, the FCC demurred, holding that the judge below had misunderstood the scope and impact of the marriage and family clause of Art 6 when viewed in tandem with the principle of equality between men and women required by Art 3(2). Even though entered into 'freely,' said the Court, the marital agreement did not represent the 'contractual parity' protected by the institution of marriage. Here a financially well-off man had exploited a financially distressed woman. The Court concluded that the constitutionally required equality between men and women may not be sacrificed within the constitutionally protected marital relationship.[89]

Structures and relationships

What is most notable about the FCC's approach to federalism and separation of powers is its contrast to the relatively non-interventionist orientation of the United States Supreme Court. With a few major exceptions in recent years, the

---

[86] 25 BVerfGE 256 (1969).

[87] P Quint 'Free Speech and Private Law in German Constitutional Law' (1989) 48 *Maryland Law Review* 277. Needless to say, 'state action' would have been required to adjudicate the free speech claim in the United States.   [88] 103 BVerfGE 89 (2001).

[89] For examples of commercial contracts voided by the Court in the light of constitutional values, see 81 BVerfGE 242 (1990) and 89 BVerfGE 214 (1993).

Supreme Court has played a minor role in resolving conflicts between levels and branches of government.[90] The Court has been content to remit their resolution to the dynamics of the national political process. By contrast, the FCC has played—and was meant to play—a vital role in reinforcing separated and divided powers. The FCC's pivotal role here can be explained by the Basic Law's complex power-sharing arrangements, its equally complex system of administrative federalism, and its detailed enumeration of exclusive and concurrent powers, not to mention provisions requiring revenue sharing among the states and between the states and the federal government, a legal framework that has generated scores of cases over the years.

Unlike Marshall's broad construction of federal power under the United States Constitution, the FCC has tended to reject implied federal power under the Basic Law. Except for two recent cases limiting the reach of Congress's commerce power,[91] the Supreme Court's nationalistic—post-1937—commerce clause jurisprudence has no equivalent in German constitutional law. Indeed, the Basic Law has had to be amended several times to ensure that certain specified subjects—such as 'the regulation of hospital charges'—fall within the federal government's concurrent power over 'economic affairs.'[92] In short, what limited exclusive powers the *Länder* do possess the FCC has vigorously defended against federal intrusion. In the field of broadcasting, for example, which falls within the state's power over cultural affairs, the Court has jealously guarded the rights of the *Länder*.[93] Early on, the Court even refused to enforce an international treaty in a *Land* whose school system conflicted with its educational provisions—a decision contrary to the anti-states rights result in the famous American case of *Missouri v Holland* (1920).[94] This absence of a strong judicial nationalism probably has something to do with the role played by the *Länder*, through the *Bundesrat*, in electing half of the FCC's members.

In fact, the Court has jealously guarded the *Bundesrat's* status and procedures. Particularly noteworthy are the *Pension Amendment* and *Immigration Act Cases*. The first, decided in 1975, effectively multiplied the laws requiring the *Bundesrat's* consent, to the point where almost 55 per cent of all federal legislation now requires the upper chamber's approval.[95] The second, decided in 2002, was the FCC's controversial decision nullifying Brandenburg's four 'yes' votes in favor of a

---

[90] Among the recent exceptions are *Immigration and Naturalization Service v Chadha*, 462 US 919 (1983); *Printz v United States*, 521 US 898 (1997); and *Clinton v City of New York*, 524 US 417 (1998).

[91] See *United States v Lopez*, 514 US 547 (1995) and *United States v Morrison*, 529 US 598 (2000).

[92] See for example GG art 74 and 19a.

[93] *Television I Case*, 12 BVerfGE 205 (1961, nullifying the effort to establish a federally-operated television station) is the seminal case.

[94] See respectively *Concordat Case*, 6 BVerfGE 309 (1957) and 252 US 416 (1920).

[95] See *Bundesrat Case*, 37 BVerGE 363 (1975). The Basic Law requires the *Bundesrat's* consent when federal law substantially alters the procedures of state administration. (Recall that most federal law is carried out by *Land* administrative agencies.) When amending the Pension Reform Act of 1972, the *Bundestag* maintained that the *Bundesrat's* consent was not required because the amendment did not change the original statute's 'essential content.' The *Bundesrat Case* ruled otherwise.

major immigration reform bill enacted by the SPD-led *Bundestag* a few months earlier. Brandenburg's vote, cast by the state's Social Democratic prime minister, was just enough to win the *Bundesrat's* consent. But the vote was cast over the initial 'no' vote of one of the *Land's* CDU delegates, the split resulting from the state's SPD-CDU coalition government. In challenging the voting procedure, CDU-led *Länder* argued that a prime minister may not constitutionally cast a state's 'unit' vote in the absence of unanimity among its delegates. Meanwhile, the Federal President, convinced that Brandenburg had cast a valid vote, had signed the bill into law. The FCC ruled otherwise. In a six to two vote, the Court invalidated the procedure, and by doing so prevented an important immigration reform measure from entering into force.[96] Interestingly, the *Immigration Act Case* was an abstract judicial review proceeding, which would not have been decided under the standing requirements of constitutional litigation in the United States.

Separation-of-powers cases feature similar contrasts between the German and American tribunals. Two examples will suffice. First, whereas the Supreme Court now rarely, if ever, strikes down a delegation of legislative power to the executive, the FCC places sharp limits on such delegations of authority. There is a textual basis for the German approach. Article 80 provides that delegations of authority to agencies must specify in law the 'content, purpose, and scope' of the power conferred. Taking this provision seriously, the FCC has struck several laws deemed to violate the principle of 'legality of administration.'[97] The second example includes cases on foreign and military affairs. Whereas the Supreme Court often regards issues raised in such cases as 'political questions' unfit for judicial resolution, the FCC has unhesitatingly applied the Basic Law to foreign and military affairs. Apropos is the recent *AWACS Case* of 2003, in which the Court agreed to hear the parliamentary FDP's application for an injunction against the government's deployment of German soldiers in Turkey, following NATO's decision to intervene militarily to protect Turkey from Iraqi attacks. The question was whether the deployment required the *Bundestag's* approval. In principle, the Court said 'yes' but here, as in related cases, the Court ruled that the constitution confers broad freedom of action on the executive, particularly when acting pursuant to transnational military agreements, to provide for the country's defense and security.[98] As mentioned earlier, the FCC has rejected the 'political question' doctrine as known in the United States. But in deciding AWACS-like cases on the merits, the Court often gives political actors considerable leeway, a perspective that may be regarded as the functional equivalent of a political question doctrine.

The FCC has had a major influence on legislative and electoral politics. Its decisions range from the *Legislative Pay Case* (1975), where the Court virtually dictated higher salaries for parliamentarians, to the recent *Wüppersahl Case* (1989)

---

[96] 106 BVerfGE 310 (2002).

[97] For a discussion of these cases, see DP Kommers *The Constitutional Jurisprudence of the Federal Republic of Germany* (2nd edn., Duke University Press, Durham, NC 1997) 137–148.

[98] 108 BVerfGE 34 (2003).

invalidating a ruling depriving a nonparty deputy of his speaking rights on the floor of the *Bundestag*. Other significant decisions include judicial rulings (1) declaring anti-democratic parties unconstitutional, (2) guarding the rights of minority parties in federal and state legislatures, (3) setting forth conditions for the public funding of political parties, (4) forbidding a party to change the order of candidates on a party list after the voting has taken place, (5) invalidating laws permitting foreign residents to vote in state and local elections, (6) sustaining in the interest of political stability the rule requiring a party to win five percent of the popular vote before being allowed to enter parliament, (7) invalidating the legal exclusion of parties not represented in the *Bundestag* from public funding in federal election campaigns, and (8) striking down provisions of a federal tax law allowing individuals and corporations to deduct their donations to political parties up to a certain percentage of their total income on the ground that these deductions unfairly discriminate against parties unable to draw support from wealthy contributors.[99]

Sources of Interpretation

Unwritten principles

Almost everything said so far in this essay about the nature of the Basic Law as a whole or of basic rights in particular raise profound problems of interpretation. Principles and theories such as the Basic Law's unity, its objective value dimension, its constitutionalization of private law, and the Constitution's integrative function have served to confer substantial interpretive authority on the FCC. These principles and theories have been judicially created, but not out of whole cloth. In the Court's view, they reflect the normative realities underlying the Basic Law, realities rooted in the dialectic between the liberal, socialist, and Christian natural law traditions that shaped the original document, particularly the provision that subjects the legislature to the 'constitutional order' and the executive and the judiciary to 'law *and justice*' (italics supplied). Owing largely to neo-Thomist influences, the FCC affirmed the existence of 'supra-positive principles of law' (*überpositive Rechtsgrundsätze*) that bind legislators and other political decision makers.[100] But as George Fletcher has pointed out, the FCC's later accents on individual autonomy, moral duty, and human rationality echo equally strong neo-Kantian influences,[101] just as the powerful strands of social welfare theory in the Court's case law may be said to reflect socialist egalitarian thought.

[99] For a discussion of these and related cases, see Kommers n 97, ch 5.

[100] *Southwest State Case*, 1 BVerfGE 14, 61 (1951), the landmark decision that has been compared to *Marbury v Madison*, 1 Cranch 137 (1803). Kommers n 97, 66–67. The relevance of these supra-positive principles was also emphasized in the *Southwest Electoral Association Case*, 1 BVerfGE 208, 233 (1953), *Matrimonial Equalization Case*, 3 BVerfGE 225, 232 (1953); and the *National Socialist Law Case*, 23 BVerfGE 98, 106 (1968).

[101] G Fletcher 'Human Dignity as a Constitutional Value' (1984) 22 *University of Western Ontario Law Review* 178–82.

These orientations have converged to produce a distinctive vision of the human person. In the famous *Life Imprisonment Case* (1977), the Court defined the human person as a 'spiritual-moral being' (*vom Menschen als einem geistig-sit-tlichen Wesen*) whose intrinsic dignity 'depends on his status as an independent [personality].'[102] But the independence affirmed here is far from the autonomous individualism of American constitutional law. 'The image of man in the Basic Law,' the FCC has declared, ' is not that of an isolated, sovereign individual; rather, the Basic Law has decided in favor of a relationship between individual and community in the sense of a person's dependence on and commitment to the community, without infringing upon a person's individual value.'[103] These words have been a constant refrain in the Court's jurisprudence. Similar lines of thought can be discerned in the Court's view of the polity, one that rejects the self-regarding individualism of *bourgeois* liberalism as well as the collectivism of Marxism. Much of the FCC's case law identifies a polity that reminds Americans of Lincoln's image of a fraternal democracy. As the abortion cases and many free speech decisions show, the social context in which men and women discover the source of their dignity—and human flourishing—cannot be ignored in a properly governed society. Accordingly, human dignity resides not only in individuality but in sociality as well.

The written Constitution

The major source of constitutional interpretation in Germany is the documentary text adopted by the *Länder* legislatures in 1949 along with 49 major amendatory Acts ratified between 1951 and 2004. The words and phrases of the constitution mean what they say, and the Court takes them seriously. It rarely interprets constitutional language in a way radically different from the common understanding of the text. But, as suggested in later subsections, the FCC has employed a wide range of interpretative approaches and guides to expound the meaning of the written text. These include legalistic modes of analysis along with an effort to determine the general purpose of textual provisions in the light of their historical, philosophical, and socio-moral determinants.

But the constitution includes more than the documentary text. What might be called the *working* text arguably extends to long-established practices whose attenuation would raise serious constitutional issues. These practices include, under Germany's system of proportional representation, the requirement that a political party garner at least five per cent of the popular vote as a condition of entering parliament. Although the Court has never declared that proportional representation itself is constitutionally required,[104] its abolition after 55 years of unbroken

---

[102] 45 BVerfGE 187, 227 (1977).

[103] *Investment Aid Case*, 4 BVerfGE 7, 15–16 (1954). Time and again over the years the Court has invoked this passage in its decisional law. For example *Conscientious Objector Case I*, 12 BVerfGE 45, 51 (1960) and *Klass Case*, 30 BVerfGE 1, 20 (1970).

[104] See for example 16 BVerfGE 130 (1963).

observance could easily be contested on constitutional grounds, especially in the light of the Court's solicitude for the rights and representational value of minority parties. An unwritten norm previously unmentioned but which is now a solid part of the working text is the principle of federal comity (*Bundestreue*), an innovative doctrine the Court has inferred from the Basic Law's federal structure. It requires more than the observance of formal constitutional legality; it also requires both levels of government to consult with each other when their interests conflict or overlap.[105] A 1992 change in the Basic Law actually formalized the principle of comity in the field of European affairs. When making agreements with the European Union, the federal government is now required to keep the *Bundesrat* informed of its negotiations.[106] Even when dealing with the European Union under one of its exclusive powers, the federal government, according to Art 23(4), 'shall take the position of the *Bundesrat* into account.' Given the FCC's jurisprudence of federal comity, there is no reason to believe that the *Bundesrat* would be unable validly to petition the FCC to hear a case when arguing that its position was not adequately taken into account by the national government. Politically loose or indeterminate language such as this would almost surely be resistant to judicial intervention in the United States.

Historical materials

The FCC occasionally draws upon historical materials to illuminate the general purpose behind a constitutionally ordained concept, value, or institution. This purpose inquiry is not always clearly differentiated from inquiry into original intent, a topic taken up in the next subsection. When appealing to purpose, the FCC usually considers the background or circumstances out of which a particular constitutional provision emerged. Because so many of the Basic Law's words and phrases have been lifted from 19th and 20th century constitutions, both state and national, the FCC often finds it useful to explore the reasons for their incorporation into these earlier documents. For example, in determining whether the inviolability of the 'home' (*Wohnung*) within the meaning of Art 13(1) extends to business offices, the Court consulted the debates and commentaries on similar provisions incorporated into the Frankfurt Constitution of 1848–49, the Prussian Constitution of 1850, and the Weimar Constitution of 1919.[107]

While admissible as sources of interpretation, these older documents pale in comparison to the significance of the Basic Law's legislative history. This history includes the report of the Herrenchiemsee conference, the body charged

---

[105] For a discussion of this principle and its application see Kommers n 97, 69–75.

[106] GG art 23(2).

[107] *Handicraft Trade Case*, 32 BverfGE 54, 69 (1971). Also EW Böckenförde 'Wie Werden in Deutchland die Grundrechte im Verfassungsrecht interpretiert' (2004) 31 *Europäische Grundrechte* 598–603. A former justice of the FCC, the author argues that issues dealing with the current interpretation of basic rights under the 1949 constitution cannot be understood in the absence of their historical development.

with preparing a working draft of the Basic Law.[108] The most fertile source for examining the background and purposes of the Basic Law, however, is the daily stenographic record of the debates and decisions of the Parliamentary Council. The protocols include the proceedings of all the Council's specialized committees, together with the arguments, decisions, and voting records of its Main Committee and plenary sessions.[109] The Court seems to find references to these protocols particularly helpful in cases involving conflicts between levels and branches of government. For example, in the famous *Flick Case* (1984), which arose out of a notorious tax and party finance scandal, the Court invoked Parliamentary Council debates to show that a parliamentary investigative committee established under Art 44 of the Basic Law could require the executive to surrender all the relevant records in the case.[110] In the equally prominent *Parliamentary Dissolution Case* (1984), the Court's majority concluded that there was nothing in the Council's proceedings that contradicted its view that the Federal President could dissolve parliament on the request of the Chancellor even though the latter had the backing of a slim parliamentary majority.[111] The dissenting opinion, however, contradicting the majority's view, was based almost entirely on lengthy quotations from the Council's members,[112] illustrating, as in American constitutional debates, that legislative history can be invoked to support more than one side of an argument over the constitution's meaning.

Judicial precedents

In Germany's codified legal system, judicial decisions do not qualify as official sources of law. But constitutional law is different. First, while the rulings of ordinary courts apply only to the parties before them, the FCC's decisions are binding on all courts and constitutional organs.[113] Second, all abstract and concrete review cases, along with decisions on whether a rule of public international law is an integral part of federal law, enjoy the force of general law. In fact, any decision declaring a law null and void or compatible or incompatible with the Basic Law must be published in the book of federal statutes known as the *Federal Law Gazette*,[114] a practice that underscores the FCC's character as a negative legislator.

[108] *Bericht über den Verfassungskonvent auf Herrenchiemsee vom 10. Bis 23. August 1948* (Richard Pflaum Verlag Munich). The Herrenchiemsee report has been cited in several opinions. See for example 16 BVerfGE 306, 318 (1963); 32 BVerfGE 54, 69 (1971); 51 BVerfGE 97, 108 (1979); and 62 BVerfGE 1, 86–105 (1984).

[109] The stenographic report of the Parliamentary Council's proceedings is available in typescript in the archives of the Bundestag and in the libraries of several law faculties. The reports have also been published. See for example *Parlamentarischer Rat: Stenographischer Bericht: Verhandlungen des Hauptausschusses* (Bonn: Bonner Universitäts-Buchdruckerei Gebr Scheur GmbH). All the protocols and documents related to the Basic Law were recently reorganized by topic and committee proceedings and published in a set of 12 volumes. See *Der Parlamentarische Rat 1948–1949* (Harald Boldt Verlag Munich). The volumes appeared periodically between 1975 and 1999. A summary of the debates on each article of the Basic Law has also been published in Volume 1 (926 pages) of *Jahrbuch des Öffentlichen Rechts*, Neue Folge (1951). [110] 67 BVerfGE 100, 130–131 (1984). [111] 62 BVerfGE 1, 44–47 (1984). [112] ibid 86–105. [113] FCCA art 31(1). [114] FCCA art 31(2).

Although the FCC rejects the principle of *stare decisis* as such, its opinions, like those of other high courts, are studded with citations to its case law. In the recent *Muslim Headscarf Case* (2003), for example, the Court supported its reasoning by reference to no fewer than 26 decisions handed down between 1957 and 1999.[115] Formally, judicial precedents do not *bind* the FCC; rather, they are marshalled to show that the FCC's established case law is consistent with its interpretation of the constitutional code (namely, the Basic Law). The German understanding of the rule of law—a central pillar of the Basic Law—requires a coherent body of decisional law in the interest of legal certainty, predictability, and the necessity of creating a stable constitutional order. In actual practice, however, the similarities in the uses (or misuses) of precedent by the FCC and other courts treated in this book are more striking than the differences.[116]

Academic writings

The work of academic lawyers carries as much if not more weight in the Basic Law's interpretation than judicial precedents. The Court relies heavily on treatises and commentaries of established legal professionals, and here it must be remembered that in code law countries such as Germany, enacted law was the work-product of legal scholars, historians, and theorists. It is no surprise, therefore, that the 'ruling opinion' (*herrschende Meinung*) in the literature takes pride of place in the interpretation of the Basic Law. The literature includes highly reputable law journals such as *Neue Juristische Wochenschrift, Monatschrift für Deutsches Recht, Juristenzeitung,* and *Zeitschrift für ausländisches öffentliches Recht und Völkerrecht.* These and other German law journals are edited not by amateurs, that is, law students, as in the United States, but by leading practitioners, judges, and professors of law. (Student-authored notes in these journals would be unheard of in Germany's legal culture.) The most often cited, and most highly regarded, commentary on the Basic Law is the loose-leaf edition of *Kommentar zum Grundgesetz* by Theodor Maunz, Günter Dürig, and Roman Herzog.[117] The latter—Herzog—was President

---

[115] 108 BVerfGE 282 (2003)

[116] The increasing importance of judicial precedents has been underscored in recent years by the publication of several casebooks in constitutional law. See for example J Schwabe (eds) *Entscheidungen des Bundesverfassungsgerichts,* (6th edn., Hamburg, 1994 [privately published and distributed]). This short paperback book is made up largely of headnotes and brief passages from relevant decisions arranged on an article-by-article basis without commentary. In addition, two former justices of the FCC have published 104 of the Court's leading opinions arranged in chronological order (again without commentary) in a two-volume paperback edition. See D Grimm and P Kirchhof (ed) *Entscheidungen des Bundesverfassungsgerichts: Studienauswahl* (2nd edn., JCB Mohr [P Siebeck], Tübingen, 1997). A third casebook, and the most useful, has been organized under 30 of the 146 articles of the Basic Law and combines brief excerpts from leading cases with annotated commentaries. See I Richter and GF Schuppert *Verfassungsrecht* (3rd edn., CH Beck'sche Verlagsbuchhandlung, Munich, 1996).

[117] In recent decades, the original authors have been joined by R Scholz, P Lerche, HJ Papier, A Randelzhofer, and E Schmidt-Aßmann, all distinguished professors of law. (Interestingly, Papier became President of the Federal Constitutional Court in 1998. He, like Herzog, was proposed by the CDU/CSU.) One other authoritative and frequently cited commentary is the three-volume set

of the FCC from 1987 to 1994 and President of the Federal Republic from 1994 to 1999.

The recent *Muslim Headscarf Case* (2003) shows how dependent the FCC is on the scholarship of the professorate and other legal experts. In the Court's closely reasoned opinion on the meaning of constitutional provisions relating to the free exercise of religion (GG Arts 4.1, 4.2, 6.2, and 7.2), the Court relied heavily on interpretive commentaries by major writers on the religion clauses such as Karl Brinkman, Axel von Campenhausen, Peter Badura, Christian Starck, Joseph Listl, Roman Herzog, and Ernst-Wolfgang Böckenförde.[118] (Böckenförde, like Herzog, was a former justice of the FCC) These authors are repeatedly cited as authoritative interpreters of the Basic Law. Perhaps a better measure of the importance of legal scholarship relative to judicial precedents is the standard practice of documentation in leading constitutional commentaries. For example, in the oft-cited commentary by Hermann von Mangoldt, Friedrich Klein, and Christian Starck, only 90 of 374 footnotes in the paragraphs devoted to Art 4.1 and 4.2 on religious freedom include references to prior case law, and many of these precedents are employed to justify the basic orientation of the commentators.[119] By contrast, a comparative examination of two leading American commentaries shows an almost exclusive reliance on the case law of the Supreme Court.[120]

Comparative and international materials

The Basic Law commits the Federal Republic to internationalism. Several constitutional provisions embody this commitment,[121] the most important of which is Art 25, the provision that makes 'general rules of international law' an integral part of domestic law. Article 25 provides that these general rules 'take precedence

by H Mangoldt, F Klein, and C Starck, *Das Bonner Grundgesetz* (4th edn., Verlag Franz Vahlen, Munich, 1999–2000). Its 8,183 pages is one measure of its scope and depth.

[118] See n 108 above. In the well-known *Jehovah's Witnesses Case*, the FCC relied almost exclusively on Böckenförde's off-the-bench writings on the relationship between the state and religious associations. Also 102 BVerfGE 370 (2000).

[119] See n 110, Vol. 1 (1999) 496–561. One commentary, however, is based exclusively on the decisions of the Federal Constitutional Court. The commentary is distinctive for this reason. See G Leibholz, HJ Rinck, and D Hesselberger *Grundgesetz für die Bundesrepublik Deutschland: Kommentar an Hand der Rechtsprechung des Bundesverfassungsgerichts* (7th edn., Schmitt, Cologne, 1993). Interestingly, both Leibholz and Rinck, long deceased, were members of the FCC. Dieter Hesselberger, a judge of the Federal Supereme Court—and now also deceased—edited later editions of the book. This book is not an *analytical* commentary of the American hornbook model. Like other commentaries, it proceeds article-by-article with extended excerpts from relevant decisions of the FCC.

[120] See LH Tribe *American Constitutional Law* Vol 1 (2nd edn., Foundation Press, New York, 2000): JE Nowak and RD Rotunda *Constitutional Law* (6th edn., St Paul MN: West Group, 2000) 1307–1428.

[121] The preamble, for example, exhorts the German people 'to promote world peace as an equal partner in a united Europe.' In addition, art 23, which in 1990 replaced the earlier article providing for the incorporation of certain German territories into the Federal Republic, commits the national government to the creation of and participation in the European Union, just as art 24 provides for the 'transfer [of] sovereign powers to international organizations.'

over statutes and directly create rights and duties for the inhabitants of the federal territory.' Accordingly, they are part of Germany's 'constitutional order' and thus binding on all branches and levels of government. So important are these rules that the Basic Law itself requires a court—any court—to obtain a decision from the FCC whenever, in the normal course of litigation, its judges doubt whether a general rule of international law is part of federal law or whether it directly creates rights and duties for individual persons.[122] Under this procedure, the FCC neither creates rules of international law nor does it resolve the particular issue before the lower court on the basis of a 'general rule' even if found to exist. It is rather engaged in what some commentators have called a 'verification proceeding' (*Verifikationsverfahren*),[123]—that is, it merely verifies whether the general principle exists in international law, after which it is up to the lower court to apply the general principle to the case at hand.[124]

The *Philippine Embassy Case* (1977) reveals the extent to which the FCC relies on customary rules of international law and other outside sources to identify a general rule of international law. In this case, the Court found such a rule in the proposition that a foreign court could not be subjected to the jurisdiction of a domestic court without the foreign state's consent when its non-sovereign activity contributes to its sovereign functions. The FCC discovered this rule by consulting practices among nations; international legal documents such as the United States Foreign Sovereign Immunities Act and the European Convention on State Immunity; the decisional law of Swiss, French, Dutch, Austrian, Scandinavian and American courts; major treatises on international law; and numerous yearbooks and essays on public international public law.[125]

The *Embassy Case* was a proceeding under the Basic Law's Article 100(2). But in dozens of other proceedings, especially those involving constitutional complaints, the FCC is required to consider whether a general rule of international law applies to a particular fact situation. Two recent examples come to mind. In the *East German Spy Case* (1995), former collaborators and agents of East Germany's Ministry of State Security challenged the validity of their convictions for spying on the Federal Republic. In their defense, the complainants cited

---

[122] GG art 100(2).

[123] See E Benda and E Klein *Lehrbuch des Verfassungsprozeßrechts* (CF Müller Verlag, Heidelberg, 1991) Rn 864, 362.

[124] The FCC has actually stretched the meaning of the Article 100(2) procedure to include doubts about the scope of a rule of public international law or about whether a clear rule of public international law rises to the level of a 'general principle' of public international law. See *Yugoslav Military Mission Case*, 15 BVerfGE 25 (1962, holding that a general rule of public international law exempting a foreign state from domestic jurisdiction does not exist). Actually, there have only been a handful of cases involving Article 100(2) verification procedure. These include cases where the Court has ruled that no general rule of public international law exists that would exempt Iran from domestic jurisdiction with respect to its non-sovereign activity—here a suit by a local heating firm against the Iranian Embassy—or that would require Germany not to prosecute a person for the same offense for which he was sentenced and incarcerated, and having served his full sentence, already in another state. See respectively *Iranian Embassy Case*, 16 BVerfGE 27 (1963) and *Fugitive Extradition Case*, 75 BverfGE 1 (1987).

[125] See 46 BVerfGE 342–404 (1977).

'binding norms of international law,' one of them allegedly being that spying activities against West Germany carried out on East German territory could not be criminally punished in reunified Germany. After examining international legal materials, including a legal opinion requested from Heidelberg's Max Planck Institute of International Public Law, the FCC held that the trial and conviction did not infringe a general rule of international law in violation of Art 25.[126] More recently, in 2003, after examining a variety of international legal materials, the FCC ruled that there was no general rule of international law that prevented the extradition of a Yemeni citizen lured to Germany by an undercover agent who had promised to put him in touch with a financial contributor willing to support his terrorist activities in the United States.[127]

It might be noted that the Court has occasionally expanded a basic right not recognized by general rules of international law. In the *Foreign Spouse Case* (1987), for example, the FCC acknowledged, as a matter of general principle, that states may control the entry of aliens into their sovereign territory. In this case, however, the FCC ruled that Art 6 of the Basic Law, obliging the state to confer its special protection on marriage and the family, and which incorporates both an institutional guarantee and an objective value, may not impose unreasonable barriers on the right of spouses living in non-European Union states (in this case Turkey and Yugoslavia) from joining their alien-worker husbands permanently resident in Germany.[128] *Foreign Spouse* recalls our previous discussion of the Basic Law's indirect horizontal effect on third parties; the FCC held that in denying these plaintiffs resident visas, the administrative courts below had failed to consider the overriding significance of Art 6 in Germany's constitutional order.

Approaches to Interpretation

Written constitutions are not self-actualizing. If they are to be maintained over time, they require interpretation and adaptation to changing circumstances. In each of the jurisdictions under study in this book, constitutional judges have developed modes of analysis and approaches to interpretation designed to keep faith with the principles and underlying values of the constitutional text. In Germany, these approaches include four methods of judicial reasoning commonly employed in both statutory and constitutional interpretation—ie, historical, grammatical, systematic, and teleological.[129] But they also embrace principles of proportionality and rationality that the state must satisfy to justify laws that limit basic rights. Still other approaches—we might call them prudential—reflect the Court's respect for the Basic Law's democratic aspirations. These include modes of

---

[126] 92 BVerfGE 320–323 (1995).   [127] *Al-M Case*, 109 BVerfGE 38 (2003)
[128] 76 BVerfGE 1 (1987).
[129] For an excellent treatment of these modes of interpretation see R Alexy and R Dreier 'Statutory Interpretation in the Federal Republic of Germany' in DN MacCormick and RS Summers (eds) *Interpreting Statutes: A Comparative Study* (Ashgate Publishing Company, Aldershot, 1995) 73–121.

judicial review that call for legislative collaboration in meeting constitutional objectives and the practice of declaring laws in conformity with the constitution when it is reasonable to do so even in the face of an alternative but reasonable interpretation in conflict with the documentary text.

Textual interpretation

The first rule of constitutional interpretation in Germany is that words mean what they say. Occasionally, words and phrases are construed in a narrow legal sense, as in cases involving the rights of criminal defendants, to satisfy the technical requirements of the law. In other instances, they tend to be interpreted in terms of their plain meaning. But plain meaning is not the same as literal meaning. Words draw meaning from their location in the text as well as from the passage of time. Then too words and phrases are regularly interpreted in the light of their putative purpose. For example, words like 'faith and 'conscience' in the clause on religious liberty are broadly construed to give maximum legal effect to the liberal spirit of the basic norm. Other terms such as 'public welfare,' 'economic affairs,' 'land law,' 'road traffic,' and 'commerce,' all subjects of the Federal Government's concurrent legislative power, have no precise meaning. In interpreting them, the Court looks to social and economic conditions, to the structural features of the Basic Law as a whole, and to the Constitution's drafting history. As the next section shows, the words and phrases of the text are often interpreted in the light of the legislative history behind their adoption.

Drafting history

Like Canada—and unlike the United States—the intentions of the Basic Law's framers are clearly secondary to other conventional approaches to constitutional interpretation. Often, when the FCC cites drafting history, it does so to support a decision arrived at by some other method of interpretation. In *Abortion Case I* (1975), for example, the Court devoted an entire section of its lengthy opinion to demonstrating that key members of the Parliamentary Council included fetal life within the protection of the general clause guaranteeing to 'everyone' the right to life.[130] By this stage of the opinion, however, the Court had already concluded that the 'human dignity' and 'right to life' clauses combined to require the state to protect the unborn. Similarly, in the *Parliamentary Committee Case*, one based largely on teleological reasoning, the FCC cited the proceedings of the Parliamentary Council to show that its decision defending the procedural rights of minority members of a parliamentary investigative committee did not contradict the will of the framers.[131]

---

[130] 39 BVerfGE 1, 38–42 (1975).

[131] 105 BVerfGE 197, 223 (2002). The case required an interpretation of the Basic Law's Article 44(1), providing for the establishment of parliamentary investigative committees upon the motion of one quarter of the *Bundestag's* members. Such a committee had been formed to look into a party finance scandal involving former Chancellor, Helmut Kohl. The question posed was whether the minority members of the committee could participate in naming witnesses and defining the scope of the investigation.

The drafting history of the Basic Law is most often cited when neither text nor context provides a clear answer to an interpretive problem. Or the Court might cite the framers to show that the drafting history does not exclude an interpretation that the text arguably forbids. For example, the Basic Law confers the state's 'special protection' on 'marriage and the family,' language that may raise doubts about the validity of same-sex civil unions. But after examining the original debates on the marriage and family clause, the Court concluded in the *Same-Sex Civil Partnership Case* (2002) that parliament may enact a civil partnership law without undermining the special constitutional protection the framers conferred on heterosexual marriage.[132] Examples of other cases citing drafting history include decisions decreeing that the Federal Government's power to regulate posts and telecommunications does not extend to the creation of a federal television station and holding that the adoption of educational standards for geriatric nursing care is within the Federal Government's concurrent power to lay down rules for 'admission to the medical profession and ancillary occupations.'[133] As these cases show, the Court frequently relies on drafting history to support—or rationalize—its resolution of conflicts between levels of government.[134]

More often than not, however, the Court ignores drafting history altogether, even where it might be invoked to illuminate arguments about the meaning of a particular textual provision, or the meaning behind the failure of the framers to adopt a particular provision. For example, the original draft of the Basic Law contained the famous *Sperrklausel* (exclusion clause), requiring a political party to secure five percent of the popular vote to gain entry into parliament under proportional representation. The striking of this provision elicited the general view that any legislative adoption of the *Sperrklausel* would be unlawful if not *expressly* permitted by the founding document.[135] The prime ministers nevertheless succeeded in inserting the clause into the law providing for the first election of the *Bundestag*, and it has remained a central feature of the electoral system ever since. Yet, in sustaining the validity of the *Sperrklausel*, the Court has chosen to rest its

---

[132] 105 BVerfGE 313 (2002).

[133] See, respectively, 12 BVerfGE 205, 236–237 (1961) and 106 BVerfGE 62, 105–107 (2002).

[134] See for example 68 BVerfGE 319, 331–332 (1984, declaring a federally imposed fee schedule for services provided by doctors to be within the Federal Government's concurrent power to regulate 'economic affairs') and 41 BVerfGE 205, 219–221 (1976, ruling that the *Länder* enjoy a monopoly over the regulation of certain fire insurance policies). Other examples of cases in which history is cited are 3 BVerfGE 225, 241 (1953, clarifying the meaning of equality between men and women within the meaning of Article 3 [2]); 51 BVerfGE 97, 108–109 (1979, holding that the protection against an unlawful seizure of property requires a warrant before a sheriff can enter the premises of a debtor for the purpose of attaching goods to satisfy a financial judgment against the latter); 83 BVerfGE 341, 354–355 (1991, finding that the special features of a religion must be taken into account when organized under the general provisions of civil law); and 85 BVerfGE 1, 12 (1991, validating a broad construction of the right to freedom of the press).

[135] 'Entstehungsgeschichte der Artikel des Grundgesetzes' (1951) 1 *Jahrbuch des Öffentlichen Rechts* (neue Folge) 349–353. See also J Frowein 'Bundesverfassungsgericht und Wahlrecht' (1974) 99 *Archiv des Öffentlichen Rechts* 90.

case on structural arguments or on a purposeful analysis rooted in the immediate or long-range needs of the political system.[136]

Structural interpretation

Another approach to constitutional interpretation is structural—or what the Germans call 'systematic' reasoning. This mode of reasoning stems from the FCC's view of the Basic Law as a unified structure of values and relationships. In its first major decision—the *Southwest State Case* (1951)—the Court underscored the critical importance of the Constitution's unity. 'No single constitutional provision may be taken out of its context and interpreted by itself,' declared the Court. 'Every constitutional provision,' it continued, 'must always be interpreted in such a way as to render it compatible with the fundamental principles of the Constitution as a whole.'[137] In its narrow sense, structural analysis focuses not on the meaning of specific, isolated clauses, but rather on the location of the clause and its relation to the whole text. In a broader sense, it seeks unity and coherence not only in the text, but in the larger political order the text signifies. There is a striking similarity between this perspective and the structural arguments advanced in leading American cases such as *McCulloch v Maryland* (1819) and *National League of Cities v Usery* (1976).[138]

But there is also a striking difference in the frequency and candor with which these approaches are used in Germany and the United States. Structural reasoning is deeply ingrained in Germany's culture of interpretation. It is as standard as doctrinal reasoning in the common law tradition, as the subsection below on 'practical concordance' teaches. Structural arguments in the Supreme Court, by contrast, are irregular or occasional and usually resorted to, but not always explicitly, when arguments from history, doctrine, precedent, and text fall short. Structural, like textual, interpretation is ostensibly oriented toward developing a consistent and predictable body of constitutional law that a state based on the rule of law requires. Actually, this approach is more open-ended and unpredictable than some justices are willing to admit.

How exactly a phrase, sentence, or article of the Basic Law is to be interpreted in the light of related provisions is anything but an exact science. Over the years, for example, the Court has had to explore the relationship between Art 21, which envisions political parties as major agencies of political representation, and Art 38,

[136] See for example 1 BVerfGE 208, 252 (1952), 4 BVerfGE 31, 41 (1954), 6 BVerfGE 84, 95 (1957), and 34 BVerfGE 81, 100 (1972).

[137] 1 BVerfGE 14, 32 (1951). Justice Gerhard Leibholz, a member of the Senate that decided *Southwest*, elaborated: 'The Court holds that each constitutional clause is in a definite relationship with all other clauses, and that together they form an entity. It considers certain constitutional principles and basic concepts to have emerged from the whole of the Basic Law to which other constitutional regulations are subordinate.' See *Politics and Law* (AW Sythoff Leiden 1965) 289.

[138] Respectively 17 US 316 (1819) and 426 US 833 (1976). Also K Ripple's discussion of structural interpretation in *Constitutional Litigation* (The Michie Company, Charlottesville VA, 1984) 14–20.

which declares members of the *Bundestag* as 'representatives of the whole people, not bound by orders or instructions, and responsible only to their conscience.' In the *Green Party Exclusion Case* (1986), the Second Senate divided six to two over whether minor parliamentary representatives could be excluded from membership on committees dealing with issues of national security.[139] The dissenting justices objected to the approved exclusion because they felt that elected members of parliament, who derive their authority from the people under the terms of Art 20 also represent the 'whole people' within the meaning of Art 38 and thus deserve some representation on parliamentary committees charged with managing the people's business.

Teleological interpretation

When construing the words, phrases, and clauses of the Basic Law, the FCC regularly adopts the teleological approach commonly used in statutory interpretation. The aim of this approach is to discover, and then to put into effect, the end or *telos* of the Constitution. In its German incarnation, the Basic Law represents a rational ordering of the polity toward its natural end, occasionally described as the 'common good,' a good discoverable in the underlying context or political morality of the constitution. Although this orientation to interpretation—one that prefers unity over multiplicity—continues to enjoy significant intellectual support on and off the Court, it is less prominent today than in the past, for three reasons often cited by its critics. First, its open-ended character tempts judges to import their political and moral views into the meaning of the Basic Law. Second, its vision of social and political harmony leaves little room for the play of political parties and interest groups in a modern pluralistic democracy. Finally, it competes with the liberal individualism that defines much of the FCC's work-product.

As applied today, however, teleological analysis is mainly an inquiry into the *function* of a rule, structure, or practice as it operates within the broad compass of contemporary social and political reality. Seeking interpretive guidance from the history and spirit of the constitution as a whole, functionalism emphasizes practical utility over abstract analysis and efficiency over textual literalism. The *Parliamentary Dissolution Case* (1984) is an illustration of this approach. The question before the Court was whether the Basic Law empowers the Federal President to dissolve the Bundestag and schedule new elections when the chancellor commands the support of a parliamentary majority, however slim. Chancellor Helmut Kohl had requested the President to dissolve parliament after he contrived to lose a vote of confidence in the expectation that new elections would increase his parliamentary majority. The constructive vote of no-confidence in tandem with the constitutional provision providing for an electoral mandate of four years for all members of the Bundestag would suggest—and this is the conventional view—that parliament cannot be dissolved before regularly scheduled

---

[139] 70 BVerfGE 324 (1986).

elections when the government enjoys majority support.[140] The Court concluded, however, over the objection of many constitutional scholars, that in the interest of effective parliamentary democracy, the President could dissolve parliament at the request of a Chancellor who feels that new elections would give him the comfortable working majority that he thinks is required to govern more effectively.[141]

An equally compelling example of teleological (or functional) reasoning is the FCC's case law under the equality provisions of Art 3. These provisions embrace the following paragraphs: (1) 'All persons are equal before the law'; (2) 'Men and women shall have equal rights'; and (3) 'No person may be disadvantaged or favored because of his sex, his parentage, his race, his language, his homeland and origin, his faith, or his religious or political opinions.' In *Nocturnal Employment*, the leading case, the FCC invalidated a federal law banning blue-collar female employees from working at night. Even when making clear that 'not every inequality based on sex offends paragraph 3,' the FCC noted that paragraph 2, when added to the ban on sex discrimination, embodies 'an affirmative command of equal opportunity [for men and women] that extends into the real social world.' The Court claimed that the purpose of paragraph 2—not to be confused with historical intent—is 'not only to do away with legal norms that base advantages or disadvantages on sex but also to bring about equal opportunity for men and women in the future.'[142] In 1994, parliament nevertheless amended paragraph 2 by adding this sentence: 'The state shall promote the actual implementation of equal rights for women and men and take steps to eliminate currently existing disadvantages.' By incorporating the FCC's teleological view into the text of paragraph 2, parliament sought to remove lingering doubts about the actual purpose behind the provision. The amendment was another example of the German tendency, as suggested earlier in this chapter, to amend the text of the Basic Law when judicial interpretations place its meaning in doubt.

Proportionality

Under the Basic Law, proportionality ranks as a major constitutional principle. Indeed, as the FCC has said in scores of cases, the test of proportionality is required by the principle of the rule of law laid down in Arts 1(3) and 20(3). Proportionality is not strictly speaking an *approach* to interpretation; it has little to do with how a judge reads a constitutional provision. Rather, the principle of proportionality is employed to justify limits on democratic rights and fundamental freedoms. Initially, of course, when interpreting specified rights, judges—in Germany and elsewhere—identify the interests or activities enclosed within these rights. But thereafter they commonly apply principles of rationality and

---

[140] See n 22.   [141] 62 BVerfGE 1 (1984).
[142] 85 BVerfGE 191, 206 (1992). See also *Fire Service Case*, 92 BVergGE 91, 109 (1995, invalidating state laws requiring men but not women to pay a fee for the support of local fire departments).

proportionality to the laws that restrict them. In Germany as in Canada, South Africa, and India, the application of these principles is at the heart of the judicial process on basic rights. As David Beatty has pointed out, '[i]ssues of justification not interpretation are what judges struggle to resolve.'[143]

Three criteria must be met in applying the principle of proportionality to an infringement of a basic right. First, a statute restricting a basic right must be an appropriate (*geeignet*) means to a legitimate end. Second, the means used to limit the right must be required (*erforderlich*) to achieve the law's purpose. Finally, the burden on the right must be proportionate (*angemessen*) to the benefit secured by the law. This reasoning resembles the enhanced scrutiny employed in American due process and equal protection law. There are differences, however. As applied by the FCC, proportionality demands less than the Supreme Court's 'strict scrutiny' but more than its 'minimum rationality' test. The supple weighing process involved in the delicate balancing of rights, duties, and public interests avoids the rigid distinctions between levels of judicial scrutiny in American law. In addition, the intensity of the FCC's analysis depends largely on the significance of a particular right on the Basic Law's scale of values.

The FCC's deft analytical approach has much to do with the Basic Law's complicated and interrelated provisions, as illustrated by cases involving the dismissal of East German teachers, professors, and other public employees for their behavior under the old regime. These cases implicate the value of human dignity (Art 1.1) as well as the rights to personality (Art 2.1), equality (Art 3.1), association (Art 9.1), and occupational freedom (Art 12), not to mention the social state clause (Art 20.1), notice and hearing requirements (Art 103.1), and the right of every German to equal eligibility for public employment (Art 33.2). Teachers and professors dismissed from their positions also invoked their right to engage in scholarship (Art 5.3). Dismissed female employees, on the other hand, depending on their personal situations, might find support in the state's duty to protect mothers, marriage, and pregnant women (Art 6). In a leading dismissal case, the Court concluded that under the Unity Treaty employment contracts of persons working in East Germany's research institutes could be terminated to protect the public's interest in the 'economical use of public funds' and 'high scholarly standards,' but pregnant women working in these same institutes could not be fired in the light of the importance of their right to occupational choice in conjunction with the high value the Basic Law places on every mother's right to the protection and care of the community.[144] The Court concluded that the

---

[143] 'Human Rights and the Rules of Law' in DM Beatty (ed) *Human Rights and Judicial Review* (Kluwer Academic Publishers, Dordrecht, 1994) 21.

[144] 85 BVerfGE 360, 375 (1992). A selected list of similar cases includes the Judgment of August 9, 1995, 93 BVerfGE 213 (upholding the disbarment of lawyers who had violated human rights principles in working for the Ministry of State Security, but overturning the law's application to persons concerning whom there was no proof of culpable conduct), Judgment of July 8, 1997, 96 BVerfGE 152 (overturning the dismissal of teachers on the basis of their rights under Art 12.1 in conjunction with Art 33.2), Judgment of July 8, 1997, 96 BVerfGE 189 (sustaining the dismissal of a professor for

dismissal of a *pregnant* woman from her job was disproportionate to the good brought about by the firings.

Practical concordance

'Practical Concordance' (*praktische Konkordanz*) is a standard feature of constitutional reasoning in Germany. The principle flows from the conception of the Basic Law as a structural unity. It demands that constitutionally protected values and rights must be harmonized with one another when they conflict or appear to conflict. Practical concordance is not clause-bound reasoning; it requires a holistic view of the constitution. It means—in theory—that one constitutional value may not be realized at the expense of another. The value of free speech, for example, rarely attains total victory over a competing constitutional value such as human dignity or the right to the development of one's personality. Professor Konrad Hesse, a former member of the Court, put it this way: 'The principle of the Constitution's unity requires the optimization of [two conflicting values]: Both legal values need to be limited so that each can attain its optimal effect. In each concrete case, therefore, the limitations must satisfy the principle of proportionality; that is, they may not go any further than necessary to produce a concordance of both legal values.'[145] In short, constitutional interpretation in the German view is anything but a zero-sum game.

The application of the principle of practical concordance may be illustrated by reference to two religious freedom cases. In the *Classroom Crucifix Case* (1995), the Court announced that Arts 7 (allowing religious instruction in the public schools) and 4 (securing freedom from religious indoctrination) 'have to be seen together and reconciled with each other through interpretation, since it is only concordance of the aspects of legal protection under both articles that can do justice to the decisions contained in the Basic Law.'[146] The FCC sought to achieve the reconciliation by requiring public schools to remove the crucifix from classrooms attended by objecting students but to permit its display in classrooms where such students are not present. The *Muslim Headscarf Case* (2003), by contrast, challenged a school regulation banning teachers from wearing headscarves. Here the positive freedom of a Muslim teacher to cover her head ran up against the negative freedom of students who might object on the ground of their faith. In the circumstances of this case, the Court required a state legislature to resolve the tension, saying that legislators 'must seek a compromise reasonably acceptable to everyone....[Constitutional] provisions must be seen together, and

collaborating with state security police), Judgement of July 8, 1997, 96 BVerfGE 171 (upholding the termination of teachers who lied about their previous relationship to the Ministry of State Security), and Judgment of the second Chamber of the First Senate, September 1, 2000, 1 B v R 661/96 (slip opinion) (overruling the removal of a former judge from the office of a notary public on the ground that her dismissal violated the right to occupational freedom.

[145] *Grundzüge des Verfassungsrechts der Bundesrepublik Deutschland* (16th edn., Verlag CF Müller, Karlsruhe, 1988) 27.   [146] 93 BVerfGE 1, 22–23 (1995).

their interpretation and influence must be coordinated with each other.' In this area, the Court noted, policies may differ from *Land* to *Land*, depending on 'school traditions, the composition of the population by religion, and whether [the population] is more or less strongly rooted in religion.'[147]

Passive virtues and dialogical techniques

Alexander Bickel, maintained that the Supreme Court is often at its best when it declines to exercise the jurisdiction it clearly has. These evasive strategies, which he calls 'passive virtues,' include 'standing' rules, case and controversy requirements, the political question doctrine, and other prudential techniques for avoiding constitutional controversies.[148] There are no exact equivalents to these rules in Germany. As noted several times in this essay, the FCC may not decline to decide cases properly before it. The Court's purpose in the German system, as also noted, is to resolve even doubtful questions of constitutionality, not to avoid them.

Yet, even while accepting jurisdiction, the Court adheres to canons of restraint that grant considerable latitude to legislative and executive decision makers.[149] One of these, familiar to Americans, is the Court's practice of upholding legislation when it can plausibly be interpreted to conform with the Constitution (*verfassungskonforme Auslegung*) even when faced with an equally plausible argument against its validity.[150] In addition, although the Court does not decline to resolve cases on the merits merely because they involve sensitive issues of foreign or military policy, it has tended to defer to the executive when exercising such authority pursuant to international treaties. As a matter of principle, the FCC has declared that the deployment of German soldiers in armed operations abroad requires parliamentary approval,[151] but even here the Court has broadly construed the executive's discretionary authority. On the domestic front, finally, the Court has taken an equally broad view of the government's discretionary authority to regulate aspects of the economy when 'necessary' under the terms of Article 72 (2). The Court's reluctance to invalidate laws passed under this provision is not unlike the Supreme Court's deferential review of socio-economic legislation under the due process clauses of the United States Constitution.

In one significant development in the field of basic rights, however, the Court has all but abdicated its authority independently to review European community regulations. In a case known as *Solange I* (1974), the FCC famously ruled that European Community law could be challenged in concrete judicial review proceedings if allegedly in conflict with fundamental rights under the Basic

---

[147] See n 115 citing *Interdenominational School Case*, 41 BVerfGE 29, 50–51 (1975) and *Classroom Crucifix Case* 93 BVerfGE 1, 22–23 (1995).

[148] *The Least Dangerous Branch* (2nd edn., Yale University Press, New Haven, 1986) ch 4.

[149] C Rau *Selbst Grenzen in der Rechtsprechung des United States Supreme Court und des Bundesverfassungsgerichts* (Duncker & Humblot, Berlin, 1996).

[150] An example is the *Rental Prepayment Case*, 95 BVerfGE 64 (1996, upholding against a property right claim the legal extension of contractual terms for the payment of rent in publicly subsidized housing).   [151] 90 BVerfGE 286 (1994).

Law.[152] The Court took the position that such challenges were permissible so long as (*solange*) the protection of fundamental rights in the European Community was below the level of protection in Germany. But twelve years later, in *Solange II* (1986), the Court ruled that fundamental rights 'in conception, substance, and manner of implementation' in the European Community is essentially equal to the protection of basic rights in Germany,[153] for which reason the Court announced that it would no longer review community laws or regulations in the light of these basic rights.

The Court reaffirmed *Solange II* in the recent *Banana Case* (2000), declaring as non-cognizable—and for the first time—an administrative court referral questioning the constitutionality of EEC regulations on the marketing of bananas as a violation of occupational and property rights.[154] The Second Senate declared: 'As long as the European Communities generally ensure the effective protection of fundamental rights and generally safeguard the essential content of fundamental rights, the Federal Constitutional Court will...no longer review [Community legislation] by the standard of fundamental rights contained in the Basic Law.'[155] After this decision, when viewed in the further light of the *Maastricht Case*,[156] the admissibility of a challenge to community law would depend only on a clear showing that the fundamental right allegedly violated 'is not generally ensured' within the Community.

Finally, we should mention the FCC's standard practice of issuing *Appellententscheidungen*, best translated as 'admonitory decisions.' An admonitory opinion has an advisory quality to it, although technically speaking it is not that at all. The FCC's admonitions fall into three categories. In the first, the Court declares a statute *unconstitutional and void* but proceeds, occasionally, to advise Parliament how to correct the deficiency. An example is the *Election Finance Case* in which the Court invalidated a law providing for the general financing of political parties. Recognizing, however, the important 'quasi-constitutional' role of parties in elections, the Court suggested the parties could be reimbursed out of public funds for actual election campaign expenses.[157] Parliament took the hint and passed a statute based on the FCC's recommendation.

In the second category the FCC declares a statute *unconstitutional but not void*. In such cases, the Court seeks to avoid the injustice or political inconvenience of a decision that nullifies a statute altogether. An example would be a sales tax statute or an income tax law that violates the principle of equality. To declare the statute unconstitutional, with *ex tunc* effect, would complicate the administration of the tax laws, not to mention the injury to persons advantaged by the laws in the first place. In these situations, the FCC *admonishes* Parliament to remove the law's

---

[152] 37 BVerfGE 27 (1974).   [153] 73 BVerfGE 339 (1986).

[154] 102 BVerfGE 147 (2000). The regulations were also challenged as a violation of GG arts 3(1) and 23(1).

[155] 21 See *Human Rights Law Journal* 254 (31 October 2000) for an English translation of the decision.   [156] 89 BVerfGE 155 (1993).

[157] 20 BVerfGE 56 (1966).

unconstitutional features or to enact a new law, usually within a specified time frame, warning Parliament that if the statute is not amended, revised, or reformed to satisfy constitutional requirements within the specified period, the bad parts of the statute will be struck down.[158] Finally, in a truer version of an admonitory decision, the Court declares a statute *incompatible with the Basic Law but not unconstitutional.* In these cases, it would be politically inexpedient to nullify a statute whose effects could not be easily undone. An example would be a challenge to the validity of an election owing to malapportioned districts. Rather than invalidating the election, the Court would require the legislature to reapportion in accord with the Constitution by the next election.[159]

Cultural and Institutional Determinants

Parliamentary Government

The structure and mode of constitutional review in Germany has been influenced by the European conception of separation of powers. Historically, the German version of separated powers, as in Europe generally, drew a bright line between legislative and judicial authority. Parliament, in which executive officials were— and are—represented, was—and is—seen as the soul of democracy, whereas courts have been reduced to apolitical civil service-like agencies entrusted with faithfully carrying out the will of legislative majorities. Unlike the American version of separation of powers, the regular judicial establishment has not been viewed as an institution equal to the legislature or the executive. But in today's strong parliamentary democracies of the German variety, separation of powers is achieved less by legislative-executive conflicts than by the opposition of minority parties to executive-dominated parliamentary majorities. In Germany, this opposition has been institutionalized by the ability of parliamentary minorities to challenge the constitutionality of laws and policies adopted by political majorities.

Accordingly, and from the beginning, Germans have recognized that the FCC, although clearly a *judicial* tribunal, plays an important political role in the Federal Republic's governmental system. In striking down legislation, often at the request of governments and parliamentary minorities, the FCC in the German view would have a major impact on the political system. There is a sense in which the Court would function as a 'quasi-legislative' institution. In the words of Hans Kelsen, the founder of Austria's Constitutional Court—on which the FCC was modeled—such a tribunal would serve as a 'negative legislator,' thus complementing the positive

---

[158] See for example the *Marriage Benefit Case*, 28 BVerfGE 324 (1970, holding unconstitutional as a violation of equality the termination of benefits to students who marry but instructing parliament to eliminate the benefits altogether or to extend them to married students.

[159] See 16 BVerfGE 130 (1963). For a discussion of these and related cases see W Rupp-vBrünneck, 'Germany: The Federal Constitutional Court' (1972) 20 *The American Journal of Comparative Law* 387–403.

law-making role of parliament.[160] Germans underscored the FCC's 'political' character by providing, as noted earlier, for the parliamentary selection and limited tenure of its members. Yet, ironically and perhaps paradoxically, the Court was expected to employ strictly judicial methods of interpretation, methods designed, in the FCC's perception of its task, to determine rationally and objectively the true meaning of the Basic Law. As *the* guardian of the Constitution empowered to keep all branches and levels of government within the bounds of their constituted authority, the FCC was calculated to bring new meaning to Germany's system of separated powers.

The Civil Law Tradition

The character of judicial review in Germany has also been influenced by its legal culture. As with other continental peoples, Germans are accustomed to a codified legal system. They tend to regard their codes as unified bodies of law covering all possible contingencies arising out of human interaction. The modern German civil code in particular is a marvel of rationally ordered rules and principles designed to regulate all private legal relationships. The fruit of stupendous labor by legal scholars, the civil code requires for its application to concrete cases a highly trained judiciary skilled in the classical techniques of statutory interpretation. The typical German judge is steeped in the ideology on which the code was originally based, namely, that written law is—or at least *was*—deemed conceptually self-sufficient and the key to the resolution of all human problems. In short, ordinary judges do not make law; they apply it *as written*. This deeply rooted view helped to nurture and accentuate Germany's positivist legal tradition.

There is a quality of caricature, however, in this description of the German judicial process. First, as noted earlier in this chapter, natural law and Kantian moral theory have had a substantial influence on the development of German constitutional law. Second, many contemporary judges see themselves as problem solvers disinclined toward judicial formalism. And in the celebrated *Soraya Case*, the FCC fully recognized, in certain circumstances, the legitimacy of judge-made law (*Richterrecht*),[161] not to mention the fact that the decisions of the FCC are

---

[160] This view of an independent constitutional court created outside the structure of the regular judiciary was put forward by Hans Kelsen, the father of Austria's Constitutional Court. See AR Brewer-Carias *Judicial Review in Comparative Law* (Cambridge University Press, Cambridge, 1989) 191–192.

[161] 34 BVerfGE 269, 287–293 1973). In this case, the ex-wife of the Shah of Iran sued a newspaper for publishing an interview with her that turned out to be fictitious. She sought monetary relief under the civil code for a violation of her personality rights, but the code failed to recognize civil actions for defamation or invasion of privacy. Such actions were normally brought in criminal courts. Owing, however, to the right to personality laid down in Article 2 of the Basic Law, German courts began to permit money damages for injuries to a person's reputation. In *Soraya*, over free speech objections, the FCC held that lower courts are permitted to extend the rules of private law when necessary to give effect to the basic values emanating from the Constitution. See also JA Frowein 'Randbemerkungen zu den Grenzen des Richterrechts in rechtsvergleichender Betrachtung' in

regarded as sources of law. Yet old attitudes linger on. First, the Basic Law itself tends to be regarded as a self-sufficient code of law. When asked where the constitutional law of their country is to be found, German law students would typically refer to the 146 articles of the Basic Law. American or Canadian students, by contrast, would point to the decisional law of their Supreme Court. Second, the principles governing statutory interpretation have been carried over into the field of constitutional law, implying that the Basic Law can be interpreted with the same consistency and dispassion as ordinary law. Finally, many judges regard the Basic Law, like the civil code, as a unified body of rules and principles that contain the right answer to almost any constitutional dispute. To underscore the law's rationality, objectivity, and depersonalization, German courts hand down singular institutional—that is, unsigned—opinions. The FCC followed this practice until 1971 when FCCA was amended to permit personalized dissents, but majority opinions remain unsigned and dissenting opinions, as noted below, are rare.

Despite feints in the direction of American-style judicial review by the Weimar Republic's Federal High Court in the 1920s, Germany's civilian-positivistic legal culture was generally antagonistic to any constitutional policy-making role for the courts. Moreover, the submissive role of the courts during the Third Reich reinforced an older German view that ordinary judges were temperamentally ill-suited to play a significant constitutional role in Germany's new democracy. This perceived reality constituted one of several reasons why Germans decided to concentrate the power of judicial review in a single institution outside the structure of the regular judiciary. A related reason for a single constitutional court was Germany's fragmented court system. In distinguishing sharply between private and public law, Germans established administrative, finance, social, and labor courts as well as courts of ordinary civil and criminal jurisdiction, each constituting a separate hierarchy beginning at the state level and ending in a final *federal* court of appeal. Coupled with the absence of a tradition of *stare decisis*, these separate hierarchies could not be expected to produce a unified body of constitutional law. Interpretive unity in such a system was thought to be more easily achieved through the creation of a single court of constitutional review whose rulings would bind all courts and all branches, levels, and agencies of government.

Legal Education and Scholarship

The legal educational system has also contributed to the structure and conception of judicial review in Germany. Here too the civil law has had a decisive influence. Although law faculties require students to participate in seminars that focus on problem-solving, legal education on the whole remains highly abstract and philosophical, a methodology well-suited to interpreting codes and resolving cases on abstract judicial review. The predominant educational perspective is one of

Richterliche Rechtsfortbildung, Festschrift der Juristischen Fakultät zur 600-Jahr-Feier der Reprecht-Karls-Universität Heidelberg (CF Müller Juristischer Verlag, Heidelberg, 1986) 555–565.

mastering pre-existing legal rules and principles. The 'formalism' of the German approach to legal education may be contrasted with the 'realism' of the American, the former emphasizing statutory interpretation, the latter reasoning from case to case.[162] Yet case law has made its way into the curriculum. While professors base their lectures on rules and principles, usually apart from and independent of cases, their assistants conduct supplementary practice sessions which emphasize problem-solving and case law. Lectures focusing on code law nevertheless constitute the chief staple of German legal education, which consists of a three year course of studies heavily oriented toward the training of judges and civil servants.

The structure of legal education reflects the civil law's emphasis on judicial training as well as law teaching. In Germany, academic study and practical training are divided into separate phases. Students begin their professional training in law upon entering the university, whereas in the United States they study law at the graduate level after completing four years of college or university. The American law school curriculum is a three-year program that combines theoretical and practical training, the successful completion of which, after students pass a state bar examination, entitles them to enter the practice of law, and most do as junior attorneys in private firms. By contrast, legal education in the German university is mainly theoretical. Here students learn how to apply the law—ie, code law—a highly valued skill desperately needed in a legal culture dominated by civil servants and judges. Students embark upon the practical or technical phase of their training after passing the *first* state bar examination. The practical training embraces a compulsory two-year program consisting of assignments in courts of law, prosecutorial offices, and administrative agencies. When completing this phase, and after passing the required *second* state bar examination, the student is eligible to apply for a judgeship. If accepted, he or she serves another three years as an apprentice in a lower court, the successful completion of which entitles him or her to permanent tenure as a professional judge.

The prevailing method of teaching law mirrors the approach to the study of constitutional law. As noted, the emphasis in legal education generally is on theory, conceptual clarification, deductive reasoning, and systematization, an approach reflected in general commentaries on the Basic Law. Although a handful of constitutional scholars have begun to organize and collect constitutional cases for publication,[163] the typical teaching tool remains the standardized commentary. These commentaries differ from their American equivalents—hornbooks—which are topically organized, case-oriented, and heavily analytical. The standard German commentary proceeds methodically, article by article (and sentence by sentence), each reinforced with extensive citations to relevant historical materials, judicial decisions, and scholarly literature. Several leading commentaries have been written

---

[162] For a general discussion of the contrast between German and American legal education, see JR Ostertag, 'Legal Education in Germany and the United States—A Structural Comparison' (1993) 26 *Vanderbilt Journal of Transnational Law* 301–340.

[163] For a description of these books see n 109.

by FCC justices. One of them is exclusively based on the decisions of the FCC,[164] although it seems not to have been consulted as much as other—and more standard—commentaries.

Style of Judicial Decision-Making

The style of FCC opinions—indeed of all judicial decisions—reflects Germany's tradition of legal scholarship. Doctrinal elaboration dominates the approach to constitutional argument and legal writing generally. The FCC's full senate opinions tend to be heavily oriented toward normative theorizing and definitional refinement. In contrast to the breathtaking brevity and incisiveness of French Constitutional Council decisions, the typical German opinion is an exercise in encyclopedic scholarship. The typical case reads like a sophisticated—and often turgid—American law student research note. 'Elegance in style and presentation,' as one commentary puts it, 'are not generally considered to be worth striving for, and a witticism would be regarded as rather frivolous. Unconventional forms of legal scholarship, like economic analysis or critical legal studies, have tended to be marginalized.'[165] It seems rather clear that these opinions, which reflect a thorough survey of the literature pertaining to a particular set of constitutional issues, are written less for the general public than for the academic legal profession.

Opinion writing on the FCC is designed largely to persuade the academic legal community—and other informed readers—of the rightness, neutrality, and integrity of decisional outcomes. The typical case begins with *Leitsätze* (leading sentences) or 'headnotes' summarizing its essential holding. The opinion then proceeds systematically (1) to describe the case's factual, legal, and procedural background, (2) to recapitulate—usually in great detail—arguments advanced by petitioners and respondents, (3) to rule on the admissibility of the complaint or the legitimacy of the issue referred to the Court, and (4) to pass upon the merits of the case in an extended judgment that seeks to resolve all relevant constitutional issues. Oral arguments before the FCC are rare and when they do occur, at the Court's invitation, they are usually conducted by a handful of law professors who

---

[164] See G Leibholz, HJ Rinck and D Hesselberger *Grundgesetz für die Bundesrepublik Deutschland: Kommentar an Hand der Rechtssprechung des Bundesverfassungsgerichts* (6th edn., 1983). Leibholz, the sole editor of the first edition, was one of the original appointees to the Court. Hans-Justus Rinck, an assistant to Leibholz for several years and later a justice himself, joined the enterprise as co-editor in subsequent editions. Both are deceased. Dieter Hesselberger, a law professor, has continued to update the commentary. In addition to the standard commentaries, large collections of essays on various constitutional topics have appeared over the years, often in the form of *Festschriften* (commemorative volumes) or general handbooks on constitutional law. Prominent examples are KD Bracher *et al Die moderne Demokratie und ihr Recht: Festschrift für Gerhard Leibholz* (JCB.Mohr [P Siebeck], Tübingen, 1966); W Fürst *et al Festschrift für Wolfgang Zeidler* (Walter de Gruyter, Berlin, 1987); J Isensee and P Kirchhof (eds) *Handbuch des Staatsrechts der Bundesrepublik Deutschland* (CF Müller Juristischer Verlag, Heidelberg published in 10 volumes between 1987 and 2000); and HJ Vogel *Handbuch des Verfassungsrechts* (Walter de Gruyter, Berlin, 1984).

[165] WF Ebke and MW Finkin *Introduction to German Law* (Kluwer Law International, The Hague, 1996) 21.

specialize in constitutional litigation. Most decisions are handed down on the basis of written briefs, many of which the FCC invites from affected groups and governmental institutions. Decisions appear in the form of unsigned institutional opinions to underscore the unity, legitimacy, and impersonal character of the decisional process, one in which the FCC often labors to distinguish, not always convincingly, between constitutional and political decision-making. Personalized dissenting opinions are rare and they seem to be written only when prompted by the serious moral reservations of their authors.

Specialization

Other institutional factors that help to explain the character of judicial review in Germany and the decisional process on the FCC are the sharp division between private and public law in civil law jurisdictions and the high degree of specialization it fosters.[166] Like German society and public life generally, the judicial system divides itself into specialized jurisdictions. They include ordinary, social, finance, labor, and administrative courts staffed by some 22,000 judges—almost equal to the total number of judges in the United States with three times the population of Germany—17,000 of whom preside over the ordinary courts of civil and criminal jurisdiction. The highest appellate courts in each of these judicial hierarchies are in turn divided into specialized panels. (All lower and intermediate courts of appeal are state courts, whereas the highest courts of appeal are federal courts.) The panels do not rotate as they do on American federal appeals courts where judges are expected to preside over a wide variety of cases. Furthermore, the final courts of appeal have large numbers of justices—there are 120 on the Federal Supreme Court—who in turn function in specialized five-judge panels. Little wonder Germans have established, apart from the reasons already cited, specialized constitutional courts at both state and federal levels.

More important for present purposes is the specialization that takes place within the FCC itself. First, the FCC's two eight-judge panels—the First and Second Senates—broadly specialize in mutually exclusive jurisdictional areas. Second, and by mutual agreement at the outset of a calendar year, each justice agrees to serve as the rapporteur (*Berichterstatter*) in cases related to his or her particular expertise or interests. For example, a justice on the Second Senate may be targeted to serve as the rapporteur in all cases involving issues of international law, asylum, extradition, and deportation. Another justice may be assigned cases on tax law and still another may receive cases dealing with issues arising out of laws relating to marriage and family. As noted, cases are initially sent to the rapporteur, not to his or her colleagues. With the help of their clerks, most of whom are themselves academics, civil servants, or professional judges on the threshold of their

---

[166] See 'The Public Law—Private Law Distinction in European and United States Law' in JH Merryman *The Loneliness of the Comparative Lawyer* (Kluwer Law International, The Hague, 1999) 76–93.

careers, these individual justices are responsible for preparing a detailed report on all aspects of the case. They summarize all relevant facts, identify the constitutional provisions under scrutiny, review the arguments advanced on both sides of the question (or questions)—with full citation to applicable statutes, constitutional decisions, and published commentary—and conclude with a proposed opinion on the merits.

The rapporteur's report—or *votum* as it is called—constitutes a crucial phase in the decisional process, and often takes weeks or even months to prepare. When finished the rapporteur distributes the *votum*, along with any accompanying documents, to other members of his or her senate. If it is well-research and convincingly argued, its statement of the issues and recommendations are likely to prevail. The justices strive for unanimity, although this is not always possible. In conference the rapporteur leads the discussion where the *votum* may undergo pruning, editing, and revision. In the unlikely event no consensus emerges, the presiding justice will formulate the questions on which votes are to be taken after which the rapporteur proceeds to draft the final opinion, one that largely mirrors the *votum* even if he or she should be in dissent on one or more of the issues. The rapporteur is expected to express the general view of the senate as a whole, although he or she may, and often does, take into account dissenting views expressed in conference. The FCC's opinions may truly be said to be exercises in collegial decision-making, a process that goes a long way in explaining the general acceptance of the Court's work-product.

Conclusion

As this essay has made clear, the FCC is at the epicenter of Germany's constitutional democracy. Already on its 10th anniversary, Rudolf Smend, a leading constitutional theorist, remarked: 'The Basic Law is now virtually identical with its interpretation by the Federal Constitutional Court.'[167] By the 1990s, Smend's view was conventional wisdom among German public lawyers and constitutional scholars. Most scholars and legal professionals accept the Court as a legitimate participant in the larger community decision-making process, a remarkable achievement of postwar institution building in the Federal Republic. The frequency and willingness with which Germans from both east and west resort to the Court for redress of their grievances is a convincing measure of its high rank as a symbol of law and justice in contemporary Germany.

But the FCC is also recognized for the important political role it plays in the Federal Republic. Germans realize that the Court walks a tight rope between law and politics, and the justices themselves are acutely aware of their political

---

[167] 'Festvortrag zur Feier des zehnjährigen Bestehens des Bundesverfassungsgerichts am 26. Januar 1962' in *Das Bundesverfassungsgericht* (Verlag CF Müller, Karlsruhe, 1963) 24.

influence. Indeed, as Jutta Limbach, a former President of the FCC, remarks in her Clifford Chance Lecture delivered at Oxford University in 1997: 'Intellectual honesty compels us to state that there is no usable catalogue of criteria that could serve as a signpost in the ridge-walking between law and politics. The two fields of action partly overlap, and cannot unambiguously be separated from each other. As the constitutional review body, the Court has a share in politics.'[168] Yet she insists on distinguishing between adjudication and lawmaking. In her view, 'finding the law'—the FCC's function—'is a matter for adjudication, while making law is by contrast a task for politics.'[169] In their public statements, other justices are equally ambivalent about their role. They seem to be aware of the personal value choices they make when they decide cases but yet are reluctant to admit publicly that they are doing anything other than engaging in objective constitutional interpretation. There is a general tendency among them to distinguish between the *process* of interpretation, which they regard as nonpolitical, and the *effects* of their interpretive choices, which they admit is often political. Some justices have compared themselves to referees who rule on plays in a sports contest.[170]

The sports analogy is not altogether inapt. After all, the justices are elected to enforce the constitutional rules of the game. In doing so, like referees in any sports contest, they make judgment calls. Not all constitutional cases involve the exercise of judicial discretion but many do, as the numerous cases discussed in this chapter make clear. Discretion is an unavoidable byproduct of judicial decision-making, especially in those hard—and not so hard—cases when the FCC functions as a balancer of constitutional values or interests. As Chief Justice John Marshall once said, '[w]e must never forget that it is a *constitution* we are expounding,' and constitutions by definition require interpretation. Constitutional interpretation— whether by the FCC or other branches of government—necessitates balancing the values of stability and change. No constitution can be maintained over time without adjusting it to 'necessity' by way of creative interpretation. The criteria by which this process is carried out are, as President Limbach herself notes, 'the structural principles of the Basic Law, which have as their object the interplay and antagonism of judicial review and political activity.'

While the FCC has been extremely active in protecting the Federal Republic's party democracy, in umpiring the federal system, and adjudicating major conflicts among the highest organs of the national government, it has arguably played its most important role in protecting guaranteed rights. But here too, as we have

---

[168] 'The Law-Making Power of the Legislature and the Judicial Review' in B Markesinis *Law Making, Law Finding and Law Shaping: The Diverse Influences* (Oxford University Press, Oxford, 1997) II 174.   [169] ibid 161.

[170] The analogy of course in not altogether inapt. Justices are elected to enforce constitutional rules. In a recent interview, a leading member of the Second Senate told the author that his role on the Court was like a referee in a soccer game. His—the justice's—job is to throw up a yellow or red card depending on the nature of the offense by a player in the game. For an account of other interviews with the justices with respect to their judicial roles see DP Kommers *Judicial Politics in West Germany* (Sage Publications, Beverly Hills, 1976) 184–186.

seen, the Court's approach has been one of balancing rights and duties, on the one hand, and of seeking 'practical concordance' between conflicting rights, on the other. This particular approach to constitutional adjudication has avoided the 'absolutist' or categorical reasoning often typical of American constitutional decisions. And the fact that constitutional interpretation is often the by-product of constructive dialogue between the FCC and parliament is still another reason for the relative stability and acceptability of judicial review in Germany's civilian legal system.

5

India: From Positivism to Structuralism

S. P. Sathe*

Introduction

The Indian Constitution

India won her freedom from British colonial rule through a mainly non-violent mass movement. To prepare a new Constitution for an independent India, a Constituent Assembly for undivided India was elected pursuant to The Government of India Act 1935, enacted by the British Parliament. This Act conferred a limited franchise based on property and educational qualifications, entitling about 28.5 per cent of the adult population to vote. The All India National Congress (Congress), which had led the movement for independence, won 69 per cent of the seats in this Constituent Assembly. In 1947, the British Parliament passed the Indian Independence Act, which created two dominions, India and Pakistan. After this partition, the Constituent Assembly of undivided India was split into two bodies, one for each dominion. Congress's representation in the Constituent Assembly for post-partition India increased to 82 per cent. Congress contained within itself the entire ideological spectrum, from the left to the right, and represented India's religious as well as ethnic pluralism.[1] The work of drafting the Constitution was done between 1946 and 1949. The drafters drew heavily on the Government of India Act 1935, the last constitutional statute made by the British Parliament for India. Some provisions of the Constitution came into force on November 23, 1949, and the rest on January 26, 1950.[2]

The preamble of the Constitution spoke in the name of the 'people of India'. India was declared a republic, and all legal ties with Britain were terminated.[3] But Indians had struggled for independence not just to achieve liberation from foreign rule, but also to secure liberty, equality and justice for the people. Independence was the result of a mass movement, of which the Constitution was a continuation,

* I thank Ms Sathya Narayan, Joint Director, IALS for providing research assistance, and Ms Aparna Tatke for providing computer assistance.

[1] GA Austin *The Indian Constitution: Cornerstone of a Nation* (Clarendon Press, Oxford, 1966) 10–13.   [2] See Constitution of India art 395.
[3] ibid.

to establish a modern, democratic, secular and humanist India. The Constitution became a symbol of national consensus. Its lengthy details and specificity were inevitable, because many interests had to be accommodated, and cautions incorporated. It is not merely a law prescribing a division of power, and limits to power, but contains a bill of rights and positive directions to the State to establish a just social order.[4] It incorporates the essential aspects of parliamentary democracy,[5] federalism,[6] provisions regarding inter-state trade, commerce and intercourse,[7] rights of various minorities and disadvantaged sections of society that require special attention,[8] provisions for government servants,[9] officers belonging to the Indian Civil Service[10] and the princes whose kingdoms had acceded to India.[11] It contains the constitution not only of the Federal government but also of the states. Consequently, it is the longest of the six constitutions discussed in this book.[12]

Salient Features

The main features of the Constitution of India are: parliamentary government; federalism; a bill of rights; directive principles of state policy; separation of powers; amendment procedures; and judicial review. These will be briefly described to provide the necessary background for a discussion of constitutional interpretation.

Parliamentary government

In a parliamentary form of government the executive is part of the legislature and responsible to it. The national Parliament consists of the President, and two Houses called the House of the People and the Council of States.[13] The President is elected by an electoral college consisting of all the elected members of the two Houses and the elected members of the Legislative Assemblies of the states.[14] Unlike other federal constitutions, the Constitution does not give the states equal representation in the Council of States. The allocation of seats in the Council, to the states and the Union territories, is determined by the Fourth Schedule.[15] The House of the People consists of representatives chosen through direct election by the people divided into various constituencies. The House has a tenure of five years, whereas one third of the members of the Council of States are elected every

---

[4] Constitution of India Part IV.   [5] Constitution of India Part V.
[6] Constitution of India Part XI.   [7] Constitution of India Part XIII.
[8] Constitution of India Part XVI.   [9] Constitution of India Part XIV.
[10] Constitution of India art 314—repealed by the Constitution (Twenty-Eighth Amendment) Act 1972.
[11] Constitution of India art 291—repealed by the Constitution (Twenty-Sixth Amendment) Act 1971.
[12] The original Constitution contained 395 articles and 8 schedules. 77 articles and 3 schedules were added and 29 articles repealed by the amendments to the Constitution bringing the total number to 443 articles and 12 schedules.   [13] Constitution of India art 79.
[14] Constitution of India art 54.   [15] Constitution of India art 80(2).

two years.[16] The President appoints the Prime Minister, who holds office during her pleasure, but the Council of Ministers is collectively responsible to the House of the People.[17] There is a similar arrangement in the states, with the Governor as the head and a council of ministers to advise her.[18] Governors are appointed by the President, and hold office during her pleasure. The Legislative Assemblies of the states are elected by the people through direct election, and with a few exceptions, are unicameral.[19]

Federalism

The Government of India Act 1935 provided for British India and the Indian princely states to be joined in a federation. This was deemed necessary due to the country's vast size, and regional and linguistic diversity. But it became operational only within British India, because the princely states refused to join. They enjoyed the protection of the British government from external enemies. When they were told by Britain that it could not protect them after its withdrawal from the sub-continent, they had no other option but to join either of the two new dominions. By the time the Constitution of India was finalized, all the contiguous princely states had acceded to India. The state of Jammu and Kashmir acceded subject to certain conditions, which were incorporated in art 370 of the Constitution.

Originally, federalism in undivided India was intended to follow the classical federal model that existed in the United States and Australia, with enumerated powers given to Parliament and residual powers to the state legislatures. But after the partition of the country, the Constitution allocated enumerated powers to both, according to three Lists in the Seventh Schedule. The subjects on which Parliament has power to legislate are enumerated in the 100 items of the Union List;[20] those on which the state legislatures may legislate are set out in the 61 items of the State's List;[21] and there is a concurrent list of 52 items on which both may legislate.[22] State legislation repugnant to a valid law made by Parliament is void,[23] and if there is an existing central law, a state legislature cannot enact a law on the same subject in the concurrent list, unless it has obtained the President's assent.[24] Residual legislative power is vested in Parliament,[25] except in the case of Jammu and Kashmir, where it is vested in the state legislature.[26]

The predominance of the federal government pervades various provisions of the Constitution that deal with relations between the Union and the states. The executive power of every state must be exercised in compliance with laws made by

---

[16] Constitution of India art 83(1).   [17] Constitution of India art 75(3).
[18] See Constitution of India art 153 and 163.
[19] The legislatures of four states, namely Bihar, Maharashtra, Karnataka and Uttar Pradesh (Northern Province) are bi-cameral.
[20] Originally 97, plus 3—2A, 92A and 92 B—added by constitutional amendments.
[21] Originally 66, less 4—11, 19, 29 and 36—deleted by constitutional amendments.
[22] Originally 47, plus 5—11A, 17A, 17B, 20A and 33A—added by constitutional amendments.
[23] Constitution of India art 254(1).   [24] Constitution of India art 254(2).
[25] Constitution of India entry 97, List I and article 248.   [26] Constitution of India art 370.

Parliament, and also without impeding or prejudicing the exercise of the executive power of the Union. The executive power of the Union includes giving such directions to a state as may appear to the Government of India to be necessary for these purposes.[27]

The Constitution requires the Union to protect every state against external aggression and internal disturbance, and to ensure that the state governments comply with the provisions of the Constitution.[28] One provision, art 356, virtually negates federalism. It provides that if the President is satisfied that the government of a state cannot be carried on in accordance with the Constitution, she may by proclamation (a) assume to herself any of the functions of the government of that state, including the powers of the Governor and any body or authority other than the state legislature; and (b) declare that the powers of the state legislature shall be exercisable by or under the authority of Parliament. A proclamation dismissing a state government must be laid before each House of Parliament, and ceases to operate after two months unless it is approved by resolutions of both Houses.[29] This presidential power seemed to be immune to judicial review until 1977, when the Supreme Court of India (hereinafter, 'the Court') held that such a proclamation would be declared invalid if it were issued with *mala fides*.[30] In *SR Bommai v India*,[31] the Court held that such a proclamation was subject to judicial review like any other administrative action, and actually held the dismissal of three state governments invalid.[32]

Bill of rights

Indians had demanded a bill of rights since 1895.[33] But British law-makers did not believe in the utility of a bill of rights: they thought it would either unnecessarily impede law-making, or be a mere string of platitudes.[34] Constitutions made by Britain for her former colonies, such as Australia, Canada and New Zealand, did not contain bills of rights. Nevertheless, the Constituent Assembly unanimously decided to incorporate a bill of rights in the Constitution, titled 'Fundamental Rights'.

Unlike the first ten, and the fourteenth, amendments of the United States Constitution, the Constitution of India does not merely list protected rights, but also spells out restrictions that may be imposed on them. Furthermore, it requires the State to take positive actions towards the realization of certain human rights. For example, art 17 declares that 'untouchability' is abolished, that its practice in

---

[27] Constitution of India art 257(1).   [28] Constitution of India art 355.
[29] Constitution of India art 356(3).
[30] *State of Rajasthan v Union of India* AIR 1977 SC 1361.
[31] AIR 1994 SC 1918; (1994) 3 SCC 1.
[32] Discussed in text to nn 193–96 and 287–89 below.
[33] See Austin (n 1) 53–55.
[34] *The Joint Committee on Indian Constitutional Reforms* (Session 1933–1934) Vol I Part I, Report (His Majesty's Stationery Office) 216 para 366.

any form is forbidden, and that the enforcement of any disability arising out of 'untouchability' shall be a punishable offence. Article 23 prohibits traffic in human beings and forced labour, and declares any contravention to be a punishable offence. Article 24 provides that no child below the age of fourteen years shall be employed to work in any factory, mine or other hazardous employment. The newly added art 21-A requires the State to provide free and compulsory education to all children aged between six and fourteen in such manner as the State may, by law, determine.[35] Such provisions are not found in traditional bills of rights, such as that of the United States. They are in the nature of mandatory directions to the State, similar to provisions in international covenants such as the Universal Declaration of Human Rights, the International Covenant on Civil and Political Rights, or the International Covenant on Economic, Social and Cultural Rights.

The Fundamental Rights are: the right to equality (art 14); the right to non-discrimination on the grounds of religion, race, caste, sex, or place of birth (art 15); the right to equality and non-discrimination in public employment (art 16); rights to freedom of speech, peaceful assembly, associations, movement and residence within any part of India, the acquisition and enjoyment of property, and the practice of any profession, trade or business (art 19); the right not to be subject to retroactive penal legislation, punishment more than once for the same offence, or compulsion to give evidence against oneself (art 20); the right not to be deprived of life or personal liberty except according to procedure established by law (art 21); the rights of an arrested person to be given the grounds for her arrest, and an opportunity to be defended by a lawyer of her choice (art 22(1)-(2)); the rights of persons held in preventive detention (arts 22(4), (5), (6) and (7)); the right to freedom of religion (art 25); rights of religious denominations (art 26); the right not to be compelled to receive religious instruction in educational institutions (art 28); the right to sustain cultural diversity (art 29(1)); the right not to be denied admission, on the ground of religion, race, caste or language, to an educational institution maintained or funded by the State (art 29(2)); the right of religious and linguistic minorities to establish and administer educational institutions of their choice (art 30), and the right to move the Court for the enforcement of Fundamental Rights (art 32).

These rights are detailed and specific. While rights such as freedom of religion or of speech are couched in absolute terms in the United States Constitution, the equivalent rights in the Indian Constitution are hedged with potential restrictions, and the courts must ensure that any restrictions imposed by legislation are reasonable and for permissible purposes. The fine detail of the Constitution has helped to avoid several pitfalls. For example, hate speech is not protected by the Constitution, since art 19(2) allows the State to impose reasonable restrictions on freedom of speech in the interests of 'public order or security of the State'. The Indian Penal Code punishes acts promoting enmity between different groups; acts

---

[35] The Constitution (Eighty-Sixth Amendment) Act, 2002 s 2.

imputing disloyalty to some class of people because of their religion; and acts intended to outrage the religious feelings of any class.[36] These provisions have been held valid.[37] Similarly the Election Law (Representation of the People) Act 1951 forbids any advocacy that appeals to the electorate on religious grounds. These provisions have also been held valid.[38] The Court upheld the prohibition of pornography,[39] and even pre-censorship of films, because art 19(2) mentions 'decency and morality' as permissible grounds for restrictions on freedom of speech.[40]

Another interesting difference between fundamental rights in India and in the United States is that the former address civil society as well as the State, whereas the latter address only the State. Article 15(2) prohibits the subjection of any citizen to any disability, liability, restriction, or condition with regard to: (a) access to shops, public restaurants, hotels and places of public entertainment; or (b) the use of wells, tanks, bathing ghats, roads and places of public resort funded by the State, or dedicated to the use of the general public. Articles 17, 23 and 24, which have been mentioned previously, are also addressed to civil society.

The Fundamental Rights are divided into two parts. While some are granted only to citizens,[41] others are granted to persons.[42] The word 'State' is defined in art 12 as including the Government and Parliament of India, the Government and the Legislature of each state, and all local or other authorities within the territory of India or under the control of the Government of India.[43] The word State has been interpreted liberally to bring within its compass all bodies or authorities that involve public investment and government control.[44]

Directive principles

The idea of Directive Principles of State Policy was borrowed from Ireland.[45] They are not enforceable by any court, but are nevertheless fundamental to the governance of the country.[46] The Constitution clearly enunciates the philosophy of the welfare state, when it enjoins the State to 'strive to promote the welfare of the people by securing and protecting as effectively as it may a social order in which justice, social, economic and political, shall inform all the institutions of the national life'.[47] In particular, the State is directed to minimize inequalities in income, and eliminate inequalities in status, facilities, and opportunities, not only

---

[36] Sections 153-A, 153-B, and 295-C.   [37] *Ramji Lal Modi v U.P.* AIR 1957 SC 650.

[38] *Dr. Dasrao Deshmukh v Kamal Kishore Kadam* (1995) 5 SCC 139; *Subhash Desai v Sharad Rao* (1994) Supp (2) SCC 446: AIR 1994 SC 2277.

[39] *Ranjit Udeshi v Maharashtra* AIR 1965 SC 881.   [40] *KA Abbas v India* AIR 1971 SC 481.

[41] See arts 15(1), 15(2), 16(1), 16(2), 16(4), 19, 29(1), 29(2).

[42] Arts 14, 17, 18, 20, 21, 22, 23, 24, 25, 26, 27, 28, 30, 31 and 32.

[43] The Court held that the words 'other authorities' mean all such authorities that are created by statute, or function as agencies or instrumentalities of the State: *Ajay Hasia v Khalid Mujib* AIR 1981 SC 487.   [44] *Som Prakash v India*, AIR 1981 SC 212: (1981) 1 SCC 449.

[45] See D Feldman *Civil Liberties and Human Rights in England and Wales* (2nd edn., Oxford University Press, Oxford, 2002) 123.   [46] Art 37.

[47] Art 38(1).

among individuals but also among groups of people residing in different areas or engaged in different vocations.[48] The Directive Principles set a constitutional agenda for the future, which envisions the social, economic and political transformation of Indian society. Some goals had to be achieved within a set time frame, such as compulsory primary education for all children below the age of 14 years.[49] Article 39(b) and (c) require the State to bring about changes in property ownership in order to avoid the concentration of wealth in a few hands, and the use of the means of production to the common detriment.

Separation of powers

The legislative power is vested in the Parliament and the state legislatures, and the executive power in the President and Council of Ministers at the federal level,[50] and the Governor and Council of Ministers at the state level.[51] The executive power is co-extensive with the legislative power.[52] The President or Governors may issue ordinances, when Parliament or the State Legislature respectively is not in session, if satisfied that immediate action is necessary.[53] The Court has held that a legislature may delegate legislative power subject to certain limitations, but may not delegate the 'essential' legislative function to the executive.[54] The essential legislative function consists 'in the determination or choice of the legislative policy and of formally enacting that policy into a binding rule of conduct'.[55] A number of laws have been invalidated on this ground.[56]

Amendment of the Constitution

The Constitution provides for its amendment in three ways: (i) a small number of provisions can be amended by a simple majority;[57] (ii) most of the other provisions can be amended only by a bill passed by two-thirds of the members present and voting in, and an absolute majority of the total membership of, both Houses of Parliament;[58] and (iii) certain provisions concerning matters of federal concern must, in addition to being passed by these special majorities, be ratified by not less than half of the state legislatures.[59] These matters include: the election of the President of India; the executive power of the Union, and of the states; the Union Judiciary, and the High Courts of the states and territories; legislative relations between the centre and the states; the Lists in the Seventh Schedule; the representation of the states in Parliament; and the provision for constitutional amendment itself.

---

[48] Art 38(2).   [49] Art 45.   [50] Art 53.   [51] Art 154.

[52] Art 73—federal Government; Art 162-state government.

[53] Art 123—President; Art 212—Governor   [54] *In re Delhi Laws Act* AIR 1951 SC 332.

[55] *Harishankar Bagla v M P* AIR 1954 SC 465, 468.

[56] See SP Sathe, *Administrative Law* (7th edn., Butterworths, 2004) 39–54.

[57] Arts 3, 4, 11, 105(3), 120, 196(3), 345 and 348. Art 4(2) clearly states that 'no such law aforesaid shall be deemed to be an amendment of this Constitution for the purpose of Article 368.'

[58] Art 368(2).   [59] Proviso to art 368(2).

The Constitution has been amended 92 times. These amendments were passed in order to: (i) clarify the meaning of existing provisions; (ii) over-ride decisions of the Court concerning the right to property; (iii) dilute democratic checks and balances during the 1975 emergency, and to restore them after the emergency lapsed; (iv) enhance democracy, for example, by devolving power on village and district governments (the third tier of federalism), and preventing unprincipled and opportunistic defections from political parties by legislators. The scope of the power of constitutional amendment became a subject of controversy in the late 1960s and early 1970s, in cases that will be discussed below.[60]

Judicial review

Courts in India performed the function of judicial review even before independence. The legislatures created by the Government of India Acts had to function within the ambit of the powers given to them by those Acts. If they exceeded their powers, their acts were held *ultra vires*.[61]

Article 13(1) and (2) of the Constitution expressly states that any law inconsistent with a Fundamental Right is void, whether the law was made before or after the Constitution came into force. In *AK Gopalan v State of Madras*,[62] Chief Justice Kania observed that these provisions had been made by way of *abundante cautela* (abundant caution), and that even in their absence, the courts would have had the power to declare laws inconsistent with Fundamental Rights to be void.[63] Even without an express provision, if Parliament makes a law on a subject within the exclusive power of a state, or a state legislature makes a law on a matter within the exclusive power of Parliament, the law is deemed to be void.

Unlike other federal constitutions, India has a single unified judiciary. It has no separate Constitutional Court as in Germany or South Africa. The Supreme Court is the highest court of appeal in civil, criminal and all other matters.[64] The hierarchy of courts commences with magistrates courts in each state, and goes up to the Court. The High Courts are appellate courts in each state that deal with all laws, whether made by Parliament or the state legislature.[65] All appeals from High Courts lie to the Court, subject to conditions laid down under various provisions of the Constitution and other laws.[66] Article 131 provides that the Court has original jurisdiction, which excludes the jurisdiction of any other court, in any dispute between states; or between a state and the Government of India, that involves a legal right.[67] Parliament has power to provide for the adjudication of any dispute respecting the use of the waters of any inter-state river or river valley, and may provide that neither the Court nor any other court shall exercise jurisdiction in respect of such disputes.[68]

---

[60] See text to nn 165–175, below.   [61] *Empress v Burah and Book Singh* ILR 3 Cal. 63, 87–88.
[62] AIR 1950 SC 27.   [63] ibid 34.   [64] Arts 132, 133, 134 and 134-A.
[65] Art 214.   [66] Arts 132, 133, 134, 134-A, 135 and 136.
   [67] This jurisdiction, however, does not extend to a dispute concerning certain treaties, agreements and covenants entered into before the Constitution came into force, or that exclude the Court's jurisdiction.
   [68] Art 262(1) and (2).

The Constitution also provides that the Court has jurisdiction with respect to any other matter if such jurisdiction was exercisable by the Federal Court of India immediately before the Constitution came into force.[69] Article 142 of the Constitution gives the Court power to make such orders as are necessary to do complete justice in any cause or matter pending before it.

In Canada, the Privy Council upheld the validity of a federal Act that enables the Governor General to obtain the advisory opinion of the Supreme Court.[70] In the United States and Australia, the courts have refused to give advisory opinions.[71] In India, the Court's advisory jurisdiction was made explicit in s 213(1) of the Government of India Act 1935, which was carried over into art 143 (1) of the Constitution. If the President believes that a question of law or fact is of such public importance that it is expedient to obtain the Court's opinion, she may refer the question to the Court, and the Court may report its opinion to the President. The word 'may' means that the Court is free to refuse to give an opinion. Until now, reference has been made 12 times to the Court, and the Court has refused to give an opinion only twice.[72] Although opinions given by the Court under art 143(1) are not, strictly speaking, binding, they have been treated as binding by lower courts, governments, and the Court itself.

At common law, courts are bound by their previous decisions, and lower courts by the decisions of higher courts. The doctrine of *stare decisis* was applied in British India as part of the common law long before the decisions of the Federal Court of India were made binding on lower courts by s 212 of the Government of India Act 1935. A similar provision now appears in art 141 of the Constitution in respect of law laid down by the Court. The minimum number of judges that may decide a question involving the interpretation of the Constitution is five.[73] When judges find it necessary to reconsider an interpretation given by a bench of five judges, they must refer the matter to a larger bench, which can overrule that decision.[74] Decisions are reached by majority.[75] Separate concurring as well as dissenting judgments are often published. Likewise, the decisions of the High Courts are binding on lower courts. A *ratio decidendi* is binding, but not an *obiter dictum*. A *ratio* is a legal principle on which a decision was based and without

---

[69] Art 135.

[70] *Attorney General For Ontario v Attorney General For Canada* (1912) AC 571. See PW Hogg, *Constitutional Law of Canada* (4th edn., Carswell, Scarborough Ont, 1997) 191 para 7.3.

[71] RD Rotunda and JE Nowak, *Treatise on Constitutional Law, Substance and Procedure* (3rd edn., West Group, St Paul Mn, 1999) vol.1 para 2.13 174–80; WA Wynes. *Legislative, Executive and Judicial Powers in Australia* (5th edn., Law Book Co, Sydney, 1976) 31.

[72] *Ismail Faruqui v India* (1994) 6 SCC 360. An opinion on art 370 of the Constitution giving special status to the state of Jammu and Kashmir was sought but not responded by the Court. Under art 143(2), the President may refer a dispute arising out of certain treaties, agreements and covenants entered into before the Constitution commenced for an opinion and the Court is obligated to report its opinion to the President. But so far, no reference has been made under this clause.

[73] Art 145(3).

[74] *Bharat Petroleum Corp Ltd. v Mumbai Shramik Sanstha* (2001) 4 SCC 488.

[75] *Harish Verma v Ajay Srivastava* (2003) 1 SCC 500.

which it could not have been reached. *Obiter dicta* are observations ancillary to the *ratio*, which normally have persuasive authority only. However, it has been held that the Court's *obiter dicta* are binding on the High Courts.[76] In view of the fact that the Court has issued *obiter dicta* on broad questions that were not strictly necessary for the disposal of a case, the distinction between *ratio* and *obiter dicta* has become rather irrelevant.

The Court once said that it was not bound by its own decisions, and could overrule itself if the circumstances so demanded.[77] Indeed, it actually overruled a previous decision—and with prospective effect—in *Golaknath v Punjab*, a case involving the validity of three constitutional amendments.[78] Parliament had amended the Constitution seventeen times until then, and three of those amendments had been designed to override judicial decisions concerning the right to property. Those three amendments excluded judicial review of certain types of laws with reference to specific Fundamental Rights. The constitutional validity of these amendments was questioned, on the ground that a constitutional amendment is a 'law' within the meaning of art 13(2), and is therefore void if it contravenes any Fundamental Right. The Court had rejected that contention in 1951, in a unanimous judgment of five judges,[79] and again in 1965, by a majority of three to two.[80] Yet in *Golaknath*,[81] the Court held, by a majority of six to five, that a constitutional amendment made in accordance with art 368 was a 'law' within the meaning of art 13(2), and therefore void if it contravened any of the Fundamental Rights. The Court overruled its previous decisions.

The Court had to soften that blow in view of the fact that, under the impugned amendments, several transactions changing property relations had taken place. It would have caused great havoc economically, socially and politically, if the overruling had retrospective effect. Therefore the majority held that its ruling, that art 13 applied to constitutional amendments, would only operate from the date of its decision. Although the three impugned constitutional amendments would otherwise have been void, they were deemed to be valid since their inception and even into the future. Speaking for himself and four other judges, Chief Justice Subba Rao called this 'prospective overruling' of the previous decisions. In his separate concurring judgment, Justice Hidayatullah reasoned that since the Court had previously acquiesced in the validity of those amendments, by upholding them, they could not now be struck down. This endorsement of prospective overruling opened up a new perspective on the judicial process. It flew in the face of the theory that the judges did not make law, but merely interpreted it. *Golaknath* was decided by a bench of eleven judges. When the decision in that case was challenged, a larger bench of thirteen judges was convened to consider the

---

[76] *Swaran Singh Lamba v India* AIR 1955 SC 1729, 1734. MP Jain, *Indian Constitutional Law* (3rd edn., NM Tripathi, Bombay, 1978) 143.

[77] *Bengal Immunity Co Ltd. v Bihar* (1955) 2 SCR 603.   [78] AIR 1967 SC 1643.

[79] *Shankari Prasad v India* AIR 1951 SC 458

[80] *Sajjan Singh v Rajasthan* AIR 1965 SC 845.   [81] AIR 1967 SC 1643.

matters afresh. That was in the case of *Kesavanand*, which is dealt with in detail below.[82]

The Judges

Article 124(2) provides that Supreme Court judges are appointed by the President, after consultation with such of the judges of the Court and of the High Courts as the President may deem necessary. They then hold office until the age of 65 years. The first proviso to this clause provides that in the appointment of a judge other than the Chief Justice, the Chief Justice must always be consulted. Article 124(3) provides that no person shall be appointed as a judge of the Court unless she is a citizen of India, and (a) has for at least five years been a judge of a High Court or of two or more such courts in succession; or (b) has for at least ten years been an advocate of a High Court or two or more such courts in succession; or (c) is, in the opinion of the President, a distinguished jurist. The second proviso to art 124(2) states that a judge may resign or be removed for misbehaviour or incapacity. A resolution for such removal may be introduced in either of House of Parliament, but is taken up for consideration only after the judge is found guilty of misbehaviour or incapacity in an inquiry conducted by a committee. A resolution for removal of a judge must be passed in each House of Parliament with the support of two-thirds of the members present and voting, and an absolute majority of all the members of the House.[83] There has been only one attempt to impeach a judge of the Court (Justice Ramaswamy), which failed due to lack of support by the required number of members of Parliament. The judges' salaries, allowances and other privileges are to be determined by a law made by Parliament, and until such a law is made, are as prescribed in the second schedule. Such privileges cannot be varied to the disadvantage of a judge after her appointment.[84]

Since the Court's inception, the most senior judge has almost always been appointed as the Chief Justice upon a vacancy arising. In 1973 and 1977, however, the most senior judges were passed over (superseded) by the government, because they had decided important cases against it. Since then, the rule of seniority has once again been followed. The Court has had 35 Chief Justices since its inception. While Chandrachud had the longest term, of more than seven years, KN Singh had the shortest term, of seventeen days. The rule of seniority is now applied even in the appointment of the Court's puisne judges. Most of them are appointed after first having served on a High Court, and then as a Chief Justice of another High Court.[85] This delays the elevation of judges to the Court, with the result that they

---

[82] See text to nn 165–175, below.

[83] Art 124(4). For the inquiry committee and its procedure, see The Judges Inquiry Act, 1968.

[84] Art 125.

[85] There have been some exceptions, for example, appointments to the Supreme Court directly from the Bar. But these preceded the *Judges cases*, discussed in the text to nn 281–85, below.

have very short terms before having to retire. This has adversely affected the individual contributions that the judges can make to the development of the law.

The Court draws judges from different states, and as far as possible its composition reflects the entire ethnic, religious and cultural diversity of India. Its gender composition is, however, poor. It has only one woman judge. The strength of the Court was seven, excluding the Chief Justice, in 1950. It rose to ten in 1956, thirteen in 1961, seventeen in 1977, and twenty-five (excluding the Chief Justice) in 1986. A cursory glance at the profiles of the judges reveals that out of 136 judges appointed until 1999, thirteen were Muslims, four Christians, two Sikhs, and two Parsis. Of the 115 judges who belonged to the majority Hindu community, 24 were identified as Bramhins, the highest caste in the Hindu caste system.[86] The judges have mainly come from urban, and higher economic, backgrounds: only two have belonged to a Scheduled Caste or Scheduled Tribe.

Problems and Methods of Interpretation

The Choice of Methods

Positivist and structuralist interpretation

There are basically two models of constitutional interpretation. One is legal positivism, 'which holds that the truth of legal propositions consists in facts about the rules that have been adopted by specific social institutions, and in nothing else'.[87] This model emanates from the 'black letter law' tradition, which seeks to interpret law as a distinct, relatively autonomous reality. Law is separated from morality, and interpreted in accordance with self-constituted principles and concepts.[88]

In the second model, which we will call structuralism, the Constitution is interpreted liberally, as a totality, in the light of the spirit pervading it and the philosophy underlying it. A structuralist interpretation aims to articulate the implicit nuances of the Constitution, but may vary according to the ideological or philosophical predilections of the judges. It accords a wider role to the judiciary, which is required to be creative. According to Justice Cardozo, a written constitution 'states or ought to state not rules for the passing hour, but principles for an expanding future'.[89] Structuralist interpretation can also be called teleological, meaning that it understands the Constitution to be intended to achieve certain purposes. It is, in that sense, result-oriented.

[86] See SP Sathe *Judicial Activism in India: Transgressing Borders and Enforcing Limits* (Oxford University Press, Oxford, 2002) 298.

[87] R Dworkin *Taking Rights Seriously* (Gerald Duckworth & Co, London, 1977) vii.

[88] R Dhavan in M Galanter *Law and Society in Modern India* (Oxford University Press, New York, 1997) xvii.

[89] BN Cardozo *The Nature of the Judicial Process* (33rd printing., Yale University Press, New Haven, 1974) 83.

The Court began by taking a positivist approach to constitutional interpretation. But judicial review under a written constitution with a bill of rights cannot remain merely positivist, because the expressions used in it are often open-textured and continue to acquire new meanings.[90] Over the years, as Indian democracy threw up unexpected challenges, the Court gradually moved to a structuralist approach. This movement was not linear, or even chronologically consistent. There were dissents during the initial period of positivism, and zig-zags forwards and backwards during later periods.

The colonial heritage

In England, Parliament being supreme, there was no judicial review of Acts of Parliament. Courts in colonial India were steeped in that tradition, and even though the colonial legislatures did not enjoy the sovereignty of the Imperial Parliament, Indian courts were reluctant to strike down statutes. In fact, they tended to construe legislative powers in the widest terms. In *Queen v Burah*, the Privy Council rejected the view that Indian legislatures were mere delegates of the Imperial Parliament, and held that they had plenary legislative power as vast as that of the Imperial Parliament itself, subject only to such restrictions as had been explicitly stated in their Acts of Incorporation.[91] This liberal interpretation of the legislatures' power was based on British tradition, and the premise that a Constitution is 'a mechanism under which laws are to be made, and not a mere Act which declares what the law is to be'.[92] Such a liberal interpretation also entailed maximum deference to the legislatures' will. The Supreme Court later held that legislative power must be construed in the widest possible terms. Unless limited by the Constitution, it includes power to legislate retrospectively and to validate otherwise invalid laws or executive acts, and all ancillary and residual powers.[93]

Liberal interpretation of legislative power was combined with a positivist interpretation of the constitutional limitations imposed on it. HM Seervai, a leading commentator on constitutional law, stated the principle as follows:

> Well established rules of interpretation require that the meaning and intention of the framers of a Constitution—be it a Parliament or a Constituent Assembly—must be ascertained from the language of the Constitution itself; with the motives of those who framed it, the Court has no concern.[94]

The constituent assembly and the role of the judiciary

The positivist model of judicial review was preferred by many leaders of the National Movement, including Prime Minister Nehru. They agreed that the

[90] For example see how the equal protection clause of the Fourteenth Amendment of the United States Constitution was interpreted differently in *Plessey v Ferguson* 163 US 537 (1896) and *Brown v Board of Education*, 347 US 483. [91] (1878) 5 IA 178, 193–94: (1878) 3 AC 889, 903–904.
[92] *A-G for NSW v Brewery Employees Union* (1908) 18 CLR 469, 611 (Higgins J).
[93] *India v Madan Gopal* AIR 1954 SC 158.
[94] HM Seervai, *Constitutional Law of India* (4th edn., NM Tripathi, Bombay, 1991) vol 1 172.

future Indian Constitution should contain a bill of rights, which would assuage the apprehensions of minorities, and protect individual liberty against the executive.[95] But the leading members of the Constituent Assembly were apprehensive of the wider role thereby given to the judiciary. A debate revolved round the scope of judicial review, and particularly articles 21 and 31 of the draft Constitution. Article 21 provided that no one shall be deprived of life or personal liberty without due process of law, and art 31 protected the right to property. The words 'due process of law' were strongly opposed by those who recalled the American experience of judicial review during President Roosevelt's New Deal program.[96] Supporters of parliamentary supremacy apprehended that since the words 'due process of law' were vague, they might be used to obstruct the agenda of economic reconstruction, leading to 'the future of the country' being 'determined not by the collective wisdom of the representatives of the people but by the whims and vagaries of lawyers elevated to the judiciary'.[97] These members of the Constituent Assembly wanted judicial review to operate in the same manner as it did in England. Nehru said:

Within limits, no judge and no Supreme Court can make itself a third chamber (of the Legislature). No Supreme Court and no judiciary can stand in judgment over the sovereign will of Parliament representing the will of the entire community. If we go wrong here and there, it can point it out but in the ultimate analysis, where the future of the community is concerned, no judiciary can come in the way. And if it comes in the way, ultimately the whole Constitution is a creature of Parliament.[98]

On the other hand, some members did have reservations about this conception of the judicial role. In particular, leaders representing minority groups could not support the doctrine of parliamentary supremacy, because they felt that it would ultimately amount to the permanent supremacy of the religious majority. Dr BR Ambedkar, a leader of the oppressed caste called 'untouchables', who had been an opponent of the Congress Party during the National Movement, was elected by the Constituent Assembly as the chairman of the Constitution's drafting committee. Expressing his apprehensions about the non-inclusion of the due process clause, he said:

In a federal constitution, it is always open to the judiciary to decide whether any particular law passed by the legislature is *ultra vires* or *intra vires* in reference to the powers of legislation

---

[95] The Congress had appointed a committee in 1928 under the chairmanship of Motilal Nehru, father of Jawaharlal Nehru, to suggest reforms in the Constitution. That committee had recommended the inclusion of a bill of rights in the Constitution. A resolution accepting that suggestion was passed at the Karachi session of the INC held in 1931. See B Shiva Rao *The Framing of India's Constitution A Study* (The Indian Institute of Public Administration, New Delhi, 1968) 173.

[96] BN Rau, the constitutional advisor had met Justice Frankfurter of the United States Supreme Court and had been advised by him not to include the due process clause in the Constitution, because the power of judicial review implied by it would be undemocratic. Shiva Rao (n 95) 235, 237.

[97] Shiva Rao (n 95) 234.

[98] CAD Vol 9, 1195. The Constituent Assembly went on to function as a Provisional Parliament under art 379 of the Constitution.

which are granted by the Constitution to the particular legislature... The 'due process clause', in my judgment, would give the judiciary the power to question the law made by the legislature on another ground. That ground would be whether that law is in keeping with certain fundamental principles relating to the rights of the individual. In other words, the judiciary would be endowed with the authority to question the law not merely on the ground whether it was in excess of the authority of the legislature, but also on the ground whether the law was good law, apart from the question of the powers of the legislature making the law.[99]

Dr Ambedkar expressed the dilemma of whether it was preferable to leave the question of liberty to a majority in Parliament, which was often motivated by partisan political considerations, or to leave it to a few judges. He further reflected:

We are therefore placed in two difficult positions. One is to give the judiciary the authority to sit in judgment over the will of the legislature and to question the law made by the legis-lature on the ground that it is not good law, in consonance with fundamental principles. Is that a desirable principle? The second position is that the legislature ought to be trusted not to make bad laws. It is very difficult to come to any definite conclusion. There are dan-gers on both sides. For myself I cannot altogether omit the possibility of a Legislature packed by party men making laws which may abrogate or violate what we regard as certain fundamental principles affecting the life and liberty of an individual. At the same time, I do not see how five or six gentlemen sitting in the Federal or Supreme Court examining laws made by the Legislature and by dint of their own individual conscience or their bias or their prejudices can be trusted to determine which law is good and which law is bad.[100]

Ultimately the words 'procedure established by law' replaced the words 'due process of law' in art 21.

The Legal Positivism of the Early Years

The first judges of the Court either had been judges of the Federal Court of India, or were elevated from the High Courts. Naturally, they were inheritors of the colonial legal tradition. In *AK Gopalan v India*,[101] the first constitutional case heard by the Court, the influence of the black letter law tradition was evident. The partition of the sub-continent, and consequent communal carnage on both sides of the new divide, had persuaded the Constituent Assembly to retain provisions for preventive detention, without trial, in the Constitution. Such provisions had existed in British India during the War, and had been severely criticized by Indian freedom fighters, despite having been strictly construed by the Privy Council.[102] Article 21 of the Constitution provides that no person shall be deprived of life or personal liberty except according to procedure established by law. Some required procedures are laid down in cls 22(1) and (2), which were described previously, but cl (3) makes these inapplicable to any person who is arrested or detained

---

[99] CAD Vol 7 1000.   [100] ibid.   [101] AIR 1950 SC 27.
[102] *Emperor v Sibnath Bannerji* AIR 1945 PC 156 overruling *Keshav Talpade v Emperor* AIR 1943 FC1.

under any law providing for preventive detention.[103] Clauses (4) to (7) prescribe the procedure to be adopted in the case of preventive detention. Article 19 guarantees seven freedoms to the citizen, including freedom of movement throughout India.[104] Power to make a law authorizing preventive detention is given to both Parliament and the state legislatures in the Seventh Schedule.[105]

In the *Gopalan* case, the validity of the Preventive Detention Act 1950 was challenged. Two questions were raised: (i) whether the Act offended art 21, and (ii) whether it offended the freedoms guaranteed by art 19. The petitioner's first objection was that the procedure provided by the Act did not satisfy the words 'procedure established by law' in art 21, which were argued to mean such procedure as conformed to the principles of natural justice. The word 'law' in the above phrase could mean either *lex* (enacted law) or *jus* (just law). If the former meaning were preferred, the clause would protect the individual against executive action but not legislative action. It was argued that to read the word 'law' as *jus* would be more consistent with the spirit of the Constitution. But the Court dismissed this argument, and held that 'law' meant enacted law. Kania CJ said:

> The courts are not at liberty to declare an Act void because in their opinion it is opposed to a spirit supposed to pervade the Constitution but not expressed in words. Where the fundamental law has not limited, either in terms or by necessary implication, the general powers conferred upon the Legislature, we cannot declare a limitation under the notion of having discovered something in the spirit of the Constitution which is not even mentioned in the instrument.[106]

The Court would not enter into the question of whether the procedure was fair. Kania CJ relied upon the absence of the word 'due' in art 21. By adopting the phrase 'procedure established by law', he said, 'the Constitution gave the Legislature the final word to determine the law'.[107]

Justice Fazl Ali, in dissent, asked whether 'the principle that no person can be condemned without a hearing by an impartial tribunal, which is well recognized in all modern civilized systems of law, cannot be regarded as part of the law of this country'.[108] The Privy Council had declared in a number of cases that it would interfere with the decisions of lower courts if they committed a breach of the principles of natural justice.[109] The Constituent Assembly had avoided the use of the words 'due process of law' because it wanted to eschew substantive, as opposed to procedural, due process. Procedural due process, according to the learned judge, had long been part of the established law.

The second question before the Court concerned the relationship between articles 19 and 21. Article 19(1)(d) granted citizens seven freedoms,[110] including freedom of movement throughout India. It was contended that the law of

---

[103] See text to nn 33–44 above.   [104] Cl. (1)(d).
[105] Entry 9—List I, Entry 3—List III.   [106] AIR 1950 SC 27, 42.
[107] AIR 1950 SC 27, 39.   [108] ibid 60.   [109] ibid.
[110] See text to n 103 above.

preventive detention offended this freedom, and that the Court should examine whether it constituted a reasonable restriction, as permitted by art 19(5).[111] All the judges, except Fazl Ali J, held that arts 19 and 21 had to be read as mutually exclusive. Only a citizen who was otherwise free was entitled to the freedoms guaranteed by art 19, whereas art 21 provided that life and personal liberty could only be taken away by law. If a person were arrested and detained, the only question the Court could ask was whether her arrest or detention had been authorized by law. The words 'personal liberty' were very narrowly construed to mean freedom from arbitrary arrest. The right to life received no attention. In dissent, Fazl Ali J laid down a seminal principle of constitutional interpretation, which has since been followed by the Court in several cases. He said:

To my mind, the scheme of the chapter dealing with the fundamental rights does not contemplate what is attributed to it, namely, that each Article is a code by itself and is independent of the others. In my opinion, it cannot be said that Arts 19, 20, 21 and 22 do not to some extent overlap each other.[112]

Fazl Ali J's approach to constitutional interpretation stands out as an alternative to the majority's positivism. It seems that the judges were in a dilemma as to the exact nature of their role. They realized that a federal constitution with a bill of rights could not be interpreted in a technocratic manner. Despite its detail and specificity, it contains expressions that are pregnant with various nuances, which must be articulated from time to time. The Constitution entrusts to the Court the responsibility of striking a balance between liberty and authority. This was implicit in art 19, whose sub-clauses allowed reasonable restrictions on freedoms guaranteed by cl (1). Referring to this, Chief Justice Patanjali Sastri once said:

In evaluating such elusive factors and forming their own conception of what is reasonable, in all the circumstances of a given case, it is inevitable that the social philosophy and the scale of values of the judges participating in the decision should play an important part, and the limit to their interference with legislative judgment in such cases can only be dictated by their sense of responsibility and self restraint and the sobering reflection that the Constitution is meant not only for people of their own way of thinking but for all, and the majority of elected representatives of the people have, in authorizing the imposition of the restrictions, considered them to be reasonable.[113]

The learned judge admitted that filling in the leeways of choice left by the constitutional text made the import of a judge's 'social philosophy' inevitable, but cautioned that the judge had to be objective and give maximum deference to the will of Parliament. The judges were in a dilemma because their tradition required them to be positivist, but the nature of the Constitution required them to look to

---

[111] Clauses (2) to (6) permit the State to impose reasonable restrictions on the rights mentioned in clauses (a) to (g) of art 19 on grounds mentioned in the respective clauses. Cl (5) permits reasonable restriction in the interests of the general public or for the protection of the interests of any Scheduled Tribe.   [112] AIR 1950 SC 27, 52.

[113] *State of Madras v VG Row* AIR 1952 SC 196, 200.

it as an organic law to be interpreted 'not simply by taking the words and a dictionary, but by considering their origin and the line of their growth'.[114]

External Aids to Interpretation

Legal positivism, strictly speaking, does not permit the use of external aids, such as debates in Parliament or the Constituent Assembly, to find out what the founders intended. But the Court has held that external aids may be used where the text of the Constitution is unclear.[115] The debates in the Constituent Assembly are well documented in 12 volumes published by the Government of India, and these may be referred to when the text of the Constitution is not explicit.[116] An example concerns the doctrine of responsible government. Although the Constitution provided that there shall be a Council of Ministers headed by the Prime Minister to aid and advise the President, it did not state that the President was bound to act according to such advice.[117] The Court held that the President was bound to act on the Council's advice.[118] This decision was based on the debates in the Constituent Assembly, and the theory of parliamentary democracy. The Constitution was subsequently amended to explicitly state that the President is bound to act on the aid and advice of the Council of Ministers.[119]

From the beginning, the Court referred to the decisions of courts in England, Australia, Canada and the United States. Lately, the Court has also cited decisions of the apex courts of other countries, such as South Africa, Sri Lanka, Pakistan and Bangladesh. As the Court's judgments have become more structuralist and sociological, the citation of academic writings has also increased.

Interpreting the Federal Distribution of Power

A major concern of judicial review in most federal polities is to keep the federal and state legislatures within their respective limits. The Indian Constitution contains an elaborate division of legislative powers in art 246, read with the three lists in the Seventh Schedule.[120] But few legal disputes concerning these powers have arisen, for three reasons. First, the powers in these lists were meticulously drafted, compared with legislative powers in Australia and Canada, which are relatively more abstract and therefore contentious. Secondly, the Indian Constitution is quite explicit about the overwhelming power of the federal legislature and

---

[114] See Justice Holmes in *Gompers v US* 233 US 604, 610 (1914).

[115] On how far the debates in the Constituent Assembly can be referred as external aids to constitutional interpretation see HM Seervai *Constitutional Law of India*, Vol I (4th edn., NM Tripathi, Bombay, 1999) 201–206.

[116] See *Golaknath v Punjab* AIR 1967 SC 1643; *Kesavanand Bharathi v Kerala* AIR 1973 SC 1461; *TMA. Pai Foundation v Karnataka* (2002) 8 SCC 481.   [117] Article 74(1).

[118] *Samsher Singh v Punjab* AIR 1974 SC 2192.

[119] Art 74(1) as amended by s 13 of the Constitution (Forty-Second Amendment) Act 1976.

[120] See text to nn 20–32 above.

government. Thirdly, because a single party (Congress) ruled at both the federal and state levels for the first two decades after Independence, conflicts between those levels rarely appeared in the courts. Most have been resolved politically, through party mechanisms, rather than through judicial procedures. Federalism has become a subject of judicial review only recently, when the Court reviewed the validity of a presidential proclamation, under art 356, dismissing a number of state governments.[121]

Since the three lists were based on the Government of India Act 1935, the Court was able to draw on interpretive principles previously laid down by the Privy Council and the Federal Court of India. The Court has also referred to American, Canadian, and Australian decisions. For example, it has held that if a law 'in pith and substance' falls within an entry in one of the three lists, any incidental encroachment on an entry in another list does not affect its validity. This principle was borrowed from Privy Council decisions in Canadian cases.[122] It requires that the law as a whole be examined to ascertain its 'true nature and character', in order to determine what entry in which List it relates to. In *Prafulla Kumar Mukherjee v Bank of Khulna*,[123] the Bengal Moneylender's Act 1940, enacted by the Bengal legislature, was challenged as being *ultra vires*. In the Government of India Act 1935, entry 27 of List II was 'money lending', whereas entry 25 of List I was 'promissory notes'. The Privy Council held that the Act dealt mainly with money lending, and was therefore not *ultra vires* the provincial legislature, even though it also dealt, incidentally, with promissory notes. Where a matter does not come within any entry in the list of a legislature's powers, but the legislature tries to deal with it in the guise of exercising one of its powers, its legislation will be struck down as being colourable.[124]

The Court held in *Bombay v Balsara*[125] that the word 'import' in entry 19 in list I must be given a restricted meaning in order to give effect to the very general words 'intoxicating liquors and narcotic drugs' in entry 31 of List II. Similarly it was held that entry 48 of list I, which provides for 'future markets', being a specific entry, must be excluded from the general entry 26 of list II, which provides for 'trade and commerce within the state'.[126] In another case, the Court observed that 'a general word used in an entry . . . must be construed to extend to all ancillary or residuary matters which can fairly and reasonably be held to be included in it'.[127]

The 'occupied field' doctrine is used to determine the validity of a state law that conflicts with a previously made central law on an item in the concurrent list. If

---

[121] *SR Bommai v India* AIR 1994 SC 1918; (1994) 3 SCC 1; discussed in the text to nn 193–96 and 287–89 below.

[122] *Citizens Insurance Co v Parsons* 7 AC 96; *Russell v The Queen* 7 AC 829; *A-G for Canada v A-G for British Columbia* AIR 1949 PC 190.

[123] (1947) 74 I-A 23, 43, AIR 1947 PC 60. See *Bombay v Narottam Jethabhai* (1951) SCR 51–64, 64–65; 72–73. [124] *KT Mopil Nair v Kerala* AIR 1961 SC 552.

[125] AIR 1951 SC 318.

[126] *Waverly Jute Mills Co Ltd v Rayman & Co (Private) Ltd* AIR 1963 SC 90.

[127] *Jagannath Baksh Singh v UP* AIR 1962 SC 1563.

Parliament has used the entire power in legislating on an item in that list, it is said that the 'field' has been wholly occupied. If, in enacting a law, Parliament intended to cover the entire field, the state law insofar as it deals with the same matter is void.[128]

Resolving Conflicts between Constitutional Provisions

The rule of harmonious construction is invoked when two provisions of the Constitution conflict. An interpretation is adopted that does not make either of them nugatory, but gives effect to both. This methodological rule is, in itself, neither positivist nor structuralist. It can be applied either in a positivist, or in a structuralist, fashion. This accounts for the different conclusions that judges have reached in applying it.

Freedom of religion

A section of the Hindu community called 'untouchables' was denied access to Hindu temples, and reformers had campaigned to give them such access. Article 25(1) guarantees freedom of religion, and cl (2)(b) provides that the State has power to open Hindu religious institutions of a public character to all sections of Hindus. But art 26(b) guarantees to religious denominations the right to manage their own affairs in matters of religion. In *Sri Venkataramana Devaru v Mysore*,[129] the validity of the Madras Temple Entry Authorization Act 1947, which provided access to a temple to all sections of Hindus, was challenged by the temple's trustees on the ground that it restricted their sect's right to manage its own affairs in matters of religion, by denying it the ability to confine access to its members. The Court took the view that the sect's right under art 26(b) was in apparent conflict with the state's power under art 25(2)(b) to open Hindu temples of a public character to all Hindus. The apparent conflict was resolved by applying the rule of harmonious construction. The Court held that while the sect could not deny entrance into the temple to the members of other castes, it could restrict entry to the inner space surrounding the deity to its own members. This was because art 25 begins with the words 'subject . . . to the other provisions of this part', which are absent in art 26.

This positivist treatment of the two articles as being in conflict was due to the Court's practice of reading each article separately, as a code in itself. The Court put arts 25 and 26 on an equal footing. If it had read the Constitution as a whole, the right of the religious denominations to manage their affairs under art 26 would have been subject to the state's power to open Hindu temples to all Hindus under art 25(2)(b). These provisions must be read in the context of the social reform movement that accompanied the national movement for independence. The

---

[128] *Orissa v Tulloch & Co* AIR 1964 SC 1284, 1291.
[129] (1958) SCR 895; AIR 1958 SC 255.

framers of the Constitution were apprehensive of the wide sweep of religion in Indian life. If freedom of religion were given an unrestricted scope, practices such as untouchability, *sati* (the burning to death of a widow on her husband's funeral pyre), or even human sacrifice, might have masqueraded as protected religious practices. Article 25 starts with the words 'subject to public order, morality and health and to other provisions of this part', specifically to make religious freedom subordinate to other rights, such as equality, the abolition of untouchability, and freedom of speech, and to the State's power under clause (2)(b) to make laws for social welfare and reform, including the opening of public Hindu religious institutions to all Hindus. The rights of religious denominations surely cannot be greater than the rights of individuals to freedom of religion. Therefore, the most legitimate interpretation would have been to treat art 26 as complementary to art 25, and subject to the qualifications and restrictive clauses included in art 25. This structuralist interpretation would have made it unnecessary to invoke the rule of harmonious construction.

Powers and privileges of legislatures

The Constitution provides that the powers, privileges and immunities of each House of Parliament, or of a state legislature, may be defined by Parliament or that legislature by law, and until so defined, are those that were enjoyed by the British Parliament at the time the Constitution commenced.[130] In *MSM Sharma v Sri Krishna Sinha*,[131] the majority held that the privileges of the legislature were not subject to freedom of speech, which includes freedom of the press, guaranteed by art 19(1)(a). The majority applied the maxim *generalia specialibus non derogant*. Since art 19(1)(a), and the later article dealing with legislatures' privileges, were both part of the Constitution, the latter, being a special provision, prevailed over the former, which is a general principle. This was a highly positivist interpretation. If Parliament or a state legislature were to enact a law defining its own privileges, that law would be subject to the Fundamental Rights. It therefore suits the Parliament and legislatures to leave their powers and privileges uncodified, so that their exercise cannot be challenged by reference to Fundamental Rights. Subba Rao J, in his dissenting judgment, held that legislative privileges must yield to freedom of the press. But although freedom of speech, and legislatures' privileges, are both protected by the Constitution, why should either of them be subordinated to the other? Should the Court not weigh up these competing interests, and decide how they should be balanced in each situation? A more empirical approach to harmonizing them would have been desirable.

The question of priority between Fundamental Rights and legislatures' privileges arose again, when the President sought an advisory opinion from the Court

---

[130] Art 105(3); Art 194(3); as originally enacted. By s 15 of the Constitution (Forty-Fourth Amendment) Act 1978, such powers and privileges remain as they were before the enactment of that Act, until they are redefined by the Parliament or legislature.   [131] AIR 1959 SC 395, 409.

concerning a dispute between the Allahabad High Court and the Legislative Assembly of the State of Uttar Pradesh. The Assembly had reprimanded one Keshav Singh for contempt, after finding that he had libeled one of its members and—when brought before it—flaunted his disrespect for it. When Singh then wrote a letter describing the Assembly's actions as a 'brutal attack on democracy', it passed a resolution sentencing him to seven days' imprisonment. A petition was filed on his behalf to the Allahabad High Court, which ordered his release on bail. The Assembly then issued a notice to Singh, his advocate, and the judges of the High Court who had heard his petition, asking why action should not be taken against them for contempt of the Assembly. The High Court, with all the judges sitting except those against whom notices had been issued, stayed the Assembly's order.

The President's reference to the Court[132] included questions regarding the competence of the Assembly to proceed against the judges for contempt, and of the courts to entertain petitions against, and to stay, orders made in the Assembly's exercise of a privilege. The majority held that the courts had power to entertain a petition seeking relief against an order for a person's arrest, on the ground of its alleged infringement of a Fundamental Right outside the precincts of the legislature. But the Court did not overrule the decision in *Sharma*, and therefore continued to allow the legislatures' privileges to override freedom of the press.

Towards Sociological Interpretation

During the early 1960s, the Court started moving towards the model of structuralist interpretation. We will briefly survey some landmarks cases that illustrate this change in its approach.

Affirmative action for the weaker sections of society

Article 46 contains a Directive Principle that requires the State to 'promote with special care the educational and economic interests of the weaker sections of the people, and, in particular, of the Scheduled Castes and the Scheduled Tribes, and [to] protect them from social injustice and all forms of exploitation'. The Scheduled Castes are those who suffered from the practice of untouchability, and the Scheduled Tribes are indigenous peoples who for centuries were excluded from access to education and gainful employment. In 1951, the Court held that if there is a conflict between a Directive Principle and a Fundamental Right, the latter must prevail. Therefore, a provision for the reservation of places in an educational institution, in pursuance of art 46, was held void for violating the Fundamental Rights in arts 15(2) and 29(2), which explicitly forbid discrimination on the grounds of religion, caste, race, place of birth, and so on.[133] They are

---

[132] *In re, Under Article 143, of the Constitution of India; In the matter of,* AIR 1965 SC 745.
[133] *Madras v Champakam Dorairajan* AIR 1951 SC 226.

species of the general guarantee, in art 14, of equality before the law and equal protection of the law.

The Constitution was immediately amended, and cl (4) was added to art 15, providing that nothing in arts 15(2) or 29(2) shall prevent the State from making any 'special provision for the advancement of socially and educationally backward classes of citizens or for the Scheduled Castes and the Scheduled Tribes'.[134] This extended the principle of affirmative action, already enshrined in art 16(4), with respect to government employment. Article 16(2) prohibits discrimination on the grounds of religion, race, caste, sex, and so on, in respect of any employment or office under the State, but cl (4) permits the State to reserve appointments in the public service in favour of any backward class of citizens, which, 'in the opinion of the State', is not adequately represented in the services under the State.

The term 'backward classes' was rather nebulous, and needed to be specified, but the government seemed to be free to decide what they were, and how many reservations were needed for them. But the Court imposed judicial control on the exercise of this power. In *Balaji v Mysore*,[135] it held that it could decide whether backwardness had been determined on the basis of relevant considerations. It held that although caste might be one of the factors, it could not be the only factor, in determining backwardness. The words 'backward classes' in art 16(4) have been read by the Court in the same sense in which the words 'socially and educationally backward classes' are used in art 15(4). Usually, the Court expects that people whose life conditions are similar to those of the Scheduled Castes and the Scheduled Tribes should be categorized as backward. The Court also imposed curbs on the extent of reservations of places in educational institutions, by holding that not more than fifty percent of the places may be reserved. In *Chitraleka v Mysore*, it extended this formula to the reservation of government jobs under art 16(4).[136]

These decisions in the early 1960s have stood the test of time. In 1989, when the government reserved 27 per cent of government jobs for the backward classes, it triggered a fierce class conflict between the advanced and the backward classes. The government responsible for this decision collapsed, and the constitutionality of the reservation was challenged in the Supreme Court. In *Indra Sawney v India*[137], the Court reaffirmed the restrictions on affirmative action laid down in *Balaji* and *Chitralekha*. It upheld the criteria of backwardness used in the Mandal Commissions's report, which had been the source of those decisions.[138] The Court further held that 'creamy layers' among the backward classes—those whose social and economic position has already been improved—should be gradually

---

[134] The Constitution (First Amendment) Act 1951 s 2.   [135] AIR 1963 SC 649.
[136] AIR 1964 SC 1823.   [137] AIR 1993 SC 417.
[138] Under art 340 of the Constitution the President can appoint a commission to investigate the conditions of socially and educationally backward classes and to make recommendations for the improvement of such conditions. The President had appointed a commission under the chairmanship of BP Mandal. This commission is known as the *Mandal Commission*.

excluded from the benefit of reservations. It also held that there should be no reservations in promotion. The logic of these decisions is that the reservations contemplated by the above provisions must be interpreted homogeneously with the right to equality. In other words, the State's power to reserve places for disadvantaged people has the same goal as the right to equality, and is therefore limited by that goal. This is a very good instance of structuralist interpretation.

Freedom of speech

Freedom of speech and expression, including freedom of the press, is of vital importance in any democracy. These freedoms are protected by art 19(1)(a), although cl (2) permits reasonable restrictions in relation to state security, public order, defamation, and other specific, competing interests.[139] Article 19(1)(g) protects the right to carry on any trade or business, but cl (6) permits reasonable restrictions 'in the interest of the general public'. *Sakal Newspapers (Private Ltd) v India*[140] concerned the validity of a price and page schedule, prescribing what price newspapers could charge for a given number of pages, how many pages they could print, and how much space they could set aside for advertisements. The purpose of the schedule was to protect small, special language newspapers from being crushed by the economies of scale enjoyed by mass circulation, English language newspapers. The schedule was challenged as being an unreasonable restriction on freedom of the press, protected by art 19(1)(a). The Union responded that the press was a trade or business, and the schedule imposed reasonable restrictions in the interest of the general public, as permitted by art 19(6).

The Court held that the press was not a mere trade or business when it disseminated news and opinion to people. It could be considered a trade or business when it dealt with its employees, and when the law required it to pay them wages at a particular rate.[141] But requiring the newspapers not to publish more pages, or to charge a lower price, than prescribed amounts, was a restriction on freedom of the press rather than on freedom to carry on a trade or business. These requirements did not come within the restrictions on freedom of speech permitted by art 19(2), which are much more specific than 'the interest of the general public' that can justify restrictions imposed on a mere trade or business under art 19(6). The Court stated that restrictions on freedom of speech would be subjected to greater scrutiny than restrictions on freedom of trade or business, which implies that the latter enjoy a stronger presumption of constitutionality than the former. This was reiterated in a later case.[142] The Court thus accorded a preferred position to freedom of speech over freedom to engage in trade or business, even though there

[139] The Court held in 1950 that freedom of speech and expression includes freedom of the press, and that prior censorship of the print media is unconstitutional: *Romesh Thapar v Madras* AIR 1950 SC 124.   [140] AIR 1962 SC 305.
[141] *Express Newspapers (P) Ltd v India* AIR 1958 SC 578.
[142] *Benett Coleman v India* AIR 1973 SC 106.

is no textual basis for the preference.[143] This is another instance of structuralist interpretation during the early 1960s.

Property rights

In property rights cases, which range from 1950 to 1973, the Court did not observe either the restraint implicit in positivism, or the dynamism ingrained in structuralism. While its methodology appeared legalistic, it was also teleological in the sense that it favoured the interests of a particular social class and maintained the status quo. We will briefly review these cases.

Land in India had for a very long time been inequitably distributed. Colonial rulers had vested property rights in people who collected revenue on their behalf. The revenue collectors extracted exploitative rents from cultivators, and after paying the required amounts to the colonial state, kept the balance for themselves. Their wealth steadily increased to the detriment of the cultivators. Congress promised land reforms during the movement for national independence. Property owners, threatened by some of these promises, persuaded the British government to include the right to property in s 299 of the Government of India Act 1935.[144]

When India became independent, the ruling Congress party had to redeem the pledges previously given regarding changes in property relations. India needed land reform, which required abolition of absentee landlordism, and the breaking up of large estates. Article 31 of the Constitution, which was repealed in 1978, was a re-incarnation of s 299 of the 1935 Act. Article 31(1) provided that no-one should be deprived of her property save by authority of law, and cl (2) required payment of compensation on the acquisition of private property by the State for a public purpose. But the Constitution also included provisions to make legislation, enacted within 18 months before the coming into force of the Constitution or six months afterwards, immune from attack on the ground that it infringed the right to property.[145] The land reform legislation that was enacted offered compensation to the landlords at varying rates, so that bigger estates received a lower rate than smaller estates. Because the legislation could not be challenged under art 31, it was challenged in the Patna High Court—successfully—on the ground that it violated the right to equality guaranteed by art 14.[146]

Without waiting for an appeal to be decided by the Court,[147] Parliament amended the Constitution by adding two articles, 31-A and 31-B. Article 31-A extended the immunity of land reform legislation from judicial review, on the ground of its alleged inconsistency with the rights given by arts 14, 19, and 31.[148] Article 31-B inserted the Ninth Schedule, which listed laws whose validity could

---

[143] This was similar to *United States v Carolene Products Co* 304 US 144 (1952).

[144] Government of India Act 1935, s 299. The Joint Committee on Indian Constitutional Reforms (n 34) 217.   [145] Clauses (4) and (6) of art 31

[146] *Kameshwar v State* AIR 1951 Pat 91.   [147] *Bihar v Kameshwar* AIR 1952 SC 252

[148] The Constitution (First Amendment) Act 1951, s 4. See SP Sathe, *Constitutional Amendments 1950–88 Law and Politics* (NM Tripathi, Bombay, 1989) Appendices 99.

not be challenged on the ground of their inconsistency with any of the Fundamental Rights.[149] Over the years, this Schedule expanded through additions made by subsequent amendments. While it originally included only 13 statutes, it now lists 284.

Article 31 provided for 'deprivation' in cl (1), and 'acquisition' in cl (2). One can be deprived of one's property, including choses in action, even if that property does not vest in the State. Such deprivation can result from the exercise of police powers, and also from the abolition of certain rights that have become obsolete and socially unjust. For example, if the State temporarily takes over management of a commercial mill or factory, to rectify inefficiency or mismanagement, this amounts to 'deprivation' within the meaning of cl (1), but not to 'acquisition' within the meaning of cl (2). So, too, if the State intervenes to require the waiver of the repayment of certain loans, by money lenders who have already earned usurious interest. Did the State have to pay compensation when it intervened to protect the public interest by way of deprivation, but not acquisition, of property? Parliament maintained that the State must have the freedom to undertake such social engineering without being burdened with this heavy liability. But the Court held that compensation was payable when a person was 'deprived' of her property, even if it was not 'acquired' by the State.[150]

In the Constituent Assembly, it had been agreed that Parliament's decisions regarding the method, the principles, or the quantum of compensation would be final, and that no court could interfere except to prevent a fraud on the Constitution. There was never any intention to expropriate private property without compensation in ordinary cases of 'petty acquisition', that is, acquisition of land for ordinary governmental purposes.[151] Nehru acknowledged that these cases would continue to be governed by the existing Land Acquisition Act 1894, which provided for acquisition of land for public purposes on payment of compensation equivalent to the market value of the property and 15 per cent solatium. Compensation at less than market value was to be reserved for exceptional cases involving the redistribution of large holdings resulting from unjust enrichment.[152] But in spite of this, the Court held that compensation must be equivalent to the market value of the property acquired.[153]

Parliament attempted to overturn these decisions by the Constitution (Fourth Amendment) Act 1955, which clearly stated (a) that compensation would be payable only when property was transferred to the State or a State corporation, and not when one was otherwise deprived of it;[154] and (b) that the adequacy of compensation would not be justiciable.[155] But despite this clear provision, the

---

149 The Constitution (First Amendment) Act 1951, s 5.
150 *West Bengal v Subodh* AIR 1954 SC 92.   151 Shiva Rao (n 95) 291.
152 CAD, Vol 9, 1192.   153 *West Bengal v Bela Bannerji* AIR 1954 SC 170.
154 Clause 2 A was added to art 31 by the Constitution (Fourth Amendment) Act 1954, s 2.
155 Article 31(2) as amended by s 2(2).

Court subsequently held that any 'compensation' must not be illusory: it must bear some relation to the value of the property.[156] On this basis it held invalid, in the Bank Nationalization Case, an Ordinance by which the government had nationalized 14 banks.[157] Had the Court applied the famous 'mischief rule', this result would have been avoided. In 1971, Parliament responded once again, amending the Constitution by replacing the word 'compensation' with the word 'amount'.[158] Despite this, the Court continued to insist that the amount given in return for acquired property must not be illusory, thereby bringing the question of adequacy in through the back door.[159]

Article 19(1)(f) guaranteed to citizens the right to acquire, hold, and dispose of property, subject to the power of the state to impose reasonable restrictions in the interest of the general public and the Scheduled Tribes. Following the principle laid down in *Gopalan*, of reading the provisions of arts 19(1)(d) and 21 of the Constitution separately, and treating each as a code by itself, the Court also read arts 19(1)(f) and 31 separately. Thus, if a person was deprived of her property or it was acquired by the state, art 31 applied and not art 19(1)(f). When restrictions were imposed on the acquisition, holding or disposal of property that a citizen otherwise continued to possess, art 19(1)(f) could be invoked.[160] But when Parliament amended art 31, to restrict judicial review, the Court changed its previous interpretation, and held that arts 19(1)(f) and 31 could be read together. This enabled a law depriving a person of her property, which could not be challenged for providing inadequate compensation, to be assailed as an unreasonable restriction on the right to hold property granted by art 19(1)(f).[161] This expanded the scope for judicial review, allowing the court to play a more creative role in deciding what constituted a 'reasonable restriction in the interest of the general public'; as permitted by art 19(5), the Court could have paid maximum deference to the will of the Parliament, and taken sociological facts into consideration. But it did not.

A strong right to property could not attain legitimacy in a country where a large number of people are poor and marginalized. The more the Court used its activism to save private property from social engineering, the greater was the loss of legitimacy suffered by the right to property. As interpreted by the Court, this right seemed to frustrate the socialist objectives reflected in the Directive Principles. Ultimately the right to property was deleted from the Fundamental Rights, and became a mere constitutional right without implying any promise of compensation for its loss. A new art 300-A protects private property only from executive action.[162] Article 19(1)(f) was also repealed by the same constitutional

---

[156] *Vajravelu Mudaliar v Sp Deputy Collector for Land Acquisition* AIR 1965 SC 1017.

[157] *RC Cooper v India* AIR 1970 SC 564.

[158] Constitution (Twenty-Fifth Amendment) Act 1971, s 2.

[159] *Kesavanand Bharati v Kerala* (n 116).   [160] *Bombay v Bhanji Munji* AIR 1955 SC 41.

[161] *KK Kochuni v Kerala* AIR 1960 SC 1080.

[162] Section 6 of the Constitution (Forty-Fourth Amendment) Act 1978 repealed art 31; s 34 of the same Act inserted ch IV, art 300-A in Part XII after ch III under the title 'Right to Property'. See

amendment.[163] The fact that the ultimate repeal of the right to property as a Fundamental Right was sponsored by the Janata government, which was an alliance of various parties that defeated the Congress party in the 1977 election, shows that the repeal had broad based political support.[164] This is confirmed by the fact that the validity of the Forty-Fourth Amendment was never challenged, and there have been no further confrontations between the Court and Parliament over the right to property.

Towards Structuralist Interpretation: the Basic Structure Doctrine

The history of the right to property shows how Parliament could override judicial decisions through the exercise of its constituent power contained in art 368. But, despite the desirability of the amendments pertaining to the right to property, a broader question concerning the scope of Parliament's power to amend the Constitution became critical. The validity of the Constitution (First Amendment) Act 1951 was challenged in *Shankari Prasad v India* (1951),[165] on the ground that since a constitutional amendment is a law, it is subject to art 13(2), which forbids the making of any law that takes away or abridges any Fundamental Right. This argument was rejected by a unanimous bench of five judges. The challenge was renewed in *Sajjan Singh v Rajasthan* (1965),[166] when the constitutional validity of the Seventeenth Amendment was challenged. While a three-two majority confirmed the earlier decision, and upheld Parliament's absolute power to amend the Constitution, the dissenting judges went beyond the question of the right to property. Hidayatullah J (as he then was) said:

I would require stronger grounds than were given in *Shakari Prasad*'s case to make me accept the view that Fundamental Rights were not really fundamental but were intended to be within the powers of amendment in common with the other parts of the Constitution.[167]

He asked whether Fundamental Rights should be 'the plaything of a special majority'.[168] This became the crux of subsequent controversies. Two years later, in *Golaknath v Punjab*,[169] the Supreme Court by a majority of six to five[170] overruled the previous decisions, and held that the power to amend the Constitution did not extend to the abrogation of any of the Fundamental Rights. The case involved the

---

SP Sathe, *Constitutional Amendments 1950–88: Law and Politics* (NM Tripathi, Bombay, 1989), Appendices, 172 and 176.

[163] ibid s 2.

[164] Hidayatullah J, who later became Chief Justice, and after retirement from the Court was elected as Vice President of India, had said in his judgment in *Golaknath* that 'of all the fundamental rights, it (right to property) is the weakest', AIR 1967 SC 1643, 1710.

[165] AIR 1951 SC 458.   [166] AIR 1965 SC 845.   [167] ibid 862.   [168] ibid.
[169] AIR 1967 SC 1643

[170] Subba Rao CJ spoke for himself and 4 other judges. Hidayatullah J, as he then was, gave a separate concurring judgment.

validity of the first, fourth, and seventeenth amendments, which had foreclosed judicial review of laws for the acquisition of property. As previously noted, the majority held that its decision would only have a prospective effect, and so those amendments were saved from invalidation.[171]

Golaknath was a big jolt for Indian constitutional lawyers. Most of them had been brought up in the black letter law tradition, and regarded the majority judgment as unsustainable. HM Seervai, author of a leading treatise on Constitutional Law and a former state Advocate-General, condemned the majority judgment as clearly wrong and 'productive of the greatest public mischief', and he called for it to be overruled at the earliest opportunity.[172] *Golaknath* was in a sense a turning point in the history of the Court, because it amounted to a major change in its interpretive methodology, and an open admission of its law-making role.[173] The majority justices plainly attempted to curb Parliament's amending power, and thereby constrain the legislative majority. The sentiment expressed in the judgments was openly counter-majoritarian. It was observed that the Fundamental Rights were the modern name 'for what has been traditionally known as natural rights',[174] and that 'absolute arbitrary power in defiance of fundamental rights exists nowhere under our Constitution, not even in the largest majority'.[175] But the majority reached this conclusion by adopting a literal, positivist interpretation of articles 13(2) and 368, which as we will see, was itself vulnerable to being over-ridden by constitutional amendment.

The government of Prime Minister Indira Gandhi was very unhappy with the decisions of the Court in the *Golaknath* and *Bank Nationalization* cases.[176] It complained that the Court would neither allow the Constitution to be amended, nor itself interpret the Fundamental Rights with a view to accommodating legitimate aspirations reflected in the Directive Principles of state policy. The Court seemed determined to stall the march towards socialism. On the Prime Minister's advice, the President dissolved the lower House of Parliament, and fresh elections were held. The Congress party's manifesto declared that if it won government, it would make basic changes to the Constitution. The party won a landslide victory, capturing more than two thirds of the seats in the lower House. It was obvious that the image of the Court, as a friend of the wealthy and defender of the status quo, had galvanized popular support for the ruling party.

Pursuant to its election manifesto, the government sponsored major constitutional amendments to reduce the power of the Court. The Twenty-fourth Amendment sought to restore to Parliament an unrestricted power of constitutional amendment, the Twenty-fifth Amendment made changes to the right to property, and the Twenty-sixth Amendment abolished the privy purses of the princes. The

---

[171] See above in the text to nn 81–2 above.
[172] HM Seervai, *Constitutional Law* (1st edn., NM Tripathi, Bombay, 1967) 1117.
[173] See text to nn 77–78 above.   [174] AIR 1967 SC 1643, 1656, (Subba Rao CJ).
[175] ibid 1698.
[176] *Golaknath v Punjab* AIR 1967 SC 1643; *RC Cooper v India* AIR 1970 SC 564.

validity of these amendments was challenged, and determined by a bench of 13 judges in *Kesavanand Bharati v Kerala*.[177]

The majority in the *Golaknath* case had held that art 368 merely provided for the procedure, and not the scope of the power, of constitutional amendment. That interpretation was based on the marginal note to art 368, which read: 'Procedure for amendment of the Constitution'. The Twenty-Fourth amendment changed the marginal note to read: 'Power of Parliament to amend the Constitution and procedure therefor'.[178] Given such explicit words, the Court could not adhere to the interpretation of art 368 as purely procedural. The *Golaknath* case majority had also held that the word 'law' in art 13(2) included a constitutional amendment. The Twenty-fourth Amendment declared otherwise.[179] All the objections taken in the *Golaknath* case were therefore disposed of, making it difficult to reject the Union's claim that Parliament's power to amend the Constitution was subject to no limitations other than those written into that article itself.[180] The Court upheld the Twenty-fourth Amendment, and barring a single clause in art 31-C, also upheld the Twenty-fifth Amendment. It left the question of the Twenty-sixth Amendment to be decided later.

The Court divided seven to six on the question of the scope of the constituent power under art 368. The majority did not concede to Parliament an unlimited power of constitutional amendment. It held that although Parliament could amend any provision, it could not destroy the basic features, or basic structure, of the Constitution. Although the text of the Constitution mentions no such limitation, and none was suggested in the Constituent Assembly, this limitation arose from the perceived necessity to sustain constitutionalism.

The majority seems to have been persuaded to impose limitations on the power of constitutional amendment by the Attorney-General's claims that Parliament could even destroy democracy and replace it by authoritarianism, or replace the secular state with a theocratic one. Could Parliament pass a single clause amendment totally repealing the Constitution? If the power under art 368 were unlimited, it could become the source of its own destruction.[181] The majority also found justification for imposing fetters on the power of constitutional amendment in the following words in art 368: 'the Constitution shall stand amended'. According to the majority, this meant that the quintessence of 'the Constitution' as originally made must survive any amendment. This 'quintessence' was what the majority described as its 'basic features' or 'basic structure'. The basic structure doctrine drew a distinction between the power of making a constitution, and the

---

[177] AIR 1973 SC 1473.

[178] The Constitution (Twenty-Fourth Amendment) Act, 1971 s 3.

[179] ibid s 2. Similar provision was made in art 368 clause (3) by s 3.

[180] 10 out of 13 judges declared that *Golaknath* had been wrongly decided. Three judges who had been party of the *Golaknath* decision observed that it was not necessary to decide whether *Golaknath* had been rightly decided. See SP Sathe 'Judicial Review in India: Limits and Policy' (1974) 35 *Ohio State Law Journal* 870.

[181] See *Kesavanand* (n 116) 1490 (Chief Justice Sikri), 1566 (Justice Shelat). See Sathe (n 86) 69.

power of amending it. While the former was *sui juris* and unlimited, the latter was limited by the basic structure of the Constitution that was sought to be amended.

This reasoning amounted to a distinct change in the Court's interpretive methodology. There is no evidence in the debates of the Constituent Assembly that any limitation on Parliament's constituent power, other than those expressed in art 368, was ever contemplated.[182] In fact, the Constitution (First Amendment) Act 1951, which imposed substantive limitations on judicial review with reference to certain Fundamental Rights, was passed by the Constituent Assembly itself, which functioned as a Provisional Parliament under art 379 of the Constitution. The Court plainly did not consider itself bound by the original intentions of the Constituent Assembly.

In *Indira Gandhi v Rajnarain*,[183] the validity of the Constitution (Thirty-Ninth Amendment) Act 1975 was challenged, against the backdrop of a draconian state of emergency proclaimed by the President under art 352, supposedly to quell 'internal disturbances' but in reality to resist agitation against Prime Minister *Indira Gandhi*.[184] Her election to Parliament had been set aside by the Allahabad High Court, on the ground that she had indulged in corrupt practices as defined by the Representation of the People Act 1951. The thirty-ninth Amendment provided that disputes regarding the election to Parliament of a person who held the office of Prime Minister at the time of the election, or was appointed as Prime Minister afterwards, should be adjudicated by whatever authority and procedure was provided by law. This meant that such disputes could not be adjudicated and determined by any court, unless Parliament authorized it to do so. The amendment further provided that any court order, made before its commencement, declaring such an election to be void, should itself be deemed null and void.

The Court held that the constituent power, being legislative in nature, could not be exercised to settle a dispute between two parties in favour of either of them, otherwise than through a judicial procedure. Three judges held that the relevant clause of the amendment was invalid because it offended the basic structure of the Constitution, and two judges held it invalid because it amounted to a usurpation of the judicial function by Parliament.[185]

It was argued on behalf of the Union that a constituent power is not a mere legislative power, but an amalgam of all three powers of government, legislative, executive, and judicial. Any division into three separate powers takes place only after a constitution is made, if it provides for such a separation (it could provide that a sovereign may exercise all three powers). A constitutional amendment is therefore an exercise of a power anterior to and independent of the separation of powers—a kind of all-embracing super power. The constituent power could therefore change the system of checks and balances upon which the separation of powers was based.[186]

---

[182] See the statement by Nehru, at n 98 above.   [183] AIR 1975 SC 2299.
[184] See section on emergency text to n 197 below.
[185] Mathew, Khanna, and Chandrachud JJ took the former view, and Chief Justice Ray and Justice Beg the latter view.   [186] ibid 2427.

This argument was rejected. The judges pointed out that whereas the power of making the Constitution might have been anterior to the separation of powers, the power of amendment is subject to it, if the Constitution so provides. The amendment power under the Constitution is a legislative power, and its exercise must result in the making of a rule or policy of general application. Legislative power could not be exercised to determine the rights or liabilities of individuals, although it can declare the basis on which such rights or liabilities may arise.

Parliament had also amended the Representation of the People Act 1951 with retrospective effect, so as to delete those actions that were held to vitiate Indira Gandhi's election from the definition of 'corrupt practices'. Taking advantage of this statutory amendment, the Court held her election to be valid. It thus avoided an immediate confrontation with her government, which had declared an emergency, while simultaneously sustaining its power of judicial review of constitutional amendments with reference to the basic structure doctrine. This was an act of subtle statesmanship on the part of the Court, comparable to that of Chief Justice Marshall in *Marbury v Madison*.[187]

A positivist interpretation is vulnerable to changes in the text. An interpretation based on the structure or spirit of the Constitution cannot be as easily dislodged. Therefore, while the *Golaknath* case's majority's interpretation was effectively nullified by the twenty-fourth amendment, no way could be found of circumventing the interpretation adopted by the majority in the *Kesavanand* case. Although this was also based on the words in art 368 that 'the Constitution shall stand amended', it was invulnerable to nullification by a subsequent constitutional amendment, because the words 'the Constitution' were construed as referring not merely to a document called the Constitution, but to a basic structure of checks and balances intended to sustain certain enduring values essential to a liberal, constitutional democracy.

Several attempts were made to revoke the basic structure doctrine. The Chief Justice constituted a bench of 13 judges to hear objections against it. But since the Government could not show that the doctrine might obstruct legitimate changes to the Constitution, or prevent progress towards social justice, the bench had to be dissolved.[188] Parliament then included provisions to bury the basic structure doctrine in the Constitution (Forty-Second) Amendment Act 1976. Section 55 of that Act sought to add clauses (4) and (5) to art 368, providing respectively that 'no amendment of the Constitution ... shall be called in question in any court on any ground', and that 'there shall be no limitation whatever on the constituent power of Parliament to amend by way of addition, variation or repeal the provisions of this Constitution'. In *Minerva Mills v India*,[189] the Court held cl (5) to be *ultra vires* the power of amendment as interpreted in *Kesavanand*, and therefore

[187] 1 *Cranch* 137 (US 1803).
[188] HM Seervai, *Constitutional Law* (3rd edn., NM Tripathi, Bombay, 1984) 1672.
[189] AIR 1980 SC 1789.

invalid. It was able to save cl (4) by applying the interpretive methodology used by courts to 'read down' finality or ouster clauses,[190] interpreting the clause to mean merely that the validity of a constitutional amendment, which did not destroy or tamper with the basic structure of the Constitution, could not be questioned in any court.

Judicial review of a constitutional amendment vests finality in the Court. In other countries, political resistance makes constitutional amendment difficult, but in India, constitutional amendments were for a long time comparatively easy. Since the emergence of a coalition government in 1989, such amendments have had to attract a national consensus. The Court has therefore been able to use its power to strike down amendments with great restraint. Since 1973, when the basic structure doctrine was laid down, the Court has struck down constitutional amendments in only four cases.[191]

The exercise of the constituent power during the 1975 emergency opened the eyes of many people who previously thought that the democratic process could be relied on to protect the rights of the people. The emergency showed that the required majority could be mustered to provide legislative sanction for draconian provisions. When *Kesavanand* was decided, it was widely believed that the majority justices based their decision on fear of a merely imaginary abuse of power by Parliament. But the constitutional amendments enacted during the emergency showed that such abuse was not imaginary. The decision in *Indira Gandhi* gave legitimacy to the basic structure doctrine.[192] For developing societies, where traditions of individual liberty and the rule of law are not yet deeply entrenched in social values, and democracy is prone to be harshly majoritarian, the safeguard of judicial review is essential.

The Court has used the Preamble of the Constitution as a basis for articulating the basic structure of the Constitution. In *SR Bommai v India*,[193] the Court held that the President's dismissal of three state governments of the Bharatiya Janata Party (BJP) under art 356 was valid, because they were incapable of complying with the principle of secularism, which is included in the Preamble to the Constitution. They had been dismissed after the demolition by Hindu extremists of an ancient Muslim mosque. Although this decision was reached by a majority of six to three, all nine judges endorsed an *obiter dictum* that secularism was part of the basic structure of the Constitution. This unanimous declaration was a warning that even if the required majority for amending the Constitution was mustered in Parliament, any amendment destructive of secularism would be held invalid. This must be seen in the context of the BJP's ideology of Hindu nationalism.

---

[190] Finality clauses means clauses which declare that the decision is final and cannot be questioned in any court.

[191] *Kesavanand Bharati v Kerala* (n 116); *Indira Gandhi v Rajnarain* AIR 1975 SC 2299; *Minerva Mills v India* AIR 1980 SC 1789; *P Sambamoorthy v AP* AIR 1987 SC 663, (1987) 1 SCC 124.

[192] SP Sathe 'Limitations on Constitutional Amendment—Basic Structure Principle Re-examined' in Dhavan, Jacob (ed) *Indian Constitution—Trends and Issues* (Indian Law Institute, Tripathi, 1978) 179.   [193] AIR 1994 SC 1918; (1994) 3 SCC 1.

'Secularism' did not exist in the Preamble of the original Constitution, but was added by the Forty-second Amendment in 1976.[194] How could an addition to the Preamble be part of the Constitution's basic, unalterable, structure?[195] The Court held that although the principle of secularism was added to the Preamble only in 1976, it existed in its essence in the original Constitution.[196] Although the basic structure doctrine was itself unknown to constitutional law when the original Constitution was enacted, it cannot be excluded from subsequent constitutional interpretations. Some constitutional changes occur through the process of formal constitutional amendment, and others through changes in constitutional interpretation. The interpretation of a constitution that has undergone 92 amendments cannot be governed by reference to the original intentions of the framers.

Emergencies

Many constitutions contain provisions dealing with emergencies arising from external aggression, war, or internal disorder. Laws concerning sedition or preventive detention operate even in normal times, but there are extraordinary situations that require an extraordinary response. The State must be empowered to combat threats to its own existence. Article 352 provides that the President, if satisfied that a grave emergency exists, in which external aggression or internal disturbance threatens India's security, may issue a proclamation of emergency.[197] Such a proclamation must be approved by resolution of both Houses of Parliament.[198] Article 358(1) provides that on the proclamation of an emergency, the rights granted by art 19 are suspended, and any law that impinges on those rights is valid for the duration of the emergency. Furthermore, art 359 empowers the President to issue an order suspending the right to move any court for the enforcement of specified Fundamental Rights, together with any proceedings pending in any court for the enforcement of such rights.

The first proclamation under art 352 was issued in 1962, when war broke out between India and China. The President also issued an order under art 359, suspending the right to seek judicial enforcement of rights under arts 14, 21, and 22. In *Makhan Singh Tarasikka v Punjab*,[199] the Court rejected an argument that, although these rights could not be enforced by a writ of *habeas corpus* issued under art 32 of the Constitution, the provision for *habeas corpus* in s 491 of the Code of Criminal Procedure 1898, which pre-date the Constitution, continued to operate. The majority took the view that the suspension of the right to move any

194 Constitution (Forth-Second) Amendment Act, 1976 s 2.

195 Seervai was the first to raise this question: Seervai *Constitutional Law* (4th edn., NM Tripathi, Bombay, 1996) vol 3 3100–01.

196 Secularism was not mentioned in the original Constitution because it was understood more as equal respect for all religions and not as separation between the state and the Church.

197 Art 352(1) as originally enacted.

198 Art 352(4). If no such resolution is passed by the House of the People within 30 days after it assembles, the proclamation ceases to be effective.   199 AIR 1964 SC 381.

court entailed the complete prohibition of access to any court for the enforcement of a Fundamental Right, whether under the Constitution or any other law.[200] On the other hand, the majority held that the validity of a preventive detention could be examined on some grounds other than an alleged breach of a Fundamental Right. Such grounds could include: (i) that the Act under which the petitioner was detained was *ultra vires* the powers of the legislature set out in the Seventh Schedule, or conferred an excessive delegation of legislative power; (ii) that the detention was *ultra vires* the Act under which it was made; and (iii) that the order of detention was made *mala fides* or without due deliberation on the merits.

The majority also observed that while art 358 suspended the rights granted by art 19, art 359 only suspended access to any court concerning breaches of rights, and did not suspend the rights themselves. Therefore, while laws enacted in contravention of art 19 after the proclamation of an emergency would be valid during the emergency, laws and executive acts inconsistent with the rights specified in the Presidential order under art 359 would be void even during the emergency, although no judicial redress was available during that period. In these respects, the Court preserved judicial review insofar as it was not foreclosed by the text of the Constitution. The Constitution was subsequently amended to provide that any law or executive action infringing rights mentioned in a Presidential order pursuant to art 359 would be valid, and would not give rise to any liability.[201]

The second proclamation of an emergency was issued in 1971, when war broke out between India and Pakistan, which led to the emergence of the new nation called Bangladesh. This emergency continued for long after the war ended. Before it expired, the President proclaimed another emergency on June 25, 1975, on the ground of internal disturbance. Parliament then passed a constitutional amendment to permit the President to issue different proclamations on different grounds, which could operate simultaneously.[202] That amendment was given retroactive effect so as to save the 1975 proclamation from any challenge to its validity.[203] The amendment also made the President's satisfaction as to the need for a proclamation 'final and conclusive', and beyond challenge in any court on any ground.[204] The 1975 emergency was declared to enable the government to survive agitation against Prime Minister Indira Gandhi, whose election to Parliament had been set aside by the Allahabad High Court. Compared to the two previous emergencies, the 1975 emergency unleashed many draconian measures, such as censorship of the press and indiscriminate detention without trial.

The question arose as to whether a person's detention could be challenged on the ground that it was unlawful. Arguably, there was a right to bring such

---

[200] Subba Rao J dissented, holding that access to the courts for *habeas corpus* under the 1898 Act survived the Presidential order.

[201] Cl. (IA) added to art 359 by s 7 of the Constitution (Thirty-Eight Amendment) Act 1975

[202] Constitution (Thirty-Eighth Amendment) Act, 1975 s 5.

[203] Constitution (Thirty-Eighth Amendment) Act, 1975 s 5, started with the words 'the following clause (Cl 4) shall be inserted, and shall be deemed always to have been inserted'.

[204] Cl. (5)(a) of art 352 inserted by s 5 of the Constitution (Thirty-Eighth Amendment) Act 1975

a challenge independently of art 21, which was suspended by an order under art 359. Nine High Courts had upheld petitions on that ground, but the government appealed to the Court in *ADM Jubalpur v Shiv Kant Shukla*.[205] The Court's decision, by majority of four to one, came as a surprise in the context of its previous decisions in the *Makhan Singh Tarasikka, Kesavanand* and *Indira Gandhi* cases. It held that while the proclamation of emergency was in force, and a Presidential order under art 359 in operation, the Court could not examine the validity of any executive action, even on the ground that it was *ultra vires* the enabling statute or *mala fides*.[206] The principle that an individual's liberty could not be taken away except by authority of law existed in India well before the Constitution came into force.[207] It continued under the Constitution by virtue of art 372. Did art 21 of the Constitution absorb the common law that pre-dated the Constitution? If rights granted by the Constitution could not be enforced by any court during the emergency, did it follow that rights arising from statutory law or common law also could not be enforced? The majority could have preserved at least the limited judicial review of executive action that is permissible under administrative law, as it had done in the *Makhan Singh* case. It seems that the majority justices read art 359 too literally, so as not to embarrass the executive government. One judge expressed hope that the power reposed by art 359 in the executive would not be abused.[208] Another said that the detained persons were treated with 'maternal care'.[209] Ray CJ characterized arguments about the possible abuse of power by the government as 'diabolic distortion and mendaciously malignant'.[210] Unlike the reasoning in the *Gopalan* case, this was not legal positivism. It is better described as escapism, helplessness, and even timidity. Ray CJ felt obliged to support the government because his appointment as Chief Justice had superseded three more senior judges. Two other members of the majority went on to become Chief Justices in order of their seniority, while the third member, Beg J, superceded Khanna J, who wrote the dissenting judgment. Khanna J's dissenting judgment was reminiscent of Lord Atkin's dissent in *Liversidge v Anderson*.[211]

The 1975 emergency was lifted after Indira Gandhi's government was voted out in elections for the House of the People held in 1977. The new Government repealed many of the constitutional amendments passed during the emergency.[212] It also amended the Constitution so as to impose curbs on the power to declare emergencies, and the power to suspend access to the courts. Henceforth, emergencies could not be declared in response to 'internal disturbances', but only

---

[205] AIR 1976 SC 1207.

[206] See Seervai, *The Emergency, Future Safeguards and the Habeas Corpus Case: A Criticism* (NM Tripathi, Bombay, 1978).

[207] *Eshugbayi v Govt of Nigeria* (1931) LR 670 (CA), (1931) All ER 44.

[208] AIR 1976 SC 1207, 1349 (Chandrachud J).   [209] ibid 1319 (Beg J).

[210] ibid 1223.   [211] (1942) AC 206: (1941) All Eng LR Vol 2 612

[212] The Constitution (Forty-Third Amendment) Act 1977; the Constitution (Forty-Fourth Amendment) Act 1978.

in response to 'armed rebellion',[213] and a Presidential order under art 359 suspending access to courts could not apply to rights granted by articles 20 and 21.[214]

While the emergency regime was repudiated in the 1977 elections, the Court was also stigmatized due to its passivity. The *Jubbalpur* decision cost it its credibility and legitimacy. The judges had to rehabilitate themselves, and this may have inspired their post-emergency activism.[215] They may have realized that the Court might lose its credibility permanently, if it were seen as a mere rubber stamp of the ruling majority. The independence of the judiciary depends on strong public support, as well as constitutional guarantees. The Court's activism in later years was directed towards both the ends.

Post-emergency Judicial Activism

The Court's post-emergency activism concerned the following main themes: (i) liberal interpretation of Fundamental Rights and Directive Principles, so as to empower the people and especially powerless minorities; (ii) procedural innovations facilitating access to the courts, and the growth of public interest litigation; (iii) transformation of judicial procedures from adversarial to polycentric and quasi-legislative; and (v) enhanced protection of the independence of the judiciary.

Liberal interpretation of fundamental rights and directive principles

Although the Court had previously held that Fundamental Rights would over-ride Directive Principles in any conflict between them,[216] in later years it moved towards a more structuralist interpretation, whereby Directive Principles were often taken into account in determining the scope of Fundamental Rights.[217] However, the real conflict was between the right to property and the Directive Principles contained in art 39(b) and (c).[218] Article 31-C was inserted by the Constitution (Twenty-fifth Amendment) Act 1971 to confer immunity on laws made pursuant to these Directive Principles from being held void on the ground of inconsistency with

---

[213] The Constitution (Forty-Fourth Amendment) Act 1978 s 37.   [214] ibid s 40.

[215] U Baxi *The Indian Supreme Court and Politics* (Eastern Book Company, 1980) 123.

[216] *Madras v Champakam Dorairajan* AIR 1951 SC 226.

[217] *Hanif Quareshi v Bihar* AIR 1958 SC 731. Here the Court considered the validity of the laws which banned cow slaughter. Article 48 asked the state to organize agriculture and animal husbandry on modern and scientific lines and take steps for banning the slaughter of cows, calves and other milch and draught cattle. The law banning cow slaughter was upheld in the light of the above Directive Principle. In the opinion of this writer, the interpretation of the Directive Principle was flawed: for a critique, see SP Sathe 'Cow Slaughter: The Legal Aspect' in AB Shah ed *Cow Slaughter: Horns of a Dilemma* (Lalvani, Bombay, 1967) 69.

[218] Art 39—The State shall, in particular, direct its policy towards securing—(b) that the ownership and control of the material resources of the community are so distributed as best to subserve the common good; (c) that the operation of the economic system does not result in the concentration of wealth and means of production to the common detriment.

arts 14, 19, and 31.[219] The Court upheld art 31-C in *Kesavanand*, with the exception of a sub-clause that conferred finality on the President's certificate that the law in question was made pursuant to those Directive Principles. Article 31-C was amended by the Constitution (Forty-second Amendment) Act 1976, to protect any law made in pursuance of any of the Directive Principles from being challenged for alleged inconsistency with any of the Fundamental Rights. In *Minerva Mills v India*,[220] the Court held, by a majority of four to one, that this amendment was void, because the total negation of either Fundamental Rights or Directive Principles would be detrimental to the basic structure of the Constitution.[221] The Court also held that both Fundamental Rights and Directive Principles were of equal importance, and that the latter ought to be taken into account when interpreting the scope of the former. Since *Minerva Mills*, the Court has adopted a policy of treating them as equally important. In fact, it has interpreted Fundamental Rights liberally so as to give effect to Directive Principles. Through liberal interpretation of art 21, the Court incorporated some Directive Principles within the right to life, such as art 45, enjoining the State to provide free and compulsory primary education within ten years.[222] The Court has held that it is no less responsible than the legislature and the executive for implementing the Directive Principles.[223]

Article 21 revisited

In *Maneka Gandhi v India* (1978),[224] the Court adopted a liberal interpretation of art 21, overriding the narrow interpretation laid down in *Gopalan*.[225] Not only did it hold that the words 'life', 'personal liberty', and 'procedure established by law' had wider meanings, thereby incorporating substantive as well as procedural due process, it also held that arts 19 and 21 had to be read together rather than as mutually exclusive. The new interpretation of art 21 was clearly inconsistent with the original intention of the Constitution's framers. The Court has since interpreted the words 'life' and 'personal liberty' to include several new rights, including a right to privacy,[226] rights of prisoners to be treated according to prison rules,[227] a right to shelter,[228] a right to education,[229] a right to sufficient food to avoid starvation,[230] a right to a healthy environment including fresh air and

---

[219] Respectively, the right to equality, rights to seven freedoms, and the right to property.

[220] AIR 1980 SC 1789.

[221] Bhagwati J, in dissent, upheld the amendment, holding that it would not lead to the erosion of Fundamental Rights.

[222] Article 21-A added by the Constitution (Eighty-Sixth Amendment) Act 2002. For examples of the cases, see the next section.   [223] *PUCL v Tamil Nadu* AIR 1997 SC 669.

[224] AIR 1978 SC 597: (1978) 1 SCC 248.   [225] See text to nn 101–112 above.

[226] *Neera Mathur v LIC* (1992) 1 SCC 286.

[227] *Sunil Batra v Delhi Administration* AIR 1978 SC 1675; *Charles Sobhraj v Supt, Central Jail, Tihar* (1979) 1 SCR 512: AIR 1978 SC 1514.

[228] *Olga Tellis v Bombay Municipal Corporation* AIR 1986 SC 180: (1985) 3 SCC 545.

[229] *Unnikrishnan v AP* (1993) 1 SCC 645.

[230] *PUCL v India* Writ Petition (Civil No. 196 of 2001) http://www.righttofood.com Also see *Kapila Hingorani v Bihar* (2003) 6 SCC 1 See Sathe *Judicial Activism in India* (Oxford India Paperbacks, New Delhi 2003) lxxi.

water,[231] and a right to health.[232] In *Francis Coralie Mullin v UT of Delhi*, Justice Bhagwati said:

The fundamental right to life which is the most precious human right and which forms the arc of all other rights must therefore be interpreted in a broad and expansive spirit so as to invest it with significance and vitality which may endure for years to come and enhance the dignity of the individual and the worth of the human person.[233]

This very broad right to life justified judicial intervention even to provide the people with food. When government storehouses were full of grain, but people were starving, the Court intervened and required the government to make the grain available. The Court said:

It is also well settled that interpretation of the Constitution of India or statutes would change from time to time. Being a living organ, it is ongoing and with the passage of time, law must change. New rights may have to be found out within the constitutional scheme. Horizons of constitutional law are expanding.[234]

The open-textured character of constitutional expressions enabled the Court to fill them with new meanings from time to time. In *India v Association For Democratic Reforms*,[235] the Court had held that the Election Commission could solicit, from a candidate offering herself for election, information about her assets and liabilities, previous convictions for criminal offences, and pending criminal prosecutions. The Court based its decision on a broad interpretation of freedom of speech, as including a right to information. Voters were held to be entitled to information regarding the antecedents of a candidate, to help them decide how to vote. Parliament then amended the Election Law to disable the Commission from soliciting any information other than that required by the amendment, and declared that notwithstanding any decision of any court, no further information could be required to be given. That amendment was challenged in *PUCL v India*.[236] The Union contended that the right to information, which was the basis of the Court's decision in the *Association For Democratic Reforms* case, was not an original right given by the Constitution, but a right derived through judicial interpretation, and therefore could be negated by legislative amendment. Rejecting this contention, Justice Shah said:

It should be understood that the fundamental rights enshrined in the Constitution, such as the right to equality and freedoms, have no fixed contents. From time to time, this Court has filled in the skeleton with soul and blood and made it vibrant. Since the last more than 50 years, this Court has interpreted Articles 14, 19 and 21 and given meaning and colour so that the nation can have a truly republic democratic society.[237]

The words 'procedure established by law' also received a liberal interpretation, and the Court insisted that any such procedure must be just and fair. On that basis

---

[231] *MC Mehta v India* AIR 1988 SC 1037
[232] *CERC v India* (1995) 3 SCC 42: AIR 1995 SC 922   [233] (1981) 1 SCC 608, 618.
[234] *Kapila Hingorani v Bihar (2003) 6 SCC 1*; (2003) SCCL.com 472, para 61.
[235] (2002) 5 SCC 294.   [236] (2003) 4 SCC 399.   [237] ibid 438–439.

it held that the death sentence could be imposed only in the rarest of rare cases.[238] It delivered several judgments against inordinately long periods of pre-trial detention, on the ground that the words 'procedure established by law' require a speedy trial.[239] The same words were held to exclude cruel and degrading punishment or torture, although no provision expressly prohibits such barbarism.[240] The court also held legal aid to be an essential aspect of criminal justice.[241]

International covenants and fundamental rights

According to English law, which is followed in India, a treaty or international convention does not apply to the domestic sphere until it is incorporated in municipal law by legislation.[242] In *Vishaka v Rajastha*,[243] the Court broke new ground in constitutional interpretation when it interpreted Fundamental Rights liberally so as to include the State's obligations under the Convention for the Elimination of All Forms of Discrimination Against Women (CEDAW). The petitioners had asked for the Court's intervention against sexual harassment of women in the work-place. The Court interpreted arts 14 (right to equality), 19(1)(g) (right to carry on any occupation, trade or business) and 21 (right to personal liberty) as including gender equality and a woman's right to work with dignity. Verma CJ observed:

The international Conventions and norms are to be read into them [Fundamental Rights] in the absence of enacted domestic law occupying the field when there is no inconsistency between them. It is now an accepted rule of judicial construction that regard must be had to international conventions and norms for construing domestic law when there is no inconsistency between them and there is a void in the domestic law.[244]

The judge further stressed that an interpretation giving effect to international conventions was implicit in the Directive Principle contained in art 51(c), to foster respect for international law and treaty obligations. The Court laid down a number of guidelines, to be observed by all authorities and bodies, to ensure the protection of women workers from sexual harassment. The Court has since used international conventions to interpret the Constitution in a number of other cases.[245]

---

[238] *Bachan Singh v Punjab* AIR 1980 SC 898.

[239] *Hussainara Khatoon v Bihar* AIR 1979 SC 1360: (1980) 1 SCC 81; *Common Cause v India* (1996) 4 SCC 33: AIR 1996 SC 1619; (1996) 6 SCC 775; AIR 1997 (Supp) SC 1539.

[240] It was held that death by hanging did not violate the procedure established by law. *Deena v India* AIR 1983 SC 1155.

[241] *Suk Das v Union Territory* AIR 1986 SC 991: (1986) 2 SCC 401.

[242] *In re Berubari Union Reference under art 143* AIR 1960 SC 845.

[243] (1997) 6 SCC 241: AIR 1997 SC 3011.   [244] ibid 3013.

[245] Also see *Geetha Hariharan v Reserve Bank of India* AIR 1999 SC 1149; *Apparel Export Promotion Council v A.K Chopra* AIR 1999 SC 625; *Madhu Kishwar v Bihar* (1996) 5 SCC 125; *Municipal Corporation of Delhi v Female Workers (Muster Roll)* (2000) 3 SCC 224; *John Vallamattam v India* (2003) 6 SCC 611.

Competing values and balancing

Structuralist interpretations vary according to the judges' value choices. Articles 105(1) and 194(1) give members of Parliament and state legislatures freedom of speech within their legislatures, and arts 105(2) and 194(2) protect them from any liability for speeches made within the legislature or for publications produced by its authority. The scope of these articles was considered in *PV Narasimha Rao v State* (CBI/SPE).[246] A 'no confidence' motion had been moved against the Rao government, which had been in a minority in the House. In order to defeat the motion, the ruling Congress party needed the support of members of another formation called the Jharkhand Mukti Morcha. After the motion was defeated, some members of Parliament were prosecuted for either giving or taking bribes to vote against it. Those prosecuted petitioned the Court, arguing that the prosecution infringed their right to freedom of speech within the House. They contended that this freedom embraced freedom of voting, including secrecy of voting, which would be breached if they were required to admit which way they had voted. The majority held that a member who bribed another member to vote in her favour, and a member who accepted such a bribe but did not vote, could be prosecuted for corruption; but a member who accepted a bribe and did vote was protected by art 105(2). Such a member could not be prosecuted, because that would involve enquiring into why and how she voted.

Unlike the citizen's freedom of speech protected by art 19(1)(a), which is subject to restrictions permitted under art 19(2), a legislator's freedom is not subject to any such restrictions. She cannot be sued for defamation, or prosecuted for any offence she might commit while exercising her freedom of speech in the House. Nevertheless, it is submitted that she also has a duty to speak fearlessly in the interests to her electorate. In construing the scope of the freedom, that duty must not be overlooked. Can the freedom be bartered away or traded off? It should be possible to hold her accountable if her exercise of the freedom is influenced by a threat or bribe. The majority's decision was contrary to the spirit of the Constitution. The dissenting judgment stated the law correctly as follows:

An interpretation of the provisions of Article 105(2) which would enable a Member of Parliament to claim immunity from prosecution in a criminal court for an offence of bribery in connection with anything said by him or a vote given by him in Parliament or any committee thereof and thereby place such Members above the law would not only be repugnant to healthy functioning of parliamentary democracy but would also be subversive of the rule of law which is also an essential part of the basic structure of the Constitution. It is settled law that in interpreting the constitutional provisions the court should adopt a construction which strengthens the foundational features and the basic structure of the Constitution.[247]

The conflicting positions of the majority and the minority judges arise from a conflict between their varying perceptions of the two competing interests, namely

[246] (1998) 4 SCC 626.   [247] ibid 673.

the member's freedom, and her accountability to the electorate. An interpretation that holds a public functionary liable and accountable is more faithful to the basic structure of the Constitution.

Procedural innovations for access to justice

The Court did not merely expand the scope of Fundamental Rights through liberal interpretation. It also adopted a broad interpretation of arts 32 and 226, which concern the courts' jurisdiction to remedy violations of Fundamental Rights, so as to do away with technicalities. Article 32 confers a Fundamental Right on a person to move the Supreme Court by 'appropriate proceedings' for the enforcement of any Fundamental Right. The Court has power to issue directions, orders or writs, including writs in the nature of *habeas corpus, mandamus,* prohibition, *quo warranto* or *certiorari,* as appropriate to enforce any Fundamental Right. Article 226 confers similar powers upon a High Court, for the enforcement of any of the Fundamental Rights or 'for any other purpose'.[248] The Constitution uses the words 'writs in the nature of' to free the courts from technicalities associated with the prerogative writs in England. The courts merely draw analogies with the prerogative writs, and issue directions, orders, or writs to mould relief to meet the peculiar requirements of each situation.[249] The Court has incorporated private law remedies, such as injunctions and stay orders, within the remedies available under these articles. Furthermore, there is no necessity for an applicant to pray for specific relief: the courts devise the appropriate relief. The words 'appropriate proceedings' have enabled the courts to design new remedies, adopt innovations such as the appointment of commissioners to research facts on behalf of an underprivileged petitioner,[250] and liberalise the rules of *locus standi* and justiciability.[251] Not only people whose interests are adversely affected, but even those who have no personal stake, can move the Court on behalf of poor and disadvantaged people whose rights have been infringed, provided that they have no ulterior motives such as the receipt of some personal reward.[252] This has come to be known as Public Interest Litigation, because the existence of a public interest is the criterion of justiciability.[253]

The Court has entertained petitions seeking protection of the Taj Mahal (a monumental palace built by a Moghul emperor) from erosion,[254] and challenging mal-governance resulting in the deaths of innocent people such as inmates of

[248] The Court has held that 'any other purpose' includes the enforcement of statutory as well as common law rights, other than those arising from contracts, torts, or crimes: *Calcutta Gas Co v West Bengal* AIR 1962 SC 1044.

[249] *TC Basappa v N Nagappa* AIR 1954 SC 440: (1955) 1 SCR. 250, 256.

[250] *Bandhua Mukti Morcha v Bihar* (1984) 3 SCC 161: AIR 1984 SC 802.

[251] Sathe (n 86) chapter VI.   [252] ibid.

[253] This is not similar to public interest law as is known in the United States. Therefore Baxi preferred to call it social action litigation. See U Baxi, 'Taking Suffering Seriously: Social Action Litigation in the Supreme Court of India' in Dhavan, Sudarshan and Khurshid (eds) *Judges and Judicial Power* (Sweet and Maxwell, Tripathi, 1985) 289.

[254] *MC Mehta v India* AIR 1997 SC 734; (2003) 8 SCC 696; (2003) 10 SCC 719.

a mental asylum,[255] starvation of the poor due to food being unavailable,[256] and the exploitation of child labour.[257] The Court has also intervened against the appropriation of public assets for private purposes by politicians through abuse of power.[258]

These innovations have made it possible for many down-trodden people to reach the Court, raising matters concerning unorganized labour,[259] bonded labour,[260] the environment[261], women's rights,[262] human rights,[263] and the rights of children[264] and other disadvantaged people.[265] Decisions upholding the rights of the poor and other socially disadvantaged people, and giving them improved access to justice, greatly enhanced the Court's image. It was no longer a court for landlords, princes, industrialists, and government servants.

Transformation from adversarial to polycentric—law making through directions

Public Interest Litigation has changed the character of the judicial process from adversarial to polycentric, and from adjudicative to quasi-legislative. Bhagwati J said in *PUDR v India*:

We wish to point out with all the emphasis at our command that public interest litigation which is a strategic arm of the legal aid movement and which is intended to bring justice within the reach of the poor masses, who constitute the low visibility area of humanity is a totally different kind of litigation from the ordinary traditional litigation which is essentially of an adversary character where there is a dispute between two litigating parties, one making claim or seeking relief against the other and that other opposing such claim or resisting such relief. Public interest litigation is brought before the Court not for the purpose of enforcing the rights of one individual against another as happens in case of ordinary litigation, but is intended to promote and vindicate public interest which demands that violations of constitutional or legal rights of a large number of people who are poor, ignorant or in a socially or economically disadvantaged position should not go unnoticed and unredressed.[266]

The judge observed that the courts existed not only for the rich and well-to-do, but also for the downtrodden and have-nots.[267] In *Bandhua Mukti Morcha v India*, Bhagwati J pointed out that the problems of the poor who now came to the

---

[255] *In re Death of 25 Chained Inmates in Asylum Fire in Tamil Nadu* (2001) 7 SCC 231. Sathe (n 230) lxx.   [256] *PUCL v India* writ petition (n 230).

[257] *PUCL v Tamil Nadu* (n 223).

[258] *BL Wadhera v India* AIR 2002 SC 1913; *MC Mehta v Kamal Nath* (2002) 3 SCC 653. See Sathe (n 230) lxviii.   [259] *PUDR v India* AIR 1982 SC 1473.

[260] *Bandhua Mukti Morcha v India* AIR 1984 SC 802.

[261] *MC Mehta v India* (1997) 2 SCC 411, (2003) 10 SCC 564.

[262] *Sakshi v India* (2004) 5 SCC 518; *Ahmedabad Women's Action Group v India* AIR 1997 SC 3614.

[263] *PUCL v India* Writ (n 230).

[264] *MC Mehta v Tamil Nadu* (1991) 1 SCC 283; (1996) 6 SCC 756.

[265] *Narmada Bachao Andolan v India* (1999) 8 SCC 308, (1998) 5 SCC 586.

[266] AIR 1982 SC 1473, 1476.   [267] ibid 1478.

Court 'were qualitatively different from those which [had] hitherto occupied the attention of the Court', and needed a 'different kind of lawyering skill and a different kind of judicial approach.'[268] Public Interest Litigation raised questions of group rights, and issues concerning the environment, governance and human rights. In *Akhil Bharatiya Shoshit Karmachari Sangh (Railway) v Union of India*, Justice Krishna Iyer explained the nature of this people-oriented jurisprudence as follows:

Our current processual jurisprudence is not of individualistic Anglo Indian mould. It is broad-based and people oriented, and envisions access to justice through 'class actions', 'public interest litigation' and 'representative proceedings'. Indeed, little Indians in large numbers seeking remedies in courts through collective proceedings, instead of being driven to an expensive plurality of litigations, is an affirmation of participative justice in our democracy. We have no hesitation in holding that the narrow concept of 'cause of action' and 'person aggrieved' and individual litigation is becoming obsolescent in some jurisdictions.[269]

The Court started to address, and award compensation to, a wider constituency than the actual litigants, when protecting human rights.[270] It has resorted to quasi-legislation through the issue of directions. The word 'directions' appears in art 32 as one available remedy. But directions are no longer merely mandates to specific respondents in litigation, but are often addressed *in rem* (against the world at large). Directions have been used to prescribe conditions for processing inter-country and intra-country adoptions, in order to protect children and prevent child trade,[271] and for managing pollution caused by traffic.[272] Directions have also been issued regarding the abolition of child labour.[273] Such directions have the force of law, although they can be replaced by legislation.[274] The Court has not only produced judicial legislation as understood in realist jurisprudence, but has actually legislated. In *Vineet Narain v India*, Chief Justice Verma once again reiterated:

[I]t is the duty of the executive to fill the vacuum by executive order because its field is coterminous with that of the legislature and where there is inaction even by the executive, for whatever reason, the judiciary must step in, in exercise of its constitutional obligations under the aforesaid provisions [articles 32 and 142] to provide a solution till such time as the legislature acts to perform its role by enacting proper legislation to cover the field.[275]

The Court abandoned its traditional insularity, and took an active part in settling disputes to achieve just results. *Azad Rikshaw Pullers Union v Punjab*[276] concerned a challenge to the validity of the Punjab Cycle Riksha (Regulation of Rikshas) Act 1955, which provided that licences to ply rikshas would be given

---

[268] AIR 1984 SC 802, 815.　　　[269] AIR 1981 SC 298, 317.

[270] See Sathe (n 86) 232–33.　　　[271] *Laxmi Kant Pandey v India* AIR 1987 SC 232.

[272] *MC Mehta v India* (n 261).　　　[273] *PUCL v Nadu* (n 223).

[274] See *Vinnet Narain v India* (1998) 6 SCC 60, 61. See also *MC Mehta v Tamil Nadu* (n 223).

[275] (1998) 1 SCC 226, 264; Sathe (n 86) 244.　　　[276] AIR 1981 SC 14.

only to those who owned them.[277] The Act was intended to enhance social justice, by eliminating the exploitation of riksha pullers, who were poor, by the riksha owners, who extracted excessive rents from them. But the Act made riksha pullers unemployed, because they did not own their vehicles, while the rikshas remained idle as their owners could not ply them. This was argued to impose an unreasonable restriction on the fundamental right of the riksha pullers to carry on their occupation, as guaranteed by art 19(1)(g). If the Act had been held invalid, the riksha pullers would have retained their livelihood, but then its intended social objective would have been frustrated. Instead of striking down the law, Krishna Iyer J arranged a loan from a nationalized bank to the riksha pullers, from which they could buy their rikshas from the owners. The loan was required to be repaid in suitable installments.

The independence of the judiciary

The Court learnt during the 1975 emergency that its independence could not be safely entrusted to the sweet will of the executive government. If the Court were to take up political issues such as the abuse of executive power, it had to be insulated from manipulation by the executive. The Court could be packed, as was attempted through the supersession of sitting judges.[278] And if the judges could be superseded, they could also be humbled in other ways. The power to appoint them rested with the government, which had already started transferring judges from one High Court to another. Some judges whose political views were disagreeable were relieved after the completion of the first two years of their temporary appointment.[279]

It is in this context that the Court was asked to clarify how judges should be appointed if judicial independence were to be preserved. Article 124(2) provides:

'Every Judge of the Supreme Court shall be appointed by the President by warrant under his hand and seal after consultation with such of the Judges of the Supreme Court and of the High Courts in the States as the President may deem necessary for the purpose..... Provided that in the case of appointment of a judge other than the Chief Justice, the Chief Justice of India shall always be consulted.'

There is no mention of any restriction on the government's power to appoint judges, except for the requirement that it consult the Chief Justice when appointing other judges.[280] But it was contended that the independence of the judiciary was part of the basic structure of the Constitution. Article 50, one of the directive principles, requires the State to separate the judiciary from the executive. In 1982,

---

[277] Riksha is a motored vehicle having three wheels. A carriage is attached to a scooter.

[278] The majority of *Kesavanand* consisted of Chief Justice and six judges. The Chief Justice retired immediately, and three judges resigned on being superseded. Another judge died, and yet another was to retire soon. Only one judge would have continued.

[279] A practice had developed that a judge was appointed as an additional judge for two years, to be made permanent as soon as a vacancy arose. No additional judge was ever discontinued. This happened only during the emergency.   [280] See text to nn 83–84 above.

in *SP Gupta v India* (known as *the First Judges case*),[281] the Court held that consultation with the Chief Justice concerning the appointment of a judge did not require her concurrence: the government was free to make the ultimate decision. But in 1993, in *Supreme Court Advocates on Record Association v India (the Second Judges case)*,[282] the Court held that the Chief Justice's opinion was binding on the Government, although before providing her advice, she was required to seek the opinion of at least two of the Court's most senior judges. On a reference by the President under art 143,[283] the Court in a third case reiterated this view, but added that the Chief Justice must consult a collegium of four of the most senior judges.

The judges acknowledged that in all democratic countries, including the United Kingdom, the United States, Australia and Canada, the appointment of judges to superior courts is in the hands of the executive and not the judiciary. But the Indian Constitution, while conferring this power on the executive, had conditioned it by requiring prior consultation with certain constitutional functionaries.[284] According to Verma J:

When the Constitution was being drafted, there was general agreement that the appointments of Judges in the superior judiciary should not be left to the absolute discretion of the executive, and this was the reason for the provision made in the Constitution imposing the obligation to consult the Chief Justice of India and the Chief Justice of the High Court. This was done to achieve independence of the Judges of the superior judiciary even at the time of their appointment... It was realized that the independence of the judiciary had to be safeguarded not merely by providing security of tenure and other conditions of service after the appointment, but also by preventing the influence of political considerations in making the appointments... It is this reason which impelled the incorporation of the obligation of consultation with the Chief Justice of India.[285]

Justice Verma also observed that the primary aim was to encourage decisions about judicial appointments to be made by consensus, in which case, no question of primacy would arise. But when opinions conflicted, the question of whose opinion had primacy arose. Since primacy could not be given to the executive, unless very good reasons existed, the opinion of the Chief Justice, in consultation with other senior judges, had to be binding. Justice Verma reasoned that the greatest significance should be attached to the opinion of the Chief Justice, who is best equipped to assess the true worth and suitability of candidates. His opinion—really a collective opinion, formed after taking into account the views of senior colleagues—would be a better way of ensuring proper appointments. This would help to achieve the constitutional purpose, without conferring an absolute

---

[281] AIR 1982 SC 149, (1981) Supp SCC 87.   [282] (1993) 4 SCC 441, AIR 1994 SC 268.
[283] *In Re Article 143 of the Constitution, Presidential Reference, 1998*. (1998) 7 SCC 739, AIR 1999 SC 1.   [284] *Second Judges* Case 1993 4 SCC 441, 596 (Justice Ahmadi).
[285] (1993) 4 SCC 441, 691.

discretion or veto on either the judiciary or the executive, much less on an individual such as the Chief Justice or the Prime Minister.

This unprecedented example of judicial activism must be understood in the context of the political events that preceded it. As long as India's politics remain fractured, and its democratic culture fragile, independent judicial review remains the only bulwark against majoritarianism. However, contrary to Verma J's opinion, a power of veto has in effect been conferred on the Chief Justice and four most senior judges, which does not seem desirable.

The Court as a Political Institution

The positivist, black letter law tradition held that judges should be completely insulated from politics, and that courts should not be concerned with policy. Structuralist interpretation requires courts to deal with politics more openly. Indian judges now have a substantial involvement in matters of social policy, as they have acknowledged in a number of cases. An example is judicial review of the President's power to dismiss state governments under art 356. This power seemed to be immune to judicial review until 1977, when in *Rajasthan v India*,[286] the Court held that such a proclamation would be declared invalid if it was issued with *mala fides*. In that case, the Court did not strike down the President's proclamation, dismissing nine state governments on the ground that the ruling party had lost in elections for the lower House of Parliament, even though that ground was totally opposed to the spirit of federalism.

In *SR Bommai v India*,[287] the Court held valid the President's dismissal of three state governments controlled by the *Bharatiya Janata Party* (BJP) on the ground that they were incapable of acting in accordance with the basic constitutional principle of 'secularism'. The Court simultaneously struck down the President's dismissal of three other state governments.[288] The Court thus acquired the power to review the act of the President under art 356, to the same extent that it could examine the validity of ordinary administrative actions. This undoubtedly enhanced the Court's role in sustaining the federal equilibrium. The case did not involve any amendment of the Constitution, and so the basic structure doctrine need not have been invoked. By raising the doctrine, the Court expanded the scope of its application: even an executive action, such as the President's under art 356, could be measured on the touchstone of the basic structure doctrine. It should be noted that three judges did not support the decision to uphold the dismissal of the three BJP governments.[289] They objected that there were no judicially manageable standards for determining the validity of the President's action. By declining jurisdiction to decide the validity of the President's action, they too would, in effect, have allowed it to stay. They perhaps wanted to avoid

---

[286] AIR 1977 SC 1361.
[287] (1994) 3 SCC 11, AIR 1994 SC 1918, previously discussed in the text to nn 193–95 above.
[288] See text to n 31 above.   [289] Ahmadi CJ, Verma and Dayal JJ.

making a manifestly political decision. Indeed, the majority's decision was rather intuitive. How could they be sure that the BJP could not abide by the principle of secularism? The BJP led government at the federal level from 1999 until 2004.

Since then, government actions have sometimes been challenged not with reference to any specific constitutional provision, but with reference to abstract principles such as secularism.[290] The Court's interpretation of secularism has not always been sound.[291] But it is no longer reluctant to admit that it deals with political issues, and has a political role. In *Indra Sawney v India*, Sawant J said:

The Constitution, being essentially a political document, has to be interpreted to meet 'the felt necessities of the time'. To interpret it ignoring the social, political, economic and cultural realities, is to interpret it not as a vibrant document alive to the social situation but as an immutable cold letter of law unconcerned with the realities.[292]

The Court has shown great courage in protecting minorities from the tyranny of fundamentalist, majoritarian forces. The victims of the communal carnage in Gujarat, in 2001, approached the Court when they could not obtain justice against the murders and rapes committed by the goons of the majority community. When all the accused were acquitted, because of a dishonest police investigation, threats to witnesses, and the lower courts' lackadaisical attitude, the Court ordered their retrial in another state.[293]

The Court's activism on social policy issues has co-existed with judicial restraint on economic issues. Since 1991, the government of India has changed its primary economic objective from a command economy to a market economy. This has required two policy changes: (1) weeding out unnecessary controls and regulations over freedom of enterprise; and (2) throwing open to private initiative, enterprises that were previously within the exclusive domain of the public sector. This has entailed disinvestment by the government in enterprises that incurred losses, or could be more efficiently managed by the private sector. Responding to these policy changes, in *Balco Employees Union (Registered) v India*, Chief Justice Kirpal said

In a democracy, it is the prerogative of each elected Government to follow its own policy. Often a change in Government may result in a shift in focus or change in economic policies. Any such change may result in adversely affecting some vested interests. Unless any illegality is committed in the execution of the policy or the same is contrary to law or mala fide, a decision bringing about change cannot per se be interfered with by the court.

Wisdom and advisability of economic policies are ordinarily not amenable in judicial review unless it can be demonstrated that the policy is contrary to any statutory provision or the Constitution. In other words, it is not for the courts to consider relative merits of different economic policies and consider whether a wiser or better one can be evolved.[294]

In this case, the Court upheld the privatization of a government company that had incurred losses. While art 19(6) expressly permits the State to operate any

---

[290] *Ismail Faruqui v India* (1994) 6 SCC 360; *Aruna Roy v India* (2002) 7 SCC 368
[291] Sathe (n 86) chapter VI.   [292] (1992) ATC p 385, 670.
[293] *Zahira v Gujarat* (2004) 4 SCC 158.   [294] (2002) 2 SCC 333, 381.

trade or business to the exclusion of any private individual, it does not oblige the State to do so. But in another case the Court objected to such disinvestment where the original investment had been authorized by an Act of Parliament. It held that disinvestment from such an enterprise could be achieved only with legislative sanction.[295]

Institutional and Cultural Factors

With a few exceptions, the judges have lacked political experience.[296] Most have been professional lawyers. Although an eminent jurist could be appointed as a judge, so far none have been. The judges are products of a legal education that emphasises what the law is, rather than the process by which it is continuously developed. Law is depicted through rote learning as a body of fixed and immutable rules, rather than something that, in the hands of a creative judiciary, always has evolutionary potential. Until recently, even academic writings in India were merely expository, consisting of section by section commentaries on statutory law with very little criticism of either the law itself or judicial decisions interpreting it.

The early generations of Supreme Court judges were trained in the English positivist tradition, and were reluctant to assume wider powers for the Court. A majority of the leaders of the Constituent Assembly agreed with their view of the proper judicial role. Therefore, there was no dispute between the political establishment and the judiciary over the Court's function. Both sides perceived it as a technocratic institution dealing with strictly legal questions. This made it easy for the political establishment to manage the Court: it simply amended the Constitution, and expected the Court to comply. During the entire Nehru period, Parliament held the initiative, and the Court merely responded. Parliament could always use its power to amend the Constitution to override the Court's decisions.

In addition, when the Constitution was first enacted, judges were compared unfavourably with politicians. The politicians had participated in the national movement for independence, and thereby acquired a halo of self-sacrifice, whereas the judges had been part of the colonial establishment. Moreover, the judges acquired a reputation for defending the rights of the wealthy classes, particularly in cases involving property rights. But since the late 1970s, the politicians have suffered a loss of public esteem. Their increasing opportunism, corruption, and populism emanating from ballot box politics, have sullied their image. The Court's activist jurisprudence during the late 1970s and 1980s, on the other hand, has earned it a greater degree of respect and trust among the people.

[295] *Centre For Public Interest Litigation v India* AIR 2003 SC 3277.
[296] Only two judges had been active in politics before joining the judiciary, namely Krishna Iyer and PB Sawant JJ Both were leftists.

In the late 1960s, the Court asserted its power to review constitutional amendments, and in the 1970s, that power was legitimized by the government's abuse of the constituent power during the 1975 emergency. The Court's decision in the *Kesavanand* case was very unorthodox, and initially seemed contrary to established, majoritarian notions of democracy. But those notions of democracy came under challenge throughout the world, as societies became more pluralistic. Even Britain, the home of parliamentary sovereignty, became a signatory to the European Convention on Human Rights, which was subsequently incorporated in the Human Rights Act 1998, thereby eroding the supremacy of Parliament.

The Court assumed a much greater responsibility for strengthening constitutionalism in the 1970s. While earlier invalidations of laws had been based on traditional positivist reasoning, subsequent ones were often based on structuralist reasoning. During the post-emergency period, the Court gave liberal and expansive interpretations to Fundamental Rights and Directive Principles, so as to expand the scope of individual liberty and include some positive social and economic rights within the canvas of the Fundamental Rights. It liberalized the rules of *locus standi* and justiciability to facilitate access by the poor to the judicial process. The growth of Public Interest Litigation, through which breaches of human rights could be remedied, increased public esteem for the Court.

Nevertheless, the Court's record has been far from perfect. The judges have mainly come from urban, and higher economic, backgrounds. Their class bias has been reflected in the early right to property cases, but also in more recent cases, such as those approving a paltry sum of compensation for victims of the Bhopal gas disaster,[297] and refusing to delay the construction of a dam until the residents of villages to be submerged by it were all resettled.[298] The Court has not been successful in realizing many social and economic rights: in particular, its declarations of the rights of the poor have not been converted into reality. It has also lacked the resources to bring about systemic changes such as speedier trials of criminal cases, and prison reforms.

In recent years, the Court seems to have been back-sliding in protecting rights. Its decision on educational institutions, giving them freedom to charge any fee without regard to its effect on access to education by the poor;[299] its declaration that workers have no right to strike;[300] its approval of the two child norm as a

---

[297] *Union Carbide Corporation v India* (1991) 4 SCC 584. A poisonous gas leaked out from the factory owned by a multi-national company resulting in deaths of large numbers of people, and those who survived suffered from various debilitating diseases. The Court approved a settlement between the UCC and the Govt. of India which provided for a paltry sum as compensation. In the earlier decision, even criminal prosecutions against the officials of the UCC were dropped. They were restored only after a writ petition was made against that decision. See (n 86) 302. Also see U Baxi and A Dhanda *Valiant Victims and Lethal Litigation: The Bhopal Case* (Indian Law Institute, NM Tripathi, Bombay, 1990).	[298] *NBA v India* (1998) 5 SCC 586; (1999) 8 SCC 308.

[299] *TMA Pai Foundation v Karnataka* (2002) 8 SCC 481, AIR 2003 SC 355.

[300] *TK Rangarajan v Tamil Nadu* (2003) 6 SCC 581.

condition of eligibility for contesting elections to panchayats;[301] are a few examples of this backward slide. Its approval of laws such as the Terrorism and Disruptive Activities Act and the Prevention of Terrorism Act, which dispense with important attributes of the due process of law, on the ground that they are necessary to combat terrorism, shows that the judges share the security concerns of the middle class.[302] All these decisions reflect their class bias.

Conclusion

Despite its shortcomings, the Court can be proud of its record. The main responsibility for defending constitutionalism in India has fallen on non-elected authorities, such as the President, the Election Commission, the National Human Rights Commission, and the judiciary. The Supreme Court, as the apex court with the power of judicial review over all other authorities, has shouldered the heaviest burden. Its assumption of power to review constitutional amendments has made it the most powerful court in the world.[303] It has evolved from a timid, positivist court into a very activist one. Its more prominent policy-making role has stemmed from its expansive interpretations of Fundamental Rights and Directive Principles, and its liberalization of procedural rules governing access to justice. Through its development of that role, the Court has earned widespread legitimacy, which has helped to ensure that its decisions have been generally obeyed.[304]

---

[301] *Javed v Haryana* (2003) 8 SCC 369. Panchayats are the grass roots, self-governing deliberative bodies, consisting of all citizens of a village or district, provided under art 243 (B) of the Constitution.

[302] *Kartar Singh v Punjab* (1994) 3 SCC 569, *PUCL v India* AIR 2004 SC 456.

[303] The Supreme Court of Bangladesh has adopted the basic structure limitation since 1989 *Anwar Hussain Chowdhary v Bangladesh* 41 DLR 1989 App Div 165. See also the decision of the Constitutional Court of South Africa in *United Democratic Movement v President of the Republic of South Africa and Others* www.concoual.gov.za/para 17, cited in T Zwart 'Review of Judicial Activism in India' in (2003) *Journal of Law and Society*.   [304] Sathe (n 86) chapter VII.

6

South Africa: From Constitutional Promise to Social Transformation

Heinz Klug

Introduction to South Africa's Constitution

South Africa's emergence as a constitutional democracy after four decades of apartheid and nearly three centuries of colonialism is rightly heralded as a miracle. With 243 sections and seven schedules South Africa's Constitution also represents an attempt to constitutionalize all the hopes, fears and conflicts of South Africa's democratic transition. This process is epitomized by the two-stage constitution-making process in which the conflicting parties first negotiated an 'interim' Constitution and then, after democratic elections, empowered the new Parliament to sit as a Constitutional Assembly in order to produce a 'final' Constitution. In order to secure the trust of the former governing white minority, and thus to enable an elected majority to produce a democratically defined Constitution, the newly created Constitutional Court was required to certify that the Constitutional Assembly had, in producing the 'final' Constitution, remained faithful to the constitutional principles adopted by the negotiators and appended to the 'interim' Constitution.

While there are important differences between the 1993 'interim' Constitution and the 1996 'final' Constitution, there are also fundamental continuities, particularly in the area of constitutional interpretation. Facilitating these continuities was the extension of constitutional jurisdiction to the Supreme Court of Appeals which means that constitutional issues may now be taken up in all the superior courts of the land. However, any court order finding that national legislation or a presidential act is inconsistent with the Constitution must be confirmed by the Constitutional Court before it takes effect. Although there is still provision for direct access to the Constitutional Court, the Court has repeatedly indicated that outside of urgent situations or compelling questions of justice it prefers a matter to be fully canvassed in the courts below before it is brought before it. The Constitutional Court, which was established in terms of the 'interim' Constitution and heard its first case in 1995, has maintained clear continuity in its approach to interpretation despite minor changes in constitutional language and the addition of some explicit interpretative guidelines in the 'final' Constitution. As a result of these continuities between the 'interim' and 'final' Constitutions, the Constitutional Court's basic approach to interpretation is still to be found outlined most explicitly in its earliest decisions under the 'interim' Constitution.

Constitution, 1996

South Africa's Constitution is the product of a legal revolution unleashed by the democratic transition from apartheid.[1] Adopted by the Constitutional Assembly in 1996 the Constitution was promulgated into law by Nelson Mandela at Sharpeville on December 10, 1996 and went into effect on February 4, 1997. Since the creation in 1910 of the Union of South Africa, by an Act of the British Parliament, the country has had three other constitutions, in 1960, 1983 and 1993. The 1996 Constitution is however the first adopted by a democratically-constituted body representing all South Africans. Not only is this democratic South Africa's founding constitution, but it also marks the shift, together with the 1993 'interim' Constitution, from parliamentary sovereignty to constitutional supremacy, thus fundamentally changing the role of the judiciary and the significance of constitutional interpretation. While there are significant continuities between the 1993 'interim' Constitution and the 1996 'final' Constitution, there are also important differences. These include such innovations as the idea of co-operative government and the explicit inclusion of socio-economic rights in the bill of rights, that mark the unique character of this Constitution as the crowning achievement of South Africa's democratic transition. Although only ten years old, South Africa's post-apartheid Constitutional order has produced a series of landmark cases in which the Constitutional Court has provided a bold and innovative vision of the rights and forms of governance guaranteed by the Constitution.

The main features of the 1996 Constitution include its founding provisions, the Bill of Rights, and the chapter on co-operative government which regulates the relationship between the national, provincial and local spheres of government. In addition the Constitution, like other post-cold war constitutions, includes specific chapters on public administration, the security services and finance. More unique are the chapters on State Institutions Supporting Constitutional Democracy and on Traditional Leaders. While the founding provisions define the nature of the post-apartheid state—emphasizing principles of democracy, human rights and equality—a key feature is the specific provision that this 'Constitution is the supreme law of the Republic' and that any 'law or conduct inconsistent with it is invalid.' Reflecting this commitment to constitutional democracy are the provisions in the chapter on State Institutions Supporting Constitutional Democracy which establish a series of independent constitutional bodies, including: a public

---

[1] A Lewis 'Revolution by Law' *New York Times* Jan 13, 1995 A15.

protector; human rights commission; auditor general; an electoral commission; as well as a commission for the promotion of the rights of cultural, religious and linguistic communities and a commission for gender equality. In contrast to these, the chapter on Traditional Leaders as well as the general provisions guaranteeing self-determination and the option of adopting additional charters of rights 'in order to deepen the culture of democracy,' reflect less the global constitutional paradigm of the late 20th century and more the rather parochial concerns flowing from South Africa's own negotiated transition.[2]

The Colonial Constitutional Order: the Union and Apartheid Constitutions

Formally, the South Africa Act passed by the British Parliament in 1909 brought together four settler colonies into a single Union of South Africa, but, in effect, it created a bifurcated state.[3] On the one hand, the Union Constitution granted the white minority parliamentary democracy while on the other it subjugated the majority—black South Africans—to autocratic administrative rule. Excluded from the 1910 'National Convention,' black leaders protested against the refusal to extend the limited franchise granted to Africans in the Cape Colony and Natal to the former Boer Republics—the Orange Free State and South African Republic—but they were rebuffed as not representative of African society.[4] Instead, African society was presented as essentially 'traditional,' to be governed separately by chiefs in a system which replicated the feudal hierarchy of European history. The Union Constitution provided that the control and administration of native affairs throughout the Union should vest in the Governor-General-in-Council, who should exercise all special powers in regard to native administration previously vested in the Governors of the several colonies. In these colonies extraordinary powers had been conferred over native affairs. For example, in Natal the Governor had taken to himself the powers of Supreme Chief over all Natives, and the Natal Code of Native Law defined these powers to include the exercise of all political power—the right to appoint and remove chiefs, to divide and amalgamate tribes and punish offenders. Finally, his actions as Supreme Chief were not cognizable by the Courts. This system was reproduced as the national model in the Native Administration Act 1927 which declared the Governor-General the Supreme Chief and vested in him all the powers arrogated by the Natal Code of Native Law. Thus through statutory enactment the white minority Parliament perpetuated colonial rule over the black majority by expressly abdicating its own

[2] H Klug *Constituting Democracy: Law, Globalism and South Africa's Political Reconstruction* (Cambridge University Press, Cambridge, 2000) and H Ebrahim *The Soul of a Nation: Constitution-Making in South Africa* (Oxford University Press, Cape Town, 1998).

[3] A Ashforth *The Politics of Official Discourse in Twentieth-Century South Africa* (Clarendon Press, Oxford, 1990) 37; See also M Mamdani *Citizen and Subject: Contemporary Africa and the Legacy of Late Colonialism* (Princeton University Press, New Jersey, 1996).   [4] Ashforth (n 3) 34.

authority over the executive in this arena and granting the executive unfettered power—free of even minimal judicial review—over the black majority.

Facing increased international criticism of its apartheid policies the government of South Africa broke with the Commonwealth and adopted a Republican Constitution in 1961. Despite the break with the United Kingdom, the main feature of this constitution was its explicit adoption of the English constitutional principle of parliamentary sovereignty. Section 59 specifically constitutionalized the exclusion of the courts from substantive review and explicitly limited any judicial review over substantive legislative enactments to those effecting the clause guaranteeing the equality of the English and Afrikaans languages. As if to emphasize the primacy of the doctrine, s 59(1) stated that '[p]arliament shall be the sovereign legislative authority in and over the Republic, and shall have full power to make laws for the peace, order and good government of the Republic.' Under this constitutional order statutory law was in effect unchallengeable as the doctrine of parliamentary sovereignty was meant to invest parliament with 'absolute power.' In the context of a white minority-controlled parliament the doctrine of parliamentary sovereignty, long justified in the English context as an expression of majoritarian democracy, was effectively perverted. This perversion was further exacerbated by the dominance of the 19th century philosophy of legal positivism among South African lawyers. Thus, while Judges were not prohibited from rejecting interpretations of the law which violated the inherited Roman-Dutch legal tradition, their deference to the will of the sovereign and strict distinction between law and morals, framed their interpretation of the law.[5]

Despite ideals of equality and other substantive criteria embedded in Roman-Dutch law, the courts, after a brief period of resistance against the removal of 'coloreds' from the voters roll in the mid-1950s,[6] recognized that the will of a racially-exclusive Parliament was to be paramount. The crude logic of this unrestrained conception of parliamentary sovereignty is summed up in a decision of the Appellate Division, South Africa's highest court at that time, in which Stratford Acting Chief Justice stated that 'arguments are sometimes advanced which do seem to me to ignore the plain principle that Parliament may make any encroachment it chooses upon the life, liberty or property of any individual subject to its sway, and that it is the function of the courts of law to enforce its will.'[7] This interpretation's impact on human rights and its 'debasement of the South African Legal System' are now part of the history of apartheid.[8]

---

[5] See J Dugard *Human Rights and the South Africa Legal Order* (Princeton University Press, New Jersey, 1978).

[6] *Harris v Minister of the Interior* 1952 (2) SA 428 (AD). See J Davidson 'The History of Judicial Oversight of Legislative and Executive Action in South Africa' (1985) 8 *Harvard JL & Public Policy* 687, 710; Dugard (n 5) 29; HR Hahlo and E Kahn, *South Africa: The Development of its Laws and Constitution* (Stevens, London, 1960) 154–9.

[7] *Sachs v Minister of Justice; Diamond v Minister of Justice* 1934 AD 11 37.

[8] Dugard (n 5) 36.

Although the policy of apartheid is identified with the nationalist party government which came to power in 1948, racial discrimination and segregation became embedded in South African society from the earliest days of colonial penetration.[9] Implementing its apartheid policy the nationalist government introduced a series of bills which together created an elaborate legislative scheme of statutory apartheid. To a great extent these laws attempted both to codify the existing practice of segregation, and to use state power to control and shape the increasing social and political pressures which were mounting as South Africa entered the post-World War II era of anti-colonial political struggles and industrialization. This statutory framework provided for: the registration of citizens by race; the prohibition of interracial sex and marriage; the provision of separate, unequal, public facilities and the racial segregation of the towns and cities of South Africa.

While apartheid legislation eventually discriminated against black South Africans in virtually all aspects of social life, from birth to death, at the same time the government introduced a second legislative scheme to address the political pressures that were developing in this period. The Bantu Authorities Act 1951 and the Promotion of Bantu Self-Government Act 1959 introduced the policy of separate development under which the black majority was to be eventually divided into ten 'ethnic' groups and granted 'self-government' or 'independence' within the overall framework of apartheid. Although this process of 'internal decolonization' led to the creation of four new constitutions between 1976 and 1983—one for each of the 'independent' *bantustans* or homelands—none of these ever gained international recognition. Instead the apartheid regime used the Suppression of Communism Act 1950 to pursue a process of political repression which included the Unlawful Organizations Act 1960, which banned the African National Congress (ANC) and Pan Africanist Congress (PAC), and culminated in continuing waves of security legislation, bannings and, ultimately, nearly continuous states of emergency.

In the face of increasing internal resistance, and international isolation, the South African government moved in the late 1970s to politically incorporate the 'Indian' and 'Coloured' communities as a means of broadening its social base. The outcome of this shift in apartheid policy was the adoption of the 1983 Constitution which extended the franchise to 'Indians' and 'Coloureds' in a tricameral legislature with its jurisdiction distributed according to a vague distinction between 'own' and 'general' affairs. Two mechanisms ensured, however, that power remained safely in the hands of the dominant white party. First, the running of government was effectively centralized under an executive State President with extraordinary powers in both the executive and legislative arenas. Second, all significant decisions within the legislature—such as the election of the President—would be automatically resolved by the 4:2:1 ratio of representatives, which ensured that even if the 'Indian' and 'Coloured' houses of parliament voted in unison, the will of the 'white' house would prevail.

[9] See M Chanock *The Making of South African Legal Culture 1902–1936: Fear, Favour and Prejudice* (Cambridge University Press, Cambridge, 2001).

The exclusion of the African majority from this scheme and resistance from within the two target communities—'Indian' and 'Coloured'—meant that the 1983 Constitution was practically still born. The escalation of resistance and rebellion which began in late 1984 and led to the imposition of repeated States of Emergency from mid-1985 sealed its fate. The ANC's publication of the Constitutional Guidelines for a Democratic South Africa[10] in mid-1988 marked the first public expression of an initiative aimed at achieving a negotiated settlement in South Africa. By publically committing itself to the adoption of a Bill of Rights enforceable through the courts the ANC assured South Africa, and the world, of its commitment to constitutional government. This led to the adoption of the Harare Declaration by the Organization of African Unity in August 1989.[11] This document used the Constitutional Guidelines as a basis for outlining the minimum principles of a post-apartheid constitution acceptable to the international community, and was later adopted by the Non-Aligned Movement, the Commonwealth and the United Nations General Assembly.[12]

Democratic Transition, Constitutional Principles and the 1993 Interim Constitution

South Africa's democratic transition was achieved through a two-stage process of constitution-making. The first stage, buffeted by ongoing violence and protests, was ultimately under the negotiating parties' control.[13] In contrast the second stage, although formally constrained by a complex set of constitutional principles contained in the 'interim' Constitution,[14] was driven by an elected Constitutional Assembly made up of a joint sitting of the National Assembly and the Senate of South Africa's first democratic parliament.[15] While South Africa's first national elections in April 1994 marks the end of apartheid, and the coming into force of the 1993 'interim' Constitution, it would take a further five years before the 1999 elections swept away the last transitional arrangements at the local level, replacing them with the first democratically-elected local governments. This election also marked the setting of the sunset clauses which had provided numerous guarantees to the old order—including a five-year government of national unity and job

[10] African National Congress, Constitutional Guidelines for a Democratic South Africa (1988) reprinted in *The Road to Peace* (ANC Dept of Political Education, June 1990) 29.

[11] See Harare Declaration, *Declaration of the OAU Ad-hoc Committee on Southern Africa on the Question of South Africa*; Harare, Zimbabwe: August 21, 1989 reprinted in *The Road to Peace* (ANC Dept of Political Education, June 1990) 34.

[12] GA Resolutions 44/27A, B and K, 22 Nov 1989; 44 GAOR, Supp. No. 49 (A/44/49), 34–35. See also, GA Resolution S-16/1, 14 Dec 1989. The Declaration is reprinted in Sec.-Gen., Second Report, U.N. Doc. A/45/1052 (1991), Annex III.

[13] H Klug 'Participating in the Design: Constitution-Making in South Africa' in P Andrews and S Ellmann (eds) *The Post-Apartheid Constitutions: Perspectives on South Africa's Basic Law* (University of the Witwatersrand Press, 2001) 146.

[14] See Constitution of the Republic of South Africa 1993 Fourth Schedule.

[15] Constitution of the Republic of South Africa 1993 s 68.

security for apartheid-era government officials—which facilitated the democratic transition.

Each of the three major protagonists negotiating South Africa's transition to democracy—the African National Congress (ANC), the National Party (NP) government and the Inkatha Freedom Party (IFP) had at first insisted on different processes of constitution-making, framed in each case by the party's substantive goals. For the ANC, a future South Africa was to be based on a common citizenship and identity which could only be achieved through a collective effort to overcome apartheid's legacy.[16] The NP government conceived of a future in which local communities would be empowered to voluntarily choose to pursue their own living arrangements without interference from the state,[17] while the IFP sought to protect its regional base of power in the province of KwaZulu/Natal, arguing for a form of 'federalism' in which regions of the country would exercise near independent authority. Central to the ANC's vision of the democratic transition was the claim of self-determination which supported the right of the people of South Africa to democratically elect a constitution-making body. In stark contrast, the NP government envisaged an extended transition period in which a future constitution could be negotiated between the parties, while the IFP viewed the very notion of a democratically-elected constituent assembly as inherently undemocratic.[18] Instead, the IFP called for a 'depoliticized' process of constitution-making, in which a group of constitutional experts would be retained to produce a draft constitution that would be adopted by parties and endorsed in a national plebiscite.[19] As the ANC campaigned for an unfettered, democratically elected, constituent assembly it was confronted with escalating violence and the eventual realization that as the holder of state power the NP government, and the white minority more generally, would refuse to relinquish power without some guarantees of the shape of the outcome.[20]

When the Conference for a Democratic South Africa (CODESA), convened in December 1991 to negotiate the transition to a new constitutional order, it was premised on a notion of consensus building between contending elites.[21] Nevertheless the NP government still refused to permit Codesa to exercise

---

[16] See ANC, *The Reconstruction and Development Programme* (1994) 1–3.

[17] See National Party *Constitutional Rule in a Participatory Democracy: The National Party's framework for a new democratic South Africa* (1991); and National Party, Constitutional Plan, *The Nationalist*, Vol 11:9, November 1991 12.

[18] See Inkatha Freedom Party, Why the Inkatha Freedom Party Objects to the Idea of the New Constitution Being Written by a Popularly Elected Assembly (Whether called 'Constituent Assembly' or called by any other name), undated submission to CODESA Working Group 2 (1992).

[19] See Position Paper of the Inkatha Freedom Party for Submission at the CODESA meeting of February 6, 1992, reprinted in AP Blaustein and GH Flanz (eds) *Constitutions of the World* (South African Supplement, Release 92-2) 173.

[20] This was recognized by the ANC from before it initiated the process of negotiations in 1987, see 'Statement of the National Executive Committee of the African National Congress on the Question of Negotiations,' Lusaka, October 9, 1987.

[21] This was given clear, if realistic, expression in the notion of sufficient consensus ie. agreement between the National Party government and the ANC.

legal powers, insisting that legal continuity required the approval of any new constitution by the NP-dominated tricameral parliament.[22] This assertion of the need for legal continuity carried the additional advantage for the NP of precluding a democratically-elected constitution-making body. In fact the apartheid government argued that there could not even be a non-racial election until a new constitution allowed a legal basis for a universal adult franchise. For the NP government any suggestion that there should be a legal break with the apartheid past raised questions about the sovereignty of the South African state and the legitimacy of its position as a de jure government and was thus non-negotiable. Acceptance of the principle of legal continuity is, in many ways, the key to understanding the emphasis on legalization in the transition from Apartheid, but it also held major implications for the shape and pace of legal change in post-apartheid South Africa.

ANC leader Joe Slovo's 'sunset clauses' proposal, adopted by the ANC National Executive Committee in February 1993,[23] represented the epitome of an elite pact. The essential feature of the 'sunset' proposal was the acceptance of a constitutionally entrenched system of executive power-sharing for five years after the first democratic election. During this period the democratically-elected parliament would be empowered to write a new Constitution which could exclude these entrenched provisions—whose sun would thus set. In accepting the NP's continued participation in government and the establishment of bilateral agreements which each party would respect in a future constituent assembly, the proposals seemed to grant the NP's basic demands—a negotiated constitution and future power-sharing.[24] However, the notion of a government of national unity articulated in the ANC proposal was clearly distinct from the NP's or other consociational power-sharing models.[25] Most importantly, where the NP had called for a compulsory coalition government with a cabinet drawn equally from the three major parties and a rotating Presidency,[26] Slovo proposed an election to determine proportional participation in executive government.[27] While initially criticized within the ANC[28] and rejected by other parties such as the Pan Africanist Congress,[29] these proposals provided the key to the political transition.

[22] Established in terms of the Republic of South Africa Constitution Act 110 of 1983.

[23] B Keller 'Mandela's Group Accepts 5 Years of Power-Sharing', *New York Times* 19 February 1993 A1. Slovo's article proposing the compromise first appeared in the *African Communist*.

[24] For an example of this misunderstanding of the proposals see S Uys 'Four rites of passage' *The Star* 16 January 1993 9.

[25] See S Ellmann 'The New South African Constitution and Ethnic Division' (1994) 26 *Columbia Human Rights Law Review* 5, 16. Ellmann notes that in 'Lijphart's terms, the new South African Constitution provides for a measure of 'executive power-sharing,' but does not, in general, offer a binding 'minority veto' even on important issues'.

[26] A Sparks 'Clever footwork as FW redefines 'power-sharing,' *The Star* 10 February, 1993 12.

[27] S Johnson & E Waugh 'Sun-set clause' offer as Slovo seeks harmony' *The Star* 1 October 1992 1.

[28] See C Smith, 'Top ANC man in scathing attack on 'sunset' Joe Slovo', *Sunday Times*, 8 November 1992 11; P Stober 'Slovo's 'sunset' debate is red hot' *The Weekly Mail*, 30 October–5 November 1992 16; P Stober 'Daggers drawn in the Slovo sunset' *The Weekly Mail* 13 November–19 November 1992 8; and F Cachalia 'Case against power sharing' *The Star* 2 February 1993 10.

[29] B Desai 'Proposed agreement can lead only to conflict' *The Star* 13 October 1992 12.

The NP's concession of an elected constituent assembly and the ANC's acceptance of a government of national unity under a transitional constitution together provided the major elements of agreement in South Africa's democratic transition. By accepting a democratic constitution-making process, the NP made it possible for the ANC to agree to the adoption of a negotiated 'interim' Constitution which would entrench a government of national unity for five years and ensure the legal continuity the NP government required. This agreement allowed the multi-party negotiations to resume at the World Trade Center outside Johannesburg concluding with the adoption of an interim Constitution by the South African Parliament in December 1993.

The 'interim' Constitution provided in turn for the creation of a 'final' Constitution within two years from the first sitting of the National Assembly.[30] Chapter 5 of the Constitution required that at least two-thirds of all the members of the Constitutional Assembly—made up by the National Assembly and Senate—vote for the new Constitution.[31] In addition, sections of a final Constitution dealing with the boundaries, powers and functions of the provinces had to be adopted by two-thirds of all the members of the regionally constituted Senate.[32] Given the possibility that the Constitutional Assembly could fail to obtain the necessary two-thirds agreement, on either a new Constitution or on the provincial arrangements, the interim Constitution provided elaborate dead-lock breaking mechanisms. First, a panel of constitutional experts[33] appointed by two-thirds of the Constitutional Assembly (or alternatively, by each party holding 40 seats in the Constitutional Assembly)[34] was required to seek amendments to resolve deadlocks within 30 days.[35] Second, if the draft text unanimously agreed upon by the panel of experts was not adopted by a two-thirds majority, then the Constitutional Assembly would be able to approve any draft text by a simple majority of its members.[36] However, in this latter case, the new text would have to be first certified by the Constitutional Court, then submitted to a national referendum, requiring ratification by at least 60 per cent of all votes cast.[37] Failure to obtain a 60 per cent ratification would force the President to dissolve Parliament and call a general election for a new Constitutional Assembly.[38] The new Constitutional Assembly would then have one year to pass a new

[30] Constitution of the Republic of South Africa 1993 s 73(1).
[31] Constitution of the Republic of South Africa 1993 s 73(2). The acceptance of a two-thirds threshold involved an important shift in position for the National Party which had attempted to require a seventy-five per cent majority to pass a new constitution within the constitution-making body. This demand led to the collapse of negotiations within the CODESA framework. See S Friedman (ed) *The Long Journey: South Africa's Quest for a Negotiated Settlement* (Raven Press, Johannesburg, 1993) 31.   [32] ibid.
[33] Constitution of the Republic of South Africa 1993 s 72(2).
[34] Constitution of the Republic of South Africa 1993 s 72(3).
[35] Constitution of the Republic of South Africa 1993 s 73(3) and (4).
[36] Constitution of the Republic of South Africa 1993 s 73(5).
[37] Constitution of the Republic of South Africa 1993 s 73(6)–(8).
[38] Constitution of the Republic of South Africa 1993 s 73(9).

Constitution;[39] however, the majority required for passage of the Constitution would be reduced from two-thirds to 60 per cent.[40]

Although the interim Constitution allowed any of these requirements to be amended by a two-thirds majority of a joint sitting of the National Assembly and Senate,[41] s 74 prohibited the repeal or amendment of both the Constitutional Principles contained in Schedule 4 of the 'interim' Constitution, and the requirement that the Constitutional Court certify that the new 'final' Constitutional text comply with those principles. The possibility of amending the constitution-making procedures thus effectively reduced the 'interim' Constitution's framework for producing the 'final' Constitution to three key elements. First, any amendment of the constitution-making procedures required a two-thirds majority of all the members of the National Assembly and Senate, requiring agreement between at least the ANC and either of the two other major parties—the NP or IFP. Second, under all circumstances the Constitutional Assembly was bound by the Constitutional Principles agreed to by the parties in the Multi-Party Negotiating Process and included in Sch 4 of the interim Constitution. And third, the Constitutional Court had to declare that the new constitutional text complies with the Constitutional Principles. Ultimately the most important issue resolved in this first round of constitution-making was how South Africa would adopt a new 'final' Constitution as the final marker of the democratic transition.

Regionalism and Cooperative Governance

Unlike traditional forms of federalism, which assume the coming together of formerly sovereign entities and their retention of certain specified powers, South Africa's 1996 'final' Constitution creates a structure in which powers are simultaneously allocated and shared among different levels of government. A key aspect of this arrangement is a complex procedure for the resolution of conflicts over governance—between the respective legislative competencies, executive powers, and in relations with other branches and levels of government. Unlike its Indian and Canadian forebears however, South Africa's Constitution follows more closely in the footsteps of the German Constitution, placing less emphasis on geographic autonomy and more on the integration of geographic jurisdictions into separate functionally determined roles in the continuum of governance over specifically defined issues.[42] While provision is made for some exclusive regional powers these are, by and large, of minor significance, all important and contested issues being included in the category of concurrent competence.

---

[39] Constitution of the Republic of South Africa 1993 s 73(10).
[40] Constitution of the Republic of South Africa 1993 s 73(11).
[41] Constitution of the Republic of South Africa 1993 s 62(1).
[42] See N Haysom, 'Federal Features of the Final Constitution' in Andrews and Ellmann (n 13) 504–524.

The 1996 Constitution entrenches three distinct levels of government—national, provincial (nine provinces) and local (including three different forms of municipal government)—and makes detailed provision for both their constitutional autonomy and interaction. Unique in this regard is the inclusion of a specific chapter detailing the governmental structure of the country and laying down general principles of interaction between these different spheres of governance.[43] Most significant among these principles is the provision requiring organs of state involved in an intergovernmental dispute to 'make every reasonable effort to settle the dispute' and to 'exhaust all other remedies before it approaches a court to resolve the dispute.'[44] Co-operative governance in this sense integrates the different geographic regions and discourages them from seeking early intervention by the courts, instead they are forced into an ongoing interaction designed to produce interregional compromises through political negotiation—as has in practice been the German experience.[45]

While the basic structure of South Africa's 'constitutional regionalism' is reflected in the division of functional areas of legislative power into areas of concurrent and exclusive legislative competence, specified in Schedules 4 and 5 of the Constitution, the substance of this constitutional design is contained in provisions: (1) requiring joint or collaborative decision-making; (2) regulating inter-jurisdictional conflict, and; (3) securing limited fiscal autonomy.

First, the Constitution transforms the former Senate, or second house, of the national parliament into the National Council of Provinces (NCOP)—a new second chamber directly representing the provinces in the national legislative process through their provincial delegations, appointed by the legislative parties and Premiers of each province.[46] The Constitution then provides that most bills must go before the NCOP although the nature of the NCOP's role in each bill's passage will depend on the subject matter involved.[47] Constitutional amendment of either the founding provisions,[48] Bill of Rights[49] or those sections dealing specifically with the provinces—the NCOP or provincial boundaries, powers, functions or institutions—all require the support of at least six of the nine provinces. Ordinary bills must also go before the NCOP, but procedure for their passage within the NCOP will depend on whether the bill involves a matter assigned by the Constitution to a particular procedure, is a matter of concurrent jurisdiction, or is an ordinary bill not affecting the provinces. Unless it is an ordinary bill not affecting the provinces, and therefore may be passed by a mere majority of the individual delegates to the NCOP, the decision will be made on the basis of single votes cast on behalf of each of the provincial delegations. Furthermore, the Constitution requires an Act of Parliament to provide a uniform procedure

---

[43] See Chapter 3 Co-operative Governance, Constitution of the Republic of South Africa, Act 108 of 1996. [44] S 41(3).
[45] See D Kommers *The Constitutional Jurisprudence of the Federal Republic of Germany* (2nd edn., Duke University Press, 1997) 61–114. [46] See ss 60–72.
[47] See ss 73–77. [48] Chapter One. [49] Chapter Two.

through which 'provincial legislatures confer authority on their delegations to cast votes on their behalf'.[50] Conflicts between the National Assembly and the NCOP over bills affecting the provinces are negotiated through a Mediation Committee consisting of nine members of the National Assembly and one from each of the nine provincial delegations in the NCOP. It is this elaborate system of structures and processes that creates a system of enforced engagement integrating provincial and national interests at the national level. The requirement that provincial legislatures mandate their NCOP delegations serves, in this context, to further integrate the legislative process, thus projecting provincial interests onto the national agenda while simultaneously requiring the regional bodies to debate nationally defined issues, both processes designed to limit provincial alienation.

Second, provision is made for the constitutional regulation of inter-jurisdictional conflict that may occur in the exercise of both legislative[51] and executive[52] powers. It is these provisions that effectively denote the limits of this new 'regionalism.' In the case of executive authority, mirror provisions allow either the national or the provincial executives to directly intervene at the provincial and local level respectively, if a province or local government 'cannot or does not fulfill an executive obligation in terms of legislation or the Constitution.'[53] Although these provisions establish numerous safeguards against their potential abuse, they nonetheless pose an important limit to provincial and local autonomy. In the case of legislative authority, a whole section of the Constitution deals specifically with the circumstances under which national legislation will prevail over provincial legislation in areas where the two levels of government enjoy concurrent authority. Significantly, however, the default position is that unless the conflicting national legislation meets the criteria laid down in the Constitution, it is the provincial legislation that will prevail.[54] While this seems to grant more authority to the provinces, in fact, the broad criteria establishing national authority over provincial competence, including where the national legislation provides for uniform national norms and standards, frameworks or policies,[55] means that provincial competence will provide a very thin shield against national legislative intrusion. It must be remembered, however, that the provinces will be significant participants in the production of such national legislation though the NCOP. Central authority is, however, further privileged by the inclusion of a provision listing particular circumstances, including the need to maintain national security, economic unity, or essential national standards, in which national legislation may be passed overriding even the exclusive subject matter competence secured for the provinces with respect to those areas defined in Sch 5 of the Constitution.[56]

The third important feature of South Africa's 'strong regionalism' is the constitutional protection of fiscal distributions to the provinces so that they might, to some extent, fulfill their constitutional mandates and provincial policies

---

[50] S 65(2).   [51] See ss 146–150.   [52] Ss 100 and 139.   [53] Ss 100 and 139.
[54] Subsection 146(5).   [55] Subsections 146 (2) and (3).   [56] S 44(2).

independent of the national government. Again, however, this mechanism is characterized by an emphasis on integration through the Financial and Fiscal Commission (FCC)—an independent constitutionally-created body which advises Parliament and the provincial legislatures on, among other things, the constitutional mandate that Parliament must provide for the equitable division of revenue among the national, provincial and local spheres of government.[57] Again, however, national government is privileged in that the taxing power of the regional and local governments are constitutionally constrained[58] and made dependent upon national legislation,[59] and as in the case of executive authority, the national government has a carefully constrained power through the national treasury to directly cutoff transfers of revenues to the provinces—at least for 120 days at a time.[60] The outcome is a system of mediating sources of authority which aims to neither guarantee total regional and local autonomy nor allow the national government to simply impose its will on these other spheres of government. For the moment, however, the dominance of the African National Congress at all levels of government—especially after the party won control of all nine provinces in the 2004 elections—provides the greatest impetus for national integration.

Rule of Law and the Bill of Rights

South Africa's Bill of Rights is often heralded as the crowning achievement of the democratic transition and as having produced 'some of the most progressive decision-making in the world, including the prohibition of the death penalty and the legalization of abortion.'[61] Discussing the Bill of Rights first introduced in the 'interim' Constitution, the late Etienne Mureinik argued that the new Constitution and the Bill of Rights in particular must serve as a 'bridge away from a culture of authority,' and must lead the country towards a 'culture of justification—a culture in which every exercise of power is expected to be justified.'[62] While there is a great deal of continuity between the Bill of Rights in the 'interim' and 'final' Constitutions, it is the inclusion of a commitment to the 'rule of law' in addition to constitutional supremacy in the founding provisions of the 'final' constitution that highlights post-apartheid South Africa's formal commitment to a particular culture of justification.

In practice the Constitutional Court has developed a two-fold analysis in applying both the rights guaranteed in the Bill of Rights, and the more general requirement of 'legality' or the rule of law, in reviewing the constitutionality of the exercise of governmental power. While the Court had held in earlier cases that Parliament must abide by the rule of law,[63] that is, it must not act capriciously or

---

[57] S 214.   [58] S 228 and 229.   [59] S 228(2)(b).   [60] See s 216.

[61] A Sparks *Beyond the Miracle: Inside the New South Africa* (Jonathan Ball, Cape Town, 2003) 7.

[62] E Mureinik 'A Bridge to Where? Introducing the Interim Bill of Rights' (1994) 10 *South African Journal on Human Rights* 31 32.

[63] See *Fedsure Life Assurance Ltd v Greater Johannesburg Transitional Metropolitan Council* 1999 (1) SA 374 (CC) and *New National Party v Government of the Republic of South Africa* 1999 (3) SA 191 (CC).

arbitrarily, the Court took the opportunity, in a case addressing the power of the President to appoint commissions of inquiry, to clarify its interpretative approach.[64] In this case the Constitutional Court rejected the claim that the President's action was subject to the administrative justice clause of the Bill of Rights. The Court argued that the administrative justice clause did not apply to the President's action as the appointment power was a political act, and did not involve the implementation of legislation—which is the subject of administrative justice. The Court nevertheless argued that the President was bound by the more general requirement of legality. In laying down its approach the Constitutional Court noted that first, 'the exercise of the powers [of the President] must not infringe any provision of the Bill of Rights; [and second] the exercise of the powers is also clearly constrained by the principle of legality and, as is implicit in the Constitution, the President must act in good faith and must not misconstrue the powers.'[65]

In a second case challenging the President's erroneously-informed decision to sign into operation a medicines law before the regulations required for the proper operation of the law had been prepared, the Constitutional Court held that the administrative justice clause did not apply because the President's decision about when to promulgate the law was a matter of political judgment—falling between the law-making process and the process of administration of the law.[66] Nevertheless, the Court went on to describe the general constraints the Constitution places on the exercise of public power arguing that 'it is a requirement of the rule of law that the exercise of public power by the executive and other functionaries should not be arbitrary. Decisions must be rationally related to the purpose for which the power was given, otherwise they are in effect arbitrary and inconsistent with this requirement.'[67] Most recently in the *Affordable Medicines Trust* case the Court has reiterated that when it comes to the exercise of governmental power, 'both the legislature and the executive are constrained by the principle that they may exercise no power and perform no function beyond that conferred upon them by law. In this sense the Constitution entrenches the principle of legality and provides the foundation for the control of public power.'[68] For Justice Ncobo 'what would have been *ultra vires* under common law by reason of a functionary exceeding his or her powers is now invalid under the Constitution as an infringement of the principle of legality.'[69]

In effect then the Court is employing the guarantee of the rule of law in the founding provisions of the Constitution to require that, in addition to respect for

[64] See *President of the Republic of South Africa v South African Rugby Football Union 2000* (1) SA 1 (CC). [65] ibid para 148.

[66] JD Waal, I Currie and G Erasmus, *The Bill of Rights Handbook* (4th edn., Juta Lansdowne, South Africa, 2001) 13.

[67] *Pharmaceutical Manufacturers Association of South Africa: In re: ex parte President of the Republic of South Africa* 2000 (2) SA 674 (CC) para 85.

[68] *The Affordable Medicines Trust, The National Convention on Dispensing, Dr. Mapata Norman Mabasa v The Minister of Health of the Republic of South Africa, Director-General of Health*, CCT 27/04, decided on 11 March 2005 (CC) para 49 [hereinafter *Affordable Medicines*].

[69] *Affordable Medicines*, para 51.

the specific rights guaranteed in the Bill of Rights, when it comes to the exercise of governmental power—legislative or executive—there must be a rational relationship between the scheme adopted and the achievement of a legitimate governmental purpose.[70] Upholding the Minister of Health's regulations pertaining to the dispensing of pharmaceuticals, the Constitutional Court recently pointed out that, the 'exercise of legislative and executive power is subject to two constraints, namely, the minimum threshold requirement of rationality and that it must not infringe any of the rights contained in the Bill of Rights. If exercise of power limits any such rights, it must pass the s 36(1) [limitations clause] test. And proportionality analysis is central to the s 36(1) enquiry.'[71] While it has been argued that the Court 'treats the provisions of the Bill of Rights as an elaboration of general principles implied by the rule of law,' and requires that these 'specific provisions which concretize, elaborate on and implement the rule of law must be applied in legal disputes before the general norm is invoked,'[72] Ncobo's judgment indicates that this is a more coterminous analysis depending on the nature of the challenged activity or decision and whether specific rights guaranteed in the Bill of Rights are directly affected.

While the Bill of Rights provides for the protection of an extraordinary range of rights, including classic political and civil rights as well as social, economic and environmental rights, it is important to recognize that, given the legacies of apartheid, it is also premised upon a deep understanding of the need to achieve substantive equality in South Africa. Not only does the Bill of Rights attempt to address some of the most egregious consequences of the legally imposed inequalities of the past—such as access to land ownership—it also adopts a broad definition of equality and provides for affirmative action as a mechanism to deal with this legacy. Listed among the more familiar grounds upon which discrimination is prohibited—such as race, sex, age and ethnic origin—are pregnancy, marital status, sexual orientation, disability and language. Furthermore, in cases of alleged discrimination on any of the listed grounds, such discrimination is assumed to be unfair, thus shifting the burden of proof to those denying that the *prima facie* effect of discrimination is the consequence of their actions. Finally, these constitutional protections are not limited to relations between the state and individuals, but rather are applied to both governmental and private conduct, with the Constitution mandating the legislature to enact law to prevent or prohibit unfair discrimination. The Promotion of Equality and Prevention of Unfair Discrimination Act, enacted in February 2000 to fulfill this constitutional mandate, is a wide ranging statute which aims to eradicate social and economic inequalities, 'especially those that are systematic in nature, which are generated in our history by colonialism, apartheid and patriarchy, and which brought pain and suffering to the great majority of our people.'[73]

---

[70] See courts discussion in New National Party para 19–24.

[71] *Affordable Medicines* para 91.   [72] De Waal, Currie and Erasmus (n 66)14–15.

[73] Preamble, Promotion of Equality and Prevention of Unfair Discrimination Act 4 2000.

Although the state is explicitly charged with the duty to 'respect, protect, promote, and fulfill the rights in the Bill of Rights,'[74] it is also important to recognize that the rights guaranteed are subject to limitations as explicitly provided for in the Bill of Rights. The general limitations clause provides that rights may only be limited by 'law of general application to the extent . . . reasonable and justifiable in an open and democratic society based on human dignity, equality and freedom, taking into account all relevant factors including: (a) the nature of the right; (b) the importance of the purpose of the limitation; (c) the nature and extent of the limitation; (d) the relation between the limitation and its purpose; and (e) less restrictive means to achieve the purpose.' In addition to various internal limitations—such as the exclusion of hate speech and propaganda for war from the right to free expression—and the more general limitation on the duty of the state to take 'reasonable legislative and other measures within its available resources, to achieve the progressive realization' of various social and economic rights, elaborate provision is made for the derogation of rights in a state of emergency. It is important to note, however, that the Bill of Rights also restricts the process of derogation by specifying a set of non-derogable rights and setting conditions which must be observed in cases where persons may be detained in the event of a state of emergency. Finally, the Bill of Rights also lays down its own internal rules of interpretation. Those with authority to interpret the rights are required to 'promote the values that underlie an open and democratic society based on human dignity, equality and freedom;' to 'consider international law;' and are allowed to consider foreign law.[75]

Amending Procedures

Apart from some specific procedural guarantees—such as notice periods and the requirement that an amending bill may not contain other subject matter—most provisions of the Constitution may be simply amended by a bill passed by a two-thirds vote in the National Assembly. In fact the Constitution was amended over 11 times in its first decade of existence. This general amending procedure does not, however, cover amendments to a number of specific clauses guaranteeing the nature and structure of the state, including the founding provisions in s 1, the Bill of Rights in Ch 2, or any provisions affecting the provinces either singularly or generally, all of which require higher majorities in the National Assembly and the NCOP. Even if these majorities are achieved the President may—as with all other legislation—refuse to give his or her assent to the Amendment Bill. In such a case the President may either send the bill back to Parliament for reconsideration or refer it to the 'Constitutional Court for a decision on its constitutionality.'[76] Furthermore, a third of the members of the National Assembly may, within 30 days of the President's assent, ask the Constitutional Court to review the constitutionality of the Act of

---

[74] S 7(2).   [75] S 39(1).   [76] S 74(4)(b).

Parliament. It is these latter provisions allowing for abstract review that raise the possibility that the Constitutional Court's role in deciding on the appropriateness of a proposed constitutional text may not have been exhausted by the Court's extra-ordinary role in Certifying that the 'final' constitution met the requirements of the constitutional principles contained in Sch 4 of the 1993 Constitution.

The founding provisions of the Constitution receive the highest degree of protection. Any bill to amend either that subsection of the amending provisions guaranteeing the founding provisions of s 1 or s 1 itself requires a 75 per cent vote in the National Assembly and the support of at least six of the nine provinces— voting as provinces in the National Council of Provinces (NCOP). Section 1 of the Constitution defines the Republic of South Africa as 'one, sovereign, democratic state,' founded on certain basic values: '(a) human dignity, the achievement of equality and the advancement of human rights and freedoms; (b) Non-racialism and non-sexism; (c) Supremacy of the constitution and the rule of law; [and] (d) Universal adult suffrage, a national common voters roll, regular elections and a multi-party system of democratic government, to ensure accountability, respons-iveness and openness.' The Bill of Rights is also entrenched, with any amendment requiring at least a two-thirds vote in the National Assembly as well as the support of six of the nine provinces. South Africa's 'federal' structure is also given greater constitutional protection. Any amendments affecting the National Council of Provinces, altering 'provincial boundaries, powers, functions or institutions,' or that deals 'specifically with a provincial matter,' requires the support of six of the nine provinces. In the event that the amendment bill 'concerns only a specific province or provinces' the NCOP may not pass the amendment unless it has been approved by the relevant provincial legislature or legislatures.[77]

Constitutional Court

Given the distrust of the old judicial order, the idea of superimposing a Constitutional Court as the final interpreter of a new constitution gained early acceptance among participants in the political transition. While the Constitutional Court first created under the 'interim' Constitution was given exclusive jurisdiction over constitutional appeals, it was initially placed in a co-equal position with the old Appellate Division of the Supreme Court of South Africa, which retained final jurisdiction for all non-constitutional matters, but had no jurisdiction over constitutional questions. The 'final' Constitution has retained this basic jurisdictional division, however the Supreme Court of Appeals, which hears appeals from the High Courts, now has appellate jurisdiction over all matters, including constitutional issues,[78] with the Constitutional Court retain-ing original jurisdiction over direct applications[79] and serving as the final court of

---

[77] S 74(8).   [78] Constitution of the Republic of South Africa (1996) s 168(3).
[79] Constitution of the Republic of South Africa (1996) s 167(6).

appeal on the Constitution.[80] Constitutional jurisdiction is however very far reaching as it not only deals with all government related activity[81] but also certain private activity[82] as well as the duty to develop the common law and indigenous law in conformity with the requirements of the Bill of Rights.[83]

Once the negotiating parties reached a compromise requiring a Constitutional Court to certify that the final constitution was consistent with the Constitutional Principles,[84] their attention quickly turned to the process of appointing judges to the Constitutional Court. Little attention was initially paid to the proposal by the technical committee to the Multi-Party Negotiating Process that Constitutional Court Judges be nominated by an all-party parliamentary committee and be appointed by a 75 per cent majority of both houses of parliament. However, as the significance of the Constitutional Court became increasingly clear, a major political conflict exploded.[85] In fact the conflict over this process brought the multi-party negotiations, once again, perilously close to deadlock. Despite this inauspicious beginning, the resolution of this conflict has, with minor changes, been essentially retained in the 'final' Constitution.

The resolution involved an elaborate compromise in which the newly elected President was required to follow three distinct processes in appointing members of the Constitutional Court for a non-renewable period of seven years.[86] First, the President appointed a president of the Constitutional Court in consultation with the Cabinet and Chief Justice.[87] Second, four members of the Court were appointed from among the existing judges of the Supreme Court after consultation between the President, Cabinet and the Chief Justice.[88] Finally, the President, in consultation with the Cabinet and the President of the Constitutional Court, appointed six members from a list submitted by the Judicial Service Commission (JSC),[89] a newly created body dominated two-to-one by lawyers.[90]

The final Constitution extended the period of non-renewable appointment from 7 to 12 years but also imposed a mandatory retirement age of 70 years. A subsequent constitutional amendment provides that the term of an individual justice may be extended by an Act of Parliament.[91] Appointments to the court are made by the President, either in consultation with the JSC and the leaders of the

[80] Constitution of the Republic of South Africa (1996) ss 167(3)–(5).
[81] Constitution of the Republic of South Africa (1996) s 8(1).
[82] Constitution of the Republic of South Africa (1996) s 8(2)–(3).
[83] Constitution of the Republic of South Africa (1996) s 39(2).
[84] Constitution of the Republic of South Africa (1993) s 71(2).
[85] See E Mureinik 'Rescued from illegitimacy?' *Weekly Mail & Guardian*, Review/Law, Supplement, Vol. 1, No. 5, Dec. 1993 1; and N Haysom 'An expedient package deal?' *Weekly Mail & Guardian*, Review/Law, Supplement, Vol. 1, No. 5, Dec. 1993 1.
[86] Constitution of the Republic of South Africa 1993 s 99(1).
[87] Constitution of the Republic of South Africa 1993 s 97(2)(a).
[88] Constitution of the Republic of South Africa 1993 s 99(3).
[89] Constitution of the Republic of South Africa 1993 s 99(3).
[90] Constitution of the Republic of South Africa 1993 s 105(1).
[91] Constitution of the Republic of South Africa 1996 s 176(1).

political parties represented in the National Assembly—in the case of the Chief Justice and the Deputy-Chief Justice—or, for the remaining positions on the court, from a list of nominees prepared by the JSC after the President consults with the Chief Justice and the leaders of political parties. The JSC is required to provide three more nominees than the number of appointments to be made, and the President may refuse to appoint some of these by giving reasons to the JSC why certain nominees are unacceptable—requiring the JSC to provide a supplemental list. The President's power of appointment is further restricted by the requirement that 'at all times, at least four members of the Constitutional Court must be persons who were judges at the time they were appointed.'[92] The President is required to remove a judge from office if the JSC 'finds that the judge suffers from an incapacity, is grossly incompetent or is guilty of gross misconduct' and the National Assembly votes by a two-thirds majority for that judge's removal.

Appointment to the Constitutional Court is also determined by the requirement that the person must be a South African citizen and that consideration must be given to the '[n]eed for the judiciary to reflect broadly the racial and gender composition of South Africa.'[93] In practice the Constitutional Court has, despite its young age, experienced a regular change in the composition of its panel. This has occurred as a result of a number of developments, including the transfer of the first Deputy-President of the Court to become Chief Justice (then head of the Supreme Court of Appeal exercising final appeal jurisdiction over non-constitutional matters), the death of Justice Didcott, numerous retirements and the fairly frequent use of acting Justices when permanent members were either seconded to international organizations or on leave. While the first appointments to the Constitutional Court were dominated by lawyers, judges and legal academics who had gained high stature during the struggle against apartheid or whose integrity was recognized nationally and internationally, concern for the need to achieve or maintain racial and ethnic representivity on the panel seems to have determined more recent appointments. Ten years after its inauguration the Justices of the Constitutional Court reflect the diversity of South Africa with two female, three white, six African, one Indian and two physically-disabled justices on the eleven person panel.

Sources of Interpretation

The 1996 Constitution is an extremely detailed document containing a comprehensive catalogue of citizen's rights as well as a clear map of government structures and duties. As far as interpretation is concerned, there are both explicit interpretative guidelines in the Bill of Rights as well as more general legal and interpretative

---

92　Constitution of the Republic of South Africa 1996 s 174(5).
93　Constitution of the Republic of South Africa 1996 ss 174(1) and (2).

principles laid out in the founding provisions and in quite extensive sets of governing principles which precede chapters on: cooperative governance; State Institutions Supporting Constitutional Democracy; Public Administration; and the Security Services. In addition to the explicit interpretation and limitations clauses in the Bill of Rights, there are numerous internal limitations and interpretative elements contained in individual rights provisions. While the Constitutional Court has increasingly referred to specific principles and general provisions in its case law, the most important focus of the interpretative exercise has been the implementation of the limitations clause in the realm of the Bill of Rights, with its concomitant emphasis on the broad interpretation of the scope of individual rights as well as its balancing of the state's power to limit the reach of rights under particular circumstances.

Constitution as Statute

While the Constitutional Court, from its earliest judgments, has rejected a purely textual approach to interpretation, there remains a tendency both on and off the bench to continue to assert the importance of the ordinary or plain meaning of the text as the primary source of constitutional rules.[94] Writing the Court's opinion in *S v Zuma*,[95] the Court's very first judgment, Acting Justice Kentridge emphasized the importance of the text, arguing that '[w]hile we must always be conscious of the values underlying the Constitution, it is nonetheless our task to interpret a written instrument.' He proceeded to cite Lord Wilberforce, warning that 'even a constitution is a legal instrument, the language of which must be respected.'[96] The Constitution itself provides statute-like definitions for three particular terms and lays out a specific scheme for interpreting the Bill of Rights. In the first instance, s 239 defines the document's use of three terms—national legislation; provincial legislation and organ of state. However, at the same time, this section contains an internal caveat to the effect that these meanings apply 'unless the context [in the Constitution] indicates otherwise.'[97] In the second instance, the Constitution lays down a set of interpretative rules that the courts, tribunals or other fora must apply when interpreting the Bill of Rights.[98] These specify the source of values[99] as well as particular sources of law which the court either must or may consider when interpreting the Bill of Rights.[100] This section also indicates that the Bill of Rights is not exhaustive and that other rights or freedoms may be recognized, from common law, customary law or statue, so long as they do not conflict with the rights guaranteed in the Bill of Rights.[101]

---

[94] See A Fagan 'In defense of the obvious—Ordinary language and the identification of constitutional rules'(1995) 11 *South African Journal on Human Rights* 545.
[95] 1995 (2) SA 642 (CC).   [96] *S v Zuma* 1995 (2) SA 642 (CC) para 17.   [97] S 239.
[98] S 39.   [99] S 39(a).   [100] S 39(b) and (c).   [101] S 39(3).

Legislative History

Evidence that capital punishment was subject to extensive debate in negotiations before and during the constitution-making process presented the Court, in *S v Makwanyane*,[102] with two problems. First, the Court had to clarify its own relationship to the constitution-making process, indicating what weight the views of the framers were due in interpreting the Constitution. Second, adducing evidence of the intent of the framers—despite their presence in society and even among members of the Court—required the Court to reconsider the status of legislative history in the interpretative process. While South African courts have traditionally limited the use of legislative history to evidence on the 'purpose and background of the legislation in question,'[103] the Constitutional Court noted that courts in England, Australia and New Zealand had subsequently relaxed the exclusionary rule.[104] Furthermore, the Court noted that in 'countries in which the constitution is similarly the supreme law, it is not unusual for the courts to have regard to the circumstances existing at the time the constitution was adopted, including the debates and writings which formed part of the process'.[105] Following these developments the Court accepted the reports of the technical committees to the Multi-Party Negotiating Process as 'equivalent to the travaux preparatoires relied upon by the international tribunals,' to provide evidence of context for the interpretation of the Constitution.[106] The Court, however, limited the scope of reliance on these materials to the specific context of this and similarly situated cases 'where the background material is clear, is not in dispute, and is relevant to showing why particular provisions were or were not included in the Constitution.'[107]

Although the founders of South Africa's new constitutional order are still present, the Constitutional Court has recognized that any attempt to ascertain their intent or to base interpretation of the Constitution on their original intent, is confounded by the constitution-making process itself. While accepting the usefulness of background evidence provided by the record of the negotiations the Court cautions against reliance on the comments of individual participants in the constitution-making process 'no matter how prominent a role they might have played,' as the Constitution is the 'product of a multiplicity of persons.'[108] The Court thus recognized from its inception the problem that most constitutional theories of original intent fail to take cognizance of—the collective nature of the constitution-making exercise. While legislative history may provide a context in which to understand why various issues, such as the restitution clauses, were included or excluded as products of political compromises and exchanges between the negotiating partners, the Court has recognized that the process of aggregation in any negotiated process provides a completely separate source of

---

[102] *S v Makwanyane and Others* 1995 (3) SA 391.   [103] ibid para 13.
[104] ibid para 14 & 15.   [105] ibid para 16.   [106] ibid para 17.   [107] ibid para 19.
[108] ibid para 18.

delegation to future generations of the need to decide on particular meanings or issues.[109]

Having accepted the salience of legislative history the Court argues that the 'clear failure to deal specifically in the Constitution with this issue [the death penalty] was not accidental.'[110] Support for this conclusion, the Court argues, is found in the 'Solomonic solution' proposed by the South African Law Commission in its *Interim Report on Group and Human Rights* in 1991, under which 'a Constitutional Court would be required to decide whether a right to life expressed in unqualified terms could be circumscribed by a limitations clause contained in a bill of rights.'[111] Thus the Court concludes that the failure of the founders to resolve this issue left to the Constitutional Court the duty to decide whether the 'provisions of the pre-constitutional law making the death penalty a competent sentence for murder and other crimes,' are consistent with the fundamental rights enshrined in the Constitution.[112]

Public Opinion and Constitutional Values

Recognition that public opinion seemed to favor the retention of the death penalty posed a separate and distinct problem for the fledgling Constitutional Court as it set out to establish its place and legitimacy as a new and unique institution in the South African legal order. Asserting its role as the protector of the Constitution and human rights in a post-apartheid South Africa, the Court chose this opportunity to make a clear declaration that it would 'not allow itself to be diverted from its duty to act as an independent arbiter of the Constitution.'[113] Discounting the significance of public opinion to its role, the Court argued that public opinion in itself is 'no substitute for the duty vested in the Courts to interpret the Constitution and to uphold its provisions without fear or favor.'[114] If public opinion were to be decisive, Justice Chaskalson declared, 'there would be no need for constitutional adjudication.'[115]

The Constitutional Court's blunt dismissal of public opinion was, however, mediated by a second line of argument which appeared in a number of the concurring opinions. Here the Court justified its rejection of the death penalty, despite opposing public opinion, by recognizing a national will to transcend the past and to uphold the standards of a 'civilized democratic' society.[116] Society's will to break with its past and to establish a community built on values antithetical to the maintenance of capital punishment is evidenced, according to the court, in the adoption of a new Constitution and Bill of Rights. As Justice O'Regan argued in her concurring opinion, the 'new Constitution stands as a monument to this society's commitment to a future in which all human beings will be accorded

---

[109] See NK Komesar 'Back to the Future—An Institutional View of Making and Interpreting Constitutions' (1987) 81 *Northwestern University Law Review* 191 203–10.
[110] *Makwanyane* (n 102) para 20.   [111] ibid para 22.   [112] ibid para 25.
[113] ibid para 89.   [114] ibid para 88.   [115] ibid.   [116] ibid para 199.

equal dignity and respect.'[117] In these arguments the Court seemed to embrace the legal fiction of the 1993 Constitution's preamble, which despite its negotiated status and formal adoption by the unrepresentative tricameral Parliament, announced that 'We, the people of South Africa declare that... [and] therefore [adopt] the following provisions... as the Constitution of the Republic of South Africa.'.[118]

Embracing the 'altruistic and humanitarian philosophy which animates the Constitution enjoyed by us nowadays,' as the true aspirations of the South African people Didcott J simultaneously rejected the undue influence of public opinion. First, Didcott J repeated Justice Chaskalson's citation[119] of the classic statements by Justices Powell and Jackson of the United States Supreme Court, who argued respectively that the 'assessment of popular opinion is essentially a legislative, not a judicial, function,' and that 'the very purpose of a bill of rights is to withdraw certain subjects from the vicissitudes of political controversy, to place them beyond the reach of majorities.' Then Didcott J goes on to argue that the decision to abolish or retain capital punishment is a constitutional question, the determination of which is the duty of the Court and not of representative institutions.[120]

This concurrent rejection of public opinion and embracing of national values is repeated by Kentridge J. Arguing that public opinion, 'even if expressed in Acts of Parliament, cannot be decisive,'[121] he suggests that while clear public opinion 'could not be entirely ignored,' the Court 'would be abdicating [its]... constitutional function' if it simply deferred to public opinion.[122] Justice Kentridge then proceeds to discount any evidence of public opinion on the grounds that there had been no referendum or recent legislation[123] and instead he suggests that the reduction in executions after 1990 and the official executive moratorium on the death penalty, 'while not evidence of general opinion, do cast serious doubt on the acceptability of capital punishment in South Africa.'[124] These counter-majoritarian concerns over the 'appeal to public opinion,'[125] are overshadowed in the Court's arguments by a reliance on the 'evolving standards of civilization'[126] which the court infers are incorporated into South African jurisprudence by the country's aspiration to be a free and democratic society.[127] It is this national ambition, contained in the constitutional commitment 'to promote the values which underlie an open and democratic society based on freedom and equality,'[128] which the Court presents as the source of social mores underlying the new constitutional dispensation. It is in this context, then, that Kentridge J concludes that the 'deliberate execution of a human, however depraved and criminal his conduct, must degrade the new society which is coming into being.'[129] A similar reliance

---

[117] *Makwanyane* (n102) para 344.
[118] Constitution of the Republic of South Africa 1993 Preamble.
[119] *Makwanyane* (n102) para 89.   [120] ibid para 188.   [121] ibid para 200.
[122] ibid.   [123] ibid para 201.   [124] ibid.   [125] ibid.   [126] ibid para 199.
[127] ibid para 198 and 199.   [128] Constitution of the Republic of South Africa 1993 s 35.
[129] *Makwanyane* (n 102) para 199.

on the Constitution's inherent morality as a source of a public or national will which supersedes simple public opinion can be found in Chief Justice Langa's argument that 'implicit in the provisions and tone of the Constitution are values of a more mature society, which relies on moral persuasion rather than force; on example rather than coercion.'[130]

International and Comparative Sources

The provisions of s 39 of the Constitution, requiring courts and other interpreters of the Bill of Rights to consider international law and explicitly allowing them to consider foreign law, are a fairly unique aspect of South Africa's interpretative project, calling as they do for interpreters to draw upon a vast range of external sources for interpretive and constitutional values. The provision in s 35 of the 1993 Constitution, admonishing the courts to 'have regard to public international law applicable to the protection of the rights entrenched...', was in fact strengthened in the second round of constitution-making. While the Constitutional Court emphasized in *S v Makwanyane* that s 35(1) of the 1993 Constitution did not require,[131] but rather permitted, the Courts to 'have regard to'[132] public international law as 'guidance as to the correct interpretation of particular provisions,'[133] s 39 of the 1996 Constitution now states that when interpreting the Bill of Rights the Court 'must consider international law.'[134] Thus, it is now mandatory for the Court to address the interpretation of rights given in international documents and by international fora.

The reference to foreign law remains however less positive. While the reference to foreign law in s 39 is permissive, the Constitutional Court has urged caution in respect of the use of comparative Bill of Rights jurisprudence and foreign case law. The Court noted in *Makwanyane* that these sources 'will no doubt be of importance, particularly in the early stages of the transition when there is no developed indigenous jurisprudence in this branch of the law,' but 'will not necessarily offer a safe guide to the interpretation' of the Bill of Rights.[135] The Court has gone on to note that international experience is to be considered 'with a view to finding principles rather than extracting rigid formulae,' with the purpose of seeking 'rationales rather than rules.'[136] Even with the recognition of the need to draw on foreign materials, until South Africa produces its own body of constitutional jurisprudence as a source of interpretation, the Court's use of both international materials and comparative law in the *Makwanyane* case is revealing. Instead of relying on the international and foreign materials in the sense of legal precedent, the Court used these materials primarily as a means to distinguish the South

---

[130] ibid para 222.
[131] ibid para 39. Cf, s39(1)(b) of the 1996 Constitution which states that the courts 'must consider international law.' [132] *Makwanyane* (n 102) para 37.
[133] ibid para 35. [134] S 39(1)(b). [135] *Makwanyane* (n 102) para 37.
[136] *Coetzee v Government of the Republic of South Africa*, 1995 (4) SA 631 (CC) para 57.

African case. The only case quoted with unqualified approval, as equivalent and possibly a source of the Court's decision, was the decision of the Hungarian Constitutional Court.[137] Instead the Court tended to use the international and comparative materials as a source for specific lines of argument and justification and in a more general sense as a source for supporting the general role of the court, and judicial review in particular.[138]

While the use of foreign case law has since leached into South Africa's constitutional jurisprudence beyond the interpretation of the Bill of Rights permitted in s 39 of the Constitution, early predictions and fears that the Constitutional Court might uncritically follow foreign jurisprudence, and particularly that of the United States Supreme Court, have proven unfounded. Even in cases dealing with the interpretation of the Bill of Rights the Constitutional Court has urged caution when using foreign case law. In *Sanderson v Attorney-General, Eastern Cape*,[139] a case dealing with the right of an accused to be tried within a reasonable time, the Constitutional Court argued that

'[c]omparative research is generally valuable, and is all the more so when dealing with problems new to our jurisprudence but well developed in mature constitutional democracies... Nevertheless the use of foreign precedent requires circumspection and acknowledgement that transplants require careful management. Thus, for example, one should not resort to the *Barker* test [US] or the *Morin* [Canadian] approach [which are triggered by the passage of time, involve balancing factors to decide whether a speedy trial has been denied and as a remedy impose a ban on continued prosecution] without recognizing that our society and our criminal justice system differ from those in North America. Nor should one, for instance, adopt the assertion of right requirement of *Barker* without making allowance for the fact that the vast majority of South African accused are unrepresented and have no conception of a right to a speedy trial. To deny them relief... because they did not assert their rights would be to strike a pen through the right as far as the most vulnerable members of our society are concerned.'[140]

This circumspection is even more evident in non-Bill of Rights cases. In such cases the Constitutional Court has been quick to point to differences in 'constitutional language and structure, as well as history and culture' as reasons for the Court to be fairly circumspect.[141] In one of the first cases dealing with the distribution of powers between the national and regional governments, involving a dispute over the National Education Policy Bill which was then before the National Assembly, the Constitutional Court drew heavily on Australian and Canadian jurisprudence yet explicitly warned against the relevance of the federal experience in the United States. This case was brought as a case of abstract review, in which a law's constitutionality may be challenged on its face by particular constitutionally-defined litigants, such as the President or Premier of a Province,

---

[137] *Makwanyane* (n 102) para 38. [138] For example ibid para 14, 15, 17, 18, and 89.
[139] 1998 (2) SA 38 (CC). [140] ibid para 26.
[141] See RC Blake 'The Frequent Irrelevance of US Judicial Decisions in South Africa' (1999) 15 *South African Journal on Human Rights* 192 197.

before a specific case arises. The petitioners focused on the claim that the 'Bill imposed national education policy on the provinces'[142] and thereby 'encroached upon the autonomy of the provinces and their executive authority.'[143] They also claimed that the 'Bill could have no application in KwaZulu-Natal because it [the province] was in a position to formulate and regulate its own policies.'[144] While all parties accepted that education was defined as a concurrent legislative function under the interim Constitution, the contending parties imagined that different consequences should flow from the determination that a subject matter is concurrently assigned by the Constitution to both provincial and national government.

KwaZulu-Natal, and the Inkatha Freedom Party which then held the majority of seats in the regional legislature, assumed a form of US-style preemption doctrine in which the National Assembly and national government would be precluded from acting in an area of concurrent jurisdiction so long as the province was capable of formulating and regulating its own policies. In rejecting this argument the Constitutional Court avoided the notion of preemption altogether and instead argued that the 'legislative competences of the provinces and Parliament to make laws in respect of schedule 6 [concurrent] matters do not depend upon section 126(3),' which the Court argued only comes into operation if it is necessary to resolve a conflict between inconsistent national and provincial laws.[145] The Court thus rejected the notion of preemption as a valid interpretation of the relationship between national and regional powers, and instead argued that cooperative governance allowed for coexistence, and even some dissonance, in the exercise of concurrent jurisdiction, so long as there is not an irreconcilable conflict. Even if there is irreconcilable conflict and the 'conflict is resolved in favour of either the provincial or national law the other is not invalidated' it is merely 'subordinated and to the extent of the conflict rendered inoperative.'[146] Supported by the comparative jurisprudence of Canada and Australia, the Court was able to make a distinction between 'laws that are inconsistent with each other and laws that are inconsistent with the Constitution'[147] and thereby argue that 'even if the National Education Policy Bill deals with matters in respect of which provincial laws would have paramountcy, it could not for that reason alone be declared unconstitutional.'[148]

While the Constitutional Court's approach clearly aimed to reduce the tensions inherent in the continuing conflict between provincial and national governments, particularly in relation to the continuing violent tensions in KwaZulu-Natal, it also took the opportunity to explicitly preclude an alternative interpretation. Focusing on argument before the Court which relied upon the United States Supreme Court's decision in *New York v United States*[149] the Court made the point

---

[142] *Ex Parte Speaker of the National Assembly: In Re Dispute Concerning the Constitutionality of Certain Provisions of the National Education Policy Bill 83 of 1995*, 1996 (3) SA 289, para 8 [hereinafter *National Education Bill Case*].   [143] ibid.

[144] ibid.   [145] *National Education Bill Case* (n 142) para 16.   [146] ibid.

[147] ibid.   [148] ibid para 20.   [149] 505 U.S. 144 (1992).

that '[u]nlike their counterparts in the United States of America, the provinces in South Africa are not sovereign states.'[150] Furthermore the Court warned that '[d]ecisions of the courts of the United States dealing with state rights are not a safe guide as to how our courts should address problems that may arise in relation to the rights of provinces under our Constitution.'[151]

Modes of Interpretation

Despite Kentridge J's admonishment in the *Zuma* case that 'the Constitution does not mean whatever we might wish it to mean,' and that '[i]f the language used by the lawgiver is ignored in favour of a general resort to 'values' the result is not interpretation but divination,' he nevertheless recognized that a constitution 'embodying fundamental principles should *as far as its language permits* be given a broad construction.'[152] This emphasis on the ordinary meaning of the language of the Constitution has raised some concern that the inherent positivism of South African lawyers may restrict, or serve as a drag on, the interpretative project so central to the transformative potential of the Constitution.[153] However, this concern is counterbalanced by the Constitutional Court's own assertion in the very next case that 'whilst paying due regard to the language that has been used,' the process of interpretation should be both generous and purposive, so as to give 'expression to the underlying values of the Constitution.'[154] It is this broader approach to constitutional interpretation that has marked the jurisprudence of the Constitutional Court thus far.

Generous Interpretation

In its first decision the Constitutional Court drew on the judgment of Lord Wilberforce in *Minister of Home Affairs (Bermuda) v Fisher*[155] to argue that a generous interpretation of rights is an appropriate approach to take as it 'gives to individuals the full measure of the fundamental rights and freedoms' guaranteed in the Bill of Rights.[156] The significance of this approach was made evident in another early case under the 'interim' Constitution when petitioners, whose cases had commenced before the adoption of the Constitution, attempted to claim their rights under the Constitution. A simple response to their claim, advocated by a minority of the Justices on the Constitutional Court, was to adopt a plain meaning approach and to deny their claims on the grounds that s 241(8) of the 'interim' Constitution stated in clear language that 'pending cases shall be dealt

---

[150] *National Education Bill Case* (n 142) para 23.　　　[151] ibid.

[152] *S v Zuma* 1995 (2) SA 642 (CC) para 17.

[153] See D Davis, *Democracy and Deliberation: Transformation and the South African Legal Order* (Juta Kenwyn, South Africa, 1999) 24–30.　　　[154] *Makwanyane* (n 102) para 9.

[155] *Minister of Home Affairs (Bermuda) v Fisher* [1980] AC 319 (PC).　　　[156] ibid 328–9.

with as if the Constitution had not been passed.'[157] The majority of the Court however rejected this approach. Justice Mahomed, for the majority, once again citing Lord Wilberforce, argued that constitutional interpretation must avoid 'the austerity of tabulated legalism' and that an 'interpretation which withholds the rights guaranteed by [the Bill of Rights] . . . from those involved in proceedings which fortuitously commenced before the operation of the Constitution would not give to [the Bill of Rights] . . . a construction which is 'most beneficial to the widest amplitude' and should therefore be avoided if the language and context of the relevant sections reasonably permits such a course.'[158]

While the choice of this approach, which simply prefers a broad interpretation of rights over a narrow interpretation, may be explained as part of the response to the previous denial of rights which characterized South African legal history, it has also been argued that this approach may be inherent in the two-phase analysis of rights that occurs in the context of a general limitations clause. Instead of having to restrict the scope of a right out of a concern that a broad reading will have implications beyond the circumstances of the case being decided, the Court is able, according to this argument, 'to adopt a broad construction of the right in the first (interpretative) stage of the enquiry, then . . . require the state or the person relying on the validity of the infringement to justify the infringement in the limitation stage of the litigation.'[159] Although the Constitutional Court continues to apply a generous interpretation[160] it also tends, when confronted with a conflict between a generous and purposive interpretation, to 'demarcate the right in terms of its purpose.'[161]

Purposive Interpretation

In addition to a generous interpretation, the Constitutional Court has repeatedly referred to the necessity of adopting a purposive approach to the interpretation of rights. The essence of this approach involves identifying the core values underlying the inclusion of a particular right in the Bill of Rights and to adopt an interpretation of the right that 'best supports and protects those values.'[162] This approach is also closely linked to a contextual understanding of the interpretative project. This linkage of purpose and context has at times made a profound impact on the scope of the right at issue and not always with the effect of expanding the right. While the Constitutional Court's development of the right to equality has clearly been enhanced by the Court's exploration of the linkages between the rights of dignity and equality, both in defining the purpose of equal treatment as the basis for individual dignity, and by emphasizing the contextual relationship of

---

[157] *S v Mhlungu* 1995 (3) SA 391 (CC) para 78.   [158] ibid para 9.
[159] Waal, Currie and Erasmus (n 66) 134.
[160] See *South African National Defence Force Union v Minister of Defence* 1999 (4) SA 469 (CC) para 28.   [161] Waal, Currie and Erasmus (n 66) 135.
[162] ibid 131.

the rights to dignity and equality in the constitutional text, the effect on the concepts of freedom and particular social and economic rights, such as health and education, have been less expansive.

In the first instance the Constitutional Court rejected an expansive reading of the right to freedom advocated by Justice Ackermann in *Ferreria v Levin*.[163] The majority of the Court in that case argued that in the text of the Constitution the right to freedom was placed alongside the rights not to be subject to detention without trial, torture or other forms of cruel, inhuman and degrading punishment, thus indicating that the core purpose of the right was to protect an individual's physical liberty. This purposive interpretation was relied upon to reject Ackermann J's definition of the right to freedom as a residual right of individuals not to have obstacles to their choices and activities placed in their way by the state.[164] Instead of a broad libertarian interpretation the right to freedom was thus anchored in the older tradition of freedom from physical restraint that is rooted in the common law jurisprudence of liberty. Thus a combined analysis of the textual context and a purposive interpretation of the right to freedom in effect restricted the scope of the right's interpretation.

Again, while it might be possible to conceptualize rights to life or education in broad purposive terms—including access to a dialysis machine for a patient who would likely die if access were denied, or requiring the provision of public education in accordance with the language, cultural and even religious convictions of communities in a multi-cultural society—the Constitutional Court has relied on the interaction of purpose and context to effectively constrain claims based on such broad readings of these rights. In the *Soobramoney* case,[165] the Court rejected such a broad definition of the right to life on the grounds that the state's positive obligations to provide access to health care are contained in s 27 and therefore the Court could not interpret the right to life to impose additional obligations [on the state] that were inconsistent with s 27.[166]

A similar strategy was adopted by Mahomed J who argued in the *Gauteng School Education Bill*[167] case that the fact that the 'interim' Constitution had separate clauses guaranteeing publically funded basic education in the language of choice where practicable on the one hand and another clause guaranteeing freedom to establish educational institutions based on culture, language or religion on the other, precluded a claim by parents who demanded a publicly funded school to serve the needs of a particular cultural, language and religious community. In his analysis of the right, Mahomed J noted both the textual context of the clause—as distinct from the clause guaranteeing funding—and argued that a purposive interpretation of the right did not require the guarantee of state

---

[163] *Ferreira v Levin NO* 1996 (1) SA 984 (CC).   [164] ibid para 69.

[165] *Soobramoney v Minister of Health* (KwaZulu-Natal) 1998 (1) SA 765 (CC).

[166] See Waal, Currie and Erasmus (n 66) 139 and *Soobramoney* (n 165) para 15.

[167] *Ex parte Gauteng Provincial Legislature: in re Dispute Concerning the Constitutionality of Certain Provisions of the Gauteng School Education Policy Bill 83 of 1995*, 1996 (3) SA 617 (CC).

resources in order for the right to serve its goal. Thus, he concluded, the right,

'is neither superfluous nor tautologous. It preserves an important freedom. The constitutional entrenchment of that freedom is particularly important because of our special history initiated during the fifties, in terms of the system of Bantu education. From that period the State actively discouraged and effectively prohibited private educational institutions from establishing or continuing private schools and insisted that such schools had to be established and administered subject to the control of the State. The execution of these policies constituted an invasion of the right of individuals in association with one another to establish and continue, at their own expense, their own educational institutions based on their own values. Such invasions would now be constitutionally impermissible....'[168]

As a result the applicants had no right to public funded schools to serve particular cultural, language or religious needs but, instead, a more limited right to establish their own schools with their own resources. In effect then, the interpretative effect of the emphasis on context and purpose is to limit the scope of the right under consideration.

Positive Obligations and Accountability

Distinct from each other, but so far closely related in the Court's jurisprudence, has been the interpretation of rights as imposing not only negative but also positive obligations on the government, and the Court's emphasis on the 'accountability of those exercising public power [as] ... one of the founding values'[169] of the new constitutional order. While the negative interpretation of rights is considered quite standard, the Court's embrace of the notion that rights impose a positive obligation on the state brings it closer to the jurisprudence of the German Constitutional Court and the European Court on Human Rights, as compared to the United States Supreme Court which has eschewed such an approach. In two cases, dealing respectively with challenges to the Prevention of Family Violence Act, and the dismissal of a civil case brought by a women who had been assaulted by an awaiting trial sex-offender granted bail on the advice of the police, the Constitutional Court has focused on the positive obligations imposed by constitutional rights. In *S v Baloyi* the Court found that the statute, when read in terms of the state's constitutional duty to 'respect, protect, promote and fulfill the rights in the Bill of Rights,'[170] obliged the 'State directly to protect the right of everyone to be free from private or domestic violence.'[171] Focusing on the rights to life, dignity, freedom and security of person the Court argued in *Carmichele v Minister of Safety and Security* that in 'some circumstances there would also be a positive component which obliges the State and its organs to provide appropriate

---

[168] ibid para 8.
[169] *Rail Commuters Action Group et al v Transnet Ltd t/a Metrorail et. al., CCT 56/03*, decided on 26 November 2004, para 74 [hereinafter *Rail Commuters*].   [170] 1996 Constitution s 7(2).
[171] *S v Baloyi*, 2000 (2) SA 425 (CC) para 11.

protection to everyone through laws and structures designed to afford such protection.'[172]

Most recently the state's positive obligation to provide protection to citizens, and the requirement that government and organs of state be accountable for their conduct, was upheld by the Court in a case which arose out of the intersection of government's policy of privatization and the escalating crime rate which has been a feature of post-apartheid South Africa. The case, *Rail Commuters Action Group v Transnet Ltd t/a Metrorail*,[173] was brought by rail commuters in the Western Cape who argued that a publically traded company in which the state is the only shareholder bore responsibility, together with the police, to protect passengers from crime on the trains. While O'Regan J recognized that the principle of accountability 'may not always give rise to a legal duty whether in private or public law,'[174] and that 'private law claims are not always the most appropriate method to enforce constitutional rights,'[175] she nevertheless concluded that the rail company, as an organ of state, bore a positive obligation 'to ensure that reasonable measurers are in place to provide for the security of rail commuters. . . . regardless of who may be implementing them. . . .'

Duty to Develop the Common Law and Customary Law

One of the central aspects of the *Carmichele* decision was the holding that 'where the common law deviates from the spirit, purport and objects of the Bill of Rights, the courts have an obligation to develop it by removing that deviation,'[176] and 'that this duty upon judges arises in respect both of the civil and criminal law, whether or not the parties in any particular case request the court to develop the common law'[177] as provided for in s 39(2) of the Constitution. While some have argued that this provision has more to do with the application of the Constitution rather then its interpretation,[178] it clearly holds major implications for the Court's interpretative project and the meaning the Bill of Rights will have in ordinary people's lives. This has been demonstrated most recently in cases involving the definition of marriage and the question of whether the principle of primogeniture, in the context of the customary law of succession, could be saved from constitutional invalidity.

In the first case,[179] two women approached the High Court requesting that the common law of marriage be developed in accordance with the Constitution's enshrinement of equality on the ground of sexual orientation, so as to allow them to marry. When their application was dismissed they appealed to the Supreme

---

[172] 2001 (4) SA 938 (CC) para 44.   [173] *Rail Commuters* (n 169).   [174] ibid para 78.
[175] ibid para 80.   [176] *Carmichele* (n 172) para 33.   [177] ibid para 34.
[178] See Waal, Currie & Erasmus (n 66) 143.
[179] *Marie Adriaana Fourie, Cecelia Johanna Bonthuys and Minister of Home Affairs, Director-General of Home Affairs and Lesbian and Gay Equality Project*, Supreme Court of Appeal of South Africa, Case no: 232/2003, decided 30 November 2004 [hereinafter *Fourie*].

Court of Appeal. There Justice Cameron held in accordance with the constitutional obligation to develop the common law and the 'strides that our equality jurisprudence has taken in respect of gays and lesbians in the last ten years,'[180] that the common law concept of marriage is developed to embrace same-sex partners as follows: 'Marriage is the union of two persons to the exclusion of all others for life.'"[181] In the second case,[182] the Constitutional Court consolidated a group of cases in which the 'customary' law of succession had led to the exclusion of female children, wives and sisters in the distribution of deceased estates. While the majority of the Court proceeded to declare the 'customary' law rule of primogenitor in violation of the constitutional right to gender equality, Justice Ngcobo argued that in his view 'the rule of male primogeniture should be developed in order to bring it in line with the rights in the Bill of Rights.'[183] Rejecting the majority's preference to have the common law-based Intestate Succession Act apply until there is legislative reform of indigenous law, Justice Ngcobo suggested that first, customary law could continue to apply where the parties agreed and in the event of a dispute the Magistrate Court having jurisdiction should consider what 'the most appropriate system of law to be applied' should be. In doing so, he argued, 'the Magistrate must have regard to what is fair, just and equitable' paying 'particular regard to the interest of the minor children and any other dependant of the deceased.'[184]

Internal Directives for Interpretation

Apart from specific definitional clauses, and the specific requirements of the limitations clause in the Bill of Rights, there are a number of other specific guides to interpretation in the Constitution. First, there are limitations internal to specific rights in the Bill of Rights, most obviously the clauses providing that freedom of expression does not extend to: propaganda for war; incitement of imminent violence; or advocacy of hatred that is based on race, ethnicity, gender or religion, and that constitutes incitement to cause harm.[185] Second, the Bill of Rights includes explicit, interpretative provisions outlining the source of values and law to be considered by the Constitutional Court in interpreting the Bill of Rights as well as the requirement that every court, tribunal or forum must, when interpreting any legislation or developing either the common law or customary law, 'promote the spirit, purpose and objects of the Bill of Rights.' Finally, the Constitution includes four specific sets of principles on: co-operative government and intergovernmental relations;[186] the establishment and governing of state

---

[180] ibid para 12.   [181] ibid para 49.
[182] *Nonkululeko Letta Bhe et al v Magistrate, Khayelitsha et al,* CCT 49/03; *Charlotte Shibi v Mantabeni Freddy Sithole et al,* CCT 69/03; *South African Human Rights Commission et al v President of the Republic of South Africa et al,* CCT 50/03, decided 15 October 2004 [hereinafter *Bhe*].
[183] ibid para 139.   [184] ibid para 240.   [185] S 16(2)(a)-(c).
[186] Section 41(1)(a)-(h) and 41(2)-(4).

institutions supporting constitutional democracy;[187] basic values and principles governing public administration;[188] and principles governing national security.[189]

While these principles are called upon to play a symbolic and pedagogical role in shaping the behavior of government departments and officials, both internally and in their relations with other governing units, the Constitutional Court has also begun to apply them in related cases. Asked to confirm a High Court declaration of unconstitutionality, in a case in which district municipalities claimed they had been excluded from receiving equitable fiscal allotments by the Division of Revenue Act 1 2001, the Constitutional Court reviewed the constitutional requirements of co-operative government in deciding whether to exercise its discretion to confirm the High Court's decision despite the parties' settlement of the case.[190] In reaching its decision the Court held that organs of state have a 'constitutional duty to foster co-operative government' and that the essence of Ch 3 of the Constitution is that 'disputes should where possible be resolved at a political level rather than through adversarial litigation.'[191] In fact, the Court argued, the requirements of co-operative government include a duty to 'avoid legal proceedings against one another,' a duty which the courts must ensure is duly performed.[192] More specifically, the Court stated that 'apart from the general duty to avoid legal proceedings against one another,' there is a two-fold duty obliging organs of state in an intergovernmental dispute to both 'make every reasonable effort to settle the dispute by means of mechanisms and procedures provided for,' and to 'exhaust all other remedies before they approach a court to resolve the dispute.'[193]

Problems of Interpretation

While South Africa has witnessed a decade of extraordinary transformation, from apartheid to democracy, with a united country enjoying a level of peace and political stability unimaginable in 1992, the stark inequalities and levels of abject poverty which frame the experiences of the majority of South Africans remain all too familiar. It is with this reality in mind that Chief Justice Pius Langa, then Deputy-Chief Justice of the Constitutional Court, has expressed concern that the Constitution must be relevant to the experience of ordinary South Africans. Justice Langa's concern is twofold: on the one hand he is concerned about the relationship between indigenous institutions and culture and the inherited forms of western law and constitutionalism; while on the other hand, he is worried about the disjuncture between the promises of legal rights contained in the Constitution and the truncated reality of law in action as it is experienced by the vast majority of citizens. Despite these concerns, the Constitutional Court has proceeded over the

---

[187] S 181(2)-(5).   [188] S 195 (1)(a)-(i).   [189] S 198(a)-(d).
[190] *Uthukela District Municipality v President of the Republic of South Africa*, CCT 7/02 (2002).
[191] ibid para 13.   [192] ibid.   [193] ibid para 19.

last decade to address some of the most difficult issues facing South Africa's new constitutional democracy, and while some if its judgments have been controversial—including its abolition of the death penalty—it has in this short time achieved an extraordinary status of respect, both nationally and globally. At the same time, the Court is only now beginning to face some of the more difficult issues posed by the new constitutional order—particularly issues arising out of the persistent levels of inequality and poverty as well as the place and role of indigenous law and traditional authorities—all of which will have profound implications for the future relevance, vibrancy and sustainability of the new order.

Certification and the Problem of Future Constitutional Amendments

The certification process, in which the Constitutional Court was required to certify that the constitutional text produced by the Constitutional Assembly met the conditions of the Constitutional Principles contained in Sch 4 of the 1993 'interim' Constitution was in some ways unique. However, it also raises issues of constitutional interpretation which may arise in the future in the context of challenges to duly enacted constitutional amendments similar to those that have been reflected in the 'basic structure' jurisprudence of the Indian Supreme Court. Declaring that it was unable to certify the text of the final constitution, despite its adoption—after last minute political compromises—by 86 per cent of the democratically-elected Constitutional Assembly, was an extraordinary assertion of the power of judicial review. Yet, the Constitutional Court's denial of certification was far more measured and subtly crafted than this bold assertion of 'unconstitutionality' implies. In fact the Constitutional Court was careful to point out in its unanimous, unattributed, opinion, that 'in general and in respect of the overwhelming majority of its provisions,' the Constitutional Assembly had met the predetermined requirements of the Constitutional Principles. In effect then, this was a very limited and circumscribed ruling. As a result the main political parties rejected attempts to use the denial of certification as a tool to reopen debates, instead the Constitutional Assembly focused solely on the issues raised by the Constitutional Court and passed an Amended Text within a short period of two months.[194]

This outcome was implicit in the Court's handling of its own role in the certification process. Instead of trumpeting its constitutional duty to review the work of the Constitutional Assembly, the Court was careful to point out that the Constitutional Assembly had a large degree of latitude in its interpretation of the principles, and that the role of the Constitutional Court was a judicial, and not a political, role. While this may be dismissed as posturing by a Court determined to hide behind legalism, in fact this deference to the democratic constitution-making process shaped the Court's approach to its task. In defining its mode of

---

[194] C Madlala 'Final fitting for the cloth of nationhood' *Sunday Times* 13 Oct 1996 4.

review the Court specifically identified two separate questions. First, the Court would examine whether the 'basic structures and premises of the [New Text] NT [was in] ... accordance with those contemplated in the CPs [constitutional principles].' Conducting this inquiry the Court established a minimum threshold which the Constitutional Assembly had to meet and found that in fact the New Text satisfied those standards. The significance of this approach is that despite arguments that the certification judgements are unique, in fact the Court is granted jurisdiction and called upon in the final Constitution to determine the constitutionality of any future Constitutional Amendment.[195] Significantly, at least two Justices of the Constitutional Court have made reference to the notion of the basic structure of the Constitution used by the Indian Supreme Court in its jurisprudence striking down validly enacted Constitutional Amendments. To this extent the Constitutional Assembly and the Court have left open the future of the Court's role in the formal amending process under the final Constitution.

Second, the Court's methodology held that only once the Court decided that the New Text accorded with the basic structure and premises would the court turn to an analysis of whether the details of the New Text complied with the Constitutional Principles. Turning to a detailed analysis of the content of the New Text the Court both asserted its power and duty to ensure compliance by testing the text against the Constitutional Principles, yet was also very careful to limit the scope of this review. This limiting strategy was accomplished by asserting the formal legal distinction between politics and law.[196] The Court noted that it 'has a judicial and not a political mandate' and that this 'judicial function, a legal exercise' meant that the Court had 'no power, no mandate and no right to express any view on the political choices made by the CA in drafting the NT'.[197] While the Court asserted that its interpretation of the Constitutional Principles was consistent with its jurisprudential commitment to a purposive and teleological application which gives expression to the commitment to 'create a new order' based on a 'Sovereign and democratic constitutional state' in which 'all citizens' are 'able to enjoy and exercise their fundamental rights and freedoms',[198] it also asserted that the Court was not concerned with the merits of the choices made by the Constitutional Assembly. In fact, the Court emphasized the scope of the Constitutional Assembly's latitude by arguing that while the new text 'may not

---

[195] Constitution of the Republic of South Africa 1996 s 167(4)(d).

[196] This strategy of judicial deference is interesting in a context where the Constitutional Assembly had, in its drafting of the new text, gone so far as to incorporate the precise language of Constitutional Court opinions where the Court had expressly addressed a constitutional question— for example, in the Constitutional Assembly's reformulation of the limitations clause so as to exclude the notion, derived from the German Basic Law, of the essential content of the right. Furthermore, despite popular political pressure to rescind the Court's holding against the death penalty the Constitutional Assermbly merely retained the previous formulation of the right relied upon by the Court in that case.

[197] *Ex parte Chairperson of the Constitutional Assembly: In re Certification of the Constitution of the Republic of South Africa*, 1996, 1996 (4) SA 744 (CC) para 27.

[198] *First Certification Judgment* paras 34–35.

transgress the fundamental discipline of the CPs... within the space created by those CPs interpreted purposively, the issue as to which of several permissible models should be adopted is not an issue for adjudication by this Court. That is a matter for the political judgment of the CA, and therefore properly falling within its discretion...'[199]

In contrast to this show of deference, however, the Court took a robust approach to its own judicial role of establishing legal precedent. Faced with the dilemma of alternative constructions in which one interpretation could be held to be in violation of the Constitutional Principles, the Court adopted the traditional judicial strategy of upholding that interpretation which would avoid a declaration of unconstitutionality. This raised the specter of a future Court revisiting the issue and adopting an interpretation which would be in violation of the Constitutional Principles. In this 'judicial' context the Court claimed the power to bind the future, holding that a 'future court should approach the meaning of the relevant provision of the NT on the basis that the meaning assigned... in the certification process... should not be departed from save in the most compelling circumstances.'[200] The Court took a similarly robust attitude to its judicial role in its second certification judgment when the Court certified the 'final' Constitution.[201] In this case the Court was faced with attempts by political parties and other interested groups to reopen issues which had not been identified as the basis for the Court's refusal to certify in the first round of the certification process. While accepting these challenges the Court noted the 'sound jurisprudential basis for the policy that a court should adhere to its previous decisions unless they are clearly wrong... [and that] having regard to the need for finality in the certification process and in view of the virtual identical composition of the Court that considered the questions barely three months ago, that policy is all the more desirable here.'[202] As a result the Court made it clear that a party wishing to extend the Court's review beyond those aspects identified in the first certification judgment would have a 'formidable task.' Through this reliance on a classic judicial strategy of deference to past decisions, the Court was able to significantly limit the scope of its role in the final certification judgment. It was this change in posture towards the certification process and the fact that the Constitutional Assembly fully addressed all but one of the Court's concerns that ensured a swift certification on the second round.

Significantly, the Court now relied less on the specifics of the Constitutional Principles and more on the fundamental elements of constitutionalism contained in the text—'founding values which include human dignity, the achievement of equality, the recognition and advancement of human rights and freedoms, the supremacy of the Constitution and the rule of law.'[203] While the Court still had to

---

[199] *First Certification Judgment* para 39.   [200] ibid para 43.
[201] *Ex parte Chairperson of the Constitutional Assembly: In re Certification of the Amended Text of the Constitution of the Republic of South Africa*, 1996, 1997 (2) SA 97 (CC).
[202] *Second Certification Judgment* para 8.   [203] ibid para 25.

recognize that the powers and functions of the provinces—the most contentious issue in the whole constitution-making process—remained in dispute between the parties, the Court held in essence that the removal of the presumption of constitutional validity of bills passed by the NCOP had tipped the balance.[204] Thus despite the recognition that provincial powers and functions in the Amended Text remained less than, or inferior to, those accorded to the provinces in the Interim Constitution, these powers and functions were not substantially so[205] and therefore this deficit was no longer a basis for denying certification.

The Constitutional Court's review of the text was permeated with its own concerns over the institutional implications of South Africa's new constitutionalism. In fact many of the grounds upon which the Court declined to certify the first text had institutional implications for the Court. For example, the Court's demands to strengthen the procedures and threshold for amendment of the Bill of Rights, its striking down of attempts to insulate the labour clause from judicial review, and its reliance on the presumption that a bill passed by the NCOP could be presumed to indicate a national interest overriding separate regional interest to tip the balance against the adequacy of the basket of regional powers. In each of these instances the New Text would have allowed the legislature to circumvent or minimize the Court's role in protecting rights, reviewing labor laws or regulating the relationship between national and regional governments as promised by the interconnected notions of judicial review and constitutional supremacy. Thus the Court's approach to the new text indicated a profound concern with guaranteeing the institutional prerogatives of the Court. It was this imperative, to secure the role of the Court as guardian of a constitutional democracy based on the explicit foundations of constitutional supremacy, that weighed the balance in the first Certification judgment.

Interpreting the Bill of Rights within the Frame of Dignity, Equality and Freedom

Dignity, equality and freedom play a foundational role in South Africa's post-apartheid constitution. Not only are these rights individually protected and included as founding values of the Constitution, but they are reiterated as the basic criteria of any open and democratic society in which a limitation of a right would be justifiable, and are also cited as the basic principles underlying the values of a democratic society which must be promoted through the interpretation of rights. At the same time the Constitutional Court has recognized the inherent connectedness of these rights, both in their substantive interpretation and when used as markers of the underlying principles of the new society. However, this recognition poses a difficult challenge for the project of constitutional interpretation. On the one hand, the Court's jurisprudence has adopted the most

---

[204] *Second Certification Judgment* at paras 153–157.   [205] ibid para 204(e).

generous interpretation of individual rights to dignity, equality and freedom, while on the other hand it recognizes that the boundaries of constitutional rights are 'limited by every other right accruing to another citizen'[206] and 'by the legitimate needs of society.'[207] It has been possible for the Court to elevate the right to dignity, particularly in the context of equality where 'the constitutional protection of dignity requires us to acknowledge the value and worth of all individuals as members of our society.' But the Court's jurisprudence on freedom, with tensions between an atomistic conception of individual freedom and a broader notion of individuals exercising their freedom within the context of their membership in a community,[208] has proved more complex. In this sense, then, there is a tension in the interpretative visions of dignity, equality and freedom which inform the Constitutional Court's jurisprudence. Sometimes these are asserted as independent criteria while at other moments they are employed in combination or as a means to inform their respective or related content.

This tension may be illustrated by focusing on the right to dignity which the Court has declared to be, together with the right to life, 'the most important of all human rights, and the source of all other personal rights in the Bill of Rights.'[209] The high status of dignity in the constitutional order is justified first by the argument that the 'Constitution asserts dignity to contradict our past . . . [i]t asserts it too to inform the future, to invest in our democracy respect for the intrinsic worth of all human beings'.[210] In fact, there are no less than five specific references to human dignity in the 1996 Constitution. First, human dignity, together with 'equality and the advancement of human rights and freedoms' is one of the founding provisions contained in s 1. This section may only be amended by a 75 per cent majority of the National Assembly supported by six of the nine provinces— making it virtually unchangeable. Second, there are four separate references to human dignity within the Bill of Rights: as a key democratic value which the state is obliged to uphold; as an explicit substantive right; as a non-derogable right in the event of a state of emergency; and as a factor for the courts to consider in deciding whether a limitation of a right is reasonable and justifiable.

The foundational status of human dignity means that it serves also as a background principle in the interpretation and development of other rights. In this sense there is a close link between the foundational aspects of human dignity and the specific right to dignity in the Court's jurisprudence. Arguing that the death penalty violates the right to dignity, O'Regan J of the Constitutional Court argued that 'the importance of dignity as a founding value of the new Constitution cannot be overemphasized . . . [t]his right therefore is the foundation of many of the other rights that are specifically entrenched in [the Bill of Rights].'[211] The link between

---

[206] *Bernstein v Bester NO* 1996 (2) SA 751 (CC) para 67.

[207] Waal, Currie & Erasmus (n 66) 140.   [208] See Davis (n 150) 65.

[209] *Makwanyane* (n 102).

[210] *Dawood and Another v Minister of Home Affairs and Others* 2000 (3) SA 936 (CC) para 35.

[211] Makwanyane (n 102) para 328.

the foundational place of the notion of dignity and the recognition of a specific constitutional right to dignity makes it difficult to disentangle a right to dignity from the protection of various associated rights. In order to explore the parameters of this interaction I will divide the jurisprudence into three general categories: first, how the substantive right itself has shaped the outer limits of acceptable criminal sanctions; second, how the right is interconnected with the rights to freedom and equality; and third, how the right interacts with the control of information and speech rights. Finally, I will consider the interaction of dignity, equality and freedom in the Court's application of the limitations clause which provides for the justified limitations of rights in the Bill of Rights.

First, in the area of criminal sanctions the substantive right to dignity has had its most profound impact. The Constitutional Court has relied on the right to dignity to guide the Court's imposition of limits on the state's ability to punish criminals. Because the death penalty was not explicitly precluded in the constitution-making process it was left to the Constitutional Court to address the fate of the nearly 400 prisoners on death row at the time the constitution was adopted. In *S v Makwanyane*, the new Court's second decision, the Court struck down the death penalty on a number of grounds including human dignity. The Court's decision addresses the relationship between dignity and capital punishment in a number of different ways. While Chaskalson J, arguing for the majority of the Court, based his decision on the prohibition of cruel and unusual punishment, he cited both Brennan J's argument that 'the punishment of death ... treats members of the human race as nonhumans,' and the Canadian Supreme Court's decision in *Kindler v Canada* in which a minority of judges described the death penalty as 'the supreme indignity to the individual, the ultimate corporal punishment, the final and complete lobotomy and the absolute and irrevocable castration ... the ultimate desecration of human dignity'.[212] In a subsequent case challenging the sentence of juvenile whipping as cruel, inhuman and degrading, the court argued in part that it is reasonable to expect the state to be

'foremost in upholding those values which are the guiding light of civilized societies. Respect for human dignity is one such value; acknowledging it includes an acceptance by society that ... even the vilest criminal remains a human being possessed of common human dignity.'[213]

Most recently, the Court struck down the common law criminalization of sodomy as inconsistent with human dignity because as

'a result of the criminal offence, gay men are at risk of arrest, prosecution and conviction of the offence of sodomy simply because they seek to engage in sexual conduct which is part of their experience of being human. Just as apartheid legislation rendered the lives of couples of different racial groups perpetually at risk, the sodomy offence builds insecurity and vulnerability into the daily lives of gay men. There can be no doubt that the existence

---

[212] See Makwanyane (n 102) paras 57 and 60.
[213] *S v Williams* 1995 (3) SA 632 (CC) para 58.

of a law which punishes a form of sexual expression for gay men degrades and devalues gay men in our broader society. As such it is a palpable invasion of their dignity...'[214]

Second, the right to dignity is closely associated with the rights to freedom and equality. In the first instance, Ackerman J drew on the link between dignity and personhood to emphasize the importance of freedom. In *Ferreira v Levin* he argued that

'human dignity cannot be fully valued or respected unless individuals are able to develop their humanity, their humanness to the full extent of its potential. Each human being is uniquely talented. Part of the dignity of every human being is the fact and awareness of this uniqueness. An individual's human dignity cannot be fully respected or valued unless the individual is permitted to develop his or her unique talents optimally.'

He concluded that '[h]uman dignity has little value without freedom . . . to deny people freedom is to deny them their dignity.'[215] While Ackerman J's atomistic conception of freedom and dignity was rejected by the majority, the Court did accept that the right to human dignity will flourish in the context of the 'multiplicity of rights with which it is associated' in the Bill of Rights. This strain of dignity jurisprudence (in which the right exists in a symbiotic relationship to other rights) has played an increasingly important role in the Court's equality jurisprudence.

Both in its definition of unfair discrimination and in its description of the purpose of the new constitutional order the Constitutional Court has directly linked dignity and equality. The Court has adopted a specific three-stage enquiry, with a basic threshold test to decide whether there has been a differentiation between people or categories of people; followed by a two-step analysis of whether the differentiation amounts to discrimination and particularly unfair discrimination; and concluding with a determination of whether such unfair discrimination may be justified under the limitations clause.[216] Yet the very idea of unfair discrimination, and hence violation of the equality clause, remains linked to the concept of dignity. Addressing the question whether a differentiation made in the Forestry Act 1984 between owners of land within a fire control area and those outside the area amounted to a violation of the equality clause, the Constitutional Court argued in *Prinsloo v Van der Linde* that unfair discrimination 'principally means treating persons differently in a way which impairs their fundamental dignity as human beings, who are inherently equal in dignity,'[217] and held that such a differentiation 'cannot by any stretch of the imagination, be seen as impairing the dignity of the owner or occupier of land outside the fire control area.'[218] The linkage between dignity and equality was also made in a case upholding President Mandela's decision to grant special remission of sentence to 'mothers in prison on 10 May 1994, with minor children under the age of twelve

---

[214] *National Coalition for Gay and Lesbian Equality v Minister of Justice* 1999 (1) SA 6 (CC) para 28.
[215] *Ferreira v Levin* 1996 (1) SA 984 (CC) para 49.
[216] See *Harksen v Lane NO*, 1998 (1) SA 300 (CC) para 53.
[217] *Prinsloo v Van der Linde*, 1997 (3) SA 1012 (CC) para 31.   [218] ibid para 41.

years,'[219] while rejecting the claim that the decision discriminated against fathers in a similar position. In that case the Court argued that

'[a]t the heart of the prohibition of unfair discrimination lies a recognition that the purpose of our new constitutional and democratic order is the establishment of a society in which all human beings will be accorded equal dignity and respect regardless of their membership in particular groups. The achievement of such a society in the context of our deeply inegalitarian past will not be easy, but that that is the goal of the Constitution...'[220]

Third, the right to dignity has intersected quite dramatically with rights to information and freedom of expression. Here the right to dignity has been used by the Constitutional Court, in terms of its mandate in section 39(2) of the Constitution to 'promote the spirit, purport and objects of the Bill of Rights' when developing the common law, to rewrite the long established common law of defamation. The defendants to a defamation suit—a popular Sunday newspaper—argued for the adoption of the rule in *New York Times v Sullivan*, which would limit the ability of public figures to claim defamation unless the publisher acted with 'actual malice.'[221] Acknowledging that '[f]reedom of expression is integral to a democratic society' as it is 'constitutive of the dignity and autonomy of human beings,' the Court argued that the right to free speech must be 'construed in the context of the other values enshrined...[i]n particular, the values of human dignity, freedom and equality.'[222] Noting that the 'value of human dignity... values both the personal sense of self-worth as well as the public's estimation of the worth or value of an individual,' the Court rejected the *Sullivan* approach and instead asked whether an appropriate balance had been struck 'between the protection of freedom of expression on the one hand, and the value of human dignity on the other.'[223] The Court found this balance in a rule adopted by the Supreme Court of Appeals which developed the common law to allow a defamation case to be brought by a public official in order to protect the individual's dignity, but also allowed a defense of reasonable publication, in which the publisher only needs to demonstrate that either the statement was true and in the public interest (an existing common law defense) or that even if it was false that publication was 'reasonable in all the circumstances.'[224]

Finally, the 'limitations clause' of the Constitution directs that the 'rights in the Bill of Rights may be limited only in terms of law of general application to the extent that the limitation is reasonable and justifiable in an open and democratic society based on human dignity, equality and freedom. ...'[225] Human dignity, equality and freedom in this context define the type of society against which any infringement of a constitutional right must be compared. Again the Constitutional Court has effectively merged these three criteria in discussing the definition of

---

[219] Presidential Act No. 17, 27 June 1994.

[220] *President of the Republic of South Africa v Hugo* 1997 (4) SA 1 (CC) para 41.

[221] *Fred Khumalo et al v Bantubonke Harrington Holomisa*, Case CCT 53/01 decided by the Constitutional Court on 14 June 2002, para 40.   [222] ibid paras 21 & 25.

[223] ibid para 28.   [224] ibid para 44.   [225] Constitution of the RSA (1996) s 36(1).

such a society. In the *Hugo* case the Constitutional Court explicitly cites the Canadian Supreme Court's judgement in *Egan v Canada*, in which that Court 'recognized that inherent human dignity is at the heart of individual rights in a free and democratic society' and that the right to equality 'means nothing if it does not represent a commitment to recognizing each person's equal worth as a human being, regardless of individual differences.'[226] Applying the limitation clause in *S v Makwanyane* the Constitutional Court argued that the

'limitation of constitutional rights for a purpose that is reasonable and necessary in a democratic society involves the weighing up of competing values, and ultimately an assessment based on proportionality . . . which calls for the balancing of different interests. In the balancing process, the relevant considerations will include the nature of the right that is limited, and its importance to an open and democratic society based on freedom and equality; the extent of the limitation, its efficacy and . . . whether the desired ends could reasonably be achieved through other means less damaging to the right in question.'[227]

These criteria are now enshrined as relevant factors in the limitations clause of the 1996 Constitution and yet the process of applying the limitations clause essentially remains a balancing test. Describing its process of interpretation the Constitutional Court in *S v Bhulwana* states that

'the Court places the purpose, effects and importance of the infringing legislation on one side of the scales and the nature and effect of the infringement caused by the legislation on the other. The more substantial the inroad into fundamental rights, the more persuasive the grounds of justification must be.'[228]

Interpretation of Socio-economic Rights

Despite a growing recognition that all human rights are inextricably linked and interconnected, among lawyers there has traditionally been an ingrained skepticism about the possibility of judicially enforcing socio-economic rights. The inclusion of justiciable socio-economic rights in the 1996 Constitution has therefore both been heralded as a mark of its extraordinary status and raised questions about how these provisions would be interpreted in a situation of vast socio-economic inequalities and limited governmental capacity. Responding to concerns about the justiciability of these rights in the *First Certification* case the Constitutional Court rejected the rigid distinction between different types of rights and instead argued that '[a]t the very minimum, socio-economic rights can be negatively protected from improper invasion.' In the defining case addressing the scope of socio-economic rights— *Grootboom*—the Court was called upon to define both the negative and positive obligations that the constitutional right to housing imposed on the government.

---

[226] ibid. *President of the Republic of South Africa v Hugo* (n 218) para 41.
[227] ibid. *Makwanyane* (n 102) para 104.
[228] *S v Bhulwana*, 1996 (1) SA 388 (CC) para 18.

In *Government of the Republic of South Africa and others v Grootboom and others* the Court was required to review a local government's action in evicting squatters from private land that was to be used for low income housing. In the process of eviction the homes the squatters had erected were destroyed and much of their personal possessions and building material had also been deliberately destroyed. While the Constitutional Court upheld the claimant's argument that the municipality's action violated the negative obligation—the duty not to deprive them of shelter—owed to them under s 26(1), the Court proceeded to extrapolate on the positive duties placed on the state under s 26(2). Although the government was able to present a well documented national housing policy which met the obligation to 'take reasonable legislative and other measures, within its available resources, to achieve the progressive realization of this right,' the Court found that the failure to have a policy to address the needs for emergency shelter meant that the policy failed 'to respond to the needs of those most desperate' and thus was unreasonable.[229] At the same time however the Court emphasized that '[t]he precise contours and content of the measures to be adopted are primarily a matter for the legislature and executive' and stated that the Court 'will not enquire whether other more desirable or favourable measures could have been adopted, or whether public money could have been better spent.'[230]

Applying these arguments in the area of health and HIV/AIDS in particular posed a major problem for the Constitutional Court. In the *Treatment Action Campaign*[231] (TAC) case the Court was asked to require the government to provide one particular treatment—to provide the antiretroviral drug Nevirapine to HIV-positive women in childbirth and their newborn babies—and not merely to have a reasonable policy to address the overwhelming HIV/AIDS pandemic within the confines of the state's resources. The Court's decision to require the provision of Nevirapine marked an important extension of the principles laid out in *Grootboom* and an extraordinary reversal in the Court's approach to health rights, which only a short time earlier had seemed to be frozen by the combination of medical prerogatives and resource scarcity.

The 1996 Constitution's introduction of a constitutional right to health in a context of vast inequality and limited resources soon produced a tragic but classic confrontation between the health authorities and a patient who required access to renal dialysis in order to prolong his life. When the *Soobramoney* case[232] reached the Constitutional Court, it denied his claim, drawing a distinction between the right not to be refused emergency medical treatment in terms of s 27(3) and the progressive realization of the right to health care guaranteed in s 27(1). In rejecting his claim of a right to receive treatment the Constitutional Court in effect recognized that certain medical decisions—in that case the decision to limit access to a dialysis machine to those patients whose medical condition made them eligible to receive kidney transplants—are best made by medical personnel and should

---

[229] 2001 (1) SA 46 (CC) para 44. [hereinafter *Grootboom*]
[230] ibid para 41.   [231] 2002 (5) SA 721 (CC).   [232] *Soobramoney* (n 165).

not be second-guessed by the courts.[233] In the *TAC* case the Constitutional Court essentially by-passed this decision by upholding a High Court decision requiring the government to provide mothers and new-borns in public health facilities access to Nevirapine, a drug which reduces the likelihood of mother-to-child transmission of HIV at birth. Relying on the constitutional guarantee of a right to the progressive realization of access to health care services, the Constitutional Court argued that under the circumstances, in which the cost of Nevirapine and the provision of appropriate testing and counseling to mothers was less burdensome to the state then the failure to provide the drug, the government had a constitutional duty to expand its program beyond the test sites already planned.

Here the Court rejected the government's attempt to draw an analogy between the 'medical decision' in the *Soobramoney* case and the question of whether Nevirapine should be made available beyond the 18 test sites established by health authorities. While the medical status of individuals who need kidney transplants might be a simple medical question, the lower court essentially held that the issue of whether public sector doctors may prescribe a registered drug, where medically indicated, is not. Even if the relationship between the availability of donated kidneys and the possibility of a successful transplant, as determined by the health condition of the donee, may be considered a medical question, the issue of whether it makes sense to provide a particular patient or group of patients with a particular treatment, available to others in a similar medical situation, is not solely a medical judgment. In its judgment the Constitutional Court held that where the public sector is failing to provide a particular treatment regime, medically indicated and available in the private sector, then the issue is clearly one of health policy and resources and thus implicates the progressive realization of the right to health care services. Here the Court was building on its central decision in the *Grootboom* case in which it placed a review of the reasonableness of government policy and implementation at the center of its socio-economic rights jurisprudence.

Interpretation of Regional and Concurrent Powers

As was the case under the interim Constitution, tensions between the central ANC government and non-ANC controlled provinces soon brought cases to the Constitutional Court in which it was called upon to define the parameters of cooperative government. Although wide-ranging in scope these early cases have addressed three issues central to the question of legislative authority under the 1996 Constitution. First, the Court was called upon to define the constitutional allocation of legislative power in a case in which the province claimed implied legislative powers to define the structure of its own civil service. Second, the Court was required to determine the scope of residual national legislative power in a

---

[233] *Soobramoney* (n 165) paras 3, 4, and 32–34.

case where the national government claimed concurrent authority over the establishment of municipal governments despite the Constitution's simultaneous allocation in this field of specific functions to different institutions and spheres of government. Finally, an attempt by the national government to extensively regulate liquor production, sale and consumption, a field in which the regions were granted at least some exclusive powers under the Constitution, required the Court to define the specific content of the exclusive legislative powers of the provinces.

One of the first such cases involved a challenge to national legislation which sought to define the structure of the public service, including all provincial public services. The Western Cape argued that the legislation infringed 'the executive power vested in the provinces by the Constitution and detracts from the legitimate autonomy of the provinces recognized in the Constitution.'[234] The Court however pointed to the fact that not only did the national Constitution provide that the public service is to be structured in accordance with national legislation, but also that the Western Cape Constitution required the Western Cape government to implement legislation in accordance with the provisions of the national constitution.[235]

Describing national framework legislation as a feature of the system of cooperative government provided for by the Constitution, the Court noted that such legislation

'is required for the raising and division of revenue, the preparation of budgets at all spheres of government, treasury control, procurements by organs of state, conditions according to which governments at all spheres may guarantee loans, the remuneration of public officials at all spheres of government and various other matters.'[236]

While the Court agreed that provincial governments are empowered to 'employ, promote, transfer and dismiss' personnel in the provincial administrations of the public service,' it rejected the idea of an implied provincial power depriving the national government of its 'competence to make laws for the structure and functioning of the civil service as a whole,' which is expressly retained in s 197(1) of the Constitution.[237]

Turning to consider whether the national government's structuring of the public service encroached on the 'geographical, functional or institutional integrity' of the provincial government in violation of s 41(1)(g), the Court considered the provisions of Ch 3 of the Constitution dealing with cooperative government. The Court's interpretation of these provisions emphasized the description of all spheres of government being 'distinctive, inter-dependent and inter-related,' yet went on to point out that the 'national legislature is more powerful than other legislatures, having a legislative competence in respect of any matter,' and that the 'national government is also given overall responsibility for ensuring that other

---

[234] *The Premier of the Province of the Western Cape v The President of the Republic of South Africa and the Minister of Public Service*, CCT 26/98 (1999), 1999 (12) BCLR 1360 (CC) para 4.
[235] *Public Service Case* para 8.   [236] ibid para 9.   [237] ibid para 11.

spheres of government carry out their obligations under the Constitution.'[238] While the Court accepted that the purpose of s 41(1)(g) is to prevent one sphere of government from using its power to undermine other spheres of government and preventing them from functioning effectively, it concluded that the section 'is concerned with the way power is exercised, not whether or not a power exists.'[239] The relevant question before the Court in this case however was whether the national government had the constitutional power to structure the public service.[240] Finding that indeed the power vests in the national sphere of government, the Court emphasized that the Constitutional Principles 'contemplated that the national government would have powers that transcend provincial boundaries and competences' and that 'legitimate provincial autonomy does not mean that the provinces can ignore [the constitutional] framework or demand to be insulated from the exercise of such power.'[241] The Court did however strike down a clause in the law empowering the national minister to direct a provincial official to transfer particular functions to another department (provincial or national) because such power encroached on the ability of the provinces to carry out the functions entrusted to them by the Constitution.

Although the Court seemed to come down strongly in favor of national legislative authority, at least when it is explicitly granted in the Constitution, the question of the allocation of legislative authority soon arose again, this time in the context of a dispute between the national government and the regional governments of the Western Cape and KwaZulu-Natal.[242] The provincial governments in this case challenged provisions of the Local Government: Municipal Structures Act 117 1998 in which the national government claimed residual concurrent powers to determine the structure of local government, despite the provisions of the local government Chapter of the Constitution which set out a comprehensive scheme for the allocation of powers between the national, provincial and local levels of government. Considering this allocation of power, the Court recognized that the Constitution left residual legislative powers to the national sphere. But the Court also determined that s 155 of the Constitution—which controls the establishment of local governments—allocates powers and functions between different spheres of government and the independent demarcation board so that:

'(a) the role of the national government is limited to establishing criteria for determining different categories of municipality, establishing criteria and procedures for determining municipal boundaries, defining different types of municipalities that may be established within each category, and making provision for how powers and functions are to be divided between municipalities with shared powers; (b) the power to determine municipal boundaries vests solely in the Demarcation Board; and (c) the role of the provincial

---

[238] *Public Service Case* para 18 and 19.   [239] ibid para 23.   [240] ibid para 23 and 24.
[241] ibid para 25.
[242] *The Executive Council of the Province of the Western Cape v The Minister for Provincial Affairs and Constitutional Development of the Republic of South Africa; Executive Council of KwaZulu-Natal v the President of the Republic of South Africa and Others*, 1999 (12) BCLR 1360 (CC).

government is limited to determining the types of municipalities that may be established within the province, and establishing municipalities 'in a manner consistent with the [national] legislation enacted in terms of subsections (2) and (3)'.[243]

Applying this scheme to the challenged legislation the court found unconstitutional the attempt in s 13 of the Municipal Structures Act to tell the provinces how they must set about exercising a power in respect of a matter falling outside of the competence of the national government. Despite claims by the national government that the provincial official was only obliged to take the guidelines into account and not to implement them, the Court argued that what mattered was that the national government legislated on a matter falling outside its competence.[244] Thus, despite the Court's earlier recognition of the predominance of the national sphere of government in the scheme of co-operative government, here it drew the line and clarified that there was a constitutional limit to the legislative power of the national government.

Although these early cases seem on the whole to have rejected the autonomy claims of the provincial governments by recognizing the commanding role of the national legislature, the Court was soon given the opportunity to explore the arena of exclusive provincial power after the national parliament passed legislation which sought to regulate the production, distribution and sale of liquor through a nationally defined licensing scheme.[245] Referred to the Constitutional Court by President Mandela, who had refused to sign the Bill on the ground that he had reservations about its constitutionality, the law sought in part to control the manufacture, wholesale distribution and retail sale of liquor, functions which, at least with respect to licensing, are expressly included as exclusive legislative powers of the provinces in Sch 5 of the Constitution. Citing a 'history of overt racism in the control of the manufacturing, distribution and sale of liquor,' the national government contended that the 'provisions of the Bill constitute a permissible exercise by Parliament of its legislative powers.'[246] The Western Cape complained however that the

'Bill exhaustively regulates the activities of persons involved in the manufacture, wholesale distribution and retail sale of liquor; and that even in the retail sphere the structures the Bill seeks to create reduce the provinces, in an area in which they would (subject to section 44(2)) have exclusive legislative and executive competence, to the role of funders and administrators.'[247]

The province went on to claim that the Bill thereby intrudes into its area of exclusive legislative competence.

Turning once again to the issue of cooperative government the Court noted that '[g]overnmental power is...distributed [at source] between the national, provincial and local

---

[243] *Municipal Structures Case* para 14.   [244] ibid para 20 and 21.
[245] *Ex Parte the President of the Republic of South Africa, In Re: Constitutionality of the Liquor Bill,* CCT 12/99, 11 November 1999, 2000 (1) BCLR 1 (CC).   [246] *Liquor Licensing Case* para 33.
[247] ibid para 37.

spheres of government, each of which is subject to the Constitution, and each of which is subordinated to the constitutional obligation to respect the requirements of cooperative governance.'[248]

The Court then proceeded to argue that cooperative governance includes the duty 'not [to] assume any power or function except those conferred on them in terms of the Constitution' and that the Constitution's 'distribution of legislative power between the various spheres of government' and its itemization of functional areas of concurrent and exclusive legislative competence, must be read in this light.[249]

Accepting that the national government enjoys the power to regulate the liquor trade in all respects because of the industry's impact on the 'determination of national economic policies, the promotion of inter-provincial commerce and the protection of the common market in respect of goods, services, capital and labour mobility,' the Court went on to conclude that the structure of the Constitution precluded the national government's regulation of liquor licensing.[250] The Court came to this conclusion by carefully defining three distinct objectives of the proposed law, and distinguishing those functions which would apply predominantly to intra-provincial regulation as opposed to those aspects of the liquor business requiring national regulation because of their extra-provincial and even international impact.

The Bill, according to the Court, divided the liquor trade into three tiers and provided distinct forms of regulation for these specific aspects of the business. It provided: first, for 'the prohibition on cross-holdings between the three tiers involved in the liquor trade, namely producers, distributors and retailers'; second, in an attempt to establish national uniformity in the trade, for 'the establishment of uniform conditions, in a single system, for the national registration of liquor manufacturers and distributors'; and third, for 'the prescription of detailed mechanisms to provincial legislatures for the establishment of retail licensing mechanisms.'[251]

Having defined an aspect of the Bill which focused primarily on the provincial level, the Court then proceeded to define the primary purpose of granting exclusive competencies to the provinces as implying power over the regulation of activities 'that take place within or can be regulated in a manner that has a direct effect upon the inhabitants of the province alone.' In relation to 'liquor licences,' it is obvious, the Court argued, 'that the retail sale of liquor will, except for a probably negligible minority of sales that are effected across provincial borders, occur solely within the province.' Given this fact the Court concluded that the heart of the exclusive competence granted to the regions in the Constitution, must in this arena 'lie in the licensing of retail sale of liquor'.[252]

Returning to an analysis of the 'three-tier' structure of the Bill, the Court argued that the manufacture or production of liquor, including wholesale trades

---

[248] *Liquor Licensing Case* para 41.   [249] ibid.   [250] ibid para 58.
[251] ibid para 69.   [252] ibid para 71.

in liquor—which have a national and international dimension—were not intended to be the primary field of 'liquor licences'[253]—as little, if any production is directed solely at the intra-provincial market.[254] This approach enabled the Court to simultaneously reject the Western Cape claim of a right to regulate and control the production and distribution of liquor,[255] as these functions clearly fall outside of the primary basis for the defining of exclusive provincial competence, while at the same time framing a clear arena in which the constitutionally guaranteed exclusive competences of the provinces could be more vigorously defended. Distinguishing between licensing retail outlets on the one hand and manufacturing and distribution on the other, the Court concluded that

'if the exclusive provincial legislative competence regarding 'liquor licences' in Schedule 5 applies to all liquor licences, the national government has made out a case in terms of section 44(2) justifying its intervention in creating a national system of registration for manufacturers and wholesale distributors of liquor and in prohibiting cross-holdings between the three tiers in the liquor trade.'

However, as the Court pointed out, the national government had failed to make a case for the necessity of such national regulation in 'regard to retail sales of liquor, whether by retailers or by manufacturers, nor for micro-manufacturers whose operations are essentially provincial.' To this extent then the national Parliament did not have the competence to enact the Liquor Bill and the Bill was therefore unconstitutional.[256]

Influences on Interpretation

South Africa's immediate past and the tension between the Constitution's promise of a broad spectrum of rights—including socio-economic, cultural and even environmental rights—and the continued salience of alternative normative orders, including traditional leaders and indigenous laws and practices as well as old patterns of ownership and privilege, are today the most pressing influences on the Court's interpretative enterprise. Yet, it is also evident from the Court's decisions, that the common law methodology shared by the judges and the incorporation of a plethora of interpretative tools—including the concepts of rationality and proportionality—as well as techniques of avoiding constitutional issues such as reading-in and reading down, also have an important influence on interpretation.

History

South Africa's colonial and apartheid history and its continuing legacy serve as constant backdrops to the Constitutional Court's interpretation of the Constitution.

---

[253] *Liquor Licensing Case* para 72.   [254] ibid paras 72–74.   [255] ibid para 78.
[256] ibid para 87.

In their first major judgment striking down the death penalty, the different Justices made repeated reference to the country's recent history as a justification for both their interpretative role and the purposive approach to interpretation. Here history serves both to explain the new constitutional order and to justify the Court's interpretative project. But at the same time, this history is used imperatively, to distinguish a particular future requiring the pursuit of a particular vision of rights as a fundamental part of this constitutionally-promised and guaranteed democracy.

The most dramatic of these statements by the newly appointed Justices of the Constitutional Court was issued by Mahomed J in his concurring opinion in the *Makwanyane* case as he contextualized his reasons for striking down the death penalty:

'In some countries, the Constitution only formalizes, in a legal instrument, a historical consensus of values and aspirations evolved incrementally from a stable and unbroken past to accommodate the needs of the future. The South African Constitution is different: it retains from the past only what is defensible and represents a decisive break from, and a ringing rejection of that part of the past which is disgracefully racist, authoritarian, insular and repressive and a vigorous identification of and commitment to a democratic, universalistic, caring and aspirationally egalitarian ethos, expressly articulated in the Constitution. The contrast between the past which it repudiates and the future to which is seeks to commit the nation is stark and dramatic. The past institutionalized and legitimized racism. The Constitution expresses in its preamble the need for a 'new order... in which there is equality between... people of all races'. Chapter 3 of the Constitution extends the contrast, in every relevant area of endeavor... The past was redolent with statutes which assaulted the human dignity of persons on the grounds of race and color alone. Section 10 constitutionally protects that dignity. The past accepted, permitted, perpetrated and institutionalized pervasive and manifestly unfair discrimination against women and persons of color; the preamble, s 8 and the postamble seek to articulate an ethos which not only rejects its rationale but unmistakenly recognizes the clear justification for the reversal of the accumulated legacy of such discrimination. The past permitted detention without trial: s 11(1) prohibits it. The past permitted degrading treatment of persons; s 11(2) renders it unconstitutional. The past arbitrarily repressed the freedoms of expression, assembly, association and movement; ss 15, 16, 17 and 18 accord to these freedoms the status of 'fundamental rights'. The past limited the right to vote to a minority; s 21 extends it to every citizen. The past arbitrarily denied to citizens on the grounds of race and color the right to hold and acquire property; s 26 expressly secures it. Such a jurisprudential past created what the postamble to the Constitution recognized as a society 'characterized by strife, conflict, untold suffering and injustice.' What the Constitution expressly aspires to do is to provide a transition from these grossly unacceptable features of the past to a conspicuously contrasting 'future founded on the recognition of human rights, democracy and peaceful co-existence and development opportunities for all South Africans, irrespective of color, race, class, belief or sex.'

In the same judgment O'Regan J argued that

'[r]espect for the dignity of all human beings is particularly important in South Africa. For apartheid was a denial of a common humanity. Black people were refused respect and dignity and thereby the dignity of all South Africans was diminished. The new Constitution rejects this past and affirms the equal worth of all South Africans. Thus recognition and protection of human dignity is the touchstone of the new political order and is fundamental to the new Constitution.'

The Historic Exclusion of Indigenous Law and the Hope of Ubuntu

Apart from history and the formal sources recognized in the Constitution, a majority of Justices have made specific reference to *ubuntu*[257] as a source of indigenous values in the interpretation of the Constitution.[258] The importance of these statements lies as much in the application of the concept of *ubuntu* to the question of the death penalty as they do in pointing to indigenous values as a source for the development of a particular South African constitutional jurisprudence. Despite these clear indications that the concept of *ubuntu*—the core of which is the notion that a person can only be a person through others—has been recognized by the Court as an important source of the values which are to be inculcated in the development of an indigenous constitutional jurisprudence, there is little commonality on either the specific content given by the Justices to *ubuntu* or the sources to which the Court may look in building its jurisprudence around the principles of *ubuntu*.

The concept of *ubuntu* is given its most direct application in the opinion of Justice Madala[259] who argues that the concept 'carries in it the ideas of humaneness, social justice and fairness,'[260] and states in his conclusion that the death penalty 'is clearly in conflict with the Constitution generally and runs counter to the concept of *ubuntu*.'[261] This notion of *ubuntu* as a general ethos giving an indigenous content to the humanitarian principles underlying the new Constitution is repeated by Mahomed J[262] and Mokgoro J who describes *ubuntu* as translatable as 'humaneness',[263] a 'shared value and ideal which runs like a golden thread across cultural lines'.[264] In this way there seems to be an attempt to define the spirit of *ubuntu* as providing a connection between indigenous value systems and universal human rights embodied in international law and comparative constitutional jurisprudence.[265]

This search for connection is tied however to a recognition that *ubuntu* may also provide the reverse, a unique connection between South Africa's new commitment to constitutionalism and the possibility of constructing a particularly South African constitutional jurisprudence, one that will resonate with the indigenous values of the majority of South Africans. This project requires that

---

[257] Translated as 'human nature, good nature' in GR Dent & CLS Nyembezi, *Scholar's Zulu Dictionary* (Shuter & Shooter, Pietermaritzburg South Africa, 1969) 441; or as 'human nature, humaneness, one's real self' in CM Doke, D McK Malcolm & JMA Sikakana *English and Zulu Dictionary* (Witwatersrand UP, Johannesburg, 1982) Part II 227.
[258] *Makwanyane* (n 102) para 130, 131, 223–27, 237, 241–45, 250, 260, 263, 307–313 and 374.
[259] ibid para 241–243.   [260] ibid para 237.   [261] ibid para 260.
[262] ibid para 263.   [263] ibid para 308.   [264] ibid para 307.
[265] ibid paras 308, 309, 311 and 313.

the Court not only make an analogy between *ubuntu* and humaneness, or human rights in general, but that the concept of *ubuntu* be more clearly elucidated. Chief Justice Langa began this process in the *Makwanyane* case by noting that *ubuntu* is not defined in the Constitution, and then proceeded to identify elements of *ubuntu* which together form a 'culture which places some emphasis on communality and on the interdependence of the members of the community'.[266] The three central elements of *ubuntu* are defined by Langa CJ as: (1) recognition of a 'person's status as a human being, entitled to unconditional respect, dignity, value and acceptance' from fellow community members; (2) a corresponding 'duty to give the same respect, dignity, value and acceptance to each member of that community'; and, (3) a regulation of the exercise of rights by laying emphasis 'on sharing and co-responsibility and the mutual enjoyment of rights by all'.[267]

Justice Sachs took the Court's turn to indigenous values and context a step further in insisting that it is possible to incorporate indigenous principles resurrected from 'the relatively well-developed judicial processes of indigenous societies'.[268] Reconstructing the evidence of 'traditional African jurisprudence'[269] Justice Sachs consciously engages in a 'search for core and enduring values consistent with the text and spirit of the Constitution'.[270] This is consistent with the long overdue recognition of 'African law and legal thinking as a source of legal ideas, values and practice',[271] and is a creative response to the failure to give due recognition to 'traditional African jurisprudence.' The problem however, lies in the need to develop a sound theory, for both the identification of the relevant sources of African jurisprudence, and for the selection and incorporation of specific values, particularly when the evidence demonstrates different and contrasting traditions. Justice Sachs addressed this problem in the *Makwanyane* case first, by identifying three contrasting aspects of the history of the death penalty in traditional African jurisprudence, and then by announcing that '[i]n seeking the kind of values which should inform our broad approach to interpreting the Constitution I have little doubt as to which of these three contrasted aspects of tradition we should follow and which we should reject. The rational and humane adjudicatory approach is entirely consistent with and re-enforcing of the fundamental rights enshrined in our Constitution; the exorcist and militarist concepts are not.'[272] While this seemed to be a clear means to achieve the aspirations of the Constitution in the face of obvious contradictions in law and practice, in fact the Court had little opportunity in its first decade to develop this line of analysis. As a result it has, until recently, avoided the difficult task of distinguishing those aspects of customary law that should be retained as part of the country's unique heritage, and those aspects which must be rejected as in violation of the promised new constitutional order.[273]

---

[266] *Makwanyane* (n 102) para 224.   [267] ibid.   [268] ibid para 381.
[269] ibid para 373.   [270] ibid para 374.   [271] ibid para 365.   [272] ibid para 382.
[273] See DD Ndima *The African law of the 21ˢᵗ century in South Africa*, XXXVI CILSA 2003, 325–345.

Legal Legacies and Popular Experience of the Law

While the Constitutional Court has made many important decisions there has been concern that it was yet to address a range of difficult issues affecting the majority of ordinary South Africans and which hold the potential of confronting some of the more ingrained aspects of inequality and conflict which continue to pervade post-apartheid society. Most recently the Court has decided a group of cases which hold profound consequences for the hopes and aspirations of the majority of South Africans. These cases include challenges to the 'customary' laws of succession on grounds of gender discrimination;[274] the KwaZulu-Natal Pound Ordinance 1947 on the grounds that it denied cattle owners rights of equality and access to the courts;[275] and the Land Claims Court's decision that a community claiming land under the Restitution of Land Rights Act had failed to prove that their dispossession was the result of discriminatory laws or practices.[276] In each of these cases the decision of the Court would hold important consequences for the relations of power: between men and women living under indigenous law; between land owners (usually white) and landless or land hungry stock owners (usually black); as well as between land owners and land claiming communities whose claims did not self-evidently fall within the terms of the Restitution of Land Rights Act 1994.

In both the *Bhe* and *Richtersveld* cases the majority of the Court acknowledged the constitutional status of indigenous law. In the first instance the Court struck down a rule of customary law which discriminated on the basis of gender while in the second instance the Court held that 'indigenous law is an independent source of norms within the legal system,' but like all other 'law is subject to the Constitution and has to be interpreted in light of its values.'[277] The result in the *Bhe* case was for the Court to directly strike down—at least with respect to intestate succession—the 'customary' rule of primogeniture held by many traditionalists and others to be a key element of the customary legal system. In effect, the Court's decision will profoundly impact the rights of wives and daughters who until now relied upon the system of extended-family obligation historically inherent in indigenous law but long since disrupted by social and economic change. On the other side, the Court's decision in the *Richtersveld* case recognized indigenous law as a source of land rights thus strengthening the claims of those who have argued that their land rights—including rights to natural resources—were not automatically extinguished by the extension of colonial sovereignty over their territories. Their dispossession, through means other then the direct application of specific, discriminatory, apartheid land laws, will thus also be recognized

---

[274] *Bhe* case (n 182).

[275] *Xolisile Zondi v Member of the Traditional Council for Traditional and Local Government Affairs et al*, CCT 73/03 [hereinafter *Zondi*].

[276] *Alexkor Ltd et al v The Richtersveld Community and Others*, CCT 19/03, decided on 14 October 2003.					[277] ibid para 51.

for the purpose of claiming restitution of their land rights. Even if not as broad in its impact, the symbolic value of this recognition of indigenous land rights makes an important contribution to legitimizing the new constitutional order among ordinary South Africans.

Finally, the *Zondi* case involved a challenge to a set of legal provisions that formed a central plank of the system of control and dispossession in the rural areas of apartheid South Africa. Under the Pound Ordinance land owners were historically empowered to seize and impound animals trespassing on their land without notice to the livestock owner, unless the owner was a neighboring land owner. Subsequently the livestock would be sold in execution if the owners (a) could not afford the impounding fees and damages claimed by the land owner or (b) could not be readily identified. Without notice requirements or judicial process the effect was that white landowners used these rules to exert power over rural communities who lived on the land as sharecroppers, labor tenants or wage laborers and held what little wealth or economic security they had in livestock. In effect, these rules, while not racially-based, interacted with the racially-based landownership rules to both structure rural social relations and to perpetuate a continuing process of dispossession as the ownership of livestock continually shifted at below market prices from black to white farmers.

Facially race-neutral the Pound Ordinance survived the dismantling of apartheid laws but nevertheless continues to have a predominantly racial effect because rural land ownership remains, even a decade after apartheid, largely in white hands. On the other side, as Ngcobo J noted in his opinion, are people such as 'Mrs Zondi, who belongs to a group of persons historically discriminated against by their government ... which still affects their ability to protect themselves under the laws of the new order.'[278] With respect to the question of notice, the Court noted that the statute did not even require anyone to tell the livestock owner of the impending sale and Ngcobo J pointed out that even a general public notice in government publications or newspapers is likely to be insufficient 'where a large portion of the population ... is illiterate and otherwise socially disadvantaged. Mrs Zondi is indeed illiterate. The thumbprint mark she affixed to her founding affidavit bears testimony to this.'[279] Furthermore, the statue permitted the landowner to 'bypass the courts and recover damages through an execution process carried out by a private businessperson or an official of a municipality without any court intervention.'[280] Holding the statutory scheme unconstitutional, among other reasons because its effect is to limit the right of access to the courts, Ngcobo J noted that the scheme removes 'from the court's scrutiny one of the sharpest and most divisive conflicts of our society. The problem of cattle trespassing on farm land ... is not merely the ordinary agrarian irritation it must be in many societies. It is a constant and bitter reminder of the process of colonial dispossession and exclusion.'[281]

---

[278] *Zondi* case (n 275) para 51.   [279] ibid.   [280] ibid para 75.   [281] ibid para 76.

Conclusion

While South Africa's experiment in constitutionalism is only a decade old, the conditions which gave rise to the new constitutional order as well as the continuing problems of a post-colonial society facing the dual challenges of extreme inequality and a devastating HIV/AIDS pandemic, has brought domestic tension as well as global interest to the interpretative work of the Constitutional Court. Caught in the cross-hairs of struggles for the realization of the extensive promise of rights entrenched in the Constitution, and the limitations of governmental capacity and resources, the Court has thus far sailed a careful, yet innovative path—steering clear of the rocks upon which popular hopes may be dashed and avoiding the winds which promise the easy declaration of rights yet fail to carry the society towards their effective realization. At the same time, the courts themselves are undergoing transformation and tensions over this process continue to simmer within the courts and between the courts, government and the legal profession.[282] The challenge facing the Court, as its composition changes and it becomes increasingly part of a 'normal society' will be whether it is able, through its interpretation of the Constitution, to continue to strike a balance between the need to address the legacy of apartheid, including the historic exclusion of the indigenous legal systems, and the need to uphold the claims of individual freedom and dignity which have become the hallmark of its first decade.

---

[282] See National Judges Symposium *The South African Law Journal* (2003) Vol 120(4) 647–718. This is a report, including many of the speeches given, to the first plenary meeting of South African judges in 70 years and took place against a background of public controversy between senior judges and politicians.

7

Conclusions

Jeffrey Goldsworthy

Introduction

The previous chapters reveal substantial differences between the interpretive philosophies of the six national courts under examination. It is convenient to characterise the differences mainly in terms of the stronger attraction of some courts to what I will call 'legalism'. This word is used in a purely descriptive sense, not to applaud or to denigrate, but merely to denote interpretive philosophies motivated by two main concerns. One is disapproval of judicial discretion—of decision-making based on judges' values and ideologies rather than objective legal norms. The other is disapproval of judicial law-making—of decision-making that changes the law instead of merely applying it. These two concerns are related, because in any legal system in which judicial decision-making is guided by precedent, decisions based on judicial values and ideologies will in practice change the law. Legalists disapprove of judicial discretion and law-making for various reasons, including equity among litigants, predictability, democracy and the rule of law. Consequently, they would prefer law to be objective, determinate and comprehensive, so that it can provide answers to every dispute, which judges can reliably ascertain and apply.

This ambition is, of course, impossible to realise in practice, because constitutions inevitably include ambiguities, vagueness, inconsistencies and 'gaps'. Since judges cannot wash their hands of a dispute and leave the parties to fight it out in the street, they must have authority to resolve indeterminacies and gaps, thereby supplementing the constitution, by resorting to their own notions of justice and public policy. Most of what is called 'constitutional law' consists of methodological principles, doctrines and interpretations of specific provisions that are consistent with, but not required by, either the bare text of the constitution or what is reliably known of its founders' intentions and purposes. They form a superstructure of judge-made law built on the foundation of the constitution itself. As judge-made law, they are open to being changed by the judges. They include most of the doctrines concerned with the interpretation and application of constitutional rights, which are usually relatively abstract, and therefore vague, principles of political morality. In the real world, legalists must accept the inevitability of legal indeterminacy.[1] They can, however, advocate maximal determinacy.

---

[1] This should be uncontroversial except, perhaps, in Germany where the Basic Law still 'tends to be regarded as a self-sufficient code of law' which 'contain[s] the right answer to almost any constitutional

Legalism in constitutional law has been associated with various tendencies, including literalism, formalism, positivism, and originalism. For present purposes, it is useful to characterise legalism as a preference for positivism rather than normativism, and for originalism rather than non-originalism. It must be emphasised that these two distinctions are not dichotomies: each pair of alternatives represents a spectrum of possibilities. Judges, courts, and legal cultures adopt positions somewhere between the two ends of each spectrum, sometimes closer to the legalist end, and sometimes closer to the opposite end. Particular interpretive philosophies could be plotted on a graph, with these distinctions forming the two axes. But they are somewhat opaque, and require further elaboration.

By 'positivism' I mean, in this context, a conception of a constitution as a set of discrete written provisions, whose authority derives from their having been formally adopted or enacted. By 'normativism', I mean a holistic conception of a constitution as more than the sum of its written provisions: as a normative structure whose provisions are, either explicitly or implicitly, based on deeper principles, and ultimately on abstract norms of political morality that are the deepest source of its authority.[2] At one extremity of this spectrum, positivism includes literalism: the meanings of the constitution's written provisions are taken to be fixed by conventional word meanings and rules of grammar, independent of the founders' purposes. Less extreme versions of positivism are purposive: they are prepared to interpret the words of express provisions in the light of their purposes, without allowing those purposes to either supplement or over-ride the words, or to have independent normative force. A stronger version of purposivism permits the recognition of implications, provided that they are necessary for express provisions to achieve their purposes. As one moves even further towards the normativist end of the spectrum, increasingly abstract formulations of purpose are preferred, and to implement them more effectively, the enacted words may be stretched or compressed, supplemented or over-ridden—in effect, rewritten. At the extreme end, the most abstract norms attributed to the constitution are directly enforced in their own right, independently of express provisions.

By 'originalism', I mean the thesis that the content of a constitution is determined partly by the intentions or purposes of its founders, or the understandings of the founding generation. 'Non-originalism' treats these considerations as either irrelevant or of little weight, and licences judges to interpret the constitutional text according to the supposed meanings, values or understandings of contemporary society. There are, again, more or less moderate versions of both alternatives. Each one is compatible with either positivism or normativism. An originalist may be a

---

dispute': Chapter 4, pp 207–8. The Basic Law is expressly based on abstract moral principles, but even if these are objective moral truths accessible to human reason, human choices are often necessary to apply such principles to specific circumstances: see, eg, J Finnis *Natural Law and Natural Rights* (Clarendon Press, Oxford, 1980) 281–9.

[2] Professor Sathe calls this 'structuralism': Ch 5, p 226.

positivist, who maintains that the meanings of express provisions are determined by original intentions or understandings, or a normativist, who equates the constitution's deepest norms with the founders' deepest purposes. Similarly, a non-originalist may be either a positivist or a normativist, regarding either the meanings of express provisions, or the constitution's deepest norms, as determined by contemporary understandings or values.

Non-originalist normativism is a particularly potent agent of substantive constitutional change through judicial interpretation. If a constitution is regarded as based on unwritten, abstract norms of political morality, which can trump the specific terms of written provisions or even be independently enforced, and if those norms can change according to the judges' impressions of contemporary values or their personal values, then the judges possess a remarkable power to reshape the constitution. Indeed, extreme non-originalist normativism may be indistinguishable from natural law philosophies that regard law as a branch of political morality, to which positive law always remains subordinate. Both positions may also be practically indistinguishable from a strong form of pragmatism, which holds that judges should be guided by positive law only insofar as that is the best option, all-things-considered. Even originalist normativism can be difficult to distinguish from these positions, if the founders' deepest purposes are formulated as abstractly as 'to achieve justice'.

The relationship between these distinctions and the objectivity, determinacy and comprehensiveness of law is debatable. Normativism makes law more comprehensive than positivism, because it offers much richer normative resources to guide decision-making. Discrete written provisions, even if they are interpreted purposively, provide less comprehensive guidance than abstract norms of political morality. But legalists believe that this greater comprehensiveness comes at the cost of objectivity and determinacy. They distrust the incorporation of moral and political norms into law, on the ground that the usual abstraction and vagueness of such norms compels judges to resort to discretionary value-judgments. This is particularly the case if these norms can be used to trump, or enforced independently of, the wording of enacted provisions.

Legalists fear that strong forms of non-originalism and normativism licence judges to change constitutions in three ways: (a) by changing the meanings of their words; (b) by in effect rewriting their express provisions to better implement deeper values; and (c) by adding to them new, 'unwritten' principles. Legalists insist that judges should be bound not only by the founders' ultimate ends, but also by the means they chose to achieve those ends. To be guided only or mainly by their ultimate ends is not to be significantly bound at all.

But legalist critiques are not necessarily persuasive. For example, there can be no doubt that implications are sometimes justified: the content of a constitution, as of any law and indeed any communication, is never completely explicit. Full comprehension of its meaning inevitably depends partly on an understanding of purpose, illuminated by contextual information, and on background assumptions that are taken for granted.[3] Just as indeterminacy gives rise to a superstructure of judge-made law built on the constitutional text, inexplicitness requires a substructure of unwritten purposes to be excavated beneath the text. Furthermore, a strong case can be made for courts sometimes making adjustments for the inability of language in an old constitution, if strictly applied, to achieve its purposes in the modern world, because of technological or social developments that its founders did not anticipate. Take the provision in the United States Constitution that vests exclusive power in Congress to raise and maintain 'armies' and 'a navy' and to regulate 'the land and naval forces'.[4] When military aircraft were developed, it would have defeated the provision's obvious purpose if Congress had been denied the power to raise an air force. It is widely accepted that in such cases, the courts may adopt a purposive rather than a literal interpretation, by stretching the provision's literal meaning to give effect to what it originally meant, in a broad sense of 'meant' that is informed by its purpose. But if 'rewriting' to this small extent is justified, where should the line be drawn?

Consider also the extent to which courts should remedy failures on the part of the constitution's founders to expressly provide for problems, even if they should have foreseen them. When interpreting statutes, judges usually refuse to rectify failures of that kind, on the ground that the legislature should do so. But when dealing with a constitution, they should arguably be more willing to provide a solution. If a constitution fails to achieve one of its main purposes, the potential consequences are grave. They include the danger of constitutional powers being abused, of the democratic process or the federal system being subverted, and of human rights being violated. If the constitution is difficult to amend formally, or if amendment requires action by the very politicians who pose the threat needing to be checked, there may be good moral reasons for judges to intervene. On the other hand, legalists worry that such reasoning can be used to justify extensive judicial rewriting of the constitution, especially if the founders' purposes are pitched at a very abstract level ('they wanted to achieve a just society, and this is necessary to achieve justice'). Legalists deny that judges are 'statesmen', appointed to fill the shoes of the founders and continue the task of constitution-making as an on-going enterprise.

One conclusion that should be drawn from this brief discussion is that constitutional interpretation is an extraordinarily difficult enterprise, which requires striking an appropriate balance between competing, weighty considerations. The distinction between legitimate and illegitimate change depends on a host of other difficult distinctions, such as between determinacy and indeterminacy, purpose used to clarify meaning and purpose used to change it, genuine implications and spurious ones, evidence of intentions or understandings that illuminates original meanings and that which does not, changes in the application of a provision and

---

[3] J Goldsworthy 'Implications in Language, Law and the Constitution' in G Lindell ed *Future Directions in Australian Constitutional Law* (Federation Press, Sydney, 1994) 150.

[4] *The Constitution of the United States of America* (1787), Art I, s 8.

changes in its meaning, and so on. The sheer difficulty of drawing such distinctions, even for philosophers after prolonged reflection, let alone for busy judges, should make anyone pause before criticising judges too forcefully. It is doubtful that the most appropriate balance is, even in principle, determined by wholly objective, 'strictly legal' considerations. Ultimately, it requires normative judgment. And how the balance should be struck no doubt varies, depending on the unique circumstances in which any constitutional court finds itself.

In what follows, I will attempt to summarise the interpretive philosophies of the various courts whose work has been examined in the previous chapters, and then offer some explanations of the differences between them. Attempting a general characterisation of the interpretive philosophy of any court is hazardous, because it can be distorted if undue prominence is given to a small number of controversial but unrepresentative decisions. I rely mainly on the selection of cases and doctrines made by the contributors.

Comparing Interpretive Methods and Philosophies

Constitutional interpretation is guided by similar considerations in all six countries. The main ones are: the words of the constitutional text, understood in the context of related provisions; other evidence of the intentions, understandings or purposes of the founders; presumptions favouring broad, and purposive, interpretations; precedent and doctrine developed from it; so-called 'structural' principles regarded as underlying particular provisions or groups of provisions; and considerations of justice, practicality and public policy.[5] Other considerations include additional presumptions and maxims of interpretation, sometimes counselling deference to long-standing practice or the other branches of government, international and comparative law, and academic opinion.

Despite these similarities, there are substantial differences in the relative priorities or weights given to these diverse considerations in the six countries. For example, precedents naturally play a much larger role in the interpretation of older constitutions, because there are more of them; academic opinion has far more influence in Germany than elsewhere; original intentions or understandings are relied on more in Australia, Germany, and the United States than in Canada and India; 'structural' principles play a more pervasive role in Canada, Germany, India and South Africa than in Australia or the United States; justice and public policy seem more influential in India than elsewhere; and comparative law is given much less attention in the United States than in the other countries.

These differences cannot be spelled out in detail here: they can be traced through use of the Index. More significant are substantial differences in the

---

[5] These can all be sorted into Philip Bobbitt's six 'modalities' of constitutional interpretation, namely, textual, historical, structural, doctrinal, ethical, and prudential: see P Bobbitt *Constitutional Fate: Theory of the Constitution* (OUP, New York, 1982).

general philosophies of interpretation currently favoured by courts in the six countries. Australian and German judges tend to be much more strongly attracted to legalist philosophies than Canadian and Indian judges, with South African judges arguably sitting somewhere in between, and American judges being more divided over these issues.

The United States

Professor Tushnet's chapter depicts constitutional interpretation in the United States as, for the most part, straightforwardly legalist. When the Supreme Court interprets a constitutional provision without the assistance of precedent, either because the issue is novel or because the Court regards existing precedents as erroneous, it starts with the constitutional text, understood in the context of related provisions, and in the light of original understandings and the political theory that the Court finds in the text.[6] But in most cases, relevant precedents do exist, and are the predominant consideration, followed by text-based and originalist considerations that 'often go hand in hand'.[7] Professor Tushnet asserts that 'some version of a jurisprudence of original understanding remains an essential element of nearly all practical resolutions of interpretive controversies.'[8] Resort to 'structural' principles is less frequent, except in separation of powers and individual rights cases, and is used mainly to support other arguments; and explicit reference to moral or political philosophy is rare except when the text expressly incorporates moral principles.[9] Where the text does so, the Court is entitled to ignore the founders' possibly mistaken expectations about the proper application of those principles; any accusation of 'activism' in such cases is therefore unfair.[10] Sometimes the Court is criticised for excessive formalism.[11]

Yet the Supreme Court has acquired a reputation for activism, because of perceived innovations such as substantive due process, the 'incorporation' of the Bill of Rights in the 14th Amendment, broad interpretation of some provisions contrary to the apparent original understanding, and unenumerated rights, such as the right to privacy recognised in *Griswold v Connecticut* and extended to abortions in *Roe v Wade*.[12] Professor Tushnet acknowledges that the Warren Court had an 'aggressive agenda', which aroused considerable controversy over its alleged activism from the 1950s onwards.[13] But he maintains that its decisions fell well within the bounds set by standards of professional competence.[14] Some if not all of those decisions can be defended on orthodox legalist grounds: substantive due process, for example, reflected a technical meaning acquired by the words 'due process' before they were inserted into the Constitution, and the

---

[6] Chapter 1, pp 40 and 48–49.   [7] ibid pp 42 and 47.   [8] ibid p 38.
[9] ibid pp 32, 39–40, 47.   [10] ibid p 39.   [11] ibid pp 21–22.
[12] See RH Bork *The Tempting of America: the Political Seduction of the Law* (Touchstone New York 1990) Part I for a critique along these lines.   [13] ibid Chapter 1, p 52.
[14] ibid pp 50–51 and 54.

implied right to privacy is arguably as legitimate as implied intergovernmental immunities.[15]

Professor Tushnet argues that orthodox interpretive considerations—text, original understanding, precedent, and so on—have been unable to significantly constrain decision-making.[16] Precedent, for example, has not provided 'stability' partly because the judges have been unwilling to subordinate their views to those expressed in the precedents. Consequently, the precedents have come to provide an array of alternatives from which current judges can choose.[17] And original understandings have failed to constrain, partly because they often merely reveal disagreements among the founders themselves, and partly because they can be specified at different levels of generality, which point to different conclusions.[18] Consequently, judges can implement their own 'values and visions' by choosing appropriate interpretive methods, without exceeding the bounds set by standards of professional competence.[19]

But to the outside observer, the impression conveyed by the political battles that now attend the confirmation of Supreme Court nominees is that interpretive standards are deeply conflicted in the United States.[20] Decisions attacked as activist fall outside the standards accepted by some sections of the profession, even though they are within the standards accepted by others. If so, American constitutional culture might best be characterised as a site of conflict over interpretive philosophies, within the profession as well as outside it.

Professor Tushnet's chapter includes some evidence that professional standards are conflicted, with many lawyers accepting normativist standards that others repudiate. First, he point outs that the early debate between Justices Iredell and Chase in *Calder v Bull*, about the legitimacy of 'unwritten principles' of reason and justice, was never resolved.[21] Consequently, a controversial strain of natural law thinking seems to have persisted in American constitutional jurisprudence. For example, Chase J's insistence that all governments in the United States are necessarily limited may have provided the crucial 'structural' pre-supposition behind the much criticised right to privacy.[22]

Second, Professor Tushnet claims that the American people have come to accept that constitutional interpretation 'is the means by which the Constitution is recurrently revised to accommodate the general values embodied in the Constitution with the realities of governance in a changing world'.[23] This view can be traced back to Marshall CJ's influential statement in *McCulloch v Maryland*, that the Constitution was 'intended to endure for ages to come, and, consequently, to be adapted to the various crises of human affairs.'[24] According to Professor Tushnet, this became 'the touchstone for everyone who defended the idea of a living Constitution.'[25] The notion of a 'living constitution' that the courts can 'adapt' to changing circumstances is ambiguous: it could mean either

---

[15] ibid pp 20, 28 and 32 esp. n 77.   [16] ibid p 50.   [17] ibid pp 17–20.
[18] ibid pp 35–38 and 50–51.   [19] ibid pp 50–51.   [20] ibid p 50.
[21] ibid pp 26–27.   [22] ibid p 32.   [23] ibid p 49; see also pp 7, 16–17 and 54.
[24] ibid p 24.   [25] ibid p 24.

that broad but unchanging meanings must be applied to new and unexpected phenomena, or that the meanings themselves must sometimes be changed for that purpose. As Professor Tushnet explains, the principal method of adapting the Constitution to external change has been to identify the general principles underlying specific constitutional terms, and then determine how those principles apply to contemporary problems.[26] This is what I have called 'originalist normativism'. If the underlying principles are couched at a sufficiently abstract level of generality, the specific terms lose their grip. That, one suspects, has been a bone of contention.

Canada

The Privy Council took almost a literal approach to the Canadian Constitution, refusing to consult legislative history to ascertain the founders' intentions or purposes. The text itself had been drafted in a deliberately ambiguous fashion, and the ambiguities were resolved according to the judges' preconceptions of the nature of a genuine federation.[27] In other words, the judges' own ideology proved decisive.[28] They generally favoured broad interpretations of provincial powers and narrow interpretations of national ones, which may have suited Canadian society better than the founders' intentions, by mollifying separatist sentiment in Quebec.[29] This is a good example of how literalism, by maximising indeterminacy, can increase rather than decrease discretionary judicial law-making.[30]

The Privy Council described the Constitution as a 'living tree capable of growth and expansion within its natural limits',[31] but probably did not have in mind changes in the meaning of the text resulting from judicial interpretation.[32] It probably intended merely to endorse 'generous', rather than 'dynamic', interpretation.[33] But the modern Supreme Court has enthusiastically employed the metaphor to justify dynamic interpretation: the notion that, without any need for formal amendment, the Constitution should be capable of 'growth, development and adjustment to changing societal needs.'[34] Professor Hogg states that originalism has 'never enjoyed any significant support in Canada', and 'indifference to the original understanding lingers on in the modern Supreme Court'.[35] Indeed, the lawyers and politicians who drafted and adopted the Charter apparently assumed that the Court would not be bound by their intentions.[36] Consequently, the Court has held that a provision embodied the American doctrine of substantive due process, even though it had been deliberately drafted so as not to do so.[37] The judicial choice of the opposite meaning to the one intended goes well beyond 'adaptation' of the provision to cope with developments unanticipated by its

---

[26] Chapter 1, p 37.　　[27] Chapter 2, p 66.　　[28] ibid pp 75–76.　　[29] ibid p 76.
[30] ibid p 104. See above, p 323.　　[31] ibid p 76.　　[32] ibid p 84.　　[33] ibid p 87.
[34] ibid p 84, quoting Lamer CJ in *Re BC Motor Vehicle Act* [1985] 2 SCR 486; see also p 85 n 122.
[35] ibid p 83; see also pp 78–79.　　[36] ibid p 87.
[37] ibid p 84. Admittedly, the choice of the words 'fundamental justice' to avoid that result was a remarkably inept piece of drafting.

framers: it involves altering the provision's intended meaning in circumstances that they fully anticipated. Professor Hogg describes the principle of 'progressive (or dynamic) interpretation' as 'the dominant theory of interpretation in Canada.'[38]

Over the last twenty years, the Supreme Court seems to have shifted from a positivist to a normativist conception of the Constitution, giving to fundamental, unwritten principles a normative force that is independent of specific provisions.[39] Professor Hogg asserts that the Court has sometimes invented, rather than discovered, these principles, thereby amending the Constitution by judicial fiat in defiance of the prescribed procedures for amendment.[40] The supposed unwritten principle of judicial independence is a product of non-originalist normativism, since the principle runs counter to textual evidence of the founders' intentions.[41] While such principles could be found 'to accommodate virtually any grievance about government policy', Professor Hogg notes that lately, the Court has shown 'some sign of reining-in its creative impulses.'[42]

The Supreme Court has interpreted Charter rights more broadly than their American equivalents have been interpreted, and has enthusiastically adopted an activist approach.[43] Its judges seem much more united in embracing non-originalism and normativism than their American counterparts.

Australia

Of the all the national courts, the High Court of Australia has been the most legalist. High Court judges have frequently expressed aversion to changing the Constitution through creative interpretation.[44] At least since 1920, the Court has devoted itself to a predominantly positivist methodology. Many of its judges have praised 'dry legal argument',[45] insisted on not straying too far from the text,[46] repudiated political and pragmatic considerations,[47] and spoken disparagingly of reasoning from such abstractions as the 'spirit' of the Constitution or 'vague and imprecise expressions of political philosophy.'[48] The Court's commitment to positivism is epitomised by Latham CJ's declaration that even if the Commonwealth used its financial supremacy to destroy the federal system, the Court might be powerless.[49]

The judges have often referred to 'underlying principles' such as federalism, representative and responsible government, the rule of law and the separation of powers, but have generally used them to aid the interpretation of express provisions. They have tended to be wary of implications, which are usually required to be 'necessary' for express provisions to achieve their purposes.[50] They have recognised a limited doctrine of implied intergovernmental immunities, and

---

[38] ibid p 87.   [39] ibid pp 90–91.   [40] ibid pp 90 and 104.   [41] ibid pp 91–92.
[42] ibid p 92.   [43] ibid pp 71, 81, 88 and 103–105.
[44] Chapter 3, pp 119–120, 121–122, 133, 141–142, 146, 151, 153 and 154–155.
[45] ibid pp 113 and 131.   [46] ibid pp 142–143.   [47] ibid p 139.
[48] ibid pp 119 and 128 respectively; see also p 154.   [49] ibid p 139.
[50] ibid pp 128 and 136.

a much more robust doctrine of the separation of judicial power, but the latter has plausible support in the constitutional text.[51] An implied freedom of political speech was 'discovered' in 1992, raising hopes that more creativity would follow, perhaps leading to an 'implied bill of rights'. But these hopes were dashed in the late 1990's.[52] Recent attempts to derive implications directly from the principle of representative government were scotched, on the ground that it must not be treated as a 'free-standing' principle.[53]

The Court has consistently endorsed a moderate version of originalism. It has maintained that the meaning of the text cannot be changed through interpretation, even though its application to external facts can change, and it has often relied on historical evidence of what a provision was originally understood to mean.[54] Its commitment to moderate originalism has been fortified in recent years by its willingness to consult the Convention Debates and other historical evidence of original understandings and purposes.[55] Only a handful of judges have endorsed the 'living tree' theory of the Constitution.[56]

While the Court was formerly criticised for excessive literalism and formalism, it has recently shifted to a more purposive and substantive approach.[57] It is now more willing to interpret and apply provisions purposively, and more candid about the need for judicial discretion on policy grounds to resolve stubborn indeterminacies. But this has not shaken its predominant positivism and originalism.

Germany

The next most legalist court, after the Australian High Court, may be Germany's Federal Constitutional Court, whose interpretive philosophy strikes an outsider as a fascinating mix of legalism and normativism.

The Basic Law virtually dictates a normativist approach. Like the other post-War constitutions, it expressly enumerates many 'structural principles' that its detailed provisions are intended to implement.[58] Opinions have differed as to the nature and source of authority of these principles, with 'higher law' conceptions—especially popular after the War—recently losing ground to originalist theories.[59] But the Court has not limited itself to the interpretation and application of enumerated principles. It has inferred other, unwritten or 'supra-positive', principles from 'the normative realities underlying the Basic Law'.[60] For example, it has inferred 'objective values' from constitutional rights, values that are taken to impose positive obligations on all organs of the state in addition to the negative obligation of not infringing the rights.[61] Moreover, the Court does not regard constitutional norms as separate from extra-legal political or social norms: the

---

[51] Chapter 3, pp 128–129.   [52] Chapter 3, p 147.   [53] ibid pp 146–147.
[54] ibid pp 124–127 and 150–152.   [55] ibid pp 126–127.   [56] ibid p 150.
[57] ibid p 144.   [58] Although these have been supplemented by the FCC: Ch 4, p 191.
[59] ibid pp 180, 182–183 and 189.   [60] ibid p 189.   [61] ibid pp 180–181.

constitutional order and the broader community are regarded as inter-dependent, each helping to define and refine the other.[62]

Professor Kommers observes that '[s]tructural reasoning is deeply ingrained in Germany's culture of interpretation.'[63] In comparison with the United States, where it is resorted to only occasionally, when other interpretive considerations are indeterminate, in Germany it is 'as standard as doctrinal reasoning in the common law tradition.'[64] According to him, the Constitutional Court has had to maintain a 'creative balance' between the many competing principles of the constitutional order, and also to creatively adjust the Basic Law to 'necessity'.[65]

Yet German lawyers are not attracted to the notion that substantive constitutional change may be brought about through interpretation. The Court frequently relies on evidence of the founders' intentions or purposes, including the Basic Law's legislative history, especially in cases involving federal-state conflicts.[66] When political or social realities begin to diverge from the founders' handiwork, Germans turn to formal amendment, which has been frequently utilised.[67] 'Any judicially imposed remodelling of the Basic Law—enduring and binding changes in particular—would diminish the clarity, precision, and predictability required of the constitutional *Rechtsstaat*.'[68]

Although many judges agree that there is no 'slide rule' to calculate how to weigh and balance the competing values set out in the Basic Law, so that some judicial discretion is inevitable, most 'are reluctant to admit publicly that they are doing anything other than engaging in objective constitutional interpretation.'[69] They generally insist that the process of interpretation is apolitical, even though most would concede that its effects are political.[70] The old civil law conception of written laws as self-sufficient codes lingers on: 'many judges regard the Basic Law, like the civil code, as a unified body of rules and principles that contain the right answer to almost any constitutional dispute.'[71] Despite the quasi-legislative nature of its role, it 'was expected to employ strictly judicial methods of interpretation, methods designed, in the FCC's perception of its task, to determine rationally and objectively the true meaning of the Basic Law.'[72]

The theory that the Basic Law embodies an 'objective order of values', which are hierarchically ordered, in itself suggests that subjective judicial value judgments and discretion are unnecessary.[73] These values are considered to be specified by the constitutional text, as informed by history, rather than a product of judicial precedent.[74] Basic constitutional doctrines, according to the Constitutional Court, 'reflect the normative realities underlying the Basic Law.'[75] Moreover, German jurisprudence continues to rely heavily on formal reasoning: 'the emphasis in legal education ... on theory, conceptual clarification, deductive reasoning, and systematization ... [is] reflected in general commentaries on the

---

[62] ibid p 178. [63] ibid p 199. [64] ibid pp 178–179 and 213–214. [65] ibid.
[66] ibid pp 191–192 and 197–198. [67] ibid p 179. [68] ibid pp 171 and 179.
[69] ibid pp 179 and 213; see also p 207.
[70] ibid p 213, which seems to qualify the statement at p 179. See also p 211. [71] ibid p 208.
[72] ibid p 207. [73] ibid pp 179–180. [74] ibid p 180 n 70. [75] ibid p 189.

Basic Law.'[76] Definitional refinement and doctrinal elaboration, as well as normative theorizing, dominate the Court's opinions, which aim to prove the 'rightness, neutrality, and integrity of decisional outcomes'.[77]

Many observers will be sceptical about this aspiration to apolitical, objective legalism. But even if German constitutional reasoning is not objective, in a strong sense of the word, it may articulate a greater degree of inter-subjective agreement than exists in, say, the United States. The key to reconciling normativism and legalism in Germany seems to be professional consensus, which is converted into judicial doctrine and then steadfastly maintained. Leading journals are edited by practitioners, judges and professors, and the Constitutional Court pays as much if not more attention to leading academic commentaries as to judicial precedents. '[T]he "ruling opinion" in the literature takes pride of place in the interpretation of the Basic Law.'[78] The process by which the Court prepares its opinions is one of genuinely collegial decision-making aimed at achieving consensus within the Court, and general acceptance outside it,[79] especially within the legal academy, which the opinions are mainly aimed at convincing.[80] The Court's standard practice of handing down single, unsigned opinions also emphasises the law's 'rationality, objectivity, and depersonalistion.'[81]

India

The Indian Supreme Court has radically changed its interpretive philosophy. For two decades, its philosophy was very similar to that of the Australian High Court. This is not surprising, since both courts initially adopted the rules of statutory interpretation that had been developed by British judges in the 19th century. The position adopted in the *Gopalan* case (1950), that courts can only enforce limits found in the Constitution by express provision or necessary implication, rather than 'a spirit supposed to pervade the Constitution but not expressed in words',[82] is identical to that adopted in the leading case of *Engineers'* (1920) in Australia.[83] The Supreme Court did not always adhere to its early positivism: in a series of cases, it adopted strained interpretations of constitutional provisions in order to protect private property from expropriation without full compensation.[84]

The Court shifted to a more normativist approach when it circumscribed Parliament's power of constitutional amendment. In the *Golakanth* case (1967), it purported to adopt a literal, positivist interpretation of the relevant provisions, but constitutional experts regarded this as obviously erroneous, and concluded that the Court had really been guided by the anti-majoritarian sentiments expressed in the judgments.[85] The Court also, for the first time, adopted prospective

---

[76] Chapter 4, p 209.   [77] ibid p 210.   [78] ibid p 193.   [79] ibid pp 211–212.
[80] ibid p 210.   [81] ibid p 208.
[82] Chapter 5, p 230, quoting Kania J in *Gopalan v India* AIR 1950 SC 27.
[83] Chapter 3, p 120.   [84] Chapter 5, pp 239–242.   [85] ibid pp 242–243.

over-ruling, which 'flew in the face of the theory that the judges did not make law, but merely interpreted it.'[86] In the *Kesavanand* case (1973), the Court read into the amending power a limitation nowhere expressed, nor contemplated by the founders.[87] Although the Court purported to rely partly on the words 'the Constitution shall stand amended', they were interpreted in the light of the underlying structure or spirit of the document, comprised of enduring constitutional values.[88]

Since then, the Court has applied the 'basic structure' doctrine in other contexts,[89] overturned government action that violated broad, unwritten principles rather than specific provisions,[90] taken the non-justiciable Directive Principles into account in interpreting Fundamental Rights,[91] interpreted an article that was deliberately drafted so as not to incorporate substantive due process as doing the opposite,[92] found many new, unenumerated, 'positive' rights to be implied by the right to life and personal liberty,[93] and interpreted several Fundamental Rights as incorporating international human rights that did not exist when the Constitution was adopted.[94]

In some of its most creative decisions, the Court relied on a 'basic structure' argument, as well as a Directive Principle, to interpret a provision requiring the government merely to 'consult' with the Chief Justice, before making judicial appointments, as requiring it to act on his recommendations. It then added a novel requirement that the Chief Justice must consult with four senior colleagues before tendering any recommendations.[95] Although this interpretation seems completely unsupported by the provision's express words, especially when understood in the light of appointment practices at the time the Constitution was adopted ('consulted' never meant 'obeyed'), the Court did claim to be guided by the founders' purposes.[96] As recently as 2001, the Court stated that 'it is the function of the Court to find out the intention of the framers of the constitution.'[97] The judges' strategy therefore seems to be to appeal to the founders' purposes at a very abstract level, and then to 'adapt' their words to give better effect to those purposes. That is very a strong form of normativism.

On several occasions, Professor Sathe comments that the Court interpreted the Constitution in ways that were clearly inconsistent with the founders' intentions.[98] It has said that the Fundamental Rights have 'no fixed contents', and acknowledged that it may be justified in finding 'new rights'.[99] It has openly embraced a creative role in interpreting the Constitution, which it has described as 'a vibrant document alive to the social situation [rather than] as an immutable cold letter of law unconcerned with the realities'—a 'living organ' that must

---

[86] ibid p 224.   [87] ibid p 244.   [88] ibid p 246.   [89] ibid pp 261–262.
[90] ibid p 262.   [91] ibid p 251.   [92] ibid pp 252–254.
[93] ibid pp 252–253.   [94] ibid p 254.   [95] ibid pp 259–260.
[96] ibid p 260.   [97] *SR Chaudhuri v Punjab* AIR 2001 SC 2707, at 2717; (2001) SCC 126.
[98] eg Chapter 5, p 252.
[99] ibid p 253, quoting, respectively, *India v Association for Democratic Reforms* (2002) 5 SCC 294, and *Kapila Hingorani v Bihar* (2003) 6 SCC 1.

change to meet the 'felt necessities of the time'.[100] In the *Golaknath* case (1967), Subba Rao CJ stated that:

Arts. 32, 141 and 142 are couched in such wide and elastic terms as to enable this court to formulate legal doctrines to meet the ends of justice. To deny this power to the Supreme Court on the basis of some outmoded theory that the Court only finds the law but does not make it is to make ineffective the powerful instrument of justice placed in the hands of the highest judiciary in this country.[101]

South Africa

It is difficult to characterise the jurisprudence of a Constitutional Court that has been in existence for less than ten years. So far, it seems to have adopted a moderately normativist approach, which does not subordinate the language of the text to underlying values.

The South African Constitution expressly incorporates abstract values and principles. Section 1, for example, declares that the state is 'founded on certain basic values' including human dignity, equality, human rights, the rule of law and democracy. Section 39(1) requires the Court to interpret constitutional rights so as 'to promote the values that underlie an open and democratic society based on human dignity, equality and freedom'. Governing principles also precede specific chapters, including those dealing with cooperative governance, public administration and the security services. In a striking innovation, s 39 requires that international law be taken into account in interpreting the Bill of Rights. This could reasonably be construed as a sign that the founders intended constitutional rights to be interpreted dynamically, in response to global developments in the understanding of human rights.

Such provisions clearly encourage a normativist approach. Concerned that this might be taken too far, Kentridge J warned that if the language of the text were ignored in favour of a general resort to values, the result would be 'divination' rather than interpretation, allowing the judges to make the Constitution mean whatever they would like it to mean.[102] The Court subsequently declared that interpretation should be 'generous and purposive', giving expression to the Constitution's underlying values, 'whilst paying due regard to the language that has been used.'[103] Professor Klug provides several examples of cases in which rights were not interpreted as broadly as they might have been, because of textual, contextual and purposive considerations.[104]

The Court takes into account the circumstances in which the Constitution was adopted, and even its legislative history, but only when this clearly illuminates the

---

[100] Chapter 5, pp 253 and 262, quoting, respectively, *Kapila Hingorani v Bihar* (2003) 6 SCC 1 and *Indra Sawney v India* (1992) ATC 385.

[101] *Golaknath v Punjab* AIR 1967 SC 1643 at 1669.

[102] Chapter 6, p 292, quoting *S v Zuma* 1995 (2) SA 642 (CC) para 17.

[103] Chapter 6, p 292, quoting *Makwanyane* 1995 (3) SA 391 (CC) para 9.

[104] Chapter 6, pp 293–295.

purpose of a provision. It does not examine the comments of individuals who participated in the constitution-making process in order to construct an 'original intent'.[105]

Some of the Court's decisions seem strongly normativist. In one case, a majority adopted a non-literal interpretation of s 241(8) of the 'interim' Constitution, which provided that 'pending cases shall be dealt with as if the Constitution had not been passed.' Although the case had commenced before the Constitution was adopted, they held that the petitioners were entitled to the benefit of new constitutional rights. They interpreted the section as including an implied qualification limiting its effect to the preservation of the jurisdiction of courts in which pending cases had been commenced.[106] Despite the apparent breadth of the enacted words, the Constitution's founding values and emphasis on rights was thought to constitute stronger evidence that a narrower meaning had been intended. Justice Mahomed expressly treated the Constitution as 'a holistic and integrated document with critical and important objectives.'[107] But the majority's reasoning exemplifies originalist rather than non-originalist normativism.[108] Justice Sachs insisted that:

> This is not a case of making the Constitution mean what we like, but of making it mean what the framers wanted it to mean; we gather their intention not from our subjective wishes, but from looking at the document as a whole.[109]

The Court has also inferred, from the reference to the rule of law in s 1, an implied requirement of legality that is independent of the administrative justice clause. Neither the Parliament nor the President may act capriciously or arbitrarily, and the President must exercise his powers in good faith.[110] This principle is treated as an additional requirement that underpins the express rights, including the right to administrative justice, which are treated as elaborations of it.[111]

Explaining the Differences

What explains these different interpretive philosophies? Judges are not, of course, automatons whose opinions are entirely 'caused' by external factors. They have reasons for their opinions, such as the principled reasons for preferring non-originalism to originalism, or vice versa. The simplest explanation would therefore be that judges in different countries just happen to have found different sets of reasons persuasive. But a deeper explanation seems called for. Why have all these groups of highly intelligent people not found the same reasons compelling, and converged on the same interpretive philosophy?

---

[105] ibid pp 286–287.
[106] *S v Mhlumgu* 1995 (3) SA 391 (CC), discussed in Ch 6, pp 292–293.
[107] *S v Mhlumgu*, para 15. [108] ibid para 100, 102. [109] ibid para 112.
[110] Chapter 6, pp 278–279. [111] ibid p 279.

Legal Culture

An obviously important factor is the legal culture in which judges receive their legal education, and practice their profession before appointment to the bench. The judges responsible for interpreting the constitutions of Canada, Australia and India—the Privy Council and the Canadian Supreme Court, the Australian High Court, and the Indian Supreme Court respectively—were all steeped in the British legal tradition, and initially set out to apply British principles of statutory interpretation.[112] By the end of the 19th century, if not before, the British legal tradition had become much more legalist than that of the United States.[113] Not that British principles of statutory interpretation were monolithic: they were themselves open to rival interpretations, which helps explain early disagreements between the Privy Council in Westminster and courts in Australia and Canada.[114] But, on any interpretation, they were strongly positivist and moderately originalist. They did not permit judges to stray far from the text: any implications had to be 'necessary'. Although they did not permit recourse to legislative history to establish the law-makers' intentions, they did allow reference to the legal and historical context in which a statute was enacted, in order to reveal the 'mischief' it was intended to remedy. And they did not permit the meanings of statutory terms to change over time, except through formal amendment.

Legal education and scholarship in Australia, Canada and India were less receptive to sociological jurisprudence and legal realism, which swept through American law schools in the early 20th century, and to the scepticism about legal determinacy that they preached. It seems likely that the post-Charter shift in Canada, to an enthusiastic form of judicial activism, is partly due to its proximity to the United States, and consequential influence of American jurisprudence on the Canadian legal academy and profession.[115] In Australia, the controversial emergence of a limited and tentative form of judicial activism in the 1990s has been attributed partly to the introduction of more pragmatic, consequentialist theories at Sydney Law School in the 1950s.[116]

In South Africa, widespread condemnation of the legal positivism that dominated legal thinking in the apartheid era, and which some feared would stunt implementation of the new Constitution, has no doubt inspired judges to adopt a more normativist approach.[117]

The importance of legal culture is also evident in the chapter on Germany. The Federal Constitutional Court's legalist philosophy clearly owes much to what Professor Kommers calls the 'civilian-positivistic' tradition, which treats legal codes as 'unified bodies of law covering all possible contingencies arising out of human interaction.'[118] He depicts legal education in Germany as highly formalistic, its main objective being mastery of pre-existing legal rules and principles, with an

---

[112] Chapter 2, p 104.   [113] Chapter 3, p 155.
[114] Chapter 2, p 75; Chapter 3, pp 115–119.   [115] Chapter 2, p 81.
[116] Chapter 3, p 155.   [117] Chapter 6, pp 269 and 292.
[118] Chapter 4, pp 208 and 207 respectively.

emphasis on 'theory, conceptual clarification, deductive reasoning, and systematization'.[119] In Germany, too, ordinary principles of statutory interpretation were carried over to the field of constitutional law.[120]

On the other hand, inherited legal culture is clearly not determinative. Professor Sathe observes that in India, a tradition of narrow, technical, 'black letter' legal education continued until quite recently. This was well after legalism in constitutional jurisprudence came to an end in the 1970s, which must be attributed to other factors.[121]

Judicial Appointments and Homogeneity

In Australia, the social and intellectual homogeneity of the High Court bench—drawn almost exclusively from the conservative Melbourne and Sydney bars—has probably helped preserve the tradition of legalism inherited from Britain, and broad judicial consensus as to the proper interpretive methodology.[122] Recent appointments to the bench have been deliberately designed by the government to preserve that consensus.[123] In Germany, judges have until recently been recruited from a broader field, including prominent politicians, civil servants, judges and academics (they are now appointed mainly from the judiciary and academia).[124] But all have had legal training of a kind that strongly encourages professional consensus.[125] Canadian judges seem less homogeneous in terms of regional and professional background than their Australian counterparts,[126] but nevertheless have generally been of unquestioned professional standing and seem broadly to agree on the Court's comparatively activist stance.

In the United States, there appears to have been even greater diversity in judicial appointments, which until recently were sometimes used to reward a President's friends and supporters, or appease powerful lobby groups.[127] One suspects that politicians such as Earl Warren, upon appointment to the bench, were less committed to professional craft norms than life-long practising lawyers or serving judges.[128] In addition, the legal profession in the United States seems, to an outsider, much more diverse—socially, culturally, politically and intellectually—than in most of the other countries studied here. Even today, when recent criticism of judicial activism has prompted a new emphasis on technical legal expertise and prior judicial experience as qualifications for appointment to the Supreme Court, intense political battles over confirmation highlight a dichotomy between rival interpretive philosophies.[129] The consequence is not that the Supreme Court is more activist than other constitutional courts: on the contrary, the Indian Supreme Court seems to deserve that title. Rather, the consequence seems to be a more sharply divided bench in the United States compared with

---

[119] Chapter 4, p 209.　　[120] Chapter 4, p 208.　　[121] Chapter 5, p 263.
[122] Chapter 3, pp 112–113 and 155.　　[123] Chapter 3, pp 157–158.
[124] Chapter 4, p 174.　　[125] Chapter 4, pp 208–209.　　[126] Chapter 2, pp 58–59.
[127] Chapter 1, p 14.　　[128] Chapter 1, p 15.　　[129] Chapter 1, pp 14–15.

other countries. Professor Tushnet points out that American judges have been socialized into a professional culture that frowns upon judicial wilfulness, making them unlikely to be wilful in any interesting sense.[130] Yet Supreme Court judges regularly attack one another for being wilful, which suggests that instead of a generally unified professional culture sharing interpretive norms, there are distinct sub-cultures—'liberal' and 'conservative'—that are almost deadlocked in a competition for influence.

It has yet to be seen how the express constitutional requirement in South Africa, that the judiciary should reflect the racial and gender composition of the nation, a requirement that the composition of the Constitutional Court already satisfies, will affect its interpretive methodology.[131]

There is some evidence that the method of judicial appointment affects the way federal distributions of powers are interpreted. The power of appointment enjoyed by national governments in Australia and the United States have probably contributed to the relatively generous interpretation of national powers in those countries.[132] Professor Tushnet argues that this is part of a broader pattern of Supreme Court decisions reflecting the 'regime principles' of the national political elite to which its judges belong.[133] In both Canada and Germany, on the other hand, a jurisprudence much more sympathetic to regional governments was constructed by judges whose appointments were either completely independent of the national government (the Privy Council), or partially dependent on the regional governments (the Federal Constitutional Court).[134] In Canada, after appeals to the Privy Council were abolished in 1949, the main lines of its federal-state jurisprudence were not changed by the Supreme Court, perhaps partly because statutory requirements and constitutional convention require the Court's judges to be representative of different regions.[135] Australia and Canada are particularly strong contrasting examples, because in both cases the result of judicial interpretation was the opposite of what the founders intended.[136] Evidence is lacking in India, where federal-state disputes have arisen less often, and have usually been resolved politically rather than legally.[137]

Political Culture

The judges charged with interpreting the Canadian, Australian and Indian constitutions had also imbibed the British constitutional tradition of parliamentary sovereignty. In these countries, the adoption of new national constitutions was not the consequence of armed struggle against perceived tyranny, but of pragmatic reform assisted by the imperial government. Although not strictly applicable to any legislature operating under a written, federal constitution, the principle of

---

[130] Chapter 1, p 54.   [131] Chapter 6, p 284.   [132] Chapter 3, p 156.
[133] Chapter 1, p 53.   [134] Chapter 2, pp 62–63, 75–76 and 104; Chapter 4, pp 187–188.
[135] Chapter 2, pp 58, 62–63 and 95.   [136] Chapter 3, p 108; Chapter 2, pp 75–76 and 104.
[137] Chapter 5, pp 232–234.

parliamentary sovereignty was nevertheless very influential. It encouraged broad interpretations of legislative power, trust in legislative rectitude, and deference to legislative will.[138] It was inhospitable both to broad interpretations of express rights, and to the imposition of new, supposedly implied, constraints on legislative power.

In the United States, on the other hand, the War of Independence was fought largely over Britain's attempt to impose the sovereignty of its Parliament over the American colonies, and in prosecuting the War, some of the new state legislatures adopted draconian measures.[139] One consequence was ingrained distrust of legislatures, which favoured narrow interpretations of their powers, broad interpretations of express rights, and the recognition of additional, implied constraints.

As for Germany, the Nazi experience profoundly disturbed the traditional European veneration of parliaments, and subordination of courts to 'apolitical civil service-like agencies entrusted with faithfully carrying out the will of legislative majorities'.[140] As the chief guardian of the constitution, the Federal Constitutional Court was accorded a constitutional status and administrative autonomy that is unique among German courts.[141] Many Germans were attracted to notions of a 'higher law' that neither positive law nor the will of the people can alter or override,[142] and at least in its early years, the Court rejected the legal positivism of the Weimar period.[143] Similarly, in South Africa, the doctrine of parliamentary sovereignty that prevailed under the former apartheid regime was decisively rejected in favour of a form of constitutionalism emphasising the protection of human rights.[144] The Constitutional Court often refers to the founders' deliberate decision to make a clean break with the values of the pre-existing legal order.[145]

Political culture can change. In India, judicial attitudes of deference to the legislature were initially reinforced by the superior prestige of elected politicians compared with that of judges. But politicians' abuses of power during the 1975 emergency, and increasing corruption, diminished the trust that had been reposed in them, not least by the judges, and their superior prestige. This provided the judges with both the motivation, and the opportunity, to act creatively to impose new limits on the executive and legislature. Public esteem for the Supreme Court was enhanced by activist decisions designed to check abuses of power by the political branches of government. Indeed, Professor Sathe suggests that one reason the Court assumed an activist stance after 1977 was to restore its credibility, by demonstrating that it was prepared to stand up to the politicians.[146]

The influence of prevailing political culture is also evident in the impact of the recent global 'rights revolution' on judicial philosophies. In Canada, the adoption of the Charter coincided with this transformation of political attitudes, propelled

---

[138] Chapter 3, pp 109–110, 148 and 156; Chapter 2, p 56; Chapter 5, p 227.
[139] J. Goldsworthy *The Sovereignty of Parliament, History and Philosophy* (Clarendon Press, Oxford, 1999) 192–97 and 204–15. [140] Chapter 4, p 206,
[141] Chapter 4, pp 172–173. [142] Chapter 4, pp 167 and 180. [143] Chapter 4, p 182.
[144] Chapter 6, p 269. [145] Chapter 6, p 315. [146] Chapter 5, p 251.

by increasing distrust of majoritarian democracy. The result has been enthusiastic judicial activism in non-Charter as well as Charter cases.[147] It is as if the Canadian Supreme Court has adopted what Professor Tushnet calls 'holistic' interpretation, whereby the adoption of an amendment (in this case, in a non-technical sense, the Charter) is taken to change the overarching 'spirit' of the entire constitution, so as to justify new readings of older, unamended provisions. This is a technique not yet accepted by the American Supreme Court.[148]   The 'rights revolution' has no doubt transformed public attitudes as well as judicial ones. Consequently, Canadian politicians are not well placed to resist perceived judicial activism. Their inability to use the 'notwithstanding clause' (s 33) to override judicial interpretations of the Charter, suggests that the general public is unlikely to condone any political attack on the judiciary.[149]

The rights revolution no doubt influenced Australian judges as well, contributing to the High Court's greater creativity in the 1990s, evident in the 'discovery' of an implied freedom of political speech. But the Court's perceived departure from its long-standing tradition of legalism did not, as in India, enhance its prestige. Australian politicians reacted to nascent judicial activism in a way that was not open to their Indian or Canadian counterparts. They were angered by it, and used their power of judicial appointment to turn the Court back to a more legalist approach.[150] This may corroborate an opinion that Australian judges have sometimes expressed, that 'strict legalism' is the best means of maintaining public confidence in the Court as a neutral umpire.[151] If that is so, the contrast with India and Canada is stark. Australia may have a more robust political culture than Canada, in terms of the willingness of politicians to denounce judicial decisions in strong language. It also differs from Canada in lacking what Charles Epp has called 'a support structure for legal mobilization': a body of well-funded human rights lobby groups that use litigation to advance their objectives. In Canada, these groups form part of a 'court party' that vigorously defends the judiciary from political attack.[152]

Another example of how political culture influences interpretive methodology is the impact in the United States of the ideology of autonomous individualism, evident in the expansive interpretation of free expression, and hostility to social and economic rights,[153] compared with the greater openness of German jurisprudence to communitarianism, which led to a strikingly different treatment of abortion.[154] The Constitutional Court in South Africa has also struggled with tensions between individualist and communitarian conceptions of freedom, which may in the future be resolved through development of the indigenous concept of *ubuntu*.[155]

---

[147] Chapter 2, p 105.   [148] Chapter 1, p 29.   [149] Chapter 2, pp 69 and 99 n 162.
[150] Chapter 3, pp 157–158.   [151] Chapter 3, p 157.
[152] C Epp and WL Morton, '*The Rights Revolution*' (U Chicago Press, Chicago, 1998); B Galligan and WL Morton, 'The Rights Revolution in Australia', in T Campbell, J Goldsworthy and A Stone, eds., '*Protecting Rights Without a Bill of Rights: Institutional Performance and Reform in Australia*' (Ashgate/Dartmouth, Aldershot, 2006); R Knopff and T Morton *The Charter Revolution and the Court Party* (Broadview Press, Peterborough Ont, 2000).   [153] Chapter 1, p 52.
[154] Chapter 4, n 60, pp 183, 190 and 213–214.   [155] Chapter 6, pp 302–303, 316–317.

Regional heterogeneity has clearly been a factor in some countries, although it can cut in different ways. In Canada, the Quebeckers' concern to protect their language and culture led them to demand provincial rights, which other Canadians accommodated due to fear of Quebec separatism.[156] On the other hand, in the United States, regional heterogeneity may have had the opposite effect. According to Professor Tushnet, the activism of the Warren Court reflected the distrust held by national political elites for white majorities in the American South, as well as distaste for 'outlier' legislation in other states that had fallen behind progressive developments in the rest of the nation.[157] Fear of religious fundamentalism and intolerance that are more prominent in some regions than others may also have been a factor in decisions of the Indian Supreme Court.[158] And no doubt differences between the Kwazulu-Natal Province and other provinces in South Africa will have an impact on interpretive methods there.[159] Strong regional variations of this kind are absent in Australia, which is more culturally homogeneous.[160]

The Nature and Age of the Constitution

The nature of a constitution is assumed to be an important factor in several chapters. Australian lawyers have often suspected that the relatively prosaic nature of their constitution, originally a British statute lacking both a ringing appeal to national aspirations and a bill of rights, has contributed to the High Court's legalist approach to its interpretation.[161] On the other hand, we have seen that all three post-War constitutions include express references to founding values and structural principles, which encourage a normativist approach to interpretation. Professors Tushnet and Sathe both regard their courts' responsibility to give meaning to abstract concepts, especially fundamental rights, as requiring a more creative approach.[162] This is corroborated by the Canadian experience. Professor Hogg shows that the adoption of the Charter of Rights in 1982 inspired a transformation in the interpretive philosophy of the Supreme Court, to a strongly normativist approach and a pattern of enthusiastic activism throughout its jurisdiction, in non-Charter as well as Charter cases.[163]

The degree of difficulty in formally amending a constitution may also be a factor. Professor Tushnet argues that because the American Constitution is inherently difficult to amend, and the political culture averse to formal amendments, the Supreme Court has felt compelled to make adaptations through creative interpretation, and the American people have accepted this as the appropriate method of updating the Constitution.[164] The Supreme Court of Canada has explicitly cited the difficulty of amending its Constitution as a justification for allowing

---

[156] Chapter 2, pp 93–94.   [157] Chapter 1, p 52.   [158] Chapter 5, p 262.
[159] Chapter 6, pp 290–291.   [160] Chapter 3, p 156.
[161] Chapter 3, pp 109, 113, 153 and 155.
[162] Chapter 5, pp 227, 231, 253; Chapter 1, pp 7 and 17.   [163] Chapter 2, pp 71, 88 and 103.
[164] Chapter 1, pp 7, 16–17 and 54.

'growth and development over time.'[165] This is corroborated by the German experience where, Professor Kommers suggests, the comparative ease of formal amendment has reinforced judicial reluctance to bring about substantial changes through interpretation.[166] But this factor can also cut the other way: in India, the Constitution was so easy for the dominant Congress Party to amend, that the Supreme Court felt compelled to act creatively to restrict the amending power.[167]

Professor Tushnet suggests that the age of the United States Constitution, as well as the difficulty of amending it, has encouraged adaptation through judicial interpretation.[168] It does seem inevitable that, as a constitution ages, its language will become less capable of fulfilling its underlying purposes, when applied to unanticipated technological and social changes. The development of an air force in the United States, mentioned previously, is an example.[169] On the other hand, the degree of difficulty of the constitution's amendment procedure is probably the more important factor. The pattern of legalism versus activism in the six countries examined here does not correlate strongly with the relative ages of their constitutions. The two most activist courts, in India and Canada, deal with a Constitution, and a Charter of Rights, that are both relatively new.

The greater age of the American Constitution is significant in two other respects. First, the fact that comparative jurisprudence is paid much less attention in the United States than elsewhere is surely due partly to that Constitution having been adopted before any of the others. To the extent that the meaning of a constitution (or a constitutional amendment) is determined by the intentions or understandings of its makers, the interpretation of constitutions adopted subsequently in other countries is of little relevance.[170] The constitutions of all the other countries studied here include provisions copied wholly or partly from other constitutions. It is often reasonable to assume that such a provision was intended to have a meaning similar to the meaning it had in the country of origin at the time it was copied. Every other chapter of this book includes evidence of considerable judicial interest in the interpretation of related provisions elsewhere. Even in the United States, British constitutional traditions up to 1789 have sometimes been examined to shed light on concepts and principles derived from them.[171]

The second respect in which relative age is significant is that precedents naturally play a much larger role in the interpretation of older constitutions, simply because there are more of them. When constitutions are young, courts have a greater need to seek guidance elsewhere, which diminishes as they build up their own stock of indigenous precedents.

The structure of a constitution can have many effects on interpretive methods. Constitutional rights appear to be interpreted more expansively in Canada and South Africa than in the United States, partly because their constitutions expressly

[165] Chapter 2, p 77, quoting *Hunter v Southam* [1884] 2 SCR 145, 155.
[166] Chapter 4, pp 171–172.   [167] Chapter 5, pp 242–245.   [168] Chapter 1, p 7.
[169] See n 4, above.
[170] Chapter 1, pp 45–46. But only 'to that extent', because the interpretation of constitutions elsewhere can be useful for other purposes: see S Choudhry, *The Migration of Constitutional Ideas* (Cambridge UP, Cambridge, 2005) (forthcoming).   [171] Chapter 1, pp 28–29 and 45.

mandate a two-stage enquiry, in which infringements of rights established at the first stage can be justified to the court at the second stage. The possibility of justification at the second stage relieves the courts of the need to adopt narrow interpretations of rights in order to accommodate legitimate competing interests.[172]

'The Felt Necessities of the Time'

There is a popular perception that no matter what their stated interpretive philosophy, judges somehow manage to find ways of adjusting their constitutions to 'the felt necessities of the time.'[173] That might explain, to take just one example, why the Privy Council consistently interpreted national powers in Canada narrowly, while the Australian High Court interpreted national powers broadly, in both cases contrary to the founders' intentions, despite both courts purporting to apply British principles of statutory interpretation.

Are the interpretive philosophies described in this chapter mainly rhetoric, that conceal essentially result-oriented decision-making? Two issues must be distinguished. The first is the extent to which law remains stubbornly indeterminate, whatever interpretive methodology is employed, thereby requiring judges to exercise discretion on moral or policy grounds. The second is the extent to which judges are willing either to misapply, or to abandon, their orthodox methodology in order to reach strongly desired conclusions.

Professor Tushnet argues that in the United States, orthodox interpretive methods have proved sufficiently indeterminate that judges have been able to 'do the jobs [they] think need to be done at any specific time.'[174] Whether his argument holds universally must be left for readers to decide. The judicial interpretation of national powers in Canada and Australia, contrary to the founders' intentions, might be examples of indeterminacy: British principles of statutory interpretation did not allow recourse to legislative history to resolve textual indeterminacy. On the other hand, many cases can be cited in which the Australian High Court's legalist methods led to very different conclusions than the American Supreme Court had previously reached. They include cases on interstate commerce, freedom of religion, and electoral equality. It is possible that such differences merely reflect the judges' different political ideologies. Alternatively, they might be the result of the larger number of abstract, and therefore less determinate, principles in the American Constitution, of a broader range of interpretive methods being accepted within the American judiciary as orthodox, or of the accumulation in the United States of a larger and more diverse body of precedents that can be used to rationalise result-oriented decisions.

As for the second issue, it is clear that judges sometimes feel they have no alternative but to act creatively in order to defuse a crisis, or to prevent or remedy

---

[172] Chapter 2, pp 70 and 103; Chapter 6, p 293.

[173] A phrase famously used by OW Holmes Jr in *The Common Law* (Little Brown, Boston, 1881) 1.

[174] Chapter 1, p 7. Tushnet acknowledges that they are not wholly indeterminate: for example, the structural provisions of the Constitution are often clear-cut: ibid pp 27–28.

what seems to them a particularly outrageous breach of some important constitutional value. When judges previously committed to legalist methods find them an obstacle in that regard, they sometimes either covertly misapply them, or abandon them (temporarily or permanently) in favour of normativism. From a legalist perspective, such cases involve a conflict, whether or not the judges perceive it, between their sense of moral responsibility, and their limited legal authority, to intervene. From a normativist perspective, especially a non-originalist one, there is less likely to be a conflict.[175]

Professor Hogg describes three examples of what he calls 'crisis management', where the Canadian Supreme Court exceeded the normal limits of its authority to craft an unorthodox solution to a looming political or legal crisis. In each case the Court adopted a normativist strategy, by resorting to 'unwritten principles'. Professor Hogg acknowledges that in one case, it is hard to see how the Court could responsibly have reached any other conclusion.[176] But he implies that in the other two cases, the Court's solution was neither necessary nor clearly desirable.[177] In one of them, it adopted a novel idea that had never been publicly suggested before or even argued by counsel.[178]

In India, the shift from a predominantly positivist to a strongly normativist approach was initially motivated by fear that the power of constitutional amendment would be abused, a fear subsequently vindicated during the 1975 emergency.[179] The Supreme Court's post-emergency activism was aimed at curbing majoritarian threats to constitutional values, political corruption, and oppression of the most marginalised and deprived segments of Indian society.[180]

Professor Tushnet notes that the American Supreme Court has sometimes relied on moral concepts to surmount limitations inherent in other interpretive approaches.[181] The Warren Court's activism was motivated by strong disapproval, shared by national political elites, of the distinctive culture of the American South, and archaic laws in a few other states that were out of step with progressive developments in the rest of the nation.[182] The paradigm example is *Brown v Board of Education*, whose moral authority even originalists have found difficult to challenge, although it is hard to defend on originalist grounds.[183] *Griswold v Connecticut* is another example.[184]

One relevant factor, then, is the number of occasions that judges are confronted, or fear they may be confronted, by executive or legislative measures they regard either as contrary to a vital national interest or as morally outrageous. One is reminded of Oliver Wendell Holmes' famous 'puke' test—any law that made him want to puke must be invalid—which Felix Frankfurter converted into a 'shocks the conscience' test.[185]

---

175 See p 323, above.
176 Chapter 2, p 98, referring to the *Manitoba Language Reference* case.
177 Chapter 2, pp 99–100.   178 Chapter 2, pp 96–100, quotation at p 100.
179 Chapter 5, pp 243, 247.   180 Chapter 5, p 262.   181 Chapter 1, p 39.
182 Chapter 1, pp 52–53.   183 Chapter 1, pp 40–41.   184 Chapter 1, p 32.
185 Letter from Justice Holmes to Harold Laski (Oct. 23, 1926), in M. Dewolfe Howe, ed., *Holmes-Laski Letters* (Harvard UP, Cambridge Mass., 1953), 888; *Rochin v California* 342 US 165, 172 (1952).

Of all potential threats to constitutional values, encroachments upon their own exclusive authority or independence often cause the greatest shock to the judicial conscience. In Australia, the most legalist of the six countries, the High Court first began to construct a doctrine of strict separation of judicial power in a case where it was contrary both to the constitutional text and the founders' intentions.[186] More recently, the Court partially extended this doctrine to most state courts, although this was inconsistent both with previous authority and with strong disapproval of 'free standing' unwritten principles expressed in recent cases.[187] In Canada, even the Privy Council before 1949 and, later, the Supreme Court, struck down laws granting judicial power to administrative tribunals, although 'the basis for the decisions was unclear or implausible.'[188] In 1997, the Supreme Court invoked an 'unwritten principle' of judicial independence, and proceeded to construct 'an elaborate edifice of doctrine with little or no basis in the text in order to protect the power, influence, salaries and perquisites of themselves and their colleagues.'[189] The Indian Supreme Court, arguably with stronger moral justification, interpreted a provision requiring the Chief Justice to be consulted before new puisne justices were appointed, as requiring his advice to be followed, and then added a requirement with no textual support whatsoever, that the Chief Justice must consult with his four most senior colleagues before tendering that advice.[190] In South Africa, many of the grounds on which the Court initially objected to the draft constitutional text related to its own jurisdiction and authority.[191]

Creative decisions that give principles highly valued by the judges greater protection than is warranted by the constitutional text, as originally understood, are not always 'progressive'. As Professors Sathe observes, judges share the values, including the prejudices, of the social class from which they are drawn.[192] In India, for example, the Supreme Court during its most legalist phase strived to limit the legislature's efforts to enhance social justice by redistributing property.[193] In the United States, the doctrines of substantive due process and freedom of contract were applied before 1937 to invalidate labour laws and other legislative reforms designed to improve social welfare. In Canada, the 'unwritten principle' of judicial independence was invoked to protect judges' salaries from public sector budget cuts that posed no conceivable threat to their independence.[194] And in Australia, an implied freedom of political speech was 'discovered' and used to invalidate legislation aimed at reducing the dependence of political parties on the wealthy individual and organizations that donate the funds needed for expensive political advertising.[195]

The object of this chapter, however, has not been to criticise the interpretive methods and philosophies described in this book. It has merely been to compare and explain them.

---

[186] Chapter 3, pp 125–126 and 128–129.   [187] Chapter 3, pp 148–149.
[188] Chapter 2, p 73.   [189] Chapter 2, p 74.   [190] Chapter 5, pp 259–261.
[191] Chapter 6, p 302.   [192] Chapter 5, p 264.   [193] Chapter 5, pp 239–241.
[194] Chapter 2, pp 73 and 92.   [195] Chapter 3, p 145.

Index